Southern Biography Series
William J. Cooper, Jr., Editor

James Henry Hammond and the Old South

James Henry Hammond as painted by William Scarborough in 1850.

JAMES HENRY HAMMOND
～ *and the* ～
OLD SOUTH

A Design for Mastery

Drew Gilpin Faust

Louisiana State University Press
Baton Rouge

Published by Louisiana State University Press
Copyright © 1982 by Louisiana State University Press
All rights reserved
Manufactured in the United States of America

Designer: *Patricia Douglas Crowder*
Typeface: *Linotron Goudy*
Typesetter: *G&S Typesetters, Inc.*

Some of the material in Chapter 5 was originally published in the *Journal of Social History*, Vol. XIV.
A version of Chapter 10 appeared in the *South Carolina Historical Magazine*, LXXXI (1980), 189–206.

Library of Congress Cataloging in Publication Data
Faust, Drew Gilpin
    James Henry Hammond and the Old South.

    (Southern biography series)
    Bibliography: p.
    Includes index.
        1.   Hammond, James Henry, 1807–1864.   2.   Slavery
    —Southern States.   3.   South Carolina—Politics
    and government—1775–1865.   4. Slaveholders—South
    Carolina—Biography.   I.   Title.   II. Series.
    F273.H25F38   1982   975.7'03'0924   [B]   82-8939
    ISBN 978-0-8071-1248-9 (paper)   AACR2

LOUISIANA PAPERBACK EDITION, 1985

The paper in this book meets the guidelines for permanence and durability of the Committee
on Production Guidelines for Book Longevity of the Council on Library Resources. ∞

Winner of the Jules F. Landry Award for 1982

For Charles

If it were all inked up into a romance it would be pronounced overstrained & improbable.

JAMES HENRY HAMMOND

Contents

Contents

Illustrations

Acknowledgments

MANY INDIVIDUALS AND INSTITUTIONS have helped me in my work on this book. The National Endowment for the Humanities, the American Council of Learned Societies, and the University of Pennsylvania all provided financial support. The staffs of the Manuscript Division of the Library of Congress, the Southern Historical Collection at the University of North Carolina at Chapel Hill, the Earl Gregg Swem Memorial Library of the College of William and Mary, the Manuscript Department of the William R. Perkins Library at Duke University, the Virginia Historical Society, the South Carolina Department of Archives and History, and the South Carolina Historical Society were unfailingly helpful. I am especially grateful to Les Inabinett, director of the South Caroliniana Library at the University of South Carolina and his staff for the many courtesies I was shown during my visits there. Fellow scholars of South Carolina Vernon Burton, David Carlton, Lacy Ford, John McCardell, George Rogers, Scott Strickland, and Tom Terrill stimulated my thinking and often challenged my conclusions. Gretchen Condran, Richard Dunn, Claudia Goldin, Margo Horn, Arthur Johnson, Barbara Kopytoff, Albert Rizzo, Peter Wood, Harold Woodman, and Michael Zuckerman read and criticized sections of the manuscript about which they had special knowledge. A number of my students helped with details of research and in preparation of the manuscript. I want to thank Marlene Heck, Sally Stephenson, and Nina Hyrnko, as well as all the members of my graduate seminars who tolerated my frequent discursions on James Henry Hammond with good humor and even enthusiasm. Carol Bleser shared with me not only her own insights into the Hammonds but numerous enlightening exchanges about our complementary projects. As editors, Beverly Jarrett and Bill Cooper were everything an author could hope. Steven Hahn read the entire text and made invaluable comments throughout. With great generosity, Eugene Genovese offered stylistic and substantive criticisms of the manuscript that helped me make this a far better book, even though much remains from which he will no doubt dissent. I owe a very special debt to Allen Stokes. Anyone who has ever worked in the South Caroliniana knows what an extraordinary manuscript librarian he is, and I have benefitted throughout this project from his sophisticated understanding of the Hammond Papers as well as a wide range of related documentary material. In addition, Allen has been a sensitive critic of the whole text, and I have been particularly grateful for his views on the complexities of Hammond's character and motivations. Charles Rosenberg has done more than I could ever hope to recount or repay, unless, perhaps, he regards getting James Henry Hammond out of our house as reward enough.

Abbreviations

DU	Manuscript Department, William R. Perkins Library, Duke University, Durham, N.C.
HBC	Hammond-Bryan-Cumming
JHH	James Henry Hammond
LC	Library of Congress
NA	National Archives
SCA	South Carolina Department of Archives and History, Columbia
SCL	South Caroliniana Library, University of South Carolina, Columbia
SHC	Southern Historical Collection, Library of the University of North Carolina at Chapel Hill
USCA	University of South Carolina Archives, Columbia

James Henry Hammond and the Old South

Introduction

O<small>N A RIDGE</small> high above the Savannah River stands Redcliffe, presiding over carefully planned avenues of magnolias and groves of hickory and pine that slope down towards Augusta, visible more than five miles away. The house was designed to dramatize the magnificence of this view. Its first floor was elevated well above ground level by brick supports, its façade graced on both upper and lower levels by wide porticoes, its roof topped by a windowed cupola. In the decade after its completion in 1858, there was much to see from the vantage point Redcliffe provided. The Savannah still served as a busy avenue of commerce and transportation, and even closer to the house stretched the young vineyards, the peach and apple orchards, and the ornamental gardens set out to embellish the mansion above them. Farther to the south lay the acres of corn and cotton fields and quarters for the three hundred slaves who made this elegance possible.

Today the cupola and second-story porch are gone; the fruit orchards and vineyards have disappeared; the magnolias have grown to a grandeur that those who planted them could have scarcely imagined. But Redcliffe seems little changed. Except for the hint of industrial smoke on the horizon above Augusta the view appears almost untouched by the passage of time. Perhaps more happened at Redcliffe in its first decade than in the century that followed, for it was these early years that witnessed the creation and destruction of a nation and the dissolution of a way of life.

During the Civil War, Redcliffe's residents heard the discharge of shore batteries on the coast, nearly fifty miles away; from the house's balconies they watched the arrival and departure of Confederate officers, come to discuss defenses for the river below; they observed the unwelcome visits of the impressment officer, appearing to seize materials necessary for support of the southern armies and sometimes leaving with a wagonload of corn or frightened slaves. And from Redcliffe they gazed out towards Georgia and the horizon to the southwest where early in 1865 the soldiers of William Tecumseh Sherman marched within fourteen miles of the house cutting their destructive swath through the countryside to bring the South to its knees.

But on the November day that Sherman set out from Atlanta toward South Carolina and the sea, the inhabitants of Redcliffe were preoccupied with other matters. For this was a day of personal grief that took precedence over national calamity. The master of Redcliffe was dead, victim of disease rather than Yankee bullets. But his family believed him a war casualty nonetheless. "Father's death," observed his son, "was largely an act of will." It was "time for me to die," James Henry Hammond had declared just before taking to his bed in mid October. By summer, he predicted, the Confederacy would be no more. A curtain would be lifted on a new world. "I do not care to see behind it. Enough, that all the efforts of my life, all my reflections & conclusions, will be upset & reversed." Hammond wished to die with the Old South, for it had given him his identity and purpose.

His funeral served as a fitting culmination to Hammond's life in this society and as a final affirmation of a social order and personal power that had nearly ceased to exist. With freedom only months away, his nearly two hundred adult slaves filed two by two up the wide steps into Redcliffe's hall to view their master's face. This was a last gesture of deference to Hammond and perhaps to the slave system as well. Ninety-five carriages and scores of horsemen and pedestrians came up the avenue of magnolias to pay tribute to the man who had been South Carolina's governor, its last United States senator, and one of the staunchest defenders of its way of life. On this autumn day, with the desolation of winter and defeat close at hand, James Henry Hammond was buried, as he had directed, near two large hickory trees "on the highest ground around." But he had insisted, "if we are subjugated run a plow over my grave."[1]

---

1. Edward Spann Hammond, "Last Moments of J. H. Hammond, November, 1864, (MS vol. bd., 1861–1909, Edward Spann Hammond Papers, SCL); Edward Spann Hammond to Loula Comer Hammond, March 11, 1903, in Clement Claiborne Clay Papers, DU; Virginia Clay-Clopton, *A Belle of the Fifties* (New York: Doubleday, Page, 1905), 231–32. Spann's quotation of his father's wish to die in "Last Moments" differs slightly from that in his letter to Loula Hammond. The citation here is from the latter.

Introduction

Hammond died in what he viewed as defeat not just for his beloved South but for his even more deeply cherished personal ambition. Although he had risen from obscurity to wealth and prominence, his desire for lasting fame had not been realized. He had hoped himself to conquer the South, to move to the very pinnacle of its master class and become, as John C. Calhoun had been before him, its regional hero, its political spokesman, its favorite son. This ambition consumed his life, directed almost his every move, and ultimately, in its calculation and rigidity, destroyed the man confined within it. Like Faulkner's Thomas Sutpen, James Henry Hammond had a "design," a compulsion to direct every effort towards self-aggrandizement and legitimation. He intended to triumph by mastering the South on its own terms and by its own rules, by excelling in the pursuits this culture had defined as most worthy. Yet such a self-conscious effort condemned him to remain always, even in success, at the margin of his society, distanced by the intellect that directed his assault upon it. As an active planter, politician, essayist, and agricultural reformer Hammond stood at the center of the South's way of life. Yet he maintained a critical perspective as well. His legacy to the twentieth century is the record of an astute participant-observer, whose keen mind was necessarily directed at understanding both the strengths and the weaknesses of southern culture and society in order to manipulate them for his own ends. Beginning at the close of the revolutionary era and ending on the eve of Confederate defeat, Hammond's life spanned the antebellum period, the rise and fall of the cotton kingdom, the prime years of the South's peculiar institution. In talent and achievement he stood far above most of his compatriots, but in the social values he acknowledged and the kinds of options he identified, Hammond was, as one friend described him, "a Representative Southern man."[2] Born with little beyond intelligence and ambition, Hammond transformed these into the kind of success most valued by his culture: plantation ownership and high political office.

Hammond's life was the pursuit of a design outlined for him by the Old South itself. His existence in many ways embodied the rules for succeeding in this society; his failures marked the penalty the South exacted of him in those

2. Suggested epitaph in loose papers, 1864, HBC Papers, SCL. I first noted the parallels between Hammond and Thomas Sutpen in A Sacred Circle: The Dilemma of the Intellectual in the Old South, 1840–1860 (Baltimore: Johns Hopkins University Press, 1977), 40, and explored these further in "James Henry Hammond's Design" (unpublished paper delivered at the Organization of American Historians convention in San Francisco, April, 1980). C. Vann Woodward elaborates upon these similarities in "Good Housekeeping," New York Review of Books, XXVIII (October 22, 1981), 47–48.

areas where he fell short, for Hammond found he was ultimately unable, as his design required, "to control myself in every particular."[3] His human tragedy is particularly one of the Old South, of the demands made upon its native sons, of the rewards granted the deserving, of the texture and meaning of both success and defeat within that unique society that existed below the Mason-Dixon Line between the Revolution and the Civil War.

3. James Henry Hammond to William Gilmore Simms, July 8, 1848, in JHH Papers, LC.

4

Part I

To Be Great Among Men

Oh God, . . . Make me great among men.
JAMES HENRY HAMMOND

CHAPTER I

A Father's Pride and Ornament

JAMES HENRY HAMMOND'S father never doubted that his firstborn son was a genius. From the time of James's birth in 1807, Elisha Hammond lived, as his son later recounted, "for me & in me." The father's hopes burdened the boy with expectations he would spend his life trying to meet. His "heart dwelt on me," James remembered, "with the fondest & alas most confident assurances, that I would one day be what he might have been, but for the blast of early hardship."[1]

Elisha's own existence represented a bitter chronicle of debt, failure, and disappointment, brightened only by dreams of a better lot for his promising son. Born in New Bedford, Massachusetts, in 1774, the elder Hammond was at the age of twenty-one earning his living building stone walls. But he aspired beyond the drudgery of manual labor. Having never so much as seen a Latin grammar, Elisha began to educate himself, working one-half of each year to support a subsequent six months of study, first at academies, then at college. In 1802 Elisha graduated from Dartmouth and embarked southward to seek his fortune. When he arrived in Charleston in November of that year, he was "Sick and a Stranger to every body I had few cloathes, and had one single ¼ of a dollar in my pocket." Out of desperation he considered becoming a Methodist minister, but more worldly ambitions prevailed. He left Charleston to seek opportunities in the growing interior of the state and established himself as a schoolmaster at Mount Bethel, a respected Methodist academy in the Newberry District of the Carolina up-country. By the spring of 1805, he had advanced remarkably, for he was ap-

1. James Henry Hammond Diary (MS in JHH Papers, LC), April 12, 1836.

pointed professor of languages in the inaugural term of the new South Carolina College in Columbia. Family legend maintains that the regularly elected professor did not appear, and so the trustees turned to nearby Mount Bethel, the source of a number of the college's students, for an emergency replacement. Hammond was well liked at the College, where students and colleagues found "his personal appearance and manners . . . very captivating." His charm soon won him a bride, Catherine Spann, of Edgefield, South Carolina, to whom he was wed in July of 1806. The Spanns were a family of middling means who owned some land and several slaves, but Catherine's meager property did not markedly improve her struggling husband's position.[2]

Soon after their marriage, Elisha resigned his professorship in Columbia and returned to rural Newberry, where he became principal of Mount Bethel. On November 15, 1807, a child was born to the schoolmaster and his young wife, and they named the boy James Henry Hammond. The early years of James's life passed amidst the secondary-school routine. The main building at Mount Bethel, built of rough-hewn stone, housed students on its second floor and the main classrooms below. The Hammonds lived in one of several surrounding cabins that served as residences for teachers and additional students who could not be accommodated in the main hall. "Among the hundred or more boys & young men there," Hammond later remembered, "I could not fail to learn something of human nature & customs even before I was eight years old." Elisha took advantage of the school environment to begin his son's academic education at an early age. "If hereafter," James mused in 1826, "ought of fame & honor shall be mine to boast of, all praise is due him who early instilled into me a 'holy thirst' for knowledge—a noble desire to excel." Elisha was soon convinced of his son's unusual endowments, for the boy quickly began to exhibit signs of great intelligence and to demonstrate as well that he had inherited his father's physical attractiveness and charm.[3]

But Elisha was not entirely satisfied by these evidences of talent. The father's hopes for his "pride and ornament" were so great that he could not entirely allay fears of ultimate disappointment. Elisha's apprehensions, his son later recalled,

2. Elisha Hammond to James Henry Hammond, March 4, April 12, 1827, in HBC Papers, SCL; Maximilian LaBorde, *History of the South Carolina College from Its Incorporation, Dec. 19, 1801, to Dec. 19, 1865; Including Sketches of Its Presidents and Professors, with an Appendix* (Charleston: Walker, Evans, and Cogswell, 1874), 27.

3. Hammond, "Thoughts and Recollections" (MS vol. bd., 1852–53), February 24, 1852, Hammond to Dear Doctor, June 26, 1826, both in JHH Papers, SCL. On Mount Bethel Academy, see Thomas H. Pope, *The History of Newberry County, South Carolina* (2 vols. projected; Columbia: University of South Carolina Press, 1973), I, 214.

"were that I would prove a prodigal & lack steadiness of purpose & many a sound flogging did he give me on these premises." His father's thrashings succeeded in alerting James both painfully and permanently to the dangers of these potential character flaws. Hammond would never forget what he came to regard as a congenital predisposition to laziness and improvidence.[4]

The secret of success, Elisha taught his son, the way for him to realize the ambition his father had awakened, was through constant and unremitting self-control. The "greatest contests that the greatest men have ever had," Elisha warned, "were with their passions to subdue and over come them." James possessed, his father assured him, "by nature and acquirement a superior Genius, health, youth, handsome address. . . . Learn, my dear Son, the government of your passions." The alternative to effective self-discipline was ignominious failure, a prospect with which Elisha terrified the boy. "More than half of the young men raised in the Southern States are sooner or later ruined by disapation [sic] but this," Elisha solemnly intoned, "I trust, will not apply to you." Even when the elder Hammond's voice was stilled by death, his warnings and evocations of disaster continued to echo within James's mind. The son internalized his father's fear of displaying impulse and emotion and throughout his life endeavored to maintain that tight self-control Elisha had prescribed. His remarkable drive, James believed, was only a façade. "I still fear myself," he confessed in 1848, "that my acting may give out some day." More than a decade later Hammond admitted how difficult he continued to find the task of self-control. "I often think I should be better if I had one of those thrashings my Father used to bestow on me—rather liberally, I thought then." Elisha was a good teacher, for his most important pupil never forgot this crucial lesson.[5]

However gifted an instructor he may have been, Elisha was not making the fortune he desired at Mount Bethel. Even efforts to supplement his school revenues with farming, a general store, and an entrepreneurial scheme to raise beans for castor oil did not provide him with sufficient income to meet the needs of his family, which increased by another child almost every year. Caroline Augusta arrived in 1810, Adeline Eliza in 1811, Juliana in 1813, and Marcus Claudius Marcellus in 1814. The year after the birth of his second son, Elisha returned to Columbia with his wife and four children. (Juliana had died at just over a year of

4. Elisha Hammond to Hammond, August 11, 1826, in JHH Papers, SCL; Hammond to William Gilmore Simms, July 8, 1848, in JHH Papers, LC.
5. Elisha Hammond to Hammond, May 9, 1828, February 11, 1827, August 17, 1828, all in JHH Papers, SCL; Hammond to Simms, July 8, 1848, October 24, 1859, both in JHH Papers, LC.

age.) At the head of the state's largest river system, Columbia had become the center of Carolina's up-country market, and Elisha was determined to make his fortune in the rapidly growing town. He invested in a sawmill, opened a sidewalk market that sold vegetables and meat, and secured the post of steward at South Carolina College, thus assuming responsibility for feeding the more than one hundred hungry youths enrolled in the institution. The students complained that Elisha's provisions were unpalatable, his hominy "disagreeable," and his meat infested with worms, but Hammond made more money at this endeavor than at any of the other schemes he undertook during his life.[6]

His family, meanwhile, continued to grow. Two babies died in infancy in 1816 and 1817, and a third son, John Fox, was born in 1820. But the arrival of Marcellus and John little diminished James's importance in his father's eyes. From the first, the younger boys seemed less gifted, less interesting to their father than his favored firstborn. Never as bright or as handsome as James, they would all their lives exhibit the heedless, impetuous "prodigality" Elisha worked so hard to thrash out of their older brother.

For James, the move to Columbia opened a new world. Rustic as it was, with a population of scarcely a thousand, the town was laid out on a monumental scale. Boulevards more than a hundred feet wide marked off four-acre blocks dotted with wooden houses regularly trimmed in yellow and grey. Because of its more central location within the state, Columbia had replaced Charleston as South Carolina's capital, and the statehouse, atop a three-hundred-foot hill covered with oaks, dominated the town. Just across the street lay the brick buildings of the college and the residential quarters of the steward and his family. James was awed by his new home, by the ambitious and sophisticated college students, and by the dramas of state politics taking place all around him.[7]

Even the meager ceremony associated with government in this provincial town must have dazzled an impressionable youth so recently arrived from an area of far greater rudeness and isolation. Hammond would no doubt have witnessed the annual fall opening of the legislative session, the parade of delegates and colorfully clad militia officers accompanying the biennial election of the new governor, and the annual commencement procession of the college, which in-

6. Faculty Minutes (in USCA), February 21, 1817. On Elisha's other Columbia ventures, see Hammond and Stillman Ledger (MS vol. bd., 1823–24, JHH Papers, SCL).

7. Lillian Adele Kibler, *Benjamin F. Perry, South Carolina Unionist* (Durham: Duke University Press, 1946), 58. See also on Columbia, Helen Kohn Hennig (ed.), *Columbia, Capital City of South Carolina, 1786–1936* (Columbia: R. L. Bryan, 1936), and Edward Hooker, *Diary of Edward Hooker, 1805–8* (Washington, D.C.: Government Printing Office, 1897).

cluded not only the scholars arrayed in academic robes but the officers of the state as well. On his way to school each morning, Hammond later remembered, he encountered the same governor's aide, en route to the capitol astride a spirited stallion. "I thought him Bucephalus & you Alexander so grand & imperial you both seemed to me." The power of office seemed represented by the force of the sleek animal that the rider so easily directed and controlled. The sight aroused a desire in the boy to be himself mounted on a similar steed, receiving the admiration of passing pedestrians. It was a concrete stimulant to his already active ambition. While the goals his father had held out to him had previously seemed abstract and unreal, in Columbia Hammond came face to face with the embodiments of success and power.[8]

But Hammond's earliest efforts to distinguish himself were not to lie in the political realm. Instead, he began to fill notebooks with essays and verse, some copied from romantic poets and others conveying his own musings in appropriately literary forms. His subjects ranged widely, but patriotic themes were a favorite. At the age of fourteen he composed a musical comedy in verse to commemorate the Battle of Eutaw, South Carolina's triumph of the Revolutionary War. In the final chorus, the cast gathered to hail the defeat of British despotism:

> Columbia's free. Oppression's oer
> The din of war will sound no more.
> South now the happy eagles soar
> And light on Carolina's shore
> This it [is] the day that freedom brings
> The Battle's past oer Eutaw Springs
> > Happy nation we are free
> > thus forever may we be
> > Time only and eternity
> > Can destroy our liberty.[9]

In the period of intense nationalism that followed the War of 1812, this young Carolinian was deeply affected by the currents of patriotic fervor. But it would not be long before Hammond, like other South Carolinians, would find that threats far more immediate and tangible than "time" and "eternity" were undermining "our liberty."

Hammond's boyhood writings displayed not only the influences of the era's pervasive nationalism but the age's closely related romanticism as well. These

8. Hammond to Beaufort T. Watts, December 6, 1859, in Beaufort T. Watts Papers, SCL.

9. Hammond, "The Deserter; or, The Battle of Eutaw," in "Selections of Poetry" (MS vol. bd., 1820–26, JHH Papers, SCL), 159.

strains are evident in the poems of Byron, Burns, and Shelley that James carefully copied into his notebook; in the boy's worshipful attention to heroes, from
Nathanael Greene to Bonaparte; and in his essays and plays. But the romantic
temper appears most clearly in the painful introspection that characterized so
much of Hammond's writing. James felt he knew a great deal about suffering, for
his father's expectations had made life a constant trial. "From my earliest recollections I now remember that I had nightmares & before I was 17 years old I
had confirmed indigestion . . . that paralyzed intellect & shattered nerves." On
paper he explored some of the dilemmas that had begun to consume him. "Every
thought and every action of man," he scribbled at age twelve, "is founded on the
broad basis of self-love . . . the hope of tranmittig to posterity his name covered with laurels." "In whatsoever situation man is placed from the highest to
the lowest his generale desire is to excel. To distinguish himself is the chief end
of all his wishes." Three years later his penmanship and spelling had improved,
but his subject matter had not changed. "No passion rules the soul with half the
force Ambition does, this the first, the primogenial ingredient of our nature."
The most inspiring embodiment of the noble force of ambition, Hammond proclaimed, was Napoleon. "No man ever rose from so low a degree to such preeminence. . . . he had no friend but his genius, no companion but his ambition, no
wealth but his mind, no power but his dignity." For the talented and aspiring,
Hammond concluded, all things are possible.[10]

For Elisha Hammond, however, almost all things seemed impossible. Exasperated by the constant complaints of the college students about their fare,
Hammond resigned as steward in 1821. Instead he determined to supplement his
growing lumbering ventures on the rivers about Columbia with a similar enterprise on the Savannah, a larger and more commercially active waterway. Leaving a partner in charge in the capital city, Elisha moved his family once again.
For most of the remaining six years of his life, Elisha struggled to make his fortune in a series of marginal enterprises in the area around Augusta, Georgia, and
the developing South Carolina town of Hamburg just across the river. When

---

10. Hammond, "Selections of Poetry"; Hammond to Simms, March 5, 1861, in JHH Papers,
LC; Hammond, "On Self Love," January, 1820, "On the Love of Fame," both in "Selections of
Poetry." See also Hammond, "Essay on Ambition, April 14, 1823" (MS in School Papers, JHH
Papers, SCL). James McLachlan has insightfully described the contribution of the romantic move-
ment to creating a "new sense of self" among the youth of the early nineteenth century. McLachlan,
"The *Choice of Hercules*: American Student Societies in the Early 19th Century," in Lawrence Stone
(ed.), *Europe, Scotland, and the United States from the 16th to the 20th Century*, Vol. II of *The University in Society* (Princeton: Princeton University Press, 1974), 483.

barges of wood destined for the coast failed to provide adequate returns, Elisha supplemented his income with the profits his wife made feeding boarders for fifty cents a day.

But this time James was spared the direct experience of his parents' struggles and disappointments. When they left Columbia in 1823, he remained behind to enter the junior class at South Carolina College. The institution had been transformed since the days of its infancy when Elisha Hammond had served as its first professor of languages. By the mid-twenties, the college boasted a president and five professors, and James's graduating class would include thirty-one members. Only one building had been completed during Elisha's term on the faculty, but since that time six additional structures had been erected to form a horseshoe around a row of trees and an expansive lawn.

In the years since its founding, the college had come to play an ever-expanding role in the political and social as well as the intellectual life of the state. The college was unquestionably an institution for the training of Carolina's leaders. Scholarship funds were scarce, and because Carolina had no system of common schools, ordinarily only the privileged advanced even to the secondary-school level. As a result, those who qualified for college were a select minority that usually included only a few youths from outside the state's aristocratic class. Some poorer pupils, such as the influential politician George McDuffie or the Presbyterian theologian James Henley Thornwell, were sponsored by wealthy benefactors. Others, like Hammond, succeeded in reaching the college through a combination of their parents' sheer determination and sacrifice with one or another fortuitous circumstance—in Hammond's case, Elisha's long connection with the institution. But such students were exceptions. The legislature funded the college with the express aims of educating and unifying the state's leadership class. The alumni's domination of state politics provoked continual complaints from less-privileged Carolinians. A pseudonymous critic protested in the Columbia *Southern Chronicle* in 1842 that many citizens looked upon "those educated at the South Carolina College as *alone* fit to fill the offices and control the destinies of the state." Twelve of the twenty-one governors between 1824 and 1865 had attended the college; three of the four state chancellors, five of the six state judges, and a majority of United States senators were former college students.[11]

11. Columbia *Southern Chronicle*, December 7, 1842, quoted in Daniel Walker Hollis, *South Carolina College*, Vol. I of *University of South Carolina* (Columbia: University of South Carolina Press, 1951), 256. See also John M. Bryan, *An Architectural History of the South Carolina College,*

In part the institution achieved this record through recruitment: sons of the state's most prominent families came to the college, and they succeeded naturally to leadership positions when they completed their academic course. But the college years were of crucial importance as well. South Carolina College socialized the upper-class youth of the state for the public service implied in their positions within the United States' most aristocratic subculture. The impact of this training is nowhere more evident than in the career of James Henry Hammond.

James's acceptance at the college with advanced standing indicated that he had already mastered the basics of Latin and Greek and was prepared to read Tacitus, Cicero, Homer, and Xenophon for semiweekly recitations. In addition he would pursue a host of other subjects, including trigonometry, quadratic equations, metaphysics, rhetoric, chemistry, mineralogy, geology, political economy, and moral philosophy. Hammond's notebooks testify to the tediousness of most of the curriculum. Lectures were, for the most part, delivered as series of propositions, which students copied almost verbatim. In language and mathematics, classes were devoted to "drill," with emphasis on exact memorization of the knowledge imparted. The most intellectually stimulating of Hammond's studies may have been the moral philosophy course that he, like almost all other students of his era, took during his senior year. This course went beyond rote learning to address questions of immediate import; moral philosophy was the science of "what ought to be." In this class Hammond imbibed lessons that made a lasting impact on his view of the world. Not only were many of Elisha's maxims reinforced but James encountered a broader political and philosophical context within which to locate his ever-growing ambition. As Professor Robert Henry led his charges through an exploration of "the true nature of man," he reiterated Elisha's exhortations to "defer not for a day, not an hour your resolution to be virtuous" and confirmed as well what James had long since suspected: that human beings were formed "to delight in the possession and exercise of power."

1801–1855 (Columbia: University of South Carolina Press, 1976); Harold S. Schultz, *Nationalism and Sectionalism in South Carolina, 1852–1860: A Study of the Movement for Southern Independence* (Durham: Duke University Press, 1950), 8; Charles W. Hutson, "The South Carolina College in the Late Fifties," *Sewanee Review*, XVIII (July, 1910), 333–43. For discussion of the aristocratic nature of the college, see Charleston *Courier*, December 3, 5, 7, 1856; reference to it as a "rich man's college" by Governor J. H. Adams, November 24, 1856, and similar remarks of Governor John L. Manning, November 25, 1853, both in Governors' Messages, Legislative Papers, 1831–59, SCA. On South Carolina College, see also Robert Henry Papers, Robert Anderson Papers, Henry Junius Nott Papers, all SCL.

But Henry opened James's eyes to a new understanding of the larger world through his detailed description of the social order in which these young men might expect to make their mark. Henry's organic conception of man's place in society offered a solid foundation for the conservative social thought that was emerging in the South of the late 1820s.[12]

In the course of the 1820s the Missouri Compromise debates in Congress, the Negro seamen controversy and the Denmark Vesey slave conspiracy had made South Carolinians nervously aware of growing threats to their peculiar institution. In its legitimation of rebellion and its assertion of the natural equality of man, the revolutionary ideology on which the nation had been founded contained ominous implications for the future of southern slavery, and now the North seemed to be gaining sufficient power within the federal government to begin to translate these abstractions into reality. Robert Henry addressed these pressing issues directly, informing his students that men were not born in freedom and equality, but in specific social situations that differentiated them from one another on a hierarchical social scale. As the antebellum period wore on, Henry left less and less of the political import of his position implicit. By the mid-thirties he began to launch overt attacks upon the philosophical underpinnings of what he saw as dangerous northern efforts to change and reform social conditions. Henry devoted considerable effort to instructing Carolina youths in how to discredit these assumptions most effectively. Anyone claiming that "there is no necessity which compels us to retain slaves," he explained, was "mistaken" because the "institutions of a country are a long length of time in being formed & therefore if they are destroyed in a day society would be uprooted." Precipitous human intervention in social processes was always bad, and he concluded, it was "absolutely necessary to keep the blacks in the present condition."[13]

Henry was not the only member of the faculty to offer instruction in the fundamentals of states' rights philosophy. The college was directed in these years

12. Hammond, "Introductory Lecture to Moral Philosophy by Rev. Robert Henry, A.M., March 6, 1824," in College Lecture Book (MS vol. bd., 1822–25, JHH Papers, SCL); John McMaster, "Questions & Answers in Moral Philosophy Not to Be Found in Paley" (Student Notebook, 1834, John McMaster Papers, SCL); Robert Julius Gage, "Lectures in Metaphysics, by Robert Henry" (Student Notes, 2 MS vols. bd., 1830–31, Robert Julius Gage Papers, SCL). On the influence of moral philosophy North and South, see D. H. Meyer, *The Instructed Conscience: The Shaping of the American National Ethic* (Philadelphia: University of Pennsylvania Press, 1972).

13. McMaster, Student Notebook, Gage, Student Notes. On the evolution of a social organicist philosophy in the South, see Theodore Dwight Bozeman, "Joseph LeConte: Organic Science and a 'Sociology' for the South," *Journal of Southern History*, XXXIX (November, 1973), 565–82.

by the illustrious—in some circles notorious—Thomas Cooper, who presided over its operation from the president's house at the center of the curve of the campus horseshoe. A British scholar, physician, and chemist, Cooper had emigrated to the United States at the end of the century and had quickly gained notoriety for his outspoken political views. Indicted and jailed in 1800 under the terms of the Alien and Sedition Acts for libel against President John Adams, Cooper gained the loyal support of Thomas Jefferson, who sponsored him for posts first at the University of Virginia, then in 1819 at South Carolina College. An increasingly vocal defender of southern liberties, Cooper has been dubbed by one historian the "Schoolmaster of State Rights." Twenty-four of his pupils went on to serve as delegates to the 1860 secession convention in South Carolina, and many more supported the agitation for sectional rights in other ways. Although Hammond later in life acknowledged Cooper's influence, he insisted that it had not been transmitted during his college years, but through the study of the old radical's writings in the years following graduation. Hammond was enrolled in one of Cooper's political economy classes, but he confessed he was "seldom present taking no interest in the subject then."[14]

In fact, Hammond seems to have paid little attention to any academic work during much of his college career. Freed from his father's oppressive exhortations, Hammond at first "gave myself up to idle associates & neither read nor studied." But Elisha's admonitions could be only partially and temporarily dismissed, for James had already internalized his father's aspirations. After a year of dissipation, Hammond found, to his alarm, that he stood about "30 to 35 in a class of 35 to 40. In fact I had no standing at all." Such a situation was intolerable, for all of life appeared to James as a contest in which the only possible outcomes were victory or abject defeat. College, he later advised his younger brother Marcellus, was a "race" in which individuals continually jockeyed for "position." "Never look behind nor yet too far before, but always be alive & ready, & you will find yourself gradually gaining ground." By the time of graduation, James had reformed his habits until he "was placed no. 4 & would have done better if I had had another session to run."[15]

Even while Hammond was neglecting his studies during a term or two of boyish self-indulgence, he did not abandon all efforts to distinguish himself. But

14. Dumas Malone, *The Public Life of Thomas Cooper, 1783–1839* (New Haven: Yale University Press, 1926), 281; Hammond to James Hamilton, March 7, 1832, in JHH Papers, LC. See also Thomas Cooper, *Lectures on Elements of Political Economy* (Columbia: D. E. Sweeny, 1826).

15. Hammond, "Thoughts and Recollections," February 24, 1852; Hammond to M. C. M. Hammond, July 6, 1833, November 30, 1832, both in JHH Papers, SCL.

his early writings show his aspirations to have been somewhat diffuse and un-focused. Hammond's first achievements were literary, and he continued to write poetry at college, even publishing some of his verse in the Columbia newspapers. Yet as he moved through the round of college activities, Hammond gradually learned that the arena in which a young Carolinian could best make his mark was not literature, but politics, not poetry, but oratory. And he was also to be trained during his college years in the personal characteristics of aggression and self-assertiveness that underlay the leadership of the South's master class.

Most of this education took place outside the classroom, and much of it in spite of the faculty, who were continually frustrated in their efforts to control the students' unruly behavior. In fact, the faculty was often the victim of the pranks that formed a central part of this assertive student culture. During Hammond's years, a group of students repeatedly removed the steps from various of the college buildings in order to enjoy the humiliating spectacle of their instructors struggling to enter on awkward ladders. Dr. Cooper, who was elderly, rotund, and, the students found, quite "clumsy," served as an object of especial mirth. Such mischief symbolically declared that whatever power these instructors might wield within the classroom, the students would and could counter with power of their own. "The relation of the Faculty and the students," one antebellum instructor reminisced, "was not the relation of friends, but in too many instances of enemies." The young men were learning to resist domination, in whatever form it appeared.[16]

These Carolinians, even as students, would not abide the slightest incursion upon their vaunted rights. The minute attention to insults to sectional honor later evident in the South's posture in the national political arena was here prefigured by the students' claims both upon the faculty and on one another, as well as in the speed with which they resorted to violence when these assumptions were challenged. Just as southerners in Congress during the late antebellum period became constitutionalists to combat northern domination and to legitimate their sectional position, so college students, threatened with disciplinary action, regularly "stood upon their rights," as one instructor observed disgustedly, "and turned lawyers." One group of youths stole the college bell, then refused to attend classes, claiming that they were required to obey only its summons. When

16. LaBorde, *History of the South Carolina College*, 133–34, 74. On unruly students in the North, see Joseph Kett, *Rites of Passage: Adolescence in America, 1790 to the Present* (New York: Basic Books, 1977). For remarks on the qualitative difference in violence in a southern college, see Thomas Cooper, "Dr. Cooper's Report," Proceedings of the Trustees, South Carolina College, April 22, 1823, USCA.

the administration substituted a portable bell rung by a slave, the young legalists were undaunted, declaring that they certainly could not be expected to heed the call of any but a white man.[17]

The most intense competition, however, took place not between students and faculty, but among the students, who were constantly vying, like Hammond, for "position" and "standing" in the eyes of their peers. Here too an over-developed notion of prerogative prevailed, for the reigning code of honor transformed every contest of wills into a challenge to manhood itself. In the dining hall one day, two students reached for a platter of trout simultaneously. Each claimed to have touched the dish first, and even though the boys were close friends, neither felt he could submit to the humiliation of yielding precedence to the other. A formal challenge ensued, and the resulting duel led to the deaths of both participants.

In this culture, students at South Carolina College quickly learned, self assertiveness was so valued that no challenge could be dismissed as trivial. The substantive import of the trout platter was irrelevant; the symbolic issue was all-important, for the power of South Carolina's master class depended to a great extent on symbols and display. This was a leadership group too widely scattered throughout the sparsely settled state to rule by means of constant surveillance and overt force. Instead, South Carolina's planters maintained their preeminence over lesser whites and a population of blacks that far outnumbered them by constantly demonstrating in their day-to-day behavior that they would permit no challenge to their omnipotence. A symbolism of violence made clear to all how quickly selective force would be invoked to reinforce the structure of power. A single duel could reaffirm both a behavioral code and an individual's status in the eyes of all who learned of the encounter; the whipping of just one slave made an unmistakable statement about race and power to an entire plantation; a young man's self-esteem could stand or fall on his control of a dish of trout.[18]

---

17. LaBorde, *History of the South Carolina College*, 278.

18. Hollis, *South Carolina College*, 92. This culture of aggressive masculinity and display affected even the most fundamental aspects of students' lives and identities. A college friend jocularly wrote Hammond after their graduation to learn "whether you yet sleep in your shirt-tail, and whether you yet have the extravagant delight of poking and punching a writhing Bedfellow with your long fleshen pole—the exquisite touches of which I have often had the honor of feeling? Let me say unto thee, that unless thou changest former habits in this particular, thou wilt be represented by every future chum as a nuisance. . . . Sir, you roughen the downy slumbers of your Bedfellow—by such hostile lunges as you are in the habit of making at him—when he is least prepared for defence against the crushing force of a Battering Ram." The "old stud, Jeff," Thomas Jefferson Withers, who

One of the primary outlets for Hammond's assertiveness and ambition lay in the activities of the two student organizations that included all South Carolina College pupils in a regular series of contests centered on the South's cherished tradition of oratory. As one historian of American education has described them, the literary societies of antebellum institutions of higher learning were "colleges within colleges" that "engrossed more of the interests and activities of the students than any other aspect of college life."[19] Courses in the regular curriculum were to be endured; the Clariosophic and Euphradian Societies of South Carolina College were where the real education took place. The intellectual influence of the debates that served as the focal activity of these organizations is far more evident in Hammond's adult life than is any of the specific knowledge he acquired in the classroom.

The Euphradian Society, to which Hammond was elected in November, 1823, met every Saturday evening after supper to "obtain a knowledge of Science in general but more particularly, to improve in Oratory." Each formal meeting included at least one and usually more prepared debates with negative and affirmative positions assigned to members two weeks in advance. In addition the Euphradians selected from their membership a monthly orator who was required to deliver a full-length address. When Hammond had been in the society only a few weeks he was chosen for this honor, and he soon had achieved a commanding position in the organization. In fact, he spoke so frequently that his fellow Euphradians finally felt compelled to consider adopting a rule that "no member be allowed to speak oftener than twice" at any meeting.[20]

The topics Hammond addressed ranged widely, but fell chiefly into the categories of private morals and public policy. Hammond successfully argued that "seduction" should not be "punishable by death," that moral rather than physi-

---

later became a prominent state jurist, was hardly referring to overt homosexual behavior, and it is unclear from his remarks exactly what passed between the two young men. Living well before the sharp differentiation and emotional internalization of distinct categories of homosexuality and heterosexuality in the post-Freudian era, Withers was concerned here less with the question of sex than that of power. Withers' language, his choice of antiquated and precious terms, as well as his play upon the word ram, indicate his bantering tone; he was teasing Hammond for his unflagging competitiveness, for the "delight" he took in dominance, even when it appeared in this somewhat inappropriate form. The physically violent expression of mastery, encouraged at every other level of life, here assumed its most elemental expression. But Withers hailed Hammond's behavior as a *reductio ad absurdum*, chastening his friend for being too absorbed in his pursuit of the values his society had held out before him. Thomas Jefferson Withers to Hammond, May 15, 1826, in JHH Papers, SCL.

19. McLachlan, "American Student Societies," 472.
20. Euphradian Society Constitution, 1806–41, Euphradian Society Minutes, 1823–33, November 20, 1824, both in USCA.

cal causes "have greatest influence on character," and that man possesses a "moral sense." He was unable to convince his fellow Euphradians that man could be "as happy without restrictions on his conduct as with them" or that eloquence could not "improve mankind."[21]

But Hammond did not always address such abstract themes. In the Euphradian Hall he first confronted the crucial political issues of his day. In March of 1825, Hammond argued unsuccessfully that an oppressive tariff could not justify rebellion in any section of the United States. In the same year he made his first and last antislavery speech when he was assigned to debate in favor of emancipation. Perhaps his heart was not in it, for the question was decided against him.[22]

When appointed debators were unprepared, Hammond often volunteered to stand in for them and speak extempore, for he relished the opportunity to display his facility in such verbal encounters. Elected treasurer of the society in 1824, Hammond soon joined a committee to spend the money in his charge in "better ornament of the Hall." Silk draperies replaced green bombazine curtains, and in accordance with this heightened sense of propriety and dignity, members were enjoined to refrain from spitting on the carpet.[23]

In January, 1825, Hammond was elevated to the Euphradian presidency. The allure of office captivated the young man, and he soon found himself electioneering for another—the highest—Euphradian honor, that of valedictory orator for the graduating class of December, 1825. The complex intrigues surrounding this election involved alliances and coalitions, threats and name-calling, but Hammond emerged triumphant from this first electoral campaign.[24]

Victory was not without its cost. Having achieved his goal, Hammond found himself almost overcome by the responsibility success entailed. Still the romantic adolescent at heart, he poured out his musings and self-doubt. "At this moment," he postured self-consciously in his diary, "the first bell is ringing to summons an audience to my valedictory oration—my voice fails me & I fear I shall acquit myself badly—The bell sounds like a death note—like the knell of departed joys—I may lose what little reputation I already possess." Hammond put

21. Euphradian Society Minutes, March 5, 1825, November 13, 1824, October 8, 1825, November 22, 1823, January 24, 1824. See also Euphradian Society Treasurer's Books, 1818–24, Euphradian Society Censor's Book, 1824–34, Euphradian Literary Society Debate Book, 1820–38, all USCA.
22. Euphradian Society Minutes, March 12, November 12, 1825. See also Hollis, "The Cult of Oratory," in *South Carolina College*, and Hutson, "The South Carolina College in the Late Fifties."
23. Euphradian Society Minutes, October 23, 1824, February 26, 1825, February 7, 1824.
24. Nell S. Graydon, *Tales of Columbia* (Columbia: R. L. Bryan, 1964), 40–41.

down his pen to gather with his fellow Euphradians in their society room, then, dressed in academic robe, marched at the head of their procession to the college chapel where he spoke. He returned to add to the page of anxious reflections he had begun earlier in the day, "It is all over & I have not disgraced myself."[25]

Far from disgracing himself, James seemed to his proud father, who had returned to Columbia for his son's graduation, to be "acquiring immortal honor by his Eloquence and composition." If achievement made James fearful of the heightened expectations it generated, his success rendered Elisha jubilant. Having left Columbia in financial embarrassment, Elisha was now a center of attention and acclaim as a result of his son's attainments. Perhaps even more important, James was hailed by those who had never deigned to acknowledge his father. "Your brother . . . ," he wrote to his daughter Eliza, "by his industrious and correct habits has acquired a popularity in and out of College, which no Scholar in this place ever obtained before he has cards every night this week to parties in the first houses of this town—The Governor notices him in every company in a very particular manner. . . . Your Mama and myself are congratulated wherever we go on account of the superior talents and correct deportment of James." Elisha added several postscripts to the letter as his gratification and joy heightened at the mounting evidence of his son's successes. James "charmed every body though the youngest scholar in his class, his manner of speaking and writing is as much superior to any in college as the brightness of the Sun beams exceeds the dim rays of the Moon."[26]

Despite the round of parties, the commencement ball, and despite his father's pride, James was more anxious than jubilant. He could well congratulate himself on his achievements, as he put it, in "gaining ground," toward fulfillment of his father's aspirations for him. In less than three years since his matriculation, James had gained not only a college degree but also a rudimentary education in the techniques and substance of southern politics and in the comportment and attitudes befitting a member of Carolina's ruling class. Hammond's years at South Carolina College and his rise to prominence within that self-contained world enabled him to transcend his humble social origins. The creation and bulwark of an aristocracy of wealth, South Carolina College nevertheless nurtured within its walls an aristocracy of talent where the most gifted and ambitious could thrive. Amongst its students, position and precedence were granted on the basis of ability, of success in its many competitive arenas, rather

25. Hammond, School Papers (JHH Papers, SCL), n.d.
26. Elisha Hammond to Eliza Hammond, December 8, 1825, in JHH Papers, SCL.

than claims of birth and social rank. In these years Hammond made friends with the men who would lead the state for the next generation. After college, Hammond was never again an outsider gazing with awe at the ceremonial displays of power in the state capital at Columbia. On the day of his graduation Hammond marched in the procession of legislators, government officials, professors, and students to the awarding of degrees. It was an important moment. No longer was he the steward's son; no longer the schoolboy staring enviously at the governor's aide on his magnificent horse. Hammond had become a person in his own right, recognized and praised by the state's chief executive, welcomed at the capital's finest houses, honored as a leading orator by his peers.

But for Hammond this remarkable success simply yielded another, more difficult agenda and amplified still further his father's original expectations of him. Just as his election as Euphradian orator overwhelmed him with fear of losing "what little reputation I already possess," so the graduation celebration that delighted Elisha made James above all tense. When the ceremony was over, young Hammond spread his academic robe upon the steps opposite the chapel and gazed across the college grounds. Since his father had become steward in 1815, a decade before, Hammond's life had been focused almost without interruption on this spot. The college had been the vehicle of his personal and intellectual growth as well as of his remarkable advancement. But, he recognized as he pondered the familiar scene before him, a new era was about to begin, for he was leaving this protected world. It was a prospect that filled him with anxiety.[27]

---

27. James Henry Hammond European Diary (MS in JHH Papers, SCL), Vol. I, December 5, 1836. On the graduation ceremony, see Charleston *Courier*, December 6, 1825.

CHAPTER 2

Ways and Means

Hammond left South Carolina College with ambition, but without voca-tion. For almost three years the institution had provided a social place and purpose. In gaining his degree, he lost the security of the academic world in which he had thrived. But James was not to be permitted the luxury of idleness while he sought an appropriate career. His father's "serious fears that my debts will ruin me before I can pay" compelled young James to seek employment at once.[1]

Like many ambitious young men of the nineteenth century, including sev-eral of the less privileged of his classmates and even his own father, Hammond turned to teaching. James grudgingly accepted a position at Poplar Spring Acad-emy, four and a half miles outside Orangeburg, a market town and district seat about fifty miles from Columbia. The role of rural schoolmaster was one the am-bitious youth had never envisioned for himself, and he chafed under the humili-ation of filling what he regarded as a demeaning position. His nine months at Poplar Spring he would later remember to have been "time most unprofitably spent." Not only did his social and intellectual advancement come to a halt, but Hammond found himself miserable and overworked as well. Many of the pupils in his charge, who were preparing for admission to South Carolina College, were hardly younger than he. Hammond feared exposure of his ignorance, especially in mathematics; he was certain his understanding of algebra was insufficient for him even to pretend to teach it to others. Beset by such anxieties, Hammond

1. Elisha Hammond to James Henry Hammond, January 1, 1826, in JHH Papers, SCL.

felt lonely and isolated as well, for he had become accustomed to the liveliness of Columbia society and to the company of his college friends. Lacking sympathetic companionship, he lapsed into romantic brooding; he poured out his unhappiness in correspondence, bemoaning "pleasures wh. have fled forever," recounting his "solitary walks" among "melancholy groves," and inquiring wistfully after the fate of a favorite "pink bonnet" in Columbia. To one former college associate, he melodramatically proclaimed, "My soul pants to throw off this weight of mortality and with it the cares & troubles of this world." Removed from the political intrigues that had begun to fascinate him in Columbia, Hammond turned once again to poetry. In the conventional romantic lament he found a congenial mode for the expression of his own feelings.

> Oh! I had once a soul as proud,
>   As proud as e'er was broke
> The future smil'd and not a cloud
>   The gathering storm bespoke
>
> I bask'd in fortune's genial beams
>   Nor long'd for pleasures gone;
> While glory and thy golden dreams,
>   Ambition lured me on.[2]

Hammond did not spare his struggling father these self-pitying effusions. Unlike James's college associates, who replied with odes to melancholy rivaling Hammond's own, Elisha had little patience with his son's complaints. The boy's situation seemed genuinely enviable to the older man. "I had rather be JHH surrounded by poverty," he declared bluntly to his son, "than any young man in the State who is only buoyed up by property and family." College, Elisha insisted, had been an unreal situation. In fact, he reminded his son, the boy had always been sheltered from the struggle for the necessities of life. "This is your first excursion into the common and illiterate world. You have always been within the walls of a seminary amongst your equals—you were a community by yourselves." But it was time James learned more of reality. "It is absolutely necessary to understand some of the drudgery of life. I know your confinement is irksome but it will help you to form a habit of business." Elisha summarily dismissed his son's dejection. "One of your age, talents & prospects low spirited pshaw

2. James Henry Hammond, "Thoughts and Recollections" (MS vol. bd., 1852–53), February 24, 1852, Hammond to Henry W. Hilliard, July 17, 1826, Hilliard to Hammond, July 15, 1826, Hammond to Dear Frank, May 26, 1826, clipping from Columbia *Telescope* (Hammond Scrapbook, MS vol. bd., 1825–40), all in JHH Papers, SCL.

Courtesy of the South Caroliniana Library
Elisha Hammond, James's father.

pshaw !!" Hammond urged James to look upon his situation as "a state of sad probation" from which he would certainly emerge "like Gold twice purified." The experience would not be devoid of opportunities if James ingratiated himself with his employers. If James succeeded in getting his charges admitted to the college, he would win the gratitude of their influential parents. James had an important service to offer. "He who believes you are in his Interest will be your friend—the great art of gaining popularity is to make every man believe so." Elisha's ultimate hopes for his son remained undiminished. "When President of the U.S.," he assured James, "you will tell many anecdotes about the Poplar Spring." [3]

3. Elisha Hammond to Hammond, January 1, August 11, June 13, July 15, 1826, all *ibid.*

James was unconsoled by his father's flattery and reassurances, for he could not abide the humiliation he felt at teaching school, at following so directly in the footsteps of his unsuccessful parent. The pretensions James had acquired at South Carolina College were hardly consistent with Elisha's urgings that he court the favor of others. Hammond sought the independence compatible with his image of himself as a person of unique gifts. "I do not like my present situation, because I really *think*, & *feel* that it is below me. I cannot reconcile it to myself & tho nothing in the conduct of those around me is *meant* to remind me of my situation, yet it does seem to me entirely too *menial*. This is not *pride*. It is nothing but an honest respect to the dignity of my character."[4]

Determined to escape both pedagogy and Poplar Spring, James began to cast about for an alternative. The profession of law offered one avenue towards economic and political advancement for a youth without wealth or family connections, but the field, Hammond knew, was becoming increasingly crowded, and so he did not settle firmly upon it. Instead, he applied for a post as surveyor general of the state and even began to consider leaving South Carolina. The rich cotton lands available on the Alabama frontier proved an irresistible attraction for many young men of ambition in the seaboard South during the 1820s and 1830s, and Hammond contemplated joining the army of migrants taking advantage of these "flush times" in the Southwest.[5]

James's first move came at the end of 1826 when he left Poplar Spring for a position as tutor with the Pegues family about five miles outside of Cheraw. Elisha had advised his son that a post "in some Genteel family" might enable him to devote "one half of your time to Study Law." Young Hammond was attracted to the new job as well by its location in the Chesterfield District not more than twenty miles from a group of his friends who lived in Society Hill.[6]

But in his new post James found little time for leisurely camaraderie. Instead he turned to his work with determination, applying himself to the study of Blackstone's *Commentaries* in every moment he could spare from the thirteen students in the two families who shared his $336 salary. This unrelieved labor soon proved "fatal to my spirits," and Hammond informed his father after three weeks that he was close to collapse from mental strain. James declared his inten-

---

4. Hammond to Elisha Hammond, February 23, 1827, *ibid.*
5. Joseph G. Baldwin, *The Flush Times of Alabama and Mississippi* (1853, reprint; New York: Sagamore Press, 1957); Alfred G. Smith, Jr., *Economic Readjustment of an Old Cotton State: South Carolina, 1820–1860* (Columbia: University of South Carolina Press, 1958).
6. Elisha Hammond to Hammond, November 16, 1826, in JHH Papers, SCL; Hammond to William Gilmore Simms, February 27, 1856, in JHH Papers, LC.

tion of "giving up every employment that requires deep thinking until I overcome if possible the demoniac spirit which preys upon me." The same force that had produced his childhood nightmares haunted him still, and Hammond felt consumed by "the gloomy broodings of a disturbed imagination." Under the circumstances, he explained to his unemployed and debt-ridden father, he could "pay little regard" to Elisha's constant demands for economy. "I shall spare no means of regaining my health." With such a vital issue at stake, James would not trifle with mere financial concerns.[7]

Because of his father's sacrifices, James had until his graduation from college been spared any real material deprivation. But Elisha encountered a spell of particularly bad luck in the late twenties and could no longer shield his son from mundane realities. The boy had completed his education, and Elisha now began to turn to him for help. It was a harsh awakening for James to recognize that his ambition for greatness required financial support, that wealth would have to be coupled with fame as a necessary personal goal.

On one level, riches seemed sordid to young men of the early nineteenth century, who sought more transcendent achievement and deplored the growing strength of the "gospel of Mammon." "Above all," Hammond inscribed in a notebook of "Fugitive Peices [sic]," "is to be admired the lofty Genius, wh. elevating itself from the grovelling mass of the world's creatures confines its vision to no place or time." Yet this age of poetic effusions and religious revivals was also an era of dynamic material progress. In the three decades before the Civil War, the United States embarked decisively upon a course of economic expansion and industrial development. Within the context of individual lives, this meant that there was money to be made, and social and political prominence came increasingly to be correlated with economic power. But the nation did not abandon its concern with the more spiritual realms of existence. Even within individual Americans intense conflict raged between the commitment to material prosperity and to more spiritual attainments. Consumed with ambition for power in all its manifestations, Hammond would struggle to reconcile these opposing loyalties all his life.[8]

Even as teenagers, Hammond and his friends recognized these dilemmas and explored them at length, filling their correspondence with personal and voca-

7. Hammond to Elisha Hammond, February 23, 1827, Elisha Hammond to Hammond, October 11, 1826, both in JHH Papers, SCL.
8. Hammond, "Fugitive Peices" (MS vol. bd. 1829–30, JHH Papers, SCL); Charles E. Rosenberg, "Sexuality, Class, and Role," *American Quarterly*, XXV (May, 1973), 131–53.

tional uncertainties. Thomas Jefferson Withers, a college classmate now teaching at Ebenezer Academy in York District, offered Hammond a significant insight into the problem. In South Carolina, he wrote, "Poverty is undoubtedly a misfortune, of grave character—for such is the . . . taste, and such the despicable principles of the society upon which we depend for half the common pleasures of life—that to meet with favour—always important to the honourable aspirations of even noble minds—the dazzling splendour of wealth is too nearly indispensable. . . . We may despise the aristocracy of wealth—and try to scorn its frowns—but they press too hard and gall too much to be treated with levity." South Carolina College had exposed them to this aristocracy of wealth and to the pleasures its money could buy. A few months of pedagogy dramatized their own comparative deprivation. Poverty thereafter assumed a far more tangible significance.[9]

Elisha had hoped that James's experience as a schoolteacher would gently introduce him to the struggle of "real life." "Difficulties," Elisha was certain, "strengthen both nerve and Resolution." Young Hammond's dissatisfaction with his pedagogical role in one sense fully realized his father's intentions, for the boy's unhappiness spurred him to find a means of escaping the injustice he felt at having to exhaust himself for the "trifling pittance" of a teacher's salary. But while Elisha at first dismissed James's grumbling, he was alarmed by the boy's account of his near collapse. He responded with sympathy and concern to James's overwrought letters. "The seat of your complaint," Elisha was convinced, "is in the Nerves; which ought to be kept as quiet as possible." If necessary, he should resign from his position and return home. "Do just as you please. I shall be satisfied. Whatever I can do for you will be done with pleasure." Elisha urged the boy to relax. He seemed to be in such an unnecessary hurry. At James's age Elisha had not yet even entered college. "You have no need of injuring yourself by hard Study," he soothed, resigning himself to assuming James's support once again.[10]

Liberated by this demonstration of parental acceptance and indulgence, James left Cheraw late in March, 1827, for Columbia, having prescribed for himself a dose of diverting society to relieve his overworked mind. This was clearly not what Elisha had intended, and he was alarmed at the thought of the expense of James's therapeutic vacation. Elisha abandoned his softened tone and resumed

9. Thomas Jefferson Withers to Hammond, November 10, 1826, in JHH Papers, SCL.

10. Elisha Hammond to Hammond, August 11, 1826, *ibid.*; Elisha Hammond to Hammond, April 12, 1827, in HBC Papers, SCL; Hammond to Elisha Hammond, February 23, 1827, Elisha Hammond to Hammond, March 18, 1827, both in JHH Papers, SCL; Elisha Hammond to Hammond, March 4, 1827, in HBC Papers, SCL.

his accustomed strictness. "*Despair!*" he wrote mockingly to James in Columbia, "at the age of nineteen—blessed with superior talents and a liberal Education, nobody to provide for but your dear self? . . . I wish I could change places with you for a few months to let you see the difference."[11]

Dutifully, James returned to his father's house late in May, 1827, and for the next year and a half devoted his efforts to qualifying for admission to the bar. Because South Carolina had no formal law school or faculty in the early nineteenth century, aspiring attorneys were instructed through the apprenticeship system, usually by reading standard texts under the supervision of an established practitioner. Occasionally lawyers offered students a private course of more formal lectures, such as those Hammond attended in the fall of 1827 given by Judge William Tracy Gould of Augusta. During the following winter James studied with Judge John McGeehee in Cambridge, South Carolina, then continued to read law with two eminent jurists, William Harper and William Campbell Preston of Columbia. "I was in all these Offices," he later recalled, "but I do not remember that any of these gentlemen asked me a question about law. I read their books & in return did some little filling of blanks for them."[12]

Too frequently Hammond found himself distracted from the problems of devises in chancery, estates on conditions, and equity courts with which he filled his notebooks. Society—especially that of young ladies—offered an almost irresistible allure to the young Carolinian. Strikingly handsome, Hammond was delighted by the powerful attraction he exerted over women. But their flattery and attentions had an equally potent effect upon him. He struggled against giving himself up to these temptations, acknowledging the truth in one friend's teasing remark that James's "lustful appetite" seemed to "have acquired complete mastery" over him. Both his father's constant exhortations and his own experience at South Carolina College had impressed James with the importance of never yielding self-control. But with charming and flirtatious women, Hammond found resistance almost impossible. The emotions of love and desire exerted their own mastery. In desperation, he decided to renounce romantic involvement altogether, and he proclaimed in a poem tellingly entitled "Independence":

> My heart is free, my heart is free
> Free as the desert air

11. Elisha Hammond to Hammond, April 7, 1827, in JHH Papers, SCL.

12. See "Gould's Lectures" (MS vol. bd., 1827), Hammond, "Thoughts and Recollections," February 24, 1852; Hammond, "Exceptions to General Rules, January 1, 1828" (MS vol. bd., 1827–28), all *ibid*.

No girl with all her flirting
Can draw it to her snare[13]

I. W. Hayne found his friend's resolution foolish, for one "so peculiarly prone" to the charms of the opposite sex could hardly forswear the company of ladies entirely. "To be plain with you," Hayne wrote in response to James's declaration of his resolve, "it is a little ridiculous to hear a youth of your complexion at nineteen talking of the eternal slumber of love in his bosom. . . . I don't like your plan of seclusion from female society."[14]

As recipients of his constant complaints about the trials of courtship and the bewildering ways of women, Hammond's friends responded generously with advice, assuring him that there was no basis for his "suicidal moments of melancholic despair." Jeff Withers believed Hammond was just too hard to please and would be dissatisfied even if he won the hand of the most eligible belle in the state. "Why, Jim," he exclaimed, "if you were to hook one of old Wade's [Hampton] daughters, I am inclined to think you would still be unhappy. You have never yet had the P——x: congratulate yourself on that good fortune." Even Elisha had his customary homilies to offer the boy on the subject of courtship. "Never marry," he advised, "unless a rich, or a poor woman raised to hard work. . . . Always have an Eye to your Ways and Means."[15]

James was indeed much concerned with his ways and means. Despite the energy he was devoting to passing the bar, he was troubled about his vocational choice. Friends continually warned him about "suffering for subsistence" as a lawyer. The profession was becoming crowded, they cautioned, and many young attorneys were unable to find adequate employment. But in South Carolina times were hard not only for lawyers. Up to 1820, the state had experienced a period of unparalleled prosperity, with short-staple cotton production and population expanding rapidly into the interior and up-country. Banking and commercial expansion followed on the heels of this boom, and citizens throughout the state thrived. But after these years, South Carolina's economy began to decline as cotton spread westward to new and more fertile soils and as increased production led to a significant drop in price. Population began to leave the state; Charleston suffered a decrease in foreign trade. The effects of this decline reverberated

13. Withers to Hammond, September 24, 1826, Hammond Scrapbook (1825–40), August 1, 1828, both in JHH Papers, SCL.
14. I. W. Hayne to Hammond, June 23, August 3, 1827, both in JHH Papers, LC.
15. Withers to Hammond, April 6, 1827, *ibid.*; Elisha Hammond to Hammond, December 21, 1827, in JHH Papers, SCL.

throughout the state economy, diminishing Elisha Hammond's entrepreneurial opportunities, curtailing the number and variety of openings for enterprising young college graduates, reducing the number of commercial transactions requiring lawyers' assistance. The legal profession had expanded rapidly in the years after the Revolution, and now, as South Carolina's growth slowed, competition among attorneys grew intense.[16]

Yet when Hammond contemplated the drawbacks to a career in the law, no clear alternative presented itself. "Law is the only road to honour," his father advised, even "if not to riches." Part of the reason for the crowding of the profession was that it did offer one avenue of mobility in a society where most money was generated through plantation agriculture, an enterprise that required considerable investments of capital. Although some individuals had made fortunes in planting during the boom years of cotton expansion before 1820, the possibilities for this sort of advancement in South Carolina had greatly diminished as new lands filled and the price of cotton declined. Unlike the North, where a variety of business opportunities had begun to open in the growing cities, the South remained overwhelmingly rural, and its economy provided a far smaller assortment of paths for social advancement. On the advice of friends, Hammond considered accepting a sinecure as the librarian of South Carolina College. But for one so jealous of his "Independence," the idea of being "continually dependent upon others caprice" was disturbing. Despite its difficulties, the law retained many attractions for the young Carolinian. Hammond was well aware of the truth of William Campbell Preston's observation, "The object of a Southern man's life is *politics* and subsidiary to this end we all practice law." If he could successfully traverse the treacherous shoals at the entrance to the legal profession, Hammond knew it offered him the best opportunity for achieving a position of social, economic, and political prominence.[17]

In the summer of 1828, however, Hammond experienced a brief setback in his professional progress when a needle broke off in his pocket and embedded itself in his leg, requiring minor surgery and leaving him lame for several weeks.

16. I. W. Hayne to Hammond, February 15, 1828, in JHH Papers, SCL; Smith, *Economic Readjustment*; Marjorie Mendenhall, "A History of Agriculture in South Carolina, 1790 to 1860: An Economic and Social Survey" (Ph.D. dissertation, University of North Carolina, Chapel Hill, 1940).
17. Elisha Hammond to Hammond, February 25, 1829, I. W. Hayne to Hammond, April 12, 1828, both in JHH Papers, SCL; William C. Preston to George Ticknor, March 2, 1834, cited in John Boyd Edmunds, "Francis W. Pickens and South Carolina Politics" (M.A. thesis, University of South Carolina, 1964), 3.

A vacation in the cool and salubrious up-country hills with his cousins hastened his recovery, but early in September misfortune struck again. His younger sister Eliza died suddenly, and James lamented in verse his absence from her side during her suffering, his inability "To catch one fond—one lingering look / And bid a last & long adieu."[18]

Eliza's death was for her father Elisha but the worst in a long string of disasters. He had hoped to escape debt with profits from shipping goods down the Savannah River in a small craft he had acquired, but the age of steamboats had arrived in Augusta, and Elisha could not compete. Unable to find any satisfactory employment, he decided to return to pedagogy. Early in 1828, he departed to direct a school in Macon, Georgia. He could not afford to move his family, and he left them behind to support themselves with revenue from boarders. Even the school in Macon failed to relieve Elisha's financial plight, for the town was poor and the few students who enrolled proved distressingly lax about paying their bills. For his first four months of teaching, Elisha received no salary at all. In October of 1828 Hammond wrote to his oldest son, informing him of his desire to reassume the position of steward at South Carolina College. Even though Elisha assured him he would refrain from butchering, James was horrified at the prospect of his father's occupying such a demeaning post in the very town where young Hammond was seeking to make his mark. Elisha defended himself, declaring the position respectable and reminding his son how much he needed the money to reunite his family and to support the boy at his legal studies. But James had his way, invoking the possibility that his father would be prosecuted for old debts if he returned to Columbia. Even though he knew "money can be made there," Elisha gave up the project and spared his son this "disgrace."[19]

In December, James's apprenticeship came to an end, and he was admitted to the bar in Columbia. Within a month he had opened a law office in the capital and had begun to advertise his services in the local newspapers. Business was slow at first, even though Hammond managed to secure an appointment as a justice of the peace for Richland County. While he waited for clients, Hammond explored the haunts of his "infancy, childhood & youth," and he enjoyed as well the company of friends in Columbia and nearby Camden. Evidently he had abandoned his earlier resolution to give up women, for he jestingly com-

18. Hammond Common Place Book (MS vol. bd., 1825–44, JHH Papers, SCL), September 13, 1828, pp. 264–65.
19. Elisha Hammond to Hammond, October 17, 1828, April 5, 1829, in JHH Papers, SCL.

plained in verse of a "Grand Larceny" resulting in the theft of his heart. One friend twitted him about the confusion engendered by his simultaneous involvement in law and romance, describing James in his home "above McFie's grocery, surrounded by gilt albums and dirty clothes, scrap books & law notes, my Lord Coke and My Lord Byron, logs of wood, well cleaned boots, a dirty basin and unemptied chamber pot." Even if his living quarters were in disarray, Hammond's boots, his friend noted, were shined, for the young lawyer's vanity required him to pay close attention to his personal appearance. A prominent judge later remembered a telling incident during these early days of Hammond's career. The two men were riding the circuit together in a stagecoach, which overturned, pinning Hammond beneath the flailing boots and arms of all the other passengers. As "we were scrambling out," James's first words came from the very bottom of the pile, "boys take care of my face."[20]

Despite his striking physical appearance and despite the legal skills he had struggled to attain, Hammond did not have an easy time establishing himself in Columbia. Much of his hardship, he believed, derived from a lack of social standing that all his personal endowments could not surmount. "I had infinite difficulties to overcome," he remembered, "in taking a position to which I had not been bred & which excited . . . much jealousy of me there." Determined to win acceptance from the town's elite, Hammond "threw off every one of my father's friends . . . to work my way among people who looked *down on me*."[21]

At last Hammond secured a case, defending a man who had been accused of forgery. Elisha was delighted when he heard his son's good news. "You can have no idea how happy it made me to hear you had one case—I could not sleep all night for joy." The elder Hammond was unable to refrain from inundating his son with advice. "Everything depends on your first appearance at the Bar," he warned. Elisha feared the case would be almost impossible to win, but he hoped James could at least take advantage of the opportunity to display his eloquence. "Let all your pleadings be full of allusions—Tropes, Figures and abound in general knowledge." The prospect of what was at stake for his son filled the elder

20. Hammond, Business Papers (JHH Papers, SCL), January 2, 1829; *South Carolina State Gazette* and Columbia *Advertiser*, both December 27, 1828; Hammond to Catherine Spann Hammond, February 22, 1829, in JHH Papers, SCL; Hammond, "An Epistle," January 3, 1829, in "Fugitive Peices"; I. W. Hayne to Hammond, July 14, 1835, John B. O'Neall to Hammond, September 22, 1860, both in JHH Papers, LC. O'Neall remembers this incident as taking place in 1833, but if it was during Hammond's lawyer days, it must have been earlier.
21. Hammond to John Fox Hammond, February 10, 1845, in JHH Papers, SCL.

Hammond with apprehension. "I feel an anxiety for your appearance at this present court that I cannot express." It was certainly not for lack of trying. [22]

On March 13, James Henry Hammond made his debut at the bar, arguing that the case was based on insufficient evidence. Effectively appealing to the localistic biases of the South Carolina jury, Hammond moved beyond the circumstances of the case to an unorthodox attack upon the relevant statute itself. He challenged the existing forgery law as English in origin and contended that it had been designed for a commercial people, "enacted for a community essentially different from ours: & upon every principle of Justice, inapplicable in its full extent, to our country." The young lawyer urged the panel of men before him not to "imitate the unbending severity of an English Jury," and to acquit his client. To the amazement at least of Hammond's father, they did. [23]

Elisha was almost as unsettled by his son's victory as he had been by the prospect of defeat. "I could not sleep all night." But the elder Hammond could not abandon his anxieties, even in this moment of triumph. "You are now on the top of the tide, beware that it dont ebb and leave you on the sand. . . . Methodize your time, guard your earnings, economize your expenses." Elisha taught his son not only how to aspire and how to achieve; he made sure James knew how to worry. [24]

Despite his initial courtroom success, young Hammond continued without clients, and considered moving out of Columbia to a district seat, such as Spartanburg, in the up-country near the North Carolina border. Slowly business began to improve, although James himself continued to complain of low spirits and despondency. "I am at this moment," he wrote in May of 1829, "One of the most unhappy wretches alive." [25]

In the spring and summer Hammond's career gradually brightened as his case load grew and his eloquence at the bar became better known. Defending one Henry Hook against a murder accusation, Hammond argued that the charge should be reduced to manslaughter, for the weapon had not been a dagger, which would have indicated clear premeditation, but a pocketknife, an imple-

22. Elisha Hammond to Hammond, February 25, 1829, *ibid.*

23. Hammond, Land Papers (JHH Papers, SCL), March 13, 1829. Eugene Genovese has suggested to me the significance of Hammond's choosing anticommercialism as the basis for a popular appeal to the jury. Certainly such a tactic would serve as evidence for Genovese's wider contentions regarding the prebourgeois nature of southern society and for southerners' own explicit perception of their world in Genovesean terms.

24. Elisha Hammond to Hammond, March 20, 1829 (see also April 5, and 25, 1829), all in JHH Papers, SCL.

25. Hammond, School Papers, May 8, 1829, *ibid.*

ment everyone carried. Mr. Hook had killed the victim after a quarrel over a debt, and had acted "upon sudden heat & with sufficient provocation" to warrant a lesser charge than murder. "I appeal to . . . your consciences," Hammond pled to the jury, "to say if this old [man] deserves a felon's death for what he has done. Is there one among you situated as he was that would not have done it." [26]

Hammond's rhetorical skills had attracted so much attention by the spring of 1829 that he was invited to serve as Fourth of July orator at the Columbia Presbyterian Church. Independence Day had become the occasion for ceremonies of patriotic self-congratulation throughout the nation, and Columbia celebrated the event in much the same way as other towns of similar size. A jubilant ringing of bells greeted the dawn and was followed by the firing of a salute of twenty-four guns—one for each of the United States. By eight in the morning, Columbia was awake and ready to attend a military parade. Recently commissioned as a second lieutenant in the militia, Hammond may well have participated in his new uniform. He was certainly a part of the procession that followed, for at ten o'clock the Rifle Company and Columbia Volunteers and the town council met near the town hall to escort the orator of the day to the services at the Columbia Presbyterian Church. Having witnessed such displays throughout his youth, Hammond now relished the satisfaction of serving as the focus of the event. [27]

After his friend I. W. Hayne read the Declaration of Independence, Hammond rose to speak on the struggle between "Freedom & oppression through the ages." Hammond must have listened attentively during the Independence Day festivities of his youth, for his address was in most respects typical of the American genre that had evolved in the fifty-three years since the Declaration had been signed. The United States, he declared, was a unique experiment in human association, different from all the tyrannical and arbitrary governments that had preceded it. The "wilds of America" had rendered the "paraphernalia of Royalty" absurd; the heroes of the Revolution had used their opportunity in this new land to stake out a claim for human freedom. Americans, he declared, in the blending of religious and nationalistic rhetoric typical of these addresses, were a chosen people "destined by providence to prove beyond all doubt that political liberty is not a chimera of the imagination." But Hammond ended on a less optimistic note, introducing a theme that was just beginning to appear in Fourth of July orations throughout the South. Long almost oblivious to politics in his preoccupation with personal difficulties, Hammond now confronted the

26. Hammond, "State vs. Henry Hook," 1828–29, Land Papers, *ibid.*
27. *South Carolina State Gazette* and Columbia *Advertiser*, both July 11, 1829.

emerging sectional conflict. For a moment he abandoned his enthusiastic paeans to American union and interjected a solemn warning. The perennial struggle between freedom and oppression, he cautioned, had not ended with the Revolution. "The people of the North," he asserted, "have been overbearing and the people of the South have become chafed. . . . We should be warned of the danger of permitting the first approaches of usurpation to pass unnoticed; Of not meeting the first efforts of unchartered power boldly, and annihilating the 'unlicked monster' of oppression at the very moment of his birth." Men had begun, Hammond noted, to question "the value of the American Union." Under such circumstances the South had only one choice: to follow the noble example of her revolutionary forbears. "Patience under usurpation is a word for slaves," Hammond proclaimed, lapsing into the language of the Founding Fathers, "and the truest prudence is, for men and nations, at all hazards to maintain their dignity and independence."[28] Having aroused his audience with these bellicose words, Hammond retreated slightly from his provocative stance and reassured his listeners that these threats to their freedom had been allayed for the time being at least. The "storm is passing away. . . . I trust," he concluded, "that our UNION is destined to survive."[29]

Hammond was not the only South Carolinian to voice doubts on this Fourth of July about the future of the South in the Union. As he spoke in Columbia, orators in Charleston were replacing the traditional appeals to national unity with similar warnings. Once a ritual affirming national identity and unity, the Fourth of July was becoming in the South an occasion for the expression of growing sectionalism. The image of the Revolution as an uprising of the oppressed against a national tyranny now served as the South's legitimation of her resistance to the encroachments of an ever-increasing federal power. Like the patriots of old, her orators declared, the South would combat any challenge to the sacred principle of liberty.[30]

The shift in the content of these orations marked a profound alteration in the attitudes of southerners generally. In the years after the War of 1812, the

28. Hammond, "Oration Delivered in the Presbyterian Church, Columbia, S.C.," July 4, 1829, JHH Papers, LC.

29. "Extracts from Lieutenant Hammond's Oration," clipping, n.d., in Hammond Scrapbook (1825–40).

30. Charleston *Mercury*, July 5, 1829. On Fourth of July orations, see A. V. Huff, "The Eagle and the Vulture: Changing Attitudes Toward Nationalism in Fourth of July Orations Delivered in Charleston, 1778–1860," *South Atlantic Quarterly*, LXXIII (Winter, 1974), 10–22; Fletcher Green, "Listen to the Eagle Scream: One Hundred Years of the Fourth of July in North Carolina (1776–1876)," *North Carolina Historical Review*, XXXI (July and October, 1954), 295–320, 529–49.

South had joined with the rest of the country in urging a strengthening of national power and unity, even at the expense of traditional local and state prerogatives. This mood found its tangible expression in movements to reorganize and enlarge the army, to protect nascent American industry with higher tariffs, and to consolidate the country through federally supported internal improvements. Such attitudes encouraged a rather loose understanding of the powers allocated to Congress under the Constitution, and thus led to what became known as "broad construction" of the federal role. By the mid-twenties, however, many southerners had come to regret their earlier nationalism. Fear was rising that a strengthened central government might interfere with slavery, and the arrival of hard times in the middle of the decade directed the attention of cotton producers to the effects of high tariffs on their profits. Because the South purchased most of its manufactured goods, tariffs seemed especially onerous. Moreover, planters worried that duties would reduce foreign demand for their agricultural crops and might even influence other nations to enact retaliatory measures against the staples on which southern livelihood depended.[31]

For South Carolinians these issues took on particular significance because of the acute economic distress the state was experiencing as the center of cotton productivity moved away from the seaboard toward the southwest. Carolinians saw in the assertion of federal power through the tariff a dangerous precedent for possible future federal action in regard to slavery. In South Carolina, where blacks were a majority, this contingency appeared especially alarming.

The year 1828 had been particularly dramatic, for passage of the so-called Tariff of Abominations, which would prove to be the nation's highest in the pre–Civil War period, had aroused at least some Carolina citizens to advocate open revolt. In December, 1828, the state legislature rejected a movement among its members for a convention to consider nullifying the right of the federal government to impose the tariff on the state. The specter of open defiance was laid to rest, if only temporarily.

In South Carolina 1829 opened amidst what one historian has called an "uneasy quiet" produced by the setback the radicals had received in the legislature and by the hopes engendered by the elevation in March of southerner Andrew Jackson and Carolinian John C. Calhoun to the two highest offices in the land. No new outrages against southern rights were committed in the spring, and thus

---

31. For a good description of these changes in attitudes and circumstances, see William W. Freehling, *Prelude to Civil War: The Nullification Controversy in South Carolina, 1816–1836* (New York: Harper and Row, 1965).

Hammond was able to end his Fourth of July oration on a note of optimism about the Union. But the fears and warnings that he had interjected into his formulaic patriotic address marked Hammond's public identification with the states' rights cause. In calling upon his audience to consider the "value of the American Union," Hammond was simply echoing a well-known militantly sectionalist speech delivered two summers before by his old teacher Thomas Cooper.[32]

During the initial years after his graduation from college, the difficulties of making a living had compelled Hammond to all but abandon his nascent political interests. But once admitted to the bar, with a practice inaugurated, if not firmly established, he redirected his attention to the questions that had so absorbed him during his years as a Euphradian. Despite the deceptive calm in 1829, these were questions that increasingly drew the concern of all Carolinians.

32. *Ibid.*, 177, 130.

CHAPTER 3

We Are with the South

IN HIS 1829 Fourth of July oration Hammond had made his first public statement for the southern cause. His audience was prophetic in its response, for
their toast following his address implored that the "display of eloquence on this
day" might "prefigure his future distinction and usefulness." But this triumph was
one his father was not to share. On July 5 James's sister Caroline wrote her
brother from Macon to inform him that Elisha was gravely ill. Before James
could leave for his father's bedside, news arrived of his death.[1]

In the fall of 1828 Elisha had become so dissatisfied with continued separation from his family that he had recklessly purchased a small farm near Macon
on credit. With never-failing hopes of making his fortune, Elisha had planted
the land in corn, and Catherine Hammond now found herself a widow with
both a mortgage to pay off and a crop to harvest. If she did not keep up the
payments, she stood to lose what her husband had already invested. Although
eager to leave Macon, where she felt a stranger, she was prohibited by law from
selling her house and land for several months. Desperate, she turned to her
eldest son for advice and help. "I never knew," she confided to him six weeks
after Elisha's death, "what the fear of suffering for common necessarys were
before."[2]

There seemed little James could do. His law practice required him to remain
in Columbia, and he could spare no sums of money large enough to aid signifi-

1. Columbia *State Gazette and Advertiser*, July 11, 1829; Caroline Hammond to James Henry
Hammond, July 5, 1829, M. Robertson to Hammond, July 12, 1829, both in JHH Papers, SCL.
2. Catherine Fox Hammond to Hammond, August 23, 1829, *ibid.*

cantly in his family's support. He urged his mother to write her rich uncle James Fox in Augusta for help, but Fox, as usual, declined to offer any assistance. Catherine Hammond's major financial assets were the several slaves she had regularly hired out to supplement her meager income from boarders, and these bondsmen may have harvested the corn crop and thus tided the family over until the Macon house was sold in February of 1830. With only forty-six dollars in cash as the profits of the sale, she moved her younger children to Augusta, where she planned to support herself by taking in lodgers. Marcellus, she thought, could be apprenticed as a clerk in a clothing store. Except for collecting a few old debts owed Elisha in Columbia, James felt able to offer his mother no help. His sense of impotence in face of his mother's desperation reinforced yet again James's already acute sensitivity to the humiliation of poverty.[3]

Despite efforts to expand his law practice, Hammond seemed unable to contract sufficient business to fill either his time or his pocket. Increasingly, James found himself devoting unoccupied moments to the compelling political questions he had addressed at the Presbyterian Church the preceding July. By the late fall of 1829, Hammond had become deeply involved with a group of Carolina radicals who supported nullification of the federal tariff, which they believed was unjustly oppressing and impoverishing the state.

After the rejection of their doctrines by the legislature in December, 1828, the leaders of the embryonic nullification movement began to work systematically to alter public opinion. The notion of stirring up the populace to exert political pressure on the legislature was itself an almost revolutionary idea within the context of traditional South Carolina politics. To a far greater extent than the rest of the nation or even the rest of the South, the Palmetto State had clung to the republican principles that had provided the ideological framework for the American Revolution. When in the 1820s and 1830s democratic assumptions and practices began to invade American political life, Carolina succeeded in resisting most of these changes, retaining the most aristocratic governmental structures in the Union until the Civil War. Although any white resident adult male could vote, he had very little to vote for. State legislators and U.S. representatives were the only elected officials, and usually a ruling clique agreed in advance upon a single candidate who ran unopposed. South Carolinians did not vote for the president, their governor, or any other state officers; these decisions were all made by the legislature. While in terms of political practices South Carolina

3. Catherine Fox Hammond to Hammond, March 14, April 14, 1830, both *ibid.*

became unique as other states reformed and democratized their constitutions in the course of the decades before the Civil War, she defended her atypicality with principles central to the American political tradition, with arguments derived directly from those advanced against the assaults of British power on colonial liberties in the years after 1763. Nineteenth-century Carolinians simply adapted this revered body of thought to new conditions, defining their relationship to the federal government as a latter-day equivalent of the colonies' resistance to Great Britain. Their opposition to Washington's despotic tendencies, they insisted, made them the truest guardians of the nation's revolutionary ideals.[4]

The strength of republican ideology in South Carolina derived not only from the state's perceptions of its external relations with the federal government; in Carolina republicanism had a special relevance to internal social and political needs as well. Joined with a growing sense of federal threat was the necessity of justifying a social order increasingly different from that of the democratizing, urbanizing, industrializing North. Both Carolina's stance within the Union and the nature of the distribution of power inside the state could be easily legitimated within the framework of classical republicanism. To combat the growth of governmental tyranny that constituted the greatest political evil, republican theorists had traditionally prescribed the rule of independent, incorruptible, and virtuous individuals. Beholden to no one, they would be free to follow the dictates of conscience; equipped to discern the common interests of the people, they would oppose every appearance of despotism. A republican order thus thrived in the organic unity characteristic of an agrarian civilization. The appearance of wealth, manufacturing, luxury, and special financial interests inevitably threatened the survival of a republic, for these forces heightened possibilities for corruption of both individuals and the state. The alliance of government with any of these powers signaled the certain demise of the disinterested virtue that made republicanism possible.

South Carolinians enthusiastically cast themselves as the embodiment of this ideal. Planters were men whose virtue and independence were firmly rooted

4. On republicanism in general, see Gordon Wood, *The Creation of the American Republic, 1776–1787* (Chapel Hill: University of North Carolina Press, 1969); J. G. A. Pocock, *The Machiavellian Moment: Florentine Political Thought and the Atlantic Republican Tradition* (Princeton: Princeton University Press, 1975). In regard to South Carolina particularly, see Robert M. Weir, "'The Harmony We Were Famous For': An Interpretation of Pre-Revolutionary South Carolina Politics," *William and Mary Quarterly*, XXVI (October, 1969), 473–501; James Banner, "The Problem of South Carolina," in Stanley Elkins and Eric McKitrick (eds.), *The Hofstadter Aegis: A Memorial* (New York: Knopf, 1974), 60–93; Kenneth S. Greenberg, "Representation and the Isolation of South Carolina, 1776–1860," *Journal of American History*, LXIV (December, 1977), 723–43.

in the soil; Carolina remained a state in which evil financial interests had made only minimal advances, and she would valiantly resist the influence of banks and manufactures within the national government. Her own political structures institutionalized republican concepts by establishing a system designed to install the "best men" in positions of power and to invest them with the responsibility to govern the less virtuous, less talented residue of the population. "Democracy" was anathema; leaders would exercise their disinterested and enlightened judgment free from any pressure exerted by the multitude. Only a few offices would be subject to popular election, and even here the will of the people would be prevented from coalescing into dangerous organized interests. The republican ideal of a harmonious organic commonality of interest legitimated the opposition of the state leadership to the development of parties within Carolina. Political intrigue and competition might inspire demagoguery and challenge the rule of virtuous disinterest—which was of course seen to be lodged in the planter class. While throughout the nation the evolution of a democratic political party system in the early nineteenth century brought important changes to the structure and distribution of power, South Carolina remained largely untouched by these currents. She was in fact the only state without a two-party system in the antebellum period.[5]

Yet while the framework of republican thought seemed on one level to fit—and to justify—the idealized self-image cherished by Carolina's planter class, it ignored essential realities of the state's social and political system, which institutionalized the subordination of lesser whites and of slaves under this guise of disinterested virtue. Planters were more the embodiment of privilege than virtue, and their increasingly aggressive defense of their slave property can hardly be seen as disinterested. Planters were themselves part of a world capitalist market, beneficiaries of a system of finance that republican ideology defined as the foremost agency of corruption. And the simple agrarian life of the American republican ideal did not comport well with the luxurious and extravagant style of many of Carolina's elite. Republicanism legitimated the rule of the planter class in South Carolina, providing them with a series of transcendent justifications for the retention and perpetuation of their slave society and for resistance to the incursions of modern, bourgeois, and democratic values into their aristocratic and precapitalist world. Yet in many ways this much-vaunted republicanism served as little more than a mask for the widespread changes that had begun to

5. On parties, see Banner, "The Problem of South Carolina."

affect even Carolina. The continuing profession of loyalty to these older ideals made behavior that contradicted these cherished abstractions psychologically and politically possible.

Within the life of a single individual like James Henry Hammond, republican ideology helped provide a framework for resolving the uncertainties he encountered in trying to find his way in a new and uncharted nineteenth-century world. By continually assuring himself that his actions met the criteria of this system of belief, he was able to reconcile himself to his ambition for wealth and power, a personal reality fundamentally at odds with the principles of republican disinterestedness. For the state, the ideology provided a basic vocabulary for political life, as well as one important vehicle for the hegemonic power of the master class. Historians have long debated the conflicts between precapitalist and bourgeois economic orders, aristocratic and democratic political structures, traditional and modern social realities within the Old South. Republican ideology offered both Hammond and his society one means of bridging this threatening chasm of change. But the discrepancies between theory and reality, between professed belief and daily action, between alleged disinterest and actual self-interest, took their toll, creating inescapable tensions within those caught like Hammond in such conflicts.[6]

The methods chosen by the nullifiers dramatically embodied these contradictions. A movement initiated by the state's elite to resist federal incursions on its power and its mastery, nullification nevertheless was compelled to turn to those very "demagogic" methods it condemned in order to mobilize Carolina in behalf of its goals. The instruments of propaganda, mass mobilization, and public agitation that were becoming standard in political contests elsewhere in the nation during the Jacksonian era paradoxically appeared in South Carolina as the tools of the aristocratic nullifiers, who regarded this whole new democratic political style as abhorrent. Yet nullifiers were so committed to their political ends that the means through which they achieved them became almost insignificant; they were ready to do whatever was necessary.

James Henry Hammond was to benefit handsomely from their need to arouse the state through a concerted plan of mobilization and propaganda. George McDuffie, an up-country congressman and leading radical, was a brilliant orator, as was William C. Preston, Hammond's former legal sponsor and another staunch

6. On the relationship of republicanism and wealth within the American context, see Drew R. McCoy, *The Elusive Republic: Political Economy in Jeffersonian America* (Chapel Hill: University of North Carolina Press, 1980).

nullifier. James Hamilton, a low-country rice planter who had led the movement in its unsuccessful 1828 effort, was a genius at political organization, and his skill in creating antitariff groups that included even the lowliest of white South Carolinians was a major factor in the movement's ultimate success. But in addition to oratory and coordination, the public relations effort required a newspaper. South Carolina's political turbulence had provided Hammond with an extraordinary opportunity.

Late in 1829, the *Southern Times* was established in the state capital by local opponents of the tariff who felt the need for an effective radical journal to serve Carolina's up-country. The two Columbians who owned and published the paper needed an articulate, hardworking figure to undertake the day-to-day editorial burden, and they selected Hammond for the task, investing him with the responsibility for producing three issues of the paper each week. He worked energetically to secure subscribers in anticipation of inaugurating publication by the first of the year. Hammond was well aware of the significance of his new commitment. "In the year 1830," he later reminisced, "I began my political career by starting a new paper in Columbia. . . . I had not up to that time been a very warm politician." As the first day of publication approached, Hammond inscribed into his private notebook a special prayer for his success, entreating God to "make me great among men—and so govern me that in all things I may use that greatness."[7]

On January 29 the first issue of the *Southern Times* appeared, boldly proclaiming its intentions. Offering his readers "a full confession of our political faith," Hammond's inaugural editorial left little doubt of the strong states' rights position the paper would assume. "We are republicans, and of the old Jeffersonian school. We are friends to the Union, and deprecate the necessity of making such an avowal. We are opposed to internal improvements. We are opposed to the Tariff in every shape, and upon every ground. We are opposed to all latitudinarian constructions of written compacts. We support the constitution of '89. We support the Union of our fathers." As in his Fourth of July oration, Hammond identified the states' rights cause with the doctrines of the Revolution. South Carolinians sought only to preserve these hallowed principles. An "awful crisis is approaching; and our blood runs cold with apprehension. . . . We are with the South. Heart and hand, soul and body, we are with the South."[8]

7. Hammond Diary (MS in JHH Papers, LC), February 7, 1841; Hammond, "A Prayer," January 10, 1830 (MS in HBC Papers, SCL).
8. Columbia *Southern Times*, January 29, 1830.

Despite this impending crisis, Hammond's aims for the paper were not restricted to the purely political. He had not abandoned his earlier romantic longing for transcendent truth, and Hammond promised to offer his readers the best of literary, philosophical, and scientific selections. In accordance with one of his particular interests, Hammond would find his "most pleasing editorial duty" to be the introduction of the "Poet's Corner," and he promised as well to enlist all available support "in the cause of letters."[9]

Hammond's discussion of his literary goals for the *Southern Times* reflected his own early ambitions for literary distinction. At college, the aspiring poet and essayist had soon learned that writing offered no road to advancement in South Carolina; it had quickly become clear, as he explained in his editorial for the *Times*, that "Literature in this country, is much more likely than politics to fall into neglect." But at the same time that his boundless ambition redirected him toward a life of public affairs, Hammond never relinquished his interest in a life of the mind. Intelligence was probably his most distinguishing personal asset, and in some other social context an intellectual role might well have provided the best framework for his desire to achieve. But in the South, as Hammond observed in an editorial consideration of regional culture, literary and cultural attainments were not encouraged and were frequently ignored. Hammond challenged this state of affairs. "We are not satisfied of the truth of the remark that the institutions of this country are not calculated to make scholars," he proclaimed. "The experiment has been by no means fully tried." In an exhortation more revealing than he knew, Hammond urged his readers to cultivate southern intellectual development. "Let us . . . make literary triumph an object of ambition, sufficient to enlist the best talents of the country." Talents, he might have added, like his own.[10]

From January, 1830, until late in the spring of 1831, Hammond entirely controlled the *Southern Times*, and its editorials reflected his particular views. In the course of these months, he developed and articulated a political philosophy that would not alter significantly for the remainder of his life. The principles of states' rights, which Hammond perceived to be the foundation of the nullification agitation, would remain the central theme of Carolina politics up to the Civil War.

The unifying feature of Hammond's defense of nullification in the *Times* during 1830 lay in his attempt to transcend the immediate crisis in order to place the disputed issues within the context of wider political, philosophical, and

9. *Ibid.*
10. *Ibid.*

moral issues. Southern opposition to the tariff, Hammond declared in an editorial at the beginning of February, "has not been conducted altogether in a proper manner. Too much stress has been laid on the effect and policy of the measure." Hammond saw his role to be the promulgation of the principles of republican virtue and disinterest that lay behind the free-trade position. His insistence that his opposition to the tariff was constitutional rather than economic in foundation represented an effort to elevate the conflict from an issue of material benefit to one of abstract justice. His later advocacy of slavery and secession would assume parallel forms. "Property is much," he declared in a February issue of the *Times*, "a leading ingredient in almost every species of human happiness—But in comparison with somethings, it is paltry. . . . it is the constitutional ground on which we must take our stand." Hammond struggled to convince his readers that the real issue was not the tariff; a compromise reduction of duties that did not directly address the broader questions of northern power and southern rights would not be an acceptable solution to the crisis. Even "if we were to be relieved by a modification of the Tariff, it is not what the South asks and contends for. We go upon higher ground. We are struggling for principle. We demand an abandonment of the power which Congress has assumed to pass the law."[11]

Hammond insisted that he and his paper were above interests or parties. Despite his active opposition to the tariff, he avoided using the term nullification for several months because of his intention never, as he self-righteously proclaimed, "to become the mouthpiece of a faction." Unquestionably the nullifiers' up-country editorial spokesman, Hammond felt compelled by the dominant republican ideology to deny—both to himself and to his readers—that he was directly connected with any organized political group. Such a relationship might make his views appear "interested" and therefore suspect.[12]

Hammond disavowed as well any desire for secession. The South Carolina radicals, he contended, were working firmly within the national tradition; they were in fact not radicals, but the nation's true conservatives, seeking to protect America from the tyrannical power of the federal government. The real danger of disunion, he emphasized, lay in accepting oppression until the "limits of endurance" were passed and no peaceable solution remained. Nullification was not revolution, but a means of preventing it. Those fearful of its doctrines, Ham-

11. *Ibid.*, February 4, June 10, 1830.
12. *Ibid.*, April 5, 1830.

mond argued, had been "alarmed without cause. They have been led into the belief that there is certain danger—when there is certain safety—that their liberties will be sacrificed by the only step that can possibly preserve them." Congress had violated South Carolinians' most sacred political precepts, showing its preference for "interests to rights, opinions to principles"; the state's citizens should act to prevent the nation's movement toward "monarchy." Nullification was the only constitutional remedy to halt this betrayal of the Founding Fathers. As he at last openly avowed his nullification views, Hammond admitted that from "the first we have been for this—for nothing more and certainly nothing less."[13]

The young editor's unflagging radical zeal soon won him the attention and approval of the state's leaders. Hammond's praise of Carolina Senator Robert Y. Hayne's actions in Washington earned him an invitation from the eminent statesman for a social evening in Columbia. Other nullifiers began to take notice of the journalist as well. Francis W. Pickens, congressman from an up-country district, confessed that he was "much pleased" with Hammond's editorial endeavors, and the two men began an intensive correspondence. Pickens wanted Hammond to print a series of his essays, and the movement more generally needed the young editor to help keep the agitation in the state at a high pitch. The *Times* began to reflect the direct influence of these more experienced statesmen; Hammond even adopted verbatim some of the political analysis they provided.[14]

As 1830 wore on, Carolina's radicals became convinced that the Jackson administration promised only disaster for the South. Vice-President John C. Calhoun, a resident of the state's up-country, seemed to be quickly falling from Jackson's favor, while the untrustworthy Martin Van Buren grew ever closer to the president. Although a southerner, Jackson was not, Hammond warned, sound in his states' rights principles. "He is not only not for us," the *Times* proclaimed, "but unequivocally against us." The nullifiers were confirmed in their fears when Congress summarily defeated a series of major tariff reductions proposed in early February by Carolinian George McDuffie. Worse still, the House of Representatives actively confronted the slavery question in April when Charles Mercer of Virginia proposed that the federal government subsidize the colonization of

13. *Ibid.*, June 17, May 10, May 27, March 8, May 10, 1830.

14. Robert Y. Hayne to Hammond, February 25, 1830, Francis W. Pickens to Hammond, March 8, 1830 (see Robert Y. Hayne to Hammond, March 30, 1829, which is echoed in the Columbia *Southern Times*, August 26, 1830), all in JHH Papers, LC.

Francis W. Pickens, painted by William Harrison Scarborough.

freed blacks in Africa. Hammond responded to this proposal, which was actually quickly tabled, with outrage. Mercer was no true son of Virginia. "He is a bastard," the editor bluntly announced, pointing out the grave dangers in the measure. "Tax us today for the transportation of our free negroes to Africa and to-morrow we will have to pay for the emancipation of our own slaves. Who can doubt this that knows how subtle are the encroachments of power?" To Hammond, any federal interference in the slavery question was tantamount to a declaration of war. The South was irrevocably committed to her peculiar institution. "We would not part with it if we could, and as it is WE NEVER WILL." All in all, the *Times* concluded, the activities of the Congress in the early months of 1830 gave dramatic testimony that the "power of the South on the floor of the National Legislature is gone forever."[15]

But at the same time that Hammond and the most radical Carolinians saw a deepening crisis, a number of events made it possible for moderates to hope that the situation was improving. Some mild tariff reductions on salt, tea, and coffee were passed—intensifying Hammond's insistence that a lowering of duties was meaningless without concessions of principle. In May, Jackson struck a blow for the strict construction of federal power in his veto of the Maysville Road Bill, a measure to provide national assistance for internal improvements. In face of these conciliatory gestures, keeping radicalism alive became an uphill endeavor.

Although the nullifiers had originally hoped to use the 1830 fall elections to fill the state legislature with their supporters, the rising tide of moderation influenced them to alter their program. The unorthodox effort to create a popular pronullification party in the state had somewhat unnerved the movement's spokesmen, who felt themselves astride a tiger that might at any moment escape from their control. As Robert Hayne confided to Hammond, "it is extremely difficult to keep up the public feeling at a proper point, and prevent its boiling over." Throughout 1830 they found themselves compelled to adjust to rapidly shifting sentiments amongst a populace they had never before sought so desperately to understand.[16]

Prevailing sentiment in the spring and summer at last dictated a shift in the radicals' public stance away from an overt demand for nullification itself toward support for an unpledged convention to be appointed by the new legislature to consider the issue. Hammond pled eloquently for this position in a Fourth of July address delivered in Lexington District. As in his oration just a year earlier, Hammond compared Carolinians to the revolutionary patriots and warned even more forcefully than before that "we must protect ourselves or forget that we are free." The crisis had now arrived.[17]

Advocacy of a convention, the radicals hoped, would rally the broadest possible support within the state. But even this new and more moderate position failed to unite the supporters of states' rights, despite an intensive campaign of

15. Columbia *Southern Times*, February 4, April 10, March 8, April 15, 1830.
16. Robert Y. Hayne to Hammond, February 25, 1830, in JHH Papers, LC.
17. Hammond, *Oration delivered at Capt. Geo. Lorick's, in Lexington District, S.C., on the Fifth of July, 1830* (Columbia: Columbia *Times & State Gazette* Office, 1830) 14.

stump speaking, barbecues, and public assemblies. Conflicts divided even the movement's leadership. John C. Calhoun, still hoping for a rapprochement with Jackson, was not ready to openly support either a convention or nullification. Senator William Smith, South Carolina's most seasoned advocate of states' rights, who was rumored to be hoping for appointment to high office in the Jackson administration, opposed the convention plan independently of Calhoun. Amidst this fragmentation, Hammond remained under the influence of nullification's most extreme supporters and consistently assumed the most aggressive position on every issue, staunchly defending states' rights principles against any dilution through compromise. As Smith and his followers began in the course of the summer to reveal their growing moderation, Hammond found himself literally risking his life in defense of his views.

In May, General James Blair, a Smith supporter and a member of Congress from the up-country district that included the town of Camden, wrote to the local newspaper expressing his satisfaction at Jackson's veto of the Maysville Road Bill. Blair considered the president's action to signal the demise of the pernicious internal improvements system, and he indicated his certainty that Carolinians need only wait patiently for the tariff system to meet a similar fate. Hammond was indignant at this show of moderation from one who professed himself an advocate of states' rights. Reprinting Blair's letter in the *Times* late in June, the editor reflected upon the congressman's folly in looking to Jackson for salvation and mocked the lack of sophistication of some of Blair's more rural constituents. Blair replied in a rage, denouncing the "illiberal irony" of the *Times* and the "wanton, rude and vulgar manner" of the "dirty piece" it had printed about him. Blair concluded by declaring Hammond a "blackguard." Hammond responded in kind, accusing Blair of "reeking foulness" and indicating his willingness to carry the conflict beyond mere words. On the last day of July the Camden *Journal* printed Blair's answer taunting Hammond about using a newspaper as his "only resort for redress," daring him, in effect, to risk a physical confrontation. On August 2, Hammond presented Blair with a request for a "personal interview." A duel was scheduled for the eighteenth of the month on the North Carolina line near Lancaster Courthouse; the weapons were to be smoothbore pistols armed with one ball each.[18]

18. *The Controversy Between General James Blair and James Henry Hammond, Esq.* (n.p., 1830), 6, 12. See Columbia *Southern Times* June 21, July 1, 1830. After July 8, the paper became the *Southern Times and State Gazette*, which see for July 15, July 31, and August 2, 1830.

Throughout this exchange of letters and insults, Hammond was careful to consult with the leaders of the radical party to ensure that he was acting with their approval, and he sought to justify his behavior as necessary and deliberate rather than capricious or ill conceived. He systematically explained his purposes in attacking Blair in the *Southern Times* of August 9, "Every man is free to have his own opinion, and free to express it, but he must also be responsible for it. If he is opposed to what we consider the *essential interests* of our country, we are opposed to him; and instead of feeling ourselves bound to laud and reverence him, be he who he may, we will contend against him might and main; we will refute his arguments if we can, and cut down his influence, *as a public man*, if we are able. It is our duty to do so."[19]

Hammond hoped in the conflict to display himself in dramatic, principled, and unselfish action. Risking life on behalf of one's principles was to Carolinians an act of supreme virtue. Hammond's recklessness became within this context the highest expression of purely disinterested action, an affirmation of cherished Carolina political values, an expression of fealty to a class and a culture by one seeking acceptance into it. In effect, he declared his loyalty to the increasingly anachronistic values of disinterested public action in face of the growing importance of an interest-based American political life. Hammond was acting from what he explained to be "a most painful sense of duty."[20]

Yet, conveniently for the ambitious young Carolinian, he could be sure that his noble action would attract considerable attention, for the general issues involved in his dispute with Blair had aroused more political interest than almost any event in the previous history of the state. Hammond was determined to appear courageous and principled and thereby to win favor for both himself and his cause, but he had lingering fears that he might have miscalculated, that his boldness might be regarded as insolence. Hammond was young, poor and socially unconnected, while Blair was an established figure in the state. In light of these realities, Blair's apostasy might seem less dangerous than Hammond's own presumption. At the height of the controversy in late July, Francis Pickens reassured the young editor about the wisdom of his course, "I do not think it will

19. Columbia *Southern Times and State Gazette*, August 9, 1830.

20. Robert M. Weir, "The South Carolinian as Extremist," *South Atlantic Quarterly*, LXXIV (Winter, 1975), 101. On dueling, see also Jack K. Williams, *Dueling in the Old South: Vignettes of Social History* (College Station: Texas A & M Press, 1980); Dickson D. Bruce, Jr., *Violence and Culture in the Antebellum South* (Austin: University of Texas Press, 1979). Columbia *Southern Times and State Gazette*, August 9, 1830.

injure your influence in the least. . . . You are a graduate of our college, a native & a member of our bar, & in every respect equal with Blair. The habit, the custom, & the opinions of the country you know as well as I do in such cases. . . . Blair has openly deserted his own avowed principles, & ought to be denounced." Public opinion in both Charleston and Columbia, friends encouraged Hammond, rested "entirely with you."[21]

As the confrontation approached, sentiment shifted decisively in the editor's favor. In early August, Pickens assured Hammond of his growing celebrity, "As it turned out nothing could have been better. You are now on the defensive entirely, and the sympathies of the whole community are with you. You could not have desired a more advantageous position for your-self." In inciting and challenging Blair, Hammond had successfully gambled that he would win the personal loyalty and support of the leaders of the nullification party. Now he had only to win the gamble he had taken with his life.[22]

Hammond did not even own a set of dueling pistols and cast about in the first week of August to find a pair with which to practice. He appointed his college friend Theodore Stark as his second, but at the advice of I. W. Hayne, who thought Stark too inexperienced, added Pierce Butler, a veteran of such frays, to the negotiations with Blair's supporters over the rules for the encounter. The participants, they determined, would take their places thirty feet apart, then be given loaded pistols, which they would hold muzzle down. At the signal "ready," they would elevate the weapons, aim, and await the command to fire. Both were required to remain erect; if one should shoot first, he must then stand firm and accept the other's fire. Each participant was permitted two or three attendants "besides the surgeon," and the fight was to continue "after the first fire so long as either of the antagonists demands it." Only the notorious inaccuracy of dueling pistols rendered such an encounter anything short of suicide.[23]

Although he had never before been a principal in a duel, Hammond was far from unfamiliar with the practice. A few months after their graduation from South Carolina College a close friend had been killed in an affair of honor, and southern newspaper editors were so frequently involved in these conflicts that Hammond might have expected at least one such confrontation as the price of

21. Pickens to Hammond, March 8, July 21, 1830, I. W. Hayne to Hammond, August, 1830, all in JHH Papers, LC; William C. Preston to Hammond, July 24, 1830, in JHH Papers, SCL.
22. Pickens to Hammond, August 9, 25, 1830, both in JHH Papers, LC.
23. Hammond to James Blair, August 2, 1830, William O. Nixon to Theodore Stark, August 7, 1830, both in JHH Papers, LC.

journalistic office. But despite his calculated decision to challenge Blair and his understanding of the consequences, Hammond was not entirely sanguine about the approaching encounter. His mother's brother, who had seen Blair perform in an earlier duel, offered consolation. "Of all the duelists I have ever seen on the field," he reported encouragingly, "I should dread him the least. He is remarkably slow. . . . I am confident if you will take sufficient time for good aim, you will run no risque of being touched. . . . From Blair's great size, it is not reasonable to expect his movements to be quick." Apparently, Hotspur had challenged Falstaff.[24]

As the appointed day approached, the friends of the two principals sought some accommodation that might avert the conflict. While the seconds were meeting on the eve of the duel, as far away as Charleston efforts were in progress to stop the encounter. James Hamilton interrupted his nullification campaigning to write in distress to Stephen Miller, an up-country radical who in the fall would run as a nullifier for William Smith's Senate seat. Hamilton begged Miller, who lived in Camden not far from Blair, to take some action to prevent the "deadly combat" of two such "useful and distinguished citizens." Hamilton himself had already penned entreaties to both antagonists. "Have not our party," he demanded of Miller, "a right almost to require of these gentlemen that they should submit their differences to the friendly arbitration of a Court of Honor." Hamilton stated his willingness to "ride 500 miles through any hazards" to prevent the encounter.[25]

But Hamilton needed to make no such sacrifice. On the night of August 17, Hammond's negotiators informed him that "*Peace is proclaimed.*" Blair had indicated that he would withdraw all "offensive expressions." Hammond's friends affirmed that the *Southern Times* had "intended no disrespect" to Blair's constituents. On the morning of the eighteenth the principals and their seconds gathered not for a duel but a celebratory breakfast. Hammond, Blair declared, was "*my friend.*"[26]

Hammond had clearly profited from the publicity surrounding the incident. As Blair himself explained to one of Hammond's seconds, "The interest taken in the affair by the Community, & particularly by such men as Major Hamilton &

24. James Spann to Hammond, August 9, 1830, *ibid.*
25. James Hamilton to Stephen Miller, August 17, 1830, in James Hamilton Papers, SHC.
26. Pierce Mason Butler to Hammond, August 17, 1830, Blair to Butler, August 30, 1830, both in JHH Papers, LC.

others that I need not name to you, together with the handsome things they have said of us, are considerations that must go far to atone for every disagreeable or unpleasant circumstance on both sides." Hamilton responded to a letter from Hammond explaining the outcome of the conflict with remittance for a subscription to the *Times* and compliments to its editor on the "early and powerful exhibition which you have made of public spirit and Talent." It was the beginning of a close political and personal alliance between Hammond and Hamilton. Francis Pickens was equally delighted and assured Hammond that he had gotten by far the better part of the compromise.[27]

The excitement over the duel was soon superseded by escalating agitation over the approaching fall elections. Hammond, less seasoned in the deferential traditions of Carolina politics than his aristocratic mentors, penned eloquent and unreserved appeals to the power and wisdom of the popular will. "It is the people, and the people only," he contended, "who possess the power surely and effectually to arrest and change the current of usurpation and oppression. To them we should appeal when it becomes necessary to make any great political movement." Warnings from Robert Hayne about the potential dangers of popular rule had little effect on Hammond's democratic sympathies in the spring, summer, and early fall of 1830. But as the October elections approached Hammond began to receive ominous reports of the unreliability of the people's voice. In Chester District, one correspondent reported, democracy meant defeat for the convention platform; the people exaggerated the dangers of nullification and would not listen to reason. In Spartanburg, the population seemed equally unamenable to truth, for they denounced the *Southern Times* as "much too violent in every respect." The widespread success of conciliation in Charleston and the more general failure of the convention position to win a decisive victory were "quite unexpected" by Hammond, and he began to reassess his support for the democratic process that had failed his cause. Universal suffrage, he declared to his readers, had given a class of people "power which they are totally incompetent to exercise—if not absolutely unworthy of it." The secret ballot, he believed, had "opened the door to much fraud and intrigue," and he called for a return to *viva voce* voting and an abandonment of the "pernicious practice" of electioneering.[28]

27. Blair to Butler, August 30, 1830, *ibid.*; Hamilton to Hammond, August 24, 1830, in Hamilton Papers; Pickens to Hammond, August 25, 1830, in JHH Papers, LC; Pickens is quoted in Spann to Hammond, September 6, 1830, in JHH Papers, SCL.
28. Columbia *Southern Times and State Gazette*, August 26, 1830; Robert Y. Hayne to Ham-

When the legislature convened in Columbia in the late fall, Hammond grew even more forceful in his appeals to the state's representatives. On November 23 he demanded the defeat of William Smith for the United States Senate, declaring that his reelection would "prostrate South Carolina in the dust." The legislature responded to the radicals' campaign almost as fully and positively as Hammond had hoped. Miller was chosen to replace Smith, and James Hamilton was elected governor. And although they failed to call a convention, the legislature passed a resolution affirming the abstract right of state interposition and nullification. Even though his goals were not fully realized, Hammond was jubilant. Before the legislature met, he explained, "we thought the question of convention would never be carried if it failed now. We are glad to say that we have seen enough to convince us that we were in error. . . . The question now assumes another aspect. The Legislature have put it upon broader and higher grounds. It is the question of Republicanism and Federalism in its old *form* and *spirit*."[29]

Yet Hammond's optimism about the ultimate success of nullification did not permit any relaxation of his vigilance. Before long he was involved in another altercation resulting from his radical political stance. During the fall and winter of 1830–1831, the editor of the *Southern Times* waged verbal warfare upon the Camden *Journal* and its "submissionist" editor, C. F. Daniels. By the first of the new year, the exchanges between the two journalists had descended to the level of personal attacks, with Hammond mocking Daniels for his peculiar food preferences and his insubstantial size. Daniels responded by ridiculing Hammond's obviously enormous ambitions and pretensions, sarcastically labelling the *Times* a "superb and beautiful vehicle of political transcendency" and its editor a "mountain of mental and corporeal magnitude" in comparison to the Camden journalist's own diminutive and humble self. The exchanges continued throughout the spring until in May, the *Journal* declared nullification to be "a doctrine that everybody will be ashamed of in a short time." The Camden editor's personal and political insults had gone too far; Hammond decided that more dramatic action was now required.

According to Daniels' report, the only account to have survived, Hammond arrived in Camden on Sunday evening May 29 "for the purpose of committing

mond, March 29, 1830, Benjamin Whitner to Hammond, September 11, 1830, Bird Pearson to Hammond, October 1, 1830, all in JHH Papers, LC; Columbia *Southern Times and State Gazette*, October 14, 1830.

29. Columbia *Southern Times and State Gazette*, November 23, 1830.

personal violence upon us." But Hammond did not judge Daniels to be of sufficient standing to warrant a challenge. Duels were only for gentlemen. Scoun-
drels should be caned or horsewhipped. Early Monday morning, Daniels related,
Hammond, armed with a club and accompanied by a friend, approached the
Camden editor and "instantaneously leveled his bludgeon upon our head." The
two men fell struggling and kicking to the ground where they wrestled until a
crowd gathered and separated them. Except for a scratch in the face and a "dis-
coloration over the right eye where in the exercise of his [Hammond's] own gen-
tlemanly, delicate and *appropriate* warfare he attempted to *gouge* us, but which
chivalrous purpose we succeeded in preventing," Daniels escaped unharmed.
The Camden newspaperman succeeded in hurling a final barb at Hammond and
his aspirations to gentility by assuring the *Journal's* readers that despite rumors to
the contrary, their editor had made no effort to bite the Columbia journalist.
"Thank you—when we turn cannibal, we shall select more savory viands."

Hammond apparently perceived the incident as a great personal triumph, for
he had "chastised" the presumptuous Daniels. Yet no record of the affray appears in any of Hammond's personal papers; he included no clippings of the two
journalists' exchanges in scrapbooks of his editorial writings. Perhaps he feared
that Daniels' resistance rendered their encounter less like a gentleman's chastisement of a scoundrel than one of the kicking, biting, gouging fights common-
place among the South's plain folk. Daniels' derision of Hammond's thin veneer
of refinement, of his scarcely concealed aspirations for social position, of the
shallowness of his claims to gentility may have come all too close to the truth.[30]

The incident with Daniels, however, seemed in no way to detract from
Hammond's growing prominence in the state. Governor Hamilton had rewarded
the editor with an invitation to become one of his aides-de-camp and had installed Hammond as a lieutenant colonel in the state militia. George McDuffie
hailed the *Times* as "decidedly the ablest journal in the State," and even John C.
Calhoun assured Hammond that he had "marked your course." From the beginning, "it has met my full approbation."[31]

Yet Hammond was not satisfied with these testimonies to his success. At the
same time the legislature was vindicating the positions he had advanced, he was

30. *Ibid.*, October 11, 1830, January 3, 1831; Camden *Journal*, March 26, May 21, June 4,
1831.
31. George McDuffie to Hammond, February 6, 1831, John C. Calhoun to Hammond, January
15, 1831, both in JHH Papers, LC.

writing to acquaintances in Alabama, inquiring about opportunities for lawyers, journalists, and men of the "middling class" in the Southwest. Despite his outspoken support for Carolina, despite his reckless risk of life in her behalf, despite his association with some of the most prominent of her citizens, Hammond still felt himself in significant ways excluded from the most intimate circles of her elite. And he was a far from patient man.[32]

32. Dixon Lewis to Hammond, December 21, 1830, *ibid.*

CHAPTER 4

A Means of Extrication

HAMMOND'S LIFE was not entirely dedicated to his law practice and editorial duties. Since late in 1829 he had been actively courting Catherine Fitzsimons, a Charleston heiress whose older sister had married Columbia's Wade Hampton II, one of the wealthiest and most politically powerful men in the state. On a visit to her up-country relatives, Catherine had met the dashing Hammond, who succeeded in winning her heart. She, in turn, captured Hammond's interest, even if she did not arouse his passion. Years later he would look back somewhat regretfully upon the decision to heed his father's repeated admonitions about marrying well. The "extreme difficulties of early life," James would remember, had led him to seize upon a "means of extrication" that involved "still greater ultimate difficulties." Hammond married out of ambition rather than love.[1]

Certainly Catherine was no belle. As a friend wrote in polite understatement to Hammond in April of 1830, "She is not I should judge from her appearance & manners calculated to make many & sudden conquests." A midtwentieth-century descendant of the Hammond family was less tactful in his report of family tradition concerning his great grandmother. "Young wags in Charleston," he related, "used to say they wouldn't marry her if every pimple on her face was worth a million dollars."[2]

Hammond was determined to give the youths of Charleston no chance at

1. James Henry Hammond Diary (MS in JHH Papers, SCL), February 23, 1853.
2. Wensley Hobby to James Henry Hammond, April 15, 1830, in JHH Papers, SCL; John Shaw Billings, "The Hammonds" (MS vol. bd., n.d., HBC Papers, SCL).

Catherine's hand or fortune, but he found himself confronted by the staunch opposition of the Fitzsimons family. Catherine's widowed mother and older brothers may well have thought her too young for such serious involvement, for she was only fifteen when Hammond began his suit. But they also disapproved of Hammond himself, fearing that he was nothing more than a fortune hunter. Hammond, however, viewed their dislike as the result not of any suspicion about his intentions, but of their contempt for his lowly social origins.

In face of this opposition, Hammond directed his energies to sweeping young Catherine off her feet. A letter of advice from a friend even suggests that Hammond may have in some way compromised the girl in his effort to ensure that she could not reject him. "If she is not one of the vilest of her sex," T. W. Brevard wrote in June, 1830, "you may rely on it that she loves you. . . . Rest assured neither the old woman [Catherine's mother] nor Paul [Catherine's brother] conjectures the whole of what passed between you and Catherine. . . . Poor Catherine is in a pack of troubles which nothing but soul can aid her in subduing . . . unless . . . you . . . shew the old folks [the Fitzsimonses] that gold and silver are not the only things that shine. . . . let her know she is prefered [sic] to all others . . . and thus may that feeling be kept alive which it seems to me you are morally bound to cherish."[3]

Throughout 1830 and into the early months of 1831, Hammond divided his time between his crusade for nullification and his campaign for Catherine Fitzsimons' hand. But he found it much easier to distinguish himself with the political leadership of the state than to impress the Fitzsimonses with his desirability as a son-in-law. While Calhoun, Hamilton, and McDuffie showered him with compliments, Catherine's mother and brothers remained unmoved.

Yet Hammond's self-assurance and determination grew in proportion to his rising prominence within the state. As Vice-President Calhoun passed through Columbia on his way home from Washington in mid-March, he summoned the young editor for "some private conversation" at seven o'clock one morning. The moment was a critical one for the future of Calhoun personally and for the fate of nullification, and the elder statesman sought Hammond's advice. Calhoun had not yet come out publicly in support of nullification doctrines; his authorship of the 1828 *Exposition* that served as the movement's intellectual manifesto would remain a secret until the following summer. In the early spring of 1831, Calhoun still hoped to be able to retain his national appeal and to win the presi-

3. Thomas W. Brevard to Hammond, June 18, 1830, in JHH Papers, SCL.

dency in 1832. Calhoun explained his strategy to Hammond. Most of Congress, he contended, had come to support him in the rupture with Jackson, who was losing popularity so rapidly that Calhoun saw some major realignment of parties as inevitable. In the privacy of a Columbia drawing room, the vice-president revealed to Hammond his scheme for using this anticipated upheaval in national politics to reconcile the three great sections of the nation. The South, the North, and the West, Calhoun explained, could be reunited through compromises and constitutional amendments that would regain the people's unalloyed confidence in national government. When Hammond rose to leave, Calhoun accompanied him partway home, confessing to the younger man his belief that as president he might be able to solve the problems confronting the South. Hammond had long insisted in the columns of the *Times* that the questions of states' rights were constitutional in nature and could not be solved simply by installing a president favorable to the South, and he politely demurred from Calhoun's proposed strategy. "I told him candidly that such a step would be imprudent at this moment . . . and should not be thought of at this time." Despite Hammond's frankness, Calhoun sought him out for both tea and dinner later in the day. The aspiring editor could not but have been impressed by these testimonies to his own growing importance.[4]

He received no such respect from the Fitzsimonses. With their wealth derived from commerce and their sympathies on the tariff largely protectionist, they may well have been not just unimpressed, but actively disturbed by Hammond's radical credentials. By the early spring, Hammond's failure to make any progress in his suit had overwhelmed him with "despondency and chagrin." His continuing rejection by the family seemed to him conclusive evidence that, no matter what his achievements, he would not be welcomed into the aristocracy of South Carolina, where family and fortune would always count more than talent. If such were the realities, he would prefer to seek his way elsewhere. He began to look seriously for a position in the Southwest. Friends in Alabama assured him that a young man of his gifts "would quickly obtain the highest honours of the State." As rumors spread that Hammond was planning to leave South Carolina, Hamilton, McDuffie, and others of prominence urged him not to abandon his vital post.[5]

4. Hammond Common Place Book (MS in JHH Papers, LC), March 18, 1831.

5. James Hamilton to Hammond, April 8, 1831, Stephen Garrett to Hammond, January 8, 1831, Hamilton to Hammond, April 8, 1831, George McDuffie to Hammond, February 6, 1831, all in JHH Papers, LC.

In mid-April, Hammond decided to push for a showdown with the Fitzsimonses. Impulsively he set out for Charleston determined to return with the promise of Catherine's hand or not to come back at all. Once again Hammond's recklessness paid off. Seeing Catherine's determination, the Fitzsimonses relented and the young couple became engaged.[6]

Hammond lost little time spreading the news of his good fortune and of his intention to retire from the *Southern Times* after his wedding in June. James Hamilton congratulated him on his "happy change of auspices." Although the governor regretted Hammond's immediate loss to the cause, he was pleased that marriage would keep Hammond in Carolina for a career of "exceptional prosperity and honor." Calhoun too was regretful, lamenting that "it will be difficult to supply your place." Yet Hammond seemed to harbor few doubts about abandoning his editorial chair, even at this critical juncture in the nullifiers' cause. Perhaps he was confident that his friend Isaac Hayne, who had agreed to replace him, would maintain the political and journalistic standards he had set. Perhaps he was simply exhausted after eighteen months of riding the circuit to maintain his law practice while publishing three editions of a newspaper every week. But whatever his other justifications, Hammond's primary reason for leaving the *Times* was to begin a new and more desirable life. No longer a struggling schoolmaster nor an ambitious lawyer nor an aspiring editor, Hammond would now be part of South Carolina's ruling class. In his final editorial of May 28, 1831, he reaffirmed both his love for the union and his dedication to the principles of states' rights. But other commitments were operating more powerfully in shaping his life.[7]

Amidst a rainstorm on June 23, James Henry Hammond and Catherine Fitzsimons were married. But Hammond's struggle with his bride's family was far from over, as the refusal of Catherine's brother to attend the wedding made clear. Having relented about her marriage to Hammond, the Fitzsimonses still remained anxious to secure Catherine's considerable property from his control by means of a marriage settlement that would enable the girl to hold her inheritance in her own name. Under South Carolina law a woman's property was automatically ceded to her husband at the time of her marriage unless other legal arrangements were made. Because Catherine was a minor, her property did not immediately devolve upon her husband, but was retained in trust by her older

6. Brevard to Hammond, April 12, 1831, in JHH Papers, SCL.

7. Hamilton to Hammond, May 3, 1831, John C. Calhoun to Hammond, May 16, 1831, both in JHH Papers, LC; Columbia *Southern Times and State Gazette*, May 28, 1831.

brother, who vigorously resisted ceding it to Hammond without some legal arrangements limiting his claims and power over it. Hammond professed outrage at the Fitzsimonses' suggestion of a formal marriage settlement, declaring that such a demand was equivalent to a charge of dishonesty against him and enlisting Catherine's support in his views. "To make this settlement," he complained, would "be to recognize & establish forever an inequality" between him and his new bride. Hammond proclaimed that he would not enjoy "all the riches of the earth" if they were held "under his wife's petticoats." After his strivings to rise to the uppermost circles of Carolina society, Hammond would not tolerate any lingering reminder of social inferiority. He had come too close to endure being turned away; he wanted to be a plantation owner in his own right.[8]

Worried lest he appear to show "too much anxiety on the subject of property," Hammond invoked more transcendent justifications for his position as well. Settlements, he piously declared, were "totally repugnant to my feelings & my principles. I have ever regarded them as at variance with the spirit & true policy of all our institutions. . . . They are relics of the English laws made for the protection of their aristocracy." When it was convenient, Hammond could still play the democrat.[9]

Instead of abating in the months after the marriage, the quarrel escalated. When Hammond asked Paul Fitzsimons to provide him with specific information about Catherine's property and with a tour of the plantation that composed the major part of her share of their father's estate, Paul refused to cooperate, threatening to invoke a "higher tribunal" to settle the issues between them. When Hammond at last gained access to Paul's accounts of Catherine's wealth, he was astounded to find that Fitzsimons had included such petty charges as ten cents for postage. Worse yet, the precise young lawyer was horrified at the sloppy records and accounts Paul had kept and at the careless way he had managed the property. For a time, Hammond even suspected Fitzsimons of having willfully cheated his sister.[10]

At the end of July, Hammond and his bride departed on a delayed wedding trip with these upsetting issues still unresolved. Traveling, as did so many privileged Carolinians of the period, to escape the midsummer heat and sickness of the lower-lying areas of the state, the Hammonds headed for the mountains near

8. Hammond to William D. Martin, July 31, 1831, in Letterpress Book, JHH Papers, SCL.
9. Hammond to Pierce Mason Butler, July 21, 1831, Hammond to Martin, July 31, 1831, both *ibid.*
10. Hammond to Butler, July 21, 1831, *ibid.*

Asheville, North Carolina. The discomforts of their journey may well have distracted them, at least temporarily, from their troubles at home. The mountain roads were "execrable," nearly destroying both their carriage and their health. Lodgings were dirty and unpleasant, and one inn seemed to Hammond to smell "like a rat hole." They continued northwards towards the Virginia Springs resorts frequented by planters from all over the South, where they were greeted not only by Carolina friends, but by an infestation of fleas.

Hammond had been too busy for the past few years to know how to enjoy this new idleness. "I am so worn out with doing nothing," he complained in a letter home, "that it fatigues me to think." Nor could he entirely banish his political interests from his mind. Elections took place during their visits in Tennessee and Virginia, and Hammond was distressed to find that few citizens had even so much as heard of nullification. But he was encouraged by the growing disenchantment with Jackson he encountered, and he hoped that these sentiments might produce sympathy for the states' rights principles of South Carolina. He worried as well about his own political future. If he and Catherine moved to her plantation, he would leave Columbia for a new district where he was an utter stranger. Anonymity threatened to mar his chances for political distinction in the approaching crisis; he feared that he would prove neither "useful nor conspicuous."[11]

Impatient to face these pressing personal and public dilemmas, Hammond was eager to return home. He and Catherine reached Columbia in early October, and Hammond immediately set about closing his law practice. Settling the rest of his private affairs would be far more difficult, however, for intense hostility still characterized his relationship with the Fitzsimonses. Although Catherine's mother had decided that the issue of a settlement should be dropped because of her daughter's opposition, Hammond's two-month absence had done little to conciliate Paul. Hammond was genuinely worried about the outcome of the conflict, for he feared a permanent rift in the family. His wife was now pregnant, and he was distressed about the effect the continued quarreling might have upon her. "My heart weeps for you Kate," he wrote her sadly. "Cut off from your family as I now am satisfied you will be forever, What have I to offer you in return for this sacrafice [sic]? Only a heart. A sincere but sorrowing heart. There is a consolation however. You delayed for two years to marry me to prevent it & when we did marry . . . I was ready to do anything to unite the family. . . . Yet

11. Hammond to Butler, July 21, 1831, Hammond to Brevard, August 26, 1831, Hammond to Butler, August 18, 1831, all *ibid.*

63

because I would not humble myself & lick the dust, all would not do. God did not make me to do that."[12]

Eager to "carry public opinion with me on this matter," and anxious to avoid the embarrassment of a court battle with the Fitzsimonses, Hammond had during the summer suggested to Paul the appointment of a panel of arbitrators to settle their differences. The two antagonists agreed upon William D. Martin, a jurist and ex-congressman, and William Harper, Hammond's former legal sponsor, the state's chancellor, and a leading nullifier. These two men were to choose a third if they found they could not agree. David Johnson, another judge, was added to the panel. Hammond wrote to each of these men, forcefully arguing his case against marriage settlements as barbaric vestiges of a bygone way of life unsuitable for a republic like South Carolina. Harper privately urged Hammond to compromise by agreeing voluntarily to restrictions on at least part of the property, but Hammond peremptorily refused. Near the end of January, 1832, the three arbiters announced their recommendation that no settlement be made. Their personal knowledge of Hammond's achievements and abilities in the public arena no doubt convinced them that the Fitzsimonses had little ground to fear that he was an unscrupulous and parasitical adventurer out to steal Catherine's fortune. Hammond's ambitions were in fact much more sweeping.[13]

Although just twenty-four, Hammond had engineered a remarkable rise from obscurity to prominence and wealth in Carolina society. He had become a political force to be reckoned with, an advisor sought out by figures as important as the nation's vice-president himself. By a fortunate marriage he had succeeded in crowning this public achievement with the personal accouterments necessary to lasting eminence in the South. Politics and planting were the two revered callings in this culture, and Hammond had now gained entry into both. Upon the resolution of his conflict with the Fitzsimonses, Hammond succeeded to control of a ten-thousand-acre plantation and well over a hundred slaves. This certainly would assure him the "independence" required for republican political virtue. Now he had only to convince those slaves, the rest of the plantation-owning Carolina elite, and perhaps himself that he had truly arrived.

Hammond's most immediate problem was to transform the neglected property Paul had released to him into a workable and profitable enterprise. Until his death, Hammond would never abandon his efforts towards the fulfillment of this

12. Hammond to Catherine Fitzsimons Hammond, November 4, 1831, in JHH Papers, SHC.
13. Hammond to Martin, December 19, 1831, Hammond to David Johnson, April 21, 1832, both in Letterpress Book, JHH Papers, SCL.

goal, and plantation management would ultimately absorb a larger portion of his energy than even his intense political ambitions. Just as the plantation itself was the central social and economic institution of the antebellum South, so too Hammond's duties as plantation master became the focus of his existence. These responsibilities were always with him; he measured himself by the effectiveness with which he executed them; he could not entirely relinquish them even in the last stages of his final illness.

But while the plantation was omnipresent in Hammond's life, ever requiring his attention and always providing the economic support for his other undertakings, it is also a story all its own. In many senses the plantation was a world unto itself, a microcosm within a larger universe. And so within the wider scope of Hammond's life, there is another tale, warranting special and separate treatment. It is the story of a man, his land, and the nearly one thousand black slaves who lived and worked on it in the last decades before the Civil War. It is, in a sense, the biography of a place and its people.

Part II

My Little Kingdom
The World of the Plantation

*But what occupation more noble than Agriculture. What one so much sought
after by the proudest characters as Despotic Sway?*
JAMES HENRY HAMMOND

James Henry Hammond's South Carolina

CHAPTER 5

In Search of Despotic Sway

Hammond as a Master of Slaves

A DOZEN MILES south of Augusta, Georgia, the Savannah curves gently, creating two bends that antebellum river captains knew as Stingy Venus and Hog Crawl Round. Close to the mouth of Boggy Gut Creek the channel narrows, and decaying wrecks of steamboats bear witness to the waterway's importance in an era long departed. Nearby, on the South Carolina shore, a cliff abruptly rises almost thirty feet above the water. Deposits of mica in the soil give the promontory a metallic tinge, and the bank and the plantation of which it was part came as early as colonial times to be called Silver Bluff.[1]

Located on an easily navigable river between Augusta and Savannah, the site played a prominent role in the early history of the up-country region. Although the focus of development in both South Carolina and Georgia remained near the coast until after the beginning of the nineteenth century, the famous botanist and traveler William Bartram in 1773 found Silver Bluff already "a very celebrated place." In the course of his mid-sixteenth-century explorations, Hernando DeSoto had discovered an Indian village flourishing on the bluff, and an Irishman, George Galphin, became the first white settler in the area when he established an Indian trading post in 1736. By the second half of the eighteenth century, blacks had added their influence to these strains of red and white. A Baptist congregation that flourished at Silver Bluff in the years just before the

---

1. These are land miles. Because of bends in the river, water distances are greater. Silver Bluff is approximately 30 river miles from Augusta and 175 from Savannah. See John Shaw Billings, "Silver Bluff, DeSoto, and Galphin" (MS vol. bd., 1955), in HBC Papers, SCL; James Henry Hammond Land and Slave Papers (MS vol. bd.), in JHH Papers, SCL.

Revolution claims the distinction of being the first separate black church in America.

With the dawning of the steamboat era and the general expansion of the up-country after the turn of the century, the region began to seem a promising area for investment. In 1814 the wealthy and enterprising Charleston merchant Christopher Fitzsimons bought two thousand acres of rich swamp land adjacent to the river for three thousand dollars, and eight years later he acquired a second tract almost four times larger. Upon Fitzsimons' death in 1825, this remote property became the share of his estate allotted to his youngest child, eleven-year-old Catherine. For the next six years, the girl's two older brothers officially managed the land, in fact abandoning it almost entirely to the neglectful supervision of a resident overseer.[2]

When James Henry Hammond arrived on December 8, 1831, to take possession of the estate his marriage had won him, he carefully noted in his diary 10,800 acres of land, which he valued at $36,100. Of this, only 967 acres, including 150 acres of swamp, were cleared for corn and cotton cultivation; 90 percent of the property remained entirely undeveloped. The land itself was of two main types: the low, boggy, and malarial tracts near the river and the red-clay soils of the wooded plateaus. Silver Bluff, he would later remark, was located "in an [sic] pine wilderness."[3]

Through these woods, the plantation livestock ran unrestrained; Hammond estimated that 95 head of cattle, 130 hogs, and 20 sheep foraged in the underbrush for roots, nuts, and shrubbery. The 25 mules needed as work animals were more carefully treated and maintained in plantation barns. In addition to food for stock, Silver Bluff's forests provided valuable firewood and timber. The plantation sawmill produced an annual crop of lumber, part of which was floated downriver to Savannah and the remainder sold as fuel to steamboat captains who stopped at the Bluff landing. In this survey of his property, Hammond recorded as well a gristmill, a cotton ginhouse, a blacksmith's shop, and a carpenter's shop. Although Hammond did not bother to list all the estate's structures,

---

2. On early history of Silver Bluff area, see Billings, "Silver Bluff," and "The Hammonds" (MS vol. bd., n.d., HBC Papers, SCL), and Dorothy K. MacDowell, "George Galphin, Nabob of the Backwoods," *South Carolina History Illustrated*, I (August, 1970), 51–56. On the early black congregation, see Albert Raboteau, *Slave Religion: The "Invisible Institution" in the Antebellum South* (New York: Oxford University Press, 1978), 139–40.

3. Hammond Plantation Diary (MS vol. bd., 1831–55, JHH Papers, SCL), December 8, 1831; James Henry Hammond to Nathaniel Beverley Tucker, August 31, 1849, in Tucker-Coleman Papers, Earl Gregg Swem Memorial Library, College of William and Mary, Williamsburg, Va.

he did note in his inventory that the property included a resident owner's dwelling. The undistinguished house was filled with rough and broken furniture and could hardly have seemed adequate to this aspiring aristocrat. But Hammond was for the time being preoccupied with other matters; he was less concerned about personal comforts than about the economic foundations of his new enterprise, about the labor force on which the prosperity of his undertaking depended.

After his brief initial survey of land and livestock, Hammond made a detailed list of the human chattel he now owned, including each individual's name and age. The 147 slaves of Silver Bluff were recorded in his inventory in family groups, as perhaps they appeared on that December day to meet their new master. Hammond had acquired seventy-four females and seventy-three males, a population with a median age of twenty-five. He would certainly have noted that forty-six, nearly a third of these slaves, were not yet fifteen, too young to be much use in the fields but a good foundation for a vigorous future labor force. Undoubtedly, too, he observed that sixty-four of the slaves were between fifteen and forty-five, the prime work years. These were the individuals upon whom Hammond would rely to plant, cultivate, and harvest the cotton and corn that would generate most of his yearly income. Seven slaves were over sixty-five and would in all likelihood not produce enough to equal the cost of their maintenance. But they could be used for chores less demanding than field labor, such as supervising the stables, selling wood to passing steamboats, or minding slave children whose mothers were at work on the crop. Despite the drain these elderly blacks represented, Hammond would have seen in the overall composition of his slave force, with its well-balanced sex ratio and comparative youth, promise of rapid natural increase, as well as of a high level of agricultural productivity. Sixty-one workers, he concluded, could be used in the fields, eight in the sawmill, one in the gristmill, seven on the wood landing, and one as stock minder.[4]

But neither Hammond's initial census, nor his first cursory examination

4. See slave census in Hammond Plantation Diary, December 8, 1831, and remarks of January 1, 1832. Unless otherwise noted, statistical compilations concerning slaves are based on this list, the birth and death registers in Hammond Plantation Diary, and Hammond, "Silver Bluff, Cathwood, Cowden, and Redcliffe" (MS vol. bd., 1856–87, JHH Papers, SCL), and on Manuscript Schedules, Seventh Census of the United States, Second Series, Slave Population, Barnwell and Edgefield Counties, South Carolina, 1850, and Manuscript Schedules, Eighth Census of the United States, Slave Population, Barnwell and Edgefield Counties, South Carolina, 1860, National Archives. Where I have seen obvious inaccuracies of transcription or arithmetic in these documents I have adjusted them. See the Appendix, Chart 1. The dependency ratio among Hammond's slaves, which is calculated as the proportion of the population under twenty and over sixty was 26.35 percent in 1831. By 1860 it had dropped to 16.1 percent.

could reveal what he all too soon realized about his newly acquired property. His efforts to shape this group of blacks into a disciplined, productive, and expanding slave force would be challenged and thwarted at nearly every turn. Hammond would be frustrated in his efforts to produce a high yield both of agricultural crops and of young blacks. His slaves, he would discover, were not only undisciplined and in "very bad subjection" as a result of careless management, but extraordinarily unhealthy as well.[5]

When Hammond took possession of Silver Bluff, he assumed a role and entered a world largely unfamiliar to him. As we have seen, his parents had owned a few slaves, whom they hired out to provide income. In the mid-twenties, Elisha had even deeded two of them—or more accurately, the profits of their rented labor—to his eldest son. But the new master at Silver Bluff was entirely inexperienced in the management of large numbers of agricultural and domestic workers. The blacks at Silver Bluff, for their part, also confronted a new situation, for they had become accustomed to living without a master in permanent residence. In 1831 Hammond and his slaves alike faced new circumstances. But it was Hammond who was the outsider, moving into a world of established patterns of behavior and interaction in the community at Silver Bluff. By law all power rested with Hammond. But in reality the situation was rather different.

Hammond quickly learned that the mastery of slaves entailed a good deal more than simply directing 147 individual lives, for he had to dominate a complex social order already in existence on the plantation. For the next three decades, he would struggle to control what he called a "system of roguery" among his slaves, a structured and organized pattern of resistance to his desire for total domination. Nevertheless, the young master was determined from the first to brook no challenge to his power. By asserting his control, he would transform Silver Bluff into a profitable enterprise and its slaves into productive workers. Hammond recognized that his effectiveness in creating a docile and tractable labor force depended upon his success in making the blacks entirely subservient to his will not just in the fields, but in every aspect of their lives. To force them to acknowledge their own weakness and his power, he would destroy the autonomy of the slave community and bring its members under his direct and total domination. Over the next several years, he developed a carefully designed plan of physical and psychological control intended to eliminate the foundations of black solidarity. Yet at the same time he sought despotic power over his slave

5. Hammond to J. W. Walker, December 27, 1836, in JHH Papers, LC.

force, Hammond from the first cherished a conception of himself as a beneficent master whose guidance and control represented the best of all possible worlds for the uncivilized and backward people entrusted to him by God. His need both to dominate and to be loved would pose insuperable difficulties within his evolving system of slave management.[6]

Hammond's slaves, so long under the desultory management of absentee owners, were not accustomed to the rigorous demands made by their new master, and they resented and resisted his drive for efficiency. "The negroes are trying me," Hammond observed on more than one occasion in the first weeks after his arrival. Under such circumstances it was hard to maintain his idealized self-image as a benevolent master surrounded by obedient and grateful servants. Instead, Hammond found himself compelled to "subdue" them, and he later recalled an initial "year of severity which cost me infinite pain" before the blacks were "broken in." If it was painful to the young master, it was undoubtedly more so to the slaves, for he resorted to frequent floggings as the most effective representation of his control. Those who performed unsatisfactory labor, left the plantation without permission, or in any other way challenged Hammond's authority were lashed, in a public display of the consequences of refusal to comply with the master's will. Eight slaves slow in returning to work after the Christmas holidays were severely whipped by the overseer. When they appealed to Hammond for sympathy, he responded by ordering them flogged again. Before he could afford to show mercy, Hammond knew he had to impress the slaves with the reality of his power.[7]

Part of this mastery consisted in extending control over the very souls of those he sought to dominate. "Intend to break up negro preaching & negro churches," he proclaimed in his plantation diary. When a slave named Ben Shubrick requested permission to "join the negro Church," Hammond refused it, but made arrangements for him to be admitted to the congregation of which Hammond was himself a member. "Ordered night meetings on the plantation to be discontinued," he noted in his plantation diary only days after his arrival at Silver Bluff. Hammond saw an implicit threat in the assemblies of fervent and devoted slaves who gathered together in praise and worship. In the authority of the black preacher lay a potential challenge to Hammond's own; in the Old Testament chronicles of Moses and the chosen people lay the germs of an ideology

---

6. Hammond Plantation Diary, October 16, 1835.

7. Hammond Plantation Diary, December 14, 13, 1831; Hammond to Walker, December 27, 1836, in JHH Papers, LC; Hammond Plantation Diary, December 28, 1831.

of black revolution. Hammond endeavored to replace independent black worship with devotions entirely under white supervision. Carefully instructed white clergymen could emphasize the less incendiary strain within Christian teachings that promoted meekness and docility. To make certain that black religion would not be transformed into a vehicle of slave revolt, Hammond visited each of his new neighbors to request that they follow his example in eliminating the black church on their plantations.[8]

Hammond soon regularized his white-controlled religious exercises by hiring itinerant ministers for Sunday afternoon slave services. Here the speakers undoubtedly emphasized the virtues of obedience to masters terrestrial as well as divine. While the whip served as the most potent symbol of physical domination, the pulpits of the Methodist and Baptist churches erected on the plantation during the 1840s became an embodiment of Hammond's crusade for ideological hegemony.

In the realm of labor, Hammond's desire for omnipotence was expressed in an unceasing pursuit of efficiency. His rigorous management quickly became evident in the fields, where the amount of labor extracted from each slave had a direct—and in Hammond's self-consciously rational eyes, even measurable—effect upon the master's purse. The new owner found his laborers accustomed to task work, a system in which a clearly defined daily job was assigned to each hand. When this duty was completed, the slave's time was his or her own. Hammond regarded such arrangements as distressingly wasteful of the labor potential of his work force, for most of the blacks, he discovered, seemed to have finished their appointed obligations by the midafternoon. Such a system, moreover, undermined not only efficiency but order, for it provided the slave too much autonomy and permitted hours of dangerous independence. The slave, Hammond explained, was motivated to work too rapidly and too carelessly in order to complete a required job. Task labor encouraged the blacks to overexert themselves, with "no rest until 3 or 4 o'clock." In a gang, under constant surveillance of the overseer, "they work moderately from sunrise to sundown stopping an hour for breakfast & 2 for dinner, go home, sleep all night & are ready & strong for an-

8. Hammond Plantation Diary, December 16, 15, 1831, May 11, 1832. On the revolutionary potential of black Christianity, see Raboteau, *Slave Religion*, Eugene Genovese, *Roll, Jordon, Roll: The World the Slaves Made* (New York: Pantheon Books, 1974), and Lawrence Levine, "Slave Songs and Slave Consciousness," in Allen Weinstein, Frank O. Gattel, and David Sarasohn (eds.), *American Negro Slavery* (New York: Oxford University Press, 1979). On white control over black religion, see Luther P. Jackson, "Religious Instruction of Negroes, 1830–1860, with Special Reference to South Carolina," *Journal of Negro History*, XV (January, 1930), 72–114.

other day." Under such a system, "they do much more," Hammond found, "and are not so apt to strain themselves." Despite the workers' clear preference for the task system, Hammond was determined to use only gang labor at Silver Bluff.[9]

While a significant part of Hammond's objection to task labor was its inefficiency, he also feared the independence it gave the laborers, both in the field, where they were free to determine the pace of their work, and during the unsupervised hours after their tasks were completed. Because Hammond wanted above all to make the slaves feel dependent, he correctly viewed encouraging any area of autonomy as counterproductive and even dangerous. As a result, he curtailed many of the privileges the slaves had enjoyed under the Fitzsimons regime, especially those that provided the blacks direct contact with the world outside the plantation. Slaves were forbidden to trade in local stores, to sell the produce of their garden patches to neighbors, to fraternize with the crews of steamboats refueling at the Bluff landing, or to visit town more than once a year. Hammond intended that his slaves have no access to a world outside his omnipotent rule.[10]

Hammond's drive to extend his power reached into nearly every realm of plantation life. The master's concern with controlling slaves' bodies logically implied a desire to manage their health, and here Hammond felt he confronted the united opposition of the blacks and of fate. Although masters always hoped for the increase in wealth that accompanied a growth of their slave population, they certainly did not pursue this goal by pampering their slaves. Efficient masters extracted as much labor as they could safely obtain without diminishing the value of their human investment and often provided slaves with the food and clothing minimally necessary for their maintenance as effective laborers. The need to adhere closely to this balance between maximum work and minimum comforts meant in practice that slavery was very often debilitating to health. Hammond shared prevailing nutritional notions that cautioned against harming slaves through too rich or elaborate a diet and prescribed a regimen made up chiefly of cornmeal, pork, and molasses. The standard weekly ration of three pounds of meat and a peck of meal for each laborer at Silver Bluff was similar to that given slaves throughout the South. Even if this diet was sufficiently high in calories to stave off hunger pangs, it provided inadequate amounts of calcium,

9. Hammond Plantation Diary, May 9, 1832, May 26, 1839, May 16, 1838. On the African origin of the slaves' preference for collective work patterns, see Genovese, *Roll, Jordan, Roll,* 322–24.

10. Hammond Plantation Diary, March 18, 1839, February 28, 1844.

magnesium, protein, iron, and vitamins; it may have contributed to deficiency diseases such as pellagra, and it certainly lowered resistance to a variety of ill-nesses, including the "fevers" and intestinal parasites, which nineteenth-century observers noted as especially prevalent among blacks and which appeared fre-quently in Hammond's discussion of sickness among his slave population.[11]

Nutritional deficiencies combined with harsh labor conditions to create in the nineteenth century, as today, a higher level of black than white mortality. All of these factors would have operated at Silver Bluff, for Hammond kept abreast of the current, albeit misguided, wisdom concerning the maintenance of slave health. But the blacks on Hammond's plantation were extraordinarily sickly. Their annual rate of death in the early 1830s averaged sixty-five per thou-sand, more than twice the rate demographers have calculated for the whole pop-ulation of U.S. slaves in 1830. Hammond was himself appalled by the level of mortality and especially alarmed by the rate of death amongst slave children. Not only was this a matter of wealth and property, but a distressing challenge to Hammond's cherished conception of himself as an effective and benevolent mas-ter. During the first decade of his management, 72 percent of slave children died before the age of five, a rate of mortality astronomical not only in terms of pres-ent day expectations but in comparison with other nineteenth-century slave communities.[12]

11. On slave health there is a voluminous and growing literature. See Todd Savitt, *Medicine and Slavery: The Diseases and Health Care of Blacks in Antebellum Virginia* (Urbana: University of Illi-nois Press, 1978); Peter Wood, *Black Majority: Negroes in Colonial South Carolina from 1670 Through the Stono Rebellion* (New York: Alfred A. Knopf, 1974); Weymouth T. Jordan, "Plantation Medicine in the Old South," *Alabama Review*, III (April, 1950), 83–107; Kenneth F. Kiple and Virginia Him-melsteib King, *Another Dimension to the Black Diaspora: Diet, Disease, and Racism* (Cambridge: Cam-bridge University Press, 1981); Richard Sutch, "The Care and Feeding of Slaves," in Paul A. David, et al. (eds.), *Reckoning with Slavery* (New York: Oxford University Press, 1976), 231–301.

12. See the Appendix, Charts 2–5. See also birth and death registers, Hammond Plantation Diary. For example, Herbert Gutman found that 20 percent of the slaves born at Good Hope, a low-country South Carolina plantation, between 1820 and 1857 died before age five. Michael Craton established a 30 percent death rate for children under five at Worthy Park in Jamaica, an island known for its high mortality and morbidity. Prevailing estimates for U.S. slaves in 1830 indicate a crude death rate of thirty per thousand and a crude birth rate of fifty-five per thousand. Hammond's slaves were thus exceptional because of high mortality rather than low fertility. See Herbert Gut-man, *The Black Family in Slavery and Freedom, 1750–1925* (New York: Pantheon Books, 1976), 47; Michael Craton, *Searching for the Invisible Man: Slaves and Plantation Life in Jamaica* (Cambridge, Mass.: Harvard University Press, 1978) 85–134, and Robert W. Fogel and Stanley L. Engerman, "Recent Findings on the Study of Slave Demography and Family Structure," *Sociology and Social Research*, LXIII (April, 1979), 566–89. For a discussion of mortality rates of combined populations of eleven plantations, including Hammond's, see Richard H. Steckel, "Slave Mortality: Analysis of Evidence from Plantation Records," *Social Science History*, III (October, 1979) 86–114; and Richard H. Steckel, "The Economics of U.S. Slave and Southern White Fertility" (Ph.D. dissertation, Uni-

For both humanitarian and economic reasons, Hammond was determined to reverse these alarming statistics. "One would think," he recorded with horror, ". . . that I was a monster of inhumanity." Late in 1841 he noted with shame, "Ten years today since I took possession. . . . It is most melancholy to record that my negroes have in that period actually decreased in the course of nature. There have been 73 births and 82 deaths. . . . And yet I have taken more pains to raise young negroes & nurse all than to do anything else. It has been forever on my mind & I have read, consulted with every one & spared no exertion—but all in vain." When he summarized his overall record of births and deaths in 1854, he found that deaths still predominated by twelve. This was, he believed, "an awful & besides a pecuniary loss a most distressing thing to me. For over 20 years I have done everything I could to preserve health. There is ample provision of clothes, food, good houses & good water & no over work. Every attention is paid to cleanliness & to the sick."[13]

From the time of his arrival at Silver Bluff in 1831 Hammond had been intensely concerned with plantation medicine. Like many slaveowners of his era, he expected to act as doctor in most cases of slave illness and to turn to formally trained physicians only when his ministrations proved ineffective. Hammond asked doctor friends to recommend readings, and he acquired a stock of common drugs and medical instruments for use at the Bluff. Soon after taking over at Silver Bluff, he stocked his medicine chest, and the remedies he procured indicate that he initially accepted the basic therapeutic assumptions of his era. His purchase of blistering ointments, tartar emetic, the purgative manna, the stimulant snakeroot, and the mercurial compound calomel reveal that Hammond clearly intended to intervene drastically in slave illness by producing vomiting, perspiration, and diarrhea in accordance with the principles of what has come to be known as "heroic treatment." Lancets for bleeding and an enema syringe, also listed among his early plantation purchases, were designed to assist the physiological operation of these drugs. Purges, cathartics, and emetics would aid the body in regaining the natural equilibrium that nineteenth-century practitioners

---

versity of Chicago, 1977). See also Jack E. Eblen, "New Estimates of the Vital Rates of the United States Black Population During the Nineteenth Century," *Demography*, XI (May, 1974), 301–319; Edward Meeker, "Mortality Trends of Southern Blacks, 1850–1910: Some Preliminary Findings," *Explorations in Economic History*, XIII (January, 1976), 13–43; Maris Vinoskis, "The Demography of the Slave Population in Antebellum America," *Journal of Interdisciplinary History*, V (Winter, 1975), 459–67.

13. Hammond Silver Bluff Diary, (MS in JHH Papers, LC), September 5, 1841; Hammond Plantation Diary, November 5, 1841, October 2, 1854.

regarded as the foundation of health. The cutting of gums during teething or the more general letting of blood were similarly regarded as means to restore systemic balance.[14]

Yet Hammond was not entirely convinced by the conventional wisdom concerning medical treatment, and the persistence of illness and death among his slaves made him willing to experiment with new therapeutic means. After only six months, he recorded his intention to forego the use of calomel and "all violent medicines," though later entries in his diary indicate his failure to keep that resolve. Although he called physicians to the Bluff with considerable frequency— an average of twice a week to treat the dysentery that erupted during his first summer of masterhood, fourteen times in less than a month during a measles epidemic, twice weekly during a winter outbreak of influenza—Hammond grew increasingly sceptical of both their diagnoses and their therapeutics. Suspicious that they often did more to harm than to cure, Hammond periodically resolved to do without the advice of physicians altogether.[15]

After reading widely in medical texts written for both doctors and laymen, Hammond in 1834 announced his intention to move away from mainstream therapeutics toward "Botanic practice," or Thomsonianism, a popular medical movement that challenged the dominance of conventional physicians and advocated a regimen of herbal remedies and harrowing steam baths. The "steam practice," Hammond believed, "prevents pretended sickness & by thoroughly cleansing the skin improves the health." Perhaps Hammond, always jealous of his own prerogative, was attracted to this system by its restoration of control over medical treatment to laymen like himself. But he also approved the movement's rejection of some of the more brutal drugs, such as mercury. While many extreme remedies were available in the botanic pharmacopoeia and while the steam treatments could be both debilitating and painful, Thomsonian remedies

14. Josiah C. Nott to Hammond, May 6, June 11, May 16, 1832, all in JHH Papers, SCL; bill of Thomas Wray, December 20, 1831, in Hammond Business Papers (JHH Papers, SCL). For uses of these drugs and the logic of this system of therapeutics, see Joseph Togno, M.D., and E. Durand, *A Manual of Materia Medica and Pharmacy Comprising a Concise Description of the Articles Used in Medicine* (Philadelphia: Carey, Lea & Carey, 1829); J. Hume Simons, *The Planter's Guide, and Family Book of Medicine* (Charleston: M'Carter and Allen, 1848); Charles E. Rosenberg, "The Therapeutic Revolution: Medicine, Meaning and Social Change in Nineteenth Century America," *Perspectives in Biology and Medicine*, XX (Summer, 1977), 485–506.

15. Hammond Plantation Diary, May 29, 1832. But Hammond used calomel against cholera two years later. Hammond Plantation Diary, September 29, 1834. See Hammond's physicians' bills, Hammond Business Papers and Hammond Business Papers, Legal Size, both in JHH Papers, SCL. Note particularly the bills of Milledge Galphin, February 23 to August 19, 1844, and February 9 to October 3, 1848, Hammond Business Papers.

tended to be at least marginally less heroic than those of the system it sought to challenge. By the late 1830s, Hammond proclaimed his maxim for medical treatment of slaves to be "*nurse well* & physic little." In his plantation hospital, Hammond had replaced high dosages of purgatives, cathartics, and emetics with prescribed rest and attentive care. "Never give horse doses," he cautioned his overseer. Even if he should suspect a slave to be "pretending," Hammond urged his manager to "let him *rest a day*, which will often save many days of real sickness."[16]

Hammond similarly reflected the concerns of his era in his growing interest in the environmental causes of slave morbidity—issues that we would regard today as part of the realm of public health. By the mid-1830s Hammond had introduced a system of "sanitary regulations" that included regular garbage removal, annual whitewashing of slave houses, the use of lime and charcoal to cover compost heaps, and careful supervision of the slaves' water supply. The master moved dwellings away from damp and low-lying areas, forbade slaves to go out before the evaporation of the morning dew, and tried to keep them from the dangerous night air.[17]

Yet even these improvements did not bring the increased health Hammond sought for his human property. The persistently high death rate, he concluded, must be a result of the "syphilitic taint" that had existed in several of the families of the original Fitzsimons slaves and of the prevalence of scrofula, or tuberculosis, in others. The population of blacks he had found at Silver Bluff, he explained, had by 1831 acquired "habits of miscarriage & . . . become so familiar with death in every form so as to be wholly demoralized." Hammond's perceptions may well have been accurate. Visiting physicians confirmed his diagnosis of "hereditary venereal" disease appearing amongst slave children, which would certainly have contributed to their higher rate of mortality. The pattern of these

16. Hammond Plantation Diary, May 23, 1834, April 19, 1835; Hammond to Walker, December 27, 1836, in JHH Papers, LC. Hammond regularly read *Southern Agriculturist, De Bow's Review, Farmer's Register,* and *Farmer and Planter,* which were replete with advice on slave health. On Thomsonianism, see James O. Breeden, "Thomsonianism in Virginia," *Virginia Magazine of History and Biography,* LXXXII (April, 1974), 150–80. Hammond's evolution away from "heroic" treatment paralleled more general developments in medicine. See M. Morton Dowler, "Remarks on Therapeutics," *New Orleans Medical and Surgical Journal,* XII (1855–56), 49; "Editorial," *ibid.,* I (1844), 247–48.

17. Hammond Plantation Diary, October 5, 1849, July 26, 1842, September 9, 26, 1849; Hammond Redcliffe Journal (MS vol. bd., 1861–64, JHH Papers, SCL); Hammond to John Fox Hammond, October 11, 1840, JHH Papers, SCL. See also "Cleaning Up," in "Governor Hammond's Instructions to His Overseer," in Willie Lee Rose (ed.), *A Documentary History of Slavery in North America* (New York: Oxford University Press, 1976), 353.

A slave house still standing in the yard at Redcliffe.

deaths, moreover, was such that some sort of familial or genetic link seems possible. Although Coober had eight recorded pregnancies between 1832 and 1849, three infants were stillborn, and the others died at ages between six weeks and nine months. Nicey, by contrast, bore seven live children of whom five survived to adulthood. Syphilis may have contributed to this pattern of high rates of miscarriage and child death in certain families.[18]

In 1854 Hammond had his son consult with his medical school professor at the University of Pennsylvania, Dr. Samuel Jackson, about the causes of infant mortality on his plantation. Hammond communicated his suspicion that heredity was playing a part, but Dr. Jackson felt not. He emphasized nutrition and urged Hammond to feed the slave children chiefly on milk and eggs. Hammond accordingly shifted the children's diet to include a larger proportion of milk. Given the high level of lactose intolerance (over 70 percent today) among people of African heritage, this was in all likelihood not beneficial to infant health.[19]

18. Bill of Milledge Galphin, M.D., July 17, 1833, in Business Papers, Legal Size, JHH Papers, SCL; Hammond Plantation Diary, October 2, 1854, July 13, 1849.
19. Nicholas Scott Cardell and Mark Myron Hopkins, "The Effect of Milk Intolerance on the

Sickle-cell anemia, unknown to nineteenth-century science and thus to Hammond, would also have had significant effects. It has been estimated that the frequency of sickle-cell trait among blacks brought from West Africa to America may have been as high as 22 percent and was probably even higher among slaves who had lived for a generation in the Carolina low country, where the resistance sickle-cell provided to the malaria endemic there would have selected in favor of the trait's perpetuation. When both parents have the sickle-cell gene, however, their offspring develop sickle-cell anemia, a disease that takes its toll in the earliest years of life if it is untreated. A 1951 study conducted in Zaire showed 50 percent mortality before age five among children with sickle-cell anemia, usually from complications of bacterial and viral infections. Such illnesses were a recurrent cause of death amongst the children at Silver Bluff, and could well have been reflecting an underlying pattern of sickle-cell disease.[20]

Despite his shift to botanic practice in the mid-thirties, Hammond continued to confront dismaying health problems in his slave population. After a number of years of a rather eclectic system of medical treatment that united his own expertise with that of local physicians and combined some Thomsonian principles with the use of more conventional measures, Hammond turned in 1854 to yet another medical fad. Homeopathy was a popular system that in its misguidedness at least had the virtue of advocating infinitesimal dosages and thus minimizing the damage a practitioner might inflict. But whatever Hammond's current enthusiasms, he never faltered in his certainty that science would eventually provide the solution to his dilemmas. His slaves, however, retained an active scepticism and stubbornly resisted his successive modes of sanitation and therapeutics. Hammond was displeased by the bondsmen's tendency to hide illness in order to escape unpleasant treatments and by their inclination to ignore many of his health regulations. But he was genuinely outraged when in 1851 he discovered that an entire alternative system of medical services thrived on his plantation amongst blacks who continued to practice African folk cures and remedies. "Traced out the negro Doctors . . . who have been giving out medicine for years here & have killed I think most of those that have died. Punished them & also their patients very severely." Hammond would permit no challenge

<hr>

Consumption of Milk by Slaves in 1860," *Journal of Interdisciplinary History*, VIII (Winter, 1978), 507–14. Harry Hammond to Hammond, November 12, 1854, in JHH Papers, SCL.

20. On sickle-cell anemia, see Savitt, *Medicine and Slavery*, 17–35, and Seth A. Ribner, "The Effects of Sickle-Cell Trait on Blacks of the Antebellum South Carolina Low Country" (unpublished seminar paper, University of Pennsylvania, 1979).

to his dominion over black bodies and, perhaps defensive about the failures of his own system of therapeutics, cited the existence of black medicine as a justification for the plantation's high level of mortality.[21]

In spite of black resistance and in spite of Hammond's frequently erroneous medical notions, his concerted effort to decrease death rates may well have proved ultimately beneficial. Although his pessimism never wavered and although mortality remained high, rates did decline during the period of his management. Child mortality decreased significantly—to 56 percent before age five in the 1840s and to 26 percent in the 1850s. Hammond expected some improvement in rates of child death as a result of his continual purchase of new, and he assumed, untainted slave stock who would produce healthy rather than sickly children. In actuality, the death statistics for children of original and newly acquired slaves are roughly comparable, and a rapid rate of intermarriage between the two groups quickly incorporated the newcomers. The major factor in the reduction in child deaths was probably Hammond's own sanitary rules, which would have had their most pronounced impact upon the health of the very young. But improvements in health were evident throughout the population and not just among children. After the late 1840s, births began to exceed deaths, and the mortality rate for the entire slave force steadily declined.

Hammond's interventions had a dramatic impact upon the demographic composition of the slave community at Silver Bluff. His medical and sanitary efforts may well have succeeded in at least partially mitigating an appalling rate of slave death. His extensive purchases, usually of young and vigorous slaves, ultimately transformed a population rendered static in size by its mortality into a slave force more than twice as large as the community of 147 Hammond found at the Bluff in 1831. From the start, Hammond purchased a few slaves to fill such skilled positions as shoemaker and horse trainer, as well as others more polished than the hands already on the plantation to serve as household slaves. As his agricultural operations expanded in the 1840s, he began to acquire workers both in gangs and as individuals from traders in Charleston, Columbia, Augusta, and Hamburg, as well as from neighbors and friends. By 1863 he had purchased 145 blacks and owned a force of 320 slaves. Yet despite his constant efforts to in-

21. Hammond Plantation Diary, October 27, 1851. On Hammond's adoption of homeopathy and on his evaluation of its effects, see Hammond to William Gilmore Simms, November 2, 1862, in JHH Papers, LC. See bills from homeopathic physician H. R. Thayer, especially bill of March 17, 1855, that includes charges for works of Smalls and Hahnemann, leading authors of the homeopathic movement, in Business Papers, JHH Papers, SCL.

crease the size and the vitality of his black population and despite the marked transformations that resulted, Hammond tended to discount his impact. Because he considered total numbers of births and deaths rather than the ratios of births and deaths to total population, Hammond remained unaware of the significance of the change in death rates. He complained that many of his new slaves had simply become "demoralized" as a result of exposure to the morbidity of the others. In his effort to control the health of his slave population Hammond felt himself continually hampered by "the hand of fate," as well as foiled in his therapeutic designs by an all too familiar "negro perversity."[22]

Hammond's intervention into what we would consider the most private domains of life was not restricted to the management of slave bodies and health; it extended to emotional and affective realms as well. Slave marriages and domestic life attracted close attention from the master, for they provided the slaveowner with yet another opportunity to display the pervasiveness of his power.

Northern abolitionists believed the disruption of family life to be perhaps the greatest outrage of the South's peculiar institution. But Hammond was able to assure one of slavery's northern critics that on his plantation the slaves "live of course in families." Indeed, kinship ties among blacks at the Bluff were already far-reaching when Hammond took control of the property. Certain surnames— Shubrick, Fuller, Goodwin—reappeared throughout the family groupings in Hammond's initial inventory, indicating that not only parents and children but extended networks including uncles, aunts, and grandparents lived together on the property. As throughout the South, there is considerable evidence of the importance with which the Hammond slaves regarded these ties. Slaves with families were far less likely to attempt escape from Silver Bluff; those who did try to leave frequently took their spouses with them; women runaways almost without exception were accompanying husbands. Black parents showed their links with a wide network of kin by frequently naming children after relatives, most often their fathers, but also after mothers, maternal and paternal grandparents, aunts and uncles, and even older siblings who had died. Filpy and Daniel had a daughter named after Daniel's mother, a son named for Filpy's father, and another son who bore his own father's name. Nicholas named a child after his sister Nelly, who returned the honor three years later by calling her own son Nicholas. When Pink died after producing a family of ten, two of her daughters

22. See Appendix, Charts 6–8; Hammond Plantation Diary, October 2, 1854; Hammond Redcliffe Journal, July 7, 1864.

named their babies for their departed mother. Even surnames, often thought to be unimportant if not entirely nonexistent among slaves, assumed a significance at Silver Bluff. Glaze was given his mother's and Goodwin his grandmother's maiden name. This active sense of familial and cultural heritage was also evident in the perpetuation of African names in the Bluff community, as for example Kizzy, who was born in 1835, and in the African custom of using day names in either their English or Akan forms, such as in the case of the slaves Monday, Quaco (Wednesday), and Cudjo (Monday). Even Hammond's anglicization of slave names in plantation records cannot entirely disguise the black origin of such appellations as Coober, Abba, and Cumba. The names of Cato, Hagar, and Hercules that appear in Bluff slave lists seem European, but may well have been creolizations of the Yoruba name Keta and the Mende names Haga and Heke.[23]

Black family ties were most obviously manifested in the overwhelming proportion of Hammond's slaves who lived out their lives in stable and apparently faithful marriages; an alliance was three times as likely to be ended by the death of one of the partners as by circumstances analogous to those we would today call divorce. Tissy Bowman was living with Isaac Goodwin and their five children when Hammond arrived at Silver Bluff, and only her death at age sixty in 1848 ended their alliance. Penny and Will had their first child in 1838, followed by eight more in the next two decades. At the time of Hammond's death the couple was still together and had become grandparents. Despite the prevalence of monogamy, some men appearing in Hammond's records seem to have had more than one wife at a time. George sired children alternately with Nancy and Binah, as Marcus did with Hannah and Justina. Possibly this was a remnant of West African polygamy. Several women also deviated from the predominant family form, producing a child by a named "outside" man amidst a long-lived marriage to another individual. For the most part, however, even the exceptions to the dominant pattern of long monogamous alliances demonstrate the strength of this mode of familial relationship. Sullivan lived with Maggy Campbell for over a decade, and the couple produced five children before Maggy left him for another man. Undaunted, Sullivan entered a second long-lived marriage with Nicey, siring six more children in the two decades that remained before emancipation.[24]

23. Hammond to Lewis Tappan, September 6, 1850, in JHH Papers, LC. See Gutman, *The Black Family*, Chap. VI, and Craton, *Searching*, 156–57. Coober was probably an anglicization of Cuba, an African day name meaning Wednesday.

24. Because of the nature of Hammond's record-keeping, a "marriage" can only be defined in terms of procreation of children. I considered a union that produced more than one child to be a

Like most southern slaveowners Hammond regarded stable family life as an essential requirement for the tranquility and smooth operation of the plantation and as an important means of social control over the slaves, whose kinship ties would necessarily bind them to the community at Silver Bluff. Hammond actively encouraged family life on the plantation; the very few blacks he sold during his period of mastery were without apparent exception individuals lacking family ties whom he had purchased and found unsatisfactory. Three of them were household servants taken on approval and then returned or exchanged. The fourth was a new slave who ran away and was sold immediately upon recovery. Not only did Hammond not separate existing family groups by sale; he often bought old or injured slaves when they came as a package with their younger and economically more desirable relatives.[25]

Marriage between slaves was not recognized in law, but Hammond formalized slave relationships by means of a ceremony, which he often conducted as part of the customary Christmas festivities. To each bride and groom he presented a cash gift of five dollars for a first marriage and three and a half dollars for a second. Such encouragement of course implied the intrusion of his own prerogative into what might seem an essentially private concern. Hammond's permission had to be secured for a marriage, and he set at least some limits on his slaves' freedom of choice by forbidding alliances with residents of other plantations. Marriages at Silver Bluff had to be approved in the eyes of Hammond as well as of God and, similarly, could be ended only by the master or by death. Hammond's support for stable family life included formal inquiries into marital friction; he acted as a kind of family court judge and meted out whippings to those whose sexual infidelity had become disruptive to plantation order. "Had a trial of Divorce & Adultery cases," he reported to his diary in 1840. "Flogged Joe Goodwyn & ordered him to go back to his wife. Ditto Gabriel & Molly & ordered them to come together again. Separated Moses & Anny finally—And flogged Tom Kollock. He had never been flogged before—Gave him 30 with my own hand [for] interfering with Maggy Campbell, Sullivan's wife."[26]

---

marriage. Of those "marriages" that ended during Hammond's administration, 76 percent were terminated by death, 24 percent by separation, usually followed by alliance and procreation with another "spouse." I have called this pattern "divorce." Relying on procreation of children as an index of marriage and divorce obviously underestimates the number of both. Given the available data, one can only hope that this underrepresentation is proportional and does not distort the percentages unduly.

25. Hammond Plantation Diary, January 23, May 31, 1845, July 8, 1835, and July 1, 1834.

26. "Governor Hammond's Instructions," 352; Hammond Plantation Diary, December 26, 1840.

But such standards of behavior did not apply to the master himself or to other whites employed on the plantation. Perhaps the most striking aspect of white intrusion into black family life was the sexual interference of masters, overseers, and even day laborers with slave women. Certainly one of the most degrading and abhorrent aspects of the slave system in the eyes of the nineteenth as well as the twentieth century, the sexual exploitation of slave women has remained largely hidden from the historian's view; its extensiveness and its meaning in the lives of both masters and slaves are subjects for speculation rather than documented analysis. But Hammond's papers reveal far more about this issue than most surviving plantation records. Birth statistics for his slaves regularly listed an infant with both mother and father. But approximately 22 percent of newborns were recorded with only a mother. As Herbert Gutman has demonstrated, young slave women throughout the South frequently produced a first child prior to wedlock or any other formal affiliation with a man, thereby indicating their fertility and thus marriageability in a manner widely accepted in many peasant cultures. A high proportion of the children with unnamed fathers at Silver Bluff fit this pattern, one in which the mothers later entered stable, long-lasting alliances and then produced children identified in birth records as belonging to two parents. But this by no means explains every instance of unlisted fathers. In some cases, later identification of fathers—by an overseer's casual notation, for example—indicates that an unattached woman was in all likelihood concealing a liaison she feared the master might punish as dangerously "adulterous." In other cases, mothers might have been hiding forbidden alliances with bondsmen from other plantations.[27]

Some women who continued to produce children with unidentified fathers, however, may well have been involved in a relationship of concubinage with either slave or white men. Next to the names of some of the children he lists without fathers in the birth record Hammond adds the explanatory word "mulatto," and one infant is included with an identified white father—the temporary stable hand J. Fudge who was fired for drunkenness before Patience even delivered his daughter Edey. But at least two of the women who had several children by unnamed fathers were Hammond's own mistresses, as he revealed in a deeply felt letter written to request his legitimate white son Harry to care for these slave women and their offspring after Hammond's own death. The seam-

27. Gutman, *The Black Family,* 75.

86

stress Sally Johnson and her daughter Louisa, whom Hammond purchased to-gether for nine hundred dollars in 1838, attended the family as household ser-vants. Hammond informed Harry in 1856:

In the last will I made I left to you . . . Sally Johnson the mother of Louisa & all the children of both. Sally says Henderson is my child. It is possible, but I do not beleive it Yet act on her's rather than my opinion. Louisa's first child *may* be mine. I think not. Her second I beleive is mine. Take care of her & her children who are both of *your* blood if not of mine & of Henderson. The services of the rest will I think compensate for indul-gence to these. I cannot free these people & send them North. It would be cruelty to them. Nor would I like that any but my own blood should own as slaves my own blood or Louisa. I leave them to your charge, beleiving that you will best appreciate & most inde-pendently carry out my wishes in regard to them. Do not let Louisa or any of my children or possible children be the Slaves of Strangers. Slavery *in the family* will be their happiest earthly condition.[28]

Clearly Hammond was involved in something quite different from casual sex. He felt strong, troubling, and conflicting emotions about these women and their offspring. But for Sally and Louisa, the situation must have been even more painful. They confronted not only the sexual and emotional demands of both their master and his son and the implicit, if not explicit, threat of physical coer-cion but also the bitter resentment of Hammond's wife, who discovered his liai-son and attempted to end it by demanding the sale or effective banishment of his slave mistresses. The two black women were, moreover, prevented from enter-ing into their own marriages. During the period of their relationship with Ham-mond, neither Sally nor Louisa lived in a household with a black man. Instead, they shared a cabin together with their children. The complex and tangled ties amongst a father and a son and a mother and daughter would be bewildering even outside the context of race and power that surrounded it in this slave so-ciety. But whatever the specific import of this relationship, whether it was repre-sentative of others of a similar type, whether such liaisons were unique or com-monplace, whether they usually were such long-standing involvements or more episodic and casual encounters, the reality and impact of white sexual demands upon slave life and family at Silver Bluff is beyond doubt. Where sex could not be separated from the wider pattern of racial domination upon which southern society rested, it was necessarily exploitative. Sally and Louisa's household, al-

28. Hammond to Harry Hammond, February 19, 1856, in JHH Papers, SCL; Hammond to Simms, December 15, 1852, in JHH Papers, LC.

most unique at Silver Bluff in its lack of a resident male, must have served as a searing reminder to the other slaves of the full significance of Hammond's ownership of their bodies and their lives.[29]

Hammond intervened between parents and children as well as between husbands and wives. He gave names to slave offspring frequently enough to remind fathers and mothers that he, not they, owned the new infants. Naming a child was not their right, he insisted, but a privilege the master could either grant or withhold. The first infant born after Hammond's assumption of power in 1831 was symbolically called Primus, as if to herald this new regime in which the master's control would extend to the slaves' very identities. In the years that followed, Hammond exercised this prerogative frequently. "Aggy had a child which I call Stark," he recorded in 1833, selecting the name to honor a college friend visiting at the Bluff. On other occasions as well, he complimented guests by giving their names to children born during their visits. The black infant Beverley was named for Virginian Nathaniel Beverley Tucker, and young Nott was called after Josiah C. Nott, another of Hammond's oldest friends. When Hammond did not like the names of slaves he purchased, especially those house servants with whom he would come in constant contact, he arbitrarily changed them. Sam Jones, acquired at the age of eight, became Wesley. But this transformation seems to have occurred only in the master's eyes. Nearly three decades later Wesley named a son Sam Jones. Hammond, who was then approaching death, may have missed the significance of this infant's name, but Wesley/Sam had clearly never abandoned his original identity and family ties.[30]

Hammond's intrusions between parents and children extended well beyond this initial question of an infant's name. Because the prosperity of the plantation depended upon the natural increase of his slave property Hammond was intensely concerned with the management of black children. His regulations about child care were intended not only to display his power but also to exercise in substantive ways what he saw as his superior judgment about the welfare of slave progeny. Hammond did all he could to encourage slave fecundity by promising gifts of extra clothing and food to mothers of new infants and endeavoring to reduce the work load of expectant women sufficiently to ensure safe child-

---

29. For the residence of Sally and Louisa Johnson, see Hammond, "The Number of Negroes and Each Family, January the 1, 1856," and "List of Negroes, 1846" (MSS in JHH Papers, LC), and "Names of Negroes on Silver Bluff Plantation the 1 January 1863, in Families" (MS in Hammond Land and Slave Papers, JHH Papers, SCL). On Hammond's quarrel with his wife, see my detailed discussion in Chapter 15.

30. Hammond Plantation Diary, May 19, 1833. See Appendix, Table 1.

birth. After the arrival of the baby, however, both his notions of plantation efficiency and his desire to control slave nurture dictated that mothers promptly
return to work. Hammond removed children of one month and over from the
care of their parents for much of each day. Until the age of about eleven, when
they began to serve as water carriers or as quarter hands in the fields, children
passed their days in a special building under the care of a "trusty nurse." Mothers
returned to suckle infants less than nine months old three times a day and
weaned children took all their meals at the nursery, eating a diet carefully prescribed by the master himself. Hammond thus attempted to ensure that his ideas
about child care and nutrition, rather than those of parents, would prevail.
After several years of experience, however, Hammond began to doubt the
wisdom of this constant intervention into family life. By stripping mothers and
fathers of these natural duties, he feared he had undermined that sense of parental responsibility upon which the well-being of the black children ultimately
rested. "I am satisfied," he confessed, "that I have endeavored to take too much
care of the negro children. It has made the parents careless. They rely entirely
on my management & will not learn to manage for themselves." Total dependence was essentially unworkable; even a slave had to be granted some measure
of human autonomy.[31]

That Hammond could make such an admission had implications for slave
management that extended well beyond the realm of child rearing. In the course
of his first decade as a plantation owner, Hammond had learned a good deal
about mastery, gradually coming to recognize the shortcomings of the unrelen-
tingly interventionist and oppressive methods he had initially embraced. Finding at Silver Bluff in 1831 an undisciplined slave force, he had sought to rule
through raw power, through the dominance of the whip and the pulpit, controlling both bodies and souls. His plan had aimed at nearly total repression, at containing and isolating the slaves on the plantation and creating there a world in
which a black could never forget that Hammond's power was absolute. He would
eliminate their church, command their labor, regulate their personal relations
and even name their children.

But Hammond gradually came to acknowledge that such a notion of plantation management was unrealistic. From the first he saw that control rested on
rewards as well as punishments, and these positive inducements evolved into an
elaborate system designed to win the slaves' allegiance. His rule, he discovered,

31. "Governor Hammond's Instructions"; Hammond Plantation Diary, May 10, 1844.

could not be based entirely on fear. While Hammond may have regarded these rewards as privileges he chose to grant, the slaves themselves increasingly looked upon them as rights. His schemes for total domination quickly proved illusory. In part this was because he needed to feel loved, not simply respected or feared; he wanted to be acknowledged as a father to his slave "family." But to an even greater extent, the blacks' determination to maintain networks of communication and community led them to challenge his design by struggling to retain elements of personal and cultural autonomy.

Hammond found certain systems of rewards already institutionalized at the Bluff. Only three weeks after his arrival he was prepared to greet his slave force on Christmas morning when they arrived at his door in search of their customary gifts. The new master responded with "a pound of tobacco each . . . & their shirts & 2 pipes" and a three-day holiday. In later years he would offer sugar and coffee as well, frocks for new mothers, cash for the slave driver, midwife, stock minder, and nurse. Another annual festival relieved the drudgeries of midsummer labor with a barbecue and a day of rest. The system of rewards extended even into the fields themselves, where Hammond introduced picking contests to honor the most diligent and productive slaves with small cash prizes. At the first of these in October, 1832, Hammond was delighted when August succeeded in amassing 216 pounds of seed cotton in a single day, staving off a challenge from Judy, who managed to pick 112 pounds before being taken sick at noon.[32]

The slaves were more than just passive recipients of these sporadic benefits; they manipulated their master for what they came to see as their due. Hammond complained that his bondsmen's demands led him against his will to countenance a slave force "too well fed & otherwise well treated," but he still could not entirely resist their claims. When, for example, after a particularly poor record of work one fall, Hammond sought to shorten the usual Christmas holiday, he ruefully recorded on December 26 that he had been "persuaded out of my decision by [the] negroes."[33]

The blacks at Silver Bluff did not limit their self-assertion to the gentle arts of persuasion. They confronted their owner with stubborn resistance and eventually compelled him to revise his conception of the meaning of mastery. After just a few days at the Bluff, Hammond had declared his intention to eliminate the black church. Yet his vigorous repressive measures over the following months

---

32. Hammond Plantation Diary, December 25, 1831, December 25, 1837, December 25, 1839, July 27, 1833, August 2, 1834, July 26, 1856, October 12, 1832.
33. *Ibid.*, October 22, 1843, December 26, 1847.

and years brought only limited success. The white-supervised Methodist and Baptist congregations that grew up on Silver Bluff did present the outward appearance of an appropriately humble piety amongst Hammond's slaves. Virginia Clay, a house guest on the plantation in the 1860s, found the services at St. Catherine's "solemn and impressive," a tribute, she felt, to Hammond's beneficent mastery. "There was the little company of white people," she recalled, "the flower of centuries of civilisation, among hundreds of blacks, but yesterday . . . in savagery, now peaceful, contented, respectful and comprehending the worship of God." There was no evidence of "religious excesses," the "mixture of hysteria and superstition" that she believed characterized most black religion. These slaves, it appeared, had abandoned religious ecstasy for the reverential passivity prescribed for them by their master.[34]

Clay's description would undoubtedly have pleased Hammond, but he knew that the decorous behavior of his slaves within the walls of St. Catherine's was but an outward compliance with his directives. He had been unable to eradicate black religious expression, evidences of which, like tips of an iceberg, betrayed an underlying pattern of independent belief and worship that persisted among his slaves. The blacks continued to hold religious meetings despite his prohibitions. Most likely the slaves at first gathered in secret, but before long they had managed to persuade the master to accept a level of black religious autonomy by permitting them to hold as many as four prayer meetings in the quarters each week. Twenty years after his initial resolve to eliminate the slave church, Hammond once again felt compelled to take action against its ever-expanding power, recording in his plantation diary that he had "ordered all church meetings to be broken up except at the Church with a white Preacher." Hammond now threatened once again to move against the black church because he feared that the intensity of religious fervor had exceeded that compromise level of moderation he and the slaves had come tacitly to accept. By 1851 "Religious troubles among the negroes"—as he described his sense of the growing disorder—revived his determination to control the very emotional and ideational sources of unruliness among his slaves. "They are running the thing into the ground," he remarked, "by being allowed too much organization—too much power to the head men & too much praying & Church meeting on the plantation." Black religious life had reemerged as an insupportable threat, for it had assumed the characteristics of a formal system with, as Hammond explicitly recognized, organization and leader-

---

34. Virginia Clay-Clopton, *A Belle of the Fifties* (New York: Doubleday, Page, 1905) 219–20.

ship to challenge his own power. But Hammond's recurrent need to act against the expanding strength of the black church indicates his failure to eliminate this organization and control his slaves' belief and worship. Hammond could periodically repress black religion, even for a time force it underground, but it ultimately remained beyond his control.[35]

Hammond's determination to eliminate task work met with similar resistance and became an issue over which master and slaves struggled until Hammond's death. Preferring the independent management of their time that task work offered, the blacks opposed the master's efforts to establish a gang form of field labor by toiling slowly and inefficiently. "Negroes dissatisfied to work in a gang & doing badly," Hammond observed. In 1839 he made a similar remark, noting that hoers were leaving "all the weeds and bunches of grass" growing around the cotton plants. "Evidently want to work task work which I will not do again," he noted firmly. But Hammond continued to record hoeing that ignored weeds, picking that passed over bulging cotton bolls, and cultivating that destroyed both mule and plough. By 1850 the slaves had clearly won a compromise, for Hammond was once again referring in his diary and correspondence to task work and complaining of blacks who left the fields by midafternoon. Hammond and his slaves arrived at a sort of accommodation on the issue of work. But in this process, Hammond had to adjust his desires and expectations as significantly as did the slaves. His abstract notions of order and absolute control were never to be fully realized. Instead, he and the blacks reached a truce that permitted a level of production acceptable to Hammond and a level of endeavor tolerable to his slaves.[36]

Black autonomy and assertiveness challenged Hammond's management in nearly every aspect of plantation life and even intruded into his own household, where, to Hammond's intense displeasure, slaves stole delicacies from his own larder. Pilfering of food and alcohol at Silver Bluff did not consist simply of random acts by slaves seeking to alleviate hunger or compensate for deprivation. Theft assumed wider significance, taking on the characteristics of a contest between master and slave in which the master was by definition always the loser. The prospect of winning the competition may well have provided the slaves with nearly as much satisfaction as did the material fruits of victory; it was

35. Hammond Plantation Diary, January 14, 1851. See also Hammond to Tappan, September 6, 1850, in JHH Papers, LC.
36. Hammond Plantation Diary, May 23, 1838, May 26, 1839; Hammond to Tappan, September 6, 1850, in JHH Papers, LC.

clearly a battle for power as well as for the specific goods in question. Although Hammond had begun immediately in 1831 to try to reduce the level of depredations against his hogs, flogging suspected thieves made little impact. Unable to prevent the disappearance of a sizable number of his pigs, he chose to define black theft as a passive "habit" rather than an assertive and powerful challenge to his control. But he recorded with grim satisfaction that the resulting reduction of the meat allowance would serve as just retribution for the slaves' conspiracy against his droves. Theirs would be, he consoled himself, a hollow victory. "The negroes," he noted in 1845, "have for . . . years killed about half my shoats & must now suffer for it." The impact of black theft was perhaps even greater on other plantation products. Hammond was resigned never to harvest his potato crop at all, for the slaves appropriated the entire yield before it was officially even removed from the ground.[37]

Alcohol, however, inspired the most carefully designed system of slave intrigue. When Hammond began to ferment wines from his own vineyards, slaves constantly tapped the bottles, then blamed the disappearance of the liquid on leaks due to faulty corking. But the slave community's most elaborate assault on Hammond's supplies of alcohol went well beyond such crude tactics to bring together a unique conjunction of engineering skill with the power of voodoo. In 1835 Hammond found that several of his slaves had dug tunnels beneath his wine cellar. A female domestic named Urana, Hammond recorded, had employed "root work" and thus "screened" the excavators by her "conjuration." Hammond determinedly "punished all who have had any thing to do with the matter far or near." But his response could not replace the lost wine nor compensate for the way the incident challenged the literal and figurative foundations of his plantation order. The force of voodoo lay entirely outside his system of control and defied his efforts to establish cultural dominance. The blacks worked patiently and ingeniously to undermine his power as well as his house.[38]

37. Hammond Plantation Diary, February 18, 1833, January 9, 1845, March 24, 1846. On hog stealing, see also Hammond's remarks on April 3, 1847, in "Record of the Proceedings of the Beech Island Agricultural Club, 1846–1862" (typescript in SCL). Despite constant complaint during the thirties and forties about the theft of hogs by slaves, Hammond was humiliated when Solon Robinson reported on slave thefts at Silver Bluff in an article for the *American Agriculturist*. Embarrassed, Hammond was quick to assure the South's eminent agriculturist Edmund Ruffin that "My negroes rarely steal a hog." Solon Robinson, "Mr. Robinson's Tour," *American Agriculturist*, IX (February, 1850), 51; Hammond to Edmund Ruffin, February 8, 1850, in Edmund Ruffin Papers, Virginia Historical Society, Richmond.

38. Hammond Redcliffe Journal, October 15, 1862; Hammond Plantation Diary, October 16, 1835.

For most of Hammond's slaves, insubordination served to establish cultural and personal autonomy within the framework of plantation demands. Resistance was a tool of negotiation, a means of extracting concessions from the master to reduce the extent of his claims over black bodies and souls. At Silver Bluff such efforts were directed more at securing necessary support for black community life than at totally overwhelming the master's power. Hammond learned that he could to a certain degree repress, but never eliminate black cultural patterns; his slaves in turn concealed much of their lives so as not to appear directly to challenge their master's hegemony.

But for some Silver Bluff residents there could be no such compromises. Instead of seeking to avoid the domination inherent in slavery, these individuals overtly challenged it, turning to arson and escape as expressions of open rebellion. Throughout the period of his management, Hammond referred to mysterious fires that would break out in the ginhouse on one occasion, the millhouse or plantation hospital on the next. While these presumed acts of sabotage were never linked to specific individuals and only minimally affected the operation of the plantation, running away offered the slave a potentially more effective means of resistance to Hammond's control. Between 1831 and 1855, when he turned most record-keeping over to his sons, Hammond noted fifty-three escape attempts by his slaves. The most striking fact about these runaways is that Hammond recorded no instance of successful flight. Thirty-five percent of the slaves who tried to escape were repeaters, although no slave was recorded as making more than three attempts. A newly purchased slave who made several efforts to escape was sold; those with long-term ties to the Silver Bluff community eventually abandoned the endeavor. The average age of runaways was thirty-three; 84 percent were male; and the median period during which a runaway had been under Hammond's domination was two years.

While the decision to run away might appear to be a rejection by the slave of the ties of black community as well as of the chains of bondage, the way in which escape functioned at Silver Bluff shows it usually operated somewhat differently. Since there were no runaways who achieved permanent freedom and since most escapees did not get far, they remained in a very real sense a part of the slave community they had seemingly fled. Forty-three percent of the runaways at the Bluff left with others. Females, who made up only 16 percent of the total, almost without exception ran with husbands or to join spouses who had already departed. Once slaves escaped they succeeded in remaining at large an average of forty-nine days. Sixty-five percent were captured and the rest returned voluntarily. The distribution of compulsory and voluntary returns over the calendar year indicates that harsh weather was a significant factor in persuading slaves to give themselves up. Seventy-seven percent of those returning in the winter months did so by choice, while in the spring and summer 80 percent were brought back against their will. Weather and work load made summer the runaway season, and more than half of all escape attempts occurred in June, July, and August.[39]

While certain individuals—notably young males, particularly those without family ties—were most likely to become runaways, the slave community as a whole provided them with assistance and support. Hammond himself recognized that runaways often went no farther than the nearby Savannah River swamps, where they survived on food provided by those remaining at home. The ties between the escapees and the community were sufficiently strong that Hammond endeavored to force runaways to return by disciplining the rest of the slave force. On at least one occasion he determined to stop the meat allowance for the entire plantation until the runaways came in. In another instance, he severely flogged four slaves harboring two runaways, hoping to break the personal and communal bonds that made prolonged absences possible.[40]

The isolation of Silver Bluff made real escape almost impossible. Some newly arrived slaves, perhaps recently separated from their families, intended to escape these new surroundings permanently, and such individuals were captured as far as a hundred miles away. The majority of runaways, however, were part of the established community on Hammond's plantation. Recognizing that they would almost certainly fail to escape the chains of bondage forever, they ran either in pursuit of a brief respite from labor or in response to uncontrollable anger. One

39. James Henry Hammond, "Silver Bluff, Cathwood, Cowden, and Redcliffe," December 6, 1856; Hammond to M. C. M. Hammond, February 12, 1847, March 3, 1864, both in JHH Papers, LC. Most existing studies of runaways have been based on advertisements for escapees. It is not clear that these individuals represent an accurate sample of runaways, for return of the more valuable slave would be more eagerly sought. More importantly, such sources cannot reveal relationships between escapees and the plantation context from which they fled. For examples of the use of advertisements in the study of runaways, see Gerald W. Mullin, *Flight and Rebellion: Slave Resistance in Eighteenth-Century Virginia* (New York: Oxford University Press, 1972), and Philip Morgan, "Black-White Interaction and Culture Change in Colonial South Carolina" (unpublished paper delivered at a Symposium on Language and Culture in South Carolina, Department of Anthropology, University of South Carolina, Columbia, March, 1979).

40. Hammond Plantation Diary, July 18, 1832.

function of the black community was to support this outlet for frustration and rage by feeding and sheltering runaways either until they were captured or until they were once again able to operate within the system of compromise that served as the basis of interaction between master and slave at Silver Bluff.

Two examples demonstrate the way runaways eventually became integrated into the plantation order. Cudjo was returned to the Bluff as a plough-hand in 1833 after a year of being hired out in Augusta. Thirty-two years old, he perhaps missed urban life or had established personal relationships that he could not bear to break. In any case, he began to run away soon after his return. He first succeeded in departing for two weeks but was seized in Augusta and imprisoned. Hammond retrieved him and put him in irons, but within days he was off again despite his fetters. Captured soon on a nearby plantation Cudjo tried again a few days later and remained at large for ten months. In March of 1834 Hammond recorded in his diary, "Cudjo came home. Just tired of running away." Although Cudjo was still on the plantation a decade later, there was no further mention of his attempting to escape.[41]

Alonzo had been with Hammond only eight months when he first fled in 1843. Thirty-four years old, he had not yet developed settled family ties on the plantation, and he ran away alone. He was captured in this first attempt and escaped twice more within the year, disappearing, Hammond recorded, "without provocation." His second absence ended when he was caught in Savannah after thirty-two days and placed in irons. After less than two months at home, he was off again, but this time he returned voluntarily within two weeks. Placed once more in shackles, Alonzo did not flee again. After 1851 Hammond recorded an ever-growing family born to Alonzo and another Silver Bluff slave named Abby. But while he stopped trying to run away and became increasingly tied to Silver Bluff, Alonzo was by no means broken of his independence. In 1864 he provoked Hammond with a final act of defiance, stubbornly refusing to supply his master with any information about the pains that were to kill him within a month. "A hale hearty man," Hammond remarked with annoyance, "killed by the negro perversity."[42]

During the initial years of his tenure at the Bluff, Hammond recorded efforts to round up runaway slaves by means of searches through the swamps on horseback or with packs of dogs. After the first decade, however, he made little men-

41. *Ibid.*, March 14, 1834, April 27, May 11, June 13, 17, 1833.
42. *Ibid.*, April 29, 1844; Hammond Redcliffe Journal, July 7, 1864.

tion of such measures and seems for the most part to have simply waited for his escapees to be captured by neighbors, turn up in nearby jails, or return home on their own. In order to encourage voluntary surrender, Hammond announced a policy of punishment for runaways that allotted ten lashes for each day absent to those recaptured by force and three lashes per day to those who returned of their own will. This standardized rule integrated the problem of runaways into the system of rewards and punishments at the Bluff and rendered it an aspect of the understanding between master and slaves. Since no one escaped permanently, the rule set forth the cost of unauthorized absence and encouraged those who had left in irrational rage to return as soon as their tempers had cooled. When the respected fifty-three-year-old driver John Shubrick was flogged for drunkenness, he fled in fury and mortification, but within a week was back exercising his customary responsibility in plantation affairs.[43]

For some, anger assumed a longer duration and significance. These individuals, like Alonzo or Cudjo, ran repeatedly until greater age or changed circumstances made life at home more bearable. Occasionally, Hammond found himself confronted with a slave whose rage seemed so deep-rooted as to be unmanageable. When Hudson escaped soon after his purchase in 1844, he was not heard of for seven months. At last, Hammond was notified that the slave was in Barnwell, on trial for arson. To protect his investment Hammond hired a lawyer to defend Hudson. But when he was acquitted, Hammond sold Hudson immediately, determining that he was an insupportable menace to plantation life. Although Hammond's understanding of power had developed to the point where he could regard most of his runaways as a part of the system of oppression, challenge, and concession that prevailed at Silver Bluff, there was no place in his regime for a revolutionary.[44]

While runaways disrupted routine, Hammond's greatest anxieties about loss of control arose from the fear that forces external to the plantation would exploit slave dissatisfaction. From the beginning of his tenure at the Bluff, he had sought to isolate his slaves from outside influences, but he was to be no more successful in this endeavor than in his efforts to eliminate the black church, end task labor, or keep his hogs and potatoes. Despite his endeavors to restrict slave access to the wider world, during the 1840s and 1850s Hammond perceived an ever-increasing threat to his power arising from challenges leveled at the pecu-

43. Hammond Plantation Diary, October 17, 1839, February 13, 1834.
44. Hammond Plantation Diary, February 19, September 19, November 5, 1844.

liar institution as a whole. To Hammond's dismay, it seemed impossible to keep information about growing abolition sentiment from the slaves. Such knowledge, Hammond feared, might provide the blacks with additional bases for ideological autonomy and greater motivation to resist his control. In an 1844 letter to John C. Calhoun, Hammond declared himself "astonished and shocked to find that some of them are aware of the opinions of the Presidential candidates on the subject of slavery and doubtless most of what the abolitionists are doing & I am sure they know as little of what is done off my place as almost any set of negroes in the state. I fancy . . . there is a growing spirit of insubordination among the slaves in this section. In the lower part of this district they have fired several houses recently. This is fearful—horrible. A quick and potent remedy must be applied."[45]

Hammond turned to his neighbors for assistance in reasserting control over the area's blacks. Together noting "a visible change . . . in the last few years in the conduct of our slaves," Hammond and other nearby residents formed the Savannah Anti-Slave Traffick Association in 1846 "for the purpose of preserving proper subordination." As its chief sponsor, Hammond hoped through this organization to spread his own deepening concern about slave behavior and to inaugurate a concerted action to close local establishments that provided blacks with liquor and news, two equally dangerous commodities. But his efforts with the grog shops enjoyed only limited success; Hammond was compelled to recognize that he could not insulate his slaves entirely from outside currents. At stressful times during the forties and fifties, he would make a renewed gesture at control, but for the most part, he learned to live with these insecurities as a necessary aspect of the South's peculiar institution. Gradually he was forced to understand that he would be unable to transform the plantation into an island kingdom in which he as lord managed information as well as bodies and souls.[46]

Early in 1861, Hammond cavalierly disclosed to a northern friend that he had at least a dozen slaves who read as well as he. Although southern law prohibited slaves from acquiring the power inherent in literacy, Hammond reported that he never interfered with the blacks' efforts to teach one another. "These people may or may not read the Tribune &c, I have never enquired," he related breezily. Those who learned to read, Hammond assured his correspondent, were

---

45. Hammond to John C. Calhoun, May 10, 1844, in John C. Calhoun Papers, Clemson University, Clemson, S.C.

46. *Preamble and Regulations of the Savannah River Anti-Slave Traffick Association*, (N.p., November 21, 1846); Hammond to Simms, September 18, 1846, in JHH Papers, LC.

not only the most intelligent but the most faithful. Hammond's tone in his letter north was undoubtedly motivated partly by a desire to appear calm and confident about the loyalty of his slaves and the future of the peculiar institution. But Hammond was also unquestionably trying to reassure himself about their docility. Unable to eliminate what he had defined as the slaves' dangerous access to society at large, he instead changed his attitudes about the dimensions of the threat such contacts implied; having failed to alter reality to conform to his original prescriptions, he reduced his own anxiety by transforming his aims to fit more closely with the existing situation.[47]

In a sense this process describes the more general evolution of his views and behavior as a slave master. Beginning with an abstract design for absolute control, Hammond turned increasingly to the art of the possible. He—as well as his slaves—learned to live with compromise, to turn to persuasion and manipulation instead of force in seeking his goals. The slaves' effective resistance to his efforts to establish total domination forced him to develop a style of mastery based to a great degree on techniques of psychological and symbolic, as well as physical, control. Although Hammond's understanding of power would continue to be refined by his experiences as slaveowner up to the moment of his death and would be particularly affected by the special circumstances of Civil War, he had as early as the mid-1840s developed a sophisticated program for control that he recorded in a formal set of plantation rules and issued to his overseers. This manual reflects the impact upon Hammond's thinking of the dynamic of oppression, challenge, and concession that he had come to know in the first decade of his struggle for mastery. Carefully calculated to win acceptance as well as compliance from the bondsmen, his system of management demonstrates how Hammond had allocated to his slaves the power to legitimate his self-image as benevolent paternalist. He had in important ways become dependent upon them.

On one level the manual was a list of detailed rules for day-to-day plantation life and for the behavior of both overseer and slaves. It summarized the injunctions Hammond had fixed upon in the course of his experience as a master and sometimes incorporated the revisions the slaves had forced in his plans. The prohibition of religious meetings was followed by the mitigating phrase "beyond singing and praying." Visits and marriages off the plantation were forbidden, but provision was made for interchange between those "living at one plantation and

47. Hammond to A. B. Allen, February 2, 1861, in JHH Papers, LC.

having wives at another." Marriage with the master's permission was "encouraged," divorce permissible but always accompanied by a hundred lashes. The
manual also presented the system of expectations, rewards, and punishments understood by all residents of the plantation. Summer barbecues, Christmas holidays, and gifts were all routinized; regular provisions of food and clothing were
detailed. Each worker could expect three pounds of bacon or pickled pork and a
peck of meal each week; a blanket, shoes, four shirts, three pairs of trousers, and
a jacket, or in the case of women, twenty-four yards of cloth and needles and
thread were provided each year. Children received one third the adult allowance
plus vegetables from a special nursery garden and were issued a pan and spoon
"placed in the charge of a nurse." Cabins had garden patches, and free time was
provided to encourage their cultivation. Except on Sundays, workers were to
leave for the fields by daylight and labor till sunset with a midday break, depending on the heat, of one to three and a half hours. "No work must ever be required after dark." Between eight-thirty and nine in the evening the sound of a
horn indicated that all slaves should be in their houses.[48]

For those who did not meet these expectations, rewards might be denied or
punishments inflicted. The most grievous offense in Hammond's eyes was running away, followed in order by getting drunk, stealing hogs, stealing other
things, leaving the plantation, absence from one's house after the horn was
blown, unclean house or person, neglect of tools, and neglect of work. "The
highest punishment must not exceed 100 lashes in one day & to that extent only
in extreme cases. The whip lash must be one inch in width . . . & never severely administered. In general 15 to 20 lashes will be a sufficient flogging. The
hands in every case must be secured by a cord. Punishment must always be given
calmly and deliberately & never when angry or excited." Hammond emphasized
to his deputies that the necessity for frequent flogging was certain evidence of
poor management. Whipping, he explained, was a last resort, to be turned to
only when other techniques of control had failed. Hammond advised a new
overseer that he would evaluate his performance "by your success in promoting
industry without flogging." In a revised version of his plantation manual Hammond reduced the maximum permissible number of lashes by half.[49]

As he gained experience, a shift occurred in Hammond's conceptions of

48. "Governor Hammond's Instructions"; Hammond Plantation Manual (MS in JHH Papers,
SCL). The second of these can be dated later than the first because of a reference to homeopathy,
which Hammond did not adopt until 1854.
49. "Governor Hammond's Instructions," 354; Hammond to Walker, February 27, 1836, in
JHH Papers, LC.

mastery from physical to psychological methods of control. These techniques were present from the first in the form of the rewards that counterbalanced punishments. But Hammond's use of psychological manipulation became far more complex than a simple system of carrot and stick. In the plantation manual of the mid-forties, it was clear that Hammond had supplemented his use of rewards with rituals and symbols designed to persuade the slaves to accept their master's definition of their own inferiority and dependence and simultaneously to acknowledge the merciful beneficence of his absolute rule. Hammond had not liked the reputation for severity his first years of mastery had gained him; gradually he sought to establish a system of domination in which he could extract willing obedience from compliant slaves, a system in which he could regard himself as benevolent father rather than cruel autocrat.

The distribution of power on the estate was designed to impress the blacks with the master's authority and to increase their loyalty to him. Lest the overseer's power seem to diminish the master's own, Hammond's plantation rules defined the role of the black driver to serve as a check upon him. Responsible for control of his fellow slaves whenever white supervision was absent, the driver was to be established as "the most important negro on the plantation." Since he could only be whipped by the master, he was removed in the eyes of his fellow slaves from the overseer's domination. "He is on no occasion to be treated with any indignity calculated to lose the respect of the other negroes," plantation regulations insisted. In addition, Hammond gave the driver the explicit right to bypass the overseer and appeal directly to the master with suggestions or complaints about plantation management—or the overseer's behavior. "The driver is permitted to visit the master at any time. . . . He is expected to communicate freely whatever attracts his attention. . . . He is a confidential agent & may be a guard against any excesses or omissions on the part of the overseer." Hammond invested the driver with sufficient power to encourage the slaves to accept as their official voice a leader Hammond had chosen and—he hoped—co-opted. It was Hammond's specific intention, moreover, to use this distribution of authority to set the driver and the overseer at odds and thus to limit the power of each in relation to his own. One of his greatest fears was that a driver would be "corrupted by bribes" from an overseer and that the two would conspire against him.[50]

As with his other designs for management, Hammond's careful allocations of

50. "Governor Hammond's Instructions," 351–52; Hammond Plantation Diary, June 14, 1849.

power fell short of achieving his goals; the slaves were not taken in by the manipulations of the master. The drivers Hammond chose did not win unquestioned acceptance as black leaders, and complaints against them were a source of recurrent conflict in the quarters. The driver himself, moreover, resisted Hammond's definition of his role by remaining in significant ways loyal to the black community and by exploiting the power inherent in his position for the slaves'— instead of the master's—ends. Although Hammond was seeking to convince the blacks of his omnipotence and their dependence, one driver at least was well aware that in important ways the situation was quite the reverse. Hammond himself recognized that the driver Tom Kollock was a far more experienced agriculturist than the master or any of his deputies. "I wish you to consult him [Tom]," Hammond instructed a new overseer, "on all occasions & in all matters of doubt take his opinion wh. you will generally find supported by good reasons." But, he warned, Kollock must be kept "in ignorance of his influence. . . . I would not have Tom injured by the supposition that he was the head manager any more than I would have you mortified by such a state of things."[51]

Yet Kollock knew more than he showed, for Hammond found two decades later that the driver had long exploited the power of which the master had presumed him ignorant. While pretending to efficient management of crops and personnel, Kollock had instead worked to undermine productivity by demanding the minimum of his laborers. Kollock had fooled Hammond, who in a fury proclaimed him a "humbug," a deceitful imposter. "I now see," Hammond declared in 1854, "that in him rests the fault of my . . . crops. He has trained his hands to do very little & that badly."[52]

While the divisions of authority at Silver Bluff were designed to emphasize the master's power, they were at the same time meant to cast him as a somewhat distant arbiter of justice, one who did not involve himself in the sordidness of day-to-day floggings. Instead, Hammond sought to portray himself as the dispenser of that mercy designed to win the grateful allegiance of the slave and to justify the plantation's social order. He tried to make himself appear not so much the creator of rules—which of course he was—but the grantor of exceptions and reprieves.[53]

51. Hammond Plantation Diary, June 18, 21, 24, 1838; Hammond to Walker, December 27, 1836, in JHH Papers, LC.
52. Hammond Plantation Diary, May 16, 1854. See William L. VanDeburg, *The Slave Drivers: Black Agricultural Labor Supervisors in the Antebellum South* (Westport, Conn.: Greenwood Press, 1979).
53. On the role of mercy in transforming power into authority, see E. P. Thompson, *Whigs and*

The distribution of provisions was an occasion for Hammond to play this paternalistic role. The event assumed the form and significance of ritual, a ceremony in which Hammond endeavored to present himself to his slaves as the source from whom all blessings flowed. The slaves were regularly required to put on clean clothes and appear before Hammond to receive their food allowance. "They should," he recorded in his plantation regulations, "be brought into that contact with the master at least once a week of receiving the means of subsistence from him." Although the overseer could perfectly well have executed such a task, the ceremonial importance of the moment demanded the master's direct participation. The special requirement for fresh apparel set the occasion off from the less sacred events of daily life, and underlined the symbolic character of this interaction between lord and bondsmen. This was plantation management as theater, with Hammond starring as the paternalist and the blacks all assembled as captive, if not appreciative, audience. The event illustrated Hammond's most idealized conception of the master-slave relationship and represented his effort to communicate this understanding to the blacks themselves, convincing them of his merciful generosity and their own humble dependence and need. The interaction was a statement designed to transform his power into legitimized authority.[54]

To a gathering of neighborhood agriculturists in 1857 Hammond's son Spann succinctly summarized the principles of slave management his father had developed in a quarter century of practical experience in plantation ownership. "Father said," he reported:

firmness, justness & moderation, in all things, were the fundamental requisites. Inspire a negro with perfect confidence in you & learn him to look to you for support, & he is your slave. A full belly quells dissension & rebellion, but too full a one breeds inordinate laziness. So in clothing, give sufficient to protect from weather, but give neither of too fine stuff, nor too abundant. Never work a negro systematically all he can do. Leave a reserve for emergencies. Their religious training must be of the most moderate sort, avoiding all excitements. Persuasion should substitute severe punishment in getting done as much as possible.[55]

In its mature form, Hammond's managerial strategy sought to undermine the

Hunters: The Origins of the Black Act (New York: Pantheon Books, 1975), and Douglas Hay, "Property, Authority and the Criminal Law," in Hay (ed.), *Albion's Fatal Tree* (New York: Pantheon Books, 1975).

54. "Governor Hammond's Instructions," 348.

55. Edward Spann Hammond Plantation Manual (MS vol. bd., 1857–58, Edward Spann Hammond Papers, SCL), July 11, 1857.

slaves' "system of roguery" by impressing them with both the master's dominance and his legitimacy. While he hoped to persuade the blacks to accept the culture of slavery—with its concomitant ideology of their own inferiority and of his benevolent paternalism—the slaves manipulated, dissimulated, and resisted to avoid affirming their master's definition of their situation. They retained, in a manner only partially visible to Hammond, essential aspects of black communal life and autonomy.

As a slaveowner, as in so many other dimensions of his life, Hammond desired to be both omnipotent and beloved. And he so cherished his illusions about ideal masterhood that he was usually able to forget he was neither kind paternalist nor all-effective manager. One of his greatest "consolations," he explained to a close friend, was to know that "my negroes . . . love & *appreciate* me." Hammond would never learn that domination is incompatible with the mutuality that serves as the foundation of genuine love. With the exigencies of Civil War and the imminence of emancipation, he would be forced to recognize that what he had regarded as devotion from his slaves had been largely a form of manipulation. The image of the benevolent master proved ultimately as empty of meaning for him as it had so long been for his slaves. Hammond had designed and promulgated an ideology through which to control his slaves. But ironically, he as much as they became its prisoner.[56]

---

56. Hammond to Simms, January 14, 1848, in JHH Papers, LC. Hammond evidently had a reputation for severity among slaves in the area around his plantation. One ex-slave interviewed by the WPA in 1938 still remembered stories of how "Governor Hammond chastise he han's." Interview with Amelia Dorsey in George Rawick (ed.), *The American Slave: A Composite Autobiography*, (Westport, Conn.: Greenwood Press, 1972), Supplement Ser. 1, Georgia, III, Pt. 1, p. 232. I am grateful to Vernon Burton for bringing this to my attention.

CHAPTER 6

Our Farms Will Be Our Factories

The Planter as Agricultural Entrepreneur

PLANTATION MANAGEMENT, Hammond once ruefully observed, was like "war without the glory." For three decades he battled with his slaves, as both master and bondsmen implemented ingenious strategies of tactical advances, surprises, and retreats. But Hammond's struggles in his role as planter were not restricted to conflicts with his black laborers. He was determined to rationalize and regularize as much of the operation of his plantation as managerial efficiency and the existing state of agricultural science would permit. "The development of your own thoughts," his son Harry once wrote him, "and their execution in the face of obstacles, and against the opinions of others was the source of all the interest you took in Planting." Like a general preparing for battle, Hammond set out to mobilize all his resources in the pursuit of victory over his slaves, over the vicissitudes of markets and weather, over the low fertility of much of his land. His ambition made him an aggressive and interventionist master; it similarly transformed him into an innovator in farming methods and a leading advocate of scientific agriculture.[1]

James Henry Hammond never forgot his father's exhortation that "Knowledge is power." On the plantation, he recognized, knowledge meant control— and in due course prosperity. Knowledge could transform Silver Bluff into a

---

1. James Henry Hammond to John C. Calhoun, September 10, 1842, in John C. Calhoun Papers, Clemson University, Clemson, S.C.; Harry Hammond to Hammond, June 29–30, 1859, in HBC Papers, SCL. The title of this chapter is from Holkham [James Henry Hammond], "Suggestions for Southern Planters," *Southern Agriculturist*, V (June, 1845), 100–205.

shining exemplar for all to admire; agricultural success could distinguish the ambitious Carolinian among all the planters of the South.[2]

When Hammond took possession of his new property in 1831, he estimated the value of land, slaves, and other plantation assets at $90,240. He had become one of the wealthiest men and largest slaveholders not only in the surrounding area but in the entire state. Yet the average net income from the Bluff over the preceding four years, he reported in disgust, had been only $775. Such a paltry sum, representing a return on investment of less than 1 percent, seemed a clear indictment of the Fitzsimons family management. The new owner was determined to increase this profit margin substantially. Always jealous of his independence, Hammond struggled to earn the right to call the plantation his own: he would always consider the increased value of Silver Bluff under his administration as evidence for the legitimacy of his ownership. He had not simply married a great plantation, he would insist, but had in good part created it.

Hammond did not wait long to introduce changes in agricultural operations at the Bluff. He at once set out to create a "business appearance," and he increased the acreage under cultivation by 16 percent in an effort to produce a more remunerative crop. On the very date of his first wedding anniversary the first cotton bolls symbolically opened, promising a rich yield for his new property. When Hammond returned to Silver Bluff in October after a late summer sojourn in the mountains, he proudly reported that "The crop is said to be by far the best ever made on the plantation."[3]

The harvest fully lived up to these preliminary expectations. With characteristic meticulousness Hammond calculated his receipts from the sale of cotton, corn, lumber, and other plantation products during his first year of management

2. Elisha Hammond to Hammond, February 25, 1829, in JHH Papers, SCL. Hammond was given the same lesson in college. See Hammond, "Introductory Lecture to Moral Philosophy by Rev. Robert Henry, A. M., March 6, 1824," in College Lecture Book (MS vol. bd., 1822–25, JHH Papers, SCL).

3. Hammond Stock and Crop Book, 1831–32 (MS in JHH Papers, LC); Hammond Plantation Diary (MS vol. bd., 1831–55), December 8, 1831, December 31, 1834, October 10, 1832; Hammond, "Silver Bluff, Cathwood, Cowden, and Redcliffe" (MS vol. bd., 1856–87), May 21, 1859, both in JHH Papers, SCL. By 1860 Hammond was one of only 88 planters in the South who owned more than three hundred slaves and one of 440 South Carolinians who owned more than a hundred. See Lewis C. Gray, *History of Agriculture in the Southern United States to 1860* (2 vols.; 1933; reprint, Gloucester, Mass.: Peter Smith, 1958), I, 482–83; Chalmers Gaston Davidson, *The Last Foray: The South Carolina Planters of 1860: A Sociological Study* (Columbia: University of South Carolina Press, 1971). Vernon Burton's analysis of the 1860 Census from Edgefield District reveals that less than 10 percent of all farms were larger than five hundred acres, that 183.2 acres was the average farm size, and that $1010 was the median personal wealth. Vernon Burton, University of Illinois, personal communication with the author, February, 1981.

to be \$11,292.99. Expenses of only \$2,754.34, which included such costs as the overseer's \$350 salary, cloth for slave garments, shoes and blankets, doctors' fees, and some new tools and equipment, left a profit of \$8,538.65—\$113.85 per full working hand. By his own calculations, this represented a return of 9.5 percent on his capital.[4]

Even though such an achievement might have seemed a tribute to his superior direction of a previously unproductive property and even though the sum was more than four times as great as his previous year's earnings as a lawyer, Hammond was not entirely satisfied. His expectations and needs had increased far more than fourfold. "I have found my wants to enlarge always faster than my means," he would later observe to his brother Marcellus. "It appears to me I have not the tenth part of my wants gratified. I find myself in this respect but little better off than when I was poor and single." Not only was he now father of a rapidly growing family, Hammond had joined the Carolina aristocracy and could no longer live in the frugal style of a bachelor attorney. A sizable income would be required to support a new and appropriate standard of living.[5]

As Hammond contemplated the future, he saw a number of options. The first and most obvious of these was simply to increase his crop—and thus his income—by expanding the acreage planted. Through the 1830s Hammond employed a portion of the off-season labor of his slaves in clearing new land and thus steadily augmented the percentage of his property under cultivation. By 1839 he had 1,651 acres in crops, more than two-thirds again as much as the 967 acres planted during the last spring of Fitzsimons management eight years before. As he increased the amount of cleared land, Hammond also found he was able to leave more fallow every year, returning it for a season to the recuperative powers of nature. While he had left no cleared land uncultivated during his first year of management, by the late 1830s he was resting as much as four hundred acres each year, and in 1840 kept six hundred acres unploughed.[6]

Hammond's efforts to extend his arable lands and rationalize his holdings led him to purchase additional tracts from neighbors and occasionally to sell off parcels of less useful land. In the first year of his ownership he bought 488 acres to the southeast of his property line, including a site for the new house he was to build for his family between 1834 and 1838.[7]

4. Hammond Plantation Diary, December 31, October 10, 1832.
5. Hammond to M. C. M. Hammond, March 19, 1840, April 1, 1841, in JHH Papers, SCL.
6. "Crop Statistics for Silver Bluff" (MS vol. bd., 1833–52, *ibid.*); "Crops of Silver Bluff Estate," in Hammond Plantation Diary.
7. See Hammond, Land Papers, Slave Lists (MS vol. bd., JHH Papers, SCL).

But Hammond soon learned that he could not entirely regulate plantation productivity. Severe storms during his second year of management destroyed much of the crop, dashing his plans for a corn surplus. In 1835 a drought defeated his calculations, and three years later weather again so diminished his cotton crop that he harvested only half what he had expected. Despite these setbacks and despite Hammond's complaints that his economic goals seemed all but unattainable, his balance sheets showed a remarkable overall growth in income throughout the 1830s. Profits per hand increased to $215.49 by 1836, and Hammond estimated in 1841 that "Exclusive of this year my income has averaged about $12,500 clear of plantation . . . expenses." At the end of a decade of ownership, Hammond reckoned that he had increased the value of his property by 50 percent. But, he remarked with the dissatisfaction he characteristically exhibited about even the most impressive of his achievements, "I should have doubled it."[8]

Hammond remained unhappy with his profits and grew increasingly aware of the inherent shortcomings of his land. Too much of it, he complained, was sandy and sterile; the rest lacked adequate drainage. Twentieth-century Soil Conservation Service surveys reveal that Hammond had an astute understanding of the grim situation he faced at Silver Bluff. Much of the area is covered with soils described as sand, loamy sand, or sandy loam, all of which tend in the southern Piedmont to be low in organic matter, in nitrogen and phosphorus, and thus, in natural fertility. Great expanses of the inland portions of Silver Bluff are classified as Troup sand, a soil with such a low moisture-holding capacity as to be critically vulnerable to drought—a condition about which Hammond constantly complained. Yet the naturally richest parts of Silver Bluff lands suffer from the opposite disadvantage—too much water. The Johnston soils, which the Department of Agriculture finds lying both close to the Savannah River and in the plantation's uplands, are characterized as "black mucky loam" and—like the Bethera clay loam and Chewacla loam also widespread at Silver Bluff—pose severe drainage problems. Hammond had good reason to feel discouraged about his plantation's prospects. The decision to increase income by expanding the percentage of land under cultivation could be at best only a partial solution to the agricultural and entrepreneurial dilemma posed by the qualities of such soils.[9]

8. Hammond to M. C. M. Hammond, January 7, 1841, Hammond Diary, November 5, 1841, both in JHH Papers, LC.

9. Soil Conservation Service, U.S. Department of Agriculture, Soil Survey Field Sheets,

As Hammond learned of more and more fortunes being made in the fresh cotton lands of the Southwest, he began to reconsider the depth of his commitment to Carolina. Throughout the 1830s, other planters were similarly growing aware of the deficiencies of their soil in comparison with lands available in Alabama, Mississippi, and Texas. Many of Carolina's most enterprising citizens abandoned their birthplace to seek opportunities elsewhere. Hammond himself remarked upon the departure "to the West of nearly every one of the young men with whom I was brought up," and he received a steady stream of letters from relocated friends who described the riches they expected to harvest in their new homes. Hammond's emerging understanding of Silver Bluff made emigration seem ever more attractive. "I have been trying to get over my desire for a western plantation," he confided to a fellow Carolinian, "but every time I see a man who has been there it puts me in a fever." Yet Hammond was reluctant to leave his political ventures and personal ties in Carolina and, as a result, put off making a final decision. At the same time as he was adding to his holdings at the Bluff, he was investing in property elsewhere. In 1836 he purchased a share of stock in the Colorado and Red River Land Company, which brought with its price of $7,500 the rights of fifty thousand acres of Texas property. Hammond fully intended to extend his speculations to include an additional "league of first rate cotton land" there. By 1838 he had declared his certainty that "I must go West and plant."[10]

But Texas seemed very far away, culturally and politically as well as geographically; it was not, Hammond noted, even part of the United States. When family and friends urged him to consider other options, Hammond was receptive, relieved to turn to possibilities closer to home. In the spring of 1838 he set off in the company of his sixteen-year-old slave Levin to explore land in Georgia and Florida described to him by friends as highly desirable. If he could acquire productive property close to Carolina, perhaps he would not be required to move his primary residence but would be able to visit these new lands frequently

---

Aiken County, South Carolina, 1978. I am grateful to Arthur Johnson, Department of Geology, University of Pennsylvania, for his assistance in interpreting these maps and extrapolating from them the conditions Hammond would have faced more than a century ago.

10. Hammond Diary (LC), February 6, 1841. See I. W. Hayne to Hammond, April 1, 1837, Josiah C. Nott to Hammond, July 21, 1840, both in JHH Papers, SCL; Hammond to Franklin H. Elmore, March 22, 1838, JHH Papers, LC; Hammond Plantation Diary, May 14, 1836, March 11, 1838. See also Alfred Smith, Jr., *Economic Readjustment of an Old Cotton State: South Carolina, 1820–1860* (Columbia: University of South Carolina, 1958); Marjorie Mendenhall, "A History of Agriculture in South Carolina, 1790 to 1860: An Economic and Social Survey" (Ph.D. dissertation, University of North Carolina, 1940).

enough to maintain close supervision without entirely disrupting his valued family and community ties.

Lodging en route in the houses of piney woods folk, Hammond found the area of cotton cultivation around Albany, Georgia, to be a "primitive place." He soon departed for the Florida home of cousins who had enthusiastically advertised their glowing prospects. The location near Tallahassee was particularly attractive. In spite of residents' tales of annual disruptions of cotton picking by Indian raids, he found this region, with its beautiful lakes and handsome houses, far more civilized than the rough frontier settlement he had visited in Georgia. Yet Hammond was uncertain about the quality of the lands he saw and afraid that the soil was of a type that would be quickly exhausted. Undecided about a course of action after a month of travel, he finally made an offer on nearly two thousand acres of land. But his indecisiveness was reflected in the low price he named, and Hammond failed to secure the property. Within a month of his return to Carolina he confessed to his brother, "I am getting every day more out of the notion of going there or sending hands there. It is too far." Hammond seemed unable to break or even to weaken his ties to South Carolina, and this deep attachment shaped all his business decisions. His public and private identity had defined him as a Carolinian, and Hammond would never escape this self-conception. His financial activities would always be molded by his wider aspirations for political and intellectual achievement. These ambitions worked decisively to keep him in South Carolina, where he had so carefully established the foundations of a public reputation. Even as he dispassionately calculated the factors of profit and loss involved in his various plans, Hammond often seemed to be using these statistics to rationalize decisions made on other—unspoken—grounds. Hammond's design encompassed far more than economic goals.[11]

Soon after his return from Florida another opportunity arose considerably closer to home. In early 1839, the young planter succeeded in selling a portion of his property known as the Lower Bluff for $5,600, thereby further rationalizing his Barnwell District holdings. In its stead, he purchased Green Valley, a 580-acre plantation in Fairfield District just north of Columbia on the Little River. The plantation, for which Hammond paid thirteen dollars an acre, included "a tolerable overseer's house" and several slave cabins. The soil seemed to Hammond so rich that he expected it to yield an average of 800 pounds of seed

11. Hammond diary (LC), April 19, 1838; Benjamin Whitner to Hammond, May 30, 1838, Hammond to M. C. M. Hammond, June 17, 1838 (see also Hammond to Whitner, June 9, 1838), all in JHH Papers, SCL.

cotton per acre, nearly twice the 481 he had averaged in his first five years as plantation master. Dispatching thirty-nine slaves from Silver Bluff, Hammond began the improvement and cultivation of the new property.[12]

By the end of the decade, Hammond had thus diversified his landholdings through the purchase of Texas and Fairfield District land, and had also begun to vary his investments more generally by acquiring $5,500 worth of railroad and bank stock. These and other nonagricultural investments in which he dabbled throughout the antebellum years had several purposes. Most such ventures were designed to provide a degree of liquidity lacking in land and slaves. Railroad stock, Hammond explained, always served as "a sort of deposit in which I can realize money in a pinch." He searched eagerly as well for opportunities in South Carolina's manufacturing sector. He invested in cotton mills as early as the 1830s, and his emerging ideological commitment to economic diversification reinforced a later interest in purchasing a share in the successful mill ventures of William Gregg at nearly Graniteville. Others of Hammond's financial schemes were more hazardous speculations, often made in cooperation with friends who, Hammond complained, seemed always to lead him to disaster. The Texas land investment company ultimately failed entirely, as did an $8,500 gold mine gamble Hammond made with one of his neighbors in the late 1850s. The planter's most expensive gesture of friendship, however, was his agreement to cosign a loan for James Hamilton, who went bankrupt in the 1840s and cost Hammond more than fifteen thousand dollars. The planter intended the loans he made to friends like Hamilton as acts of generous patronage. They were designed to advertise Hammond's great wealth and to enhance his appearance of philanthropic benevolence; Hammond expected these debts to be risk-free investments in social status. It was simply his misfortune that this particular transaction had such a costly outcome, diminishing Hammond's wealth as well as his affection for an improvident friend.[13]

12. "Green Valley," Hammond Plantation Diary, December 10, 1839, pp. 410–11. William Cooper offers the following yields as characteristic in 1850: 131 pounds lint per acre in Alabama, 125 pounds in Georgia, and 163 pounds in Mississippi. The ratio of seed to lint cotton is usually calculated at three to one. See Cooper, "The Cotton Crisis in the Antebellum South: Another Look," *Agricultural History*, XL (April, 1975), 381–91. Hammond also considered purchasing a low-country plantation and growing long-staple cotton and perhaps moving to Charleston where he could "raise my children among people." See Hammond to M. C. M. Hammond, June 6, 1841, March 4, 1838, both in JHH Papers, SCL.

13. Hammond to M. C. M. Hammond, February 20, 1849, Hammond, "Silver Bluff, Cathwood, Cowden, and Redcliffe" (MS vol. bd., 1856–87), June 28, 1859, Hammond Plantation Diary, May 14, 1836, all in JHH Papers, SCL. On the Hamilton debt, see Hammond Account Book (MS vol. bd., 1838–51, JHH Papers, SCL), May 27, June 7, 1845; James Hamilton to Hammond,

But in spite of these ventures, Hammond retained the bulk of his wealth in his plantations. Just as investments in or with friends seemed so often to fail, so any kind of dependence on the wisdom or management of others always struck Hammond as highly risky. "Never tried to help a friend," he reflected in 1859, "but what he failed & I had to pay for the piping. Never made a venture beyond my personal superintendence that ended otherwise." Temperamentally, Hammond preferred the "despotic sway" that a planter could at least aspire to establish over his landed investments. Yet his drive for a modern, rationalized system of management, for a plantation that would be like a factory, created important underlying tensions in view of Hammond's decidedly prebourgeois notions of lordlike mastery. There could be no genuine delegation of authority or division of responsibility at Silver Bluff; the idea of bureaucracy was entirely inconsistent with Hammond's understanding of his power. "I only succeed," he explained, "when everything is under my control."[14]

By the late 1830s, agricultural operations at Silver Bluff were indeed coming more tightly under Hammond's control. He had increased the value of the property by rationalizing acreage and by making a variety of improvements, clearing additional arable land, and building a new dwelling for himself, as well as new slave cabins, a ginhouse, and a slave hospital. Hammond had worked carefully to make the plantation both efficient and self-sufficient, ensuring that it produced enough corn to feed the slaves and sufficient fodder to fatten the livestock that were slaughtered as the plantation meat supply. Not only cotton production but every detail of plantation output was to be included in his entrepreneurial design.

But like businessmen and investors throughout the nation, Hammond was deeply worried about financial prospects in the early 1840s. Despite the many indications of his wealth, Hammond was well aware of the troubling economic conditions North and South that had followed the nationwide financial panic of 1837. These forces exerted their fullest impact on the Carolina cotton market in 1840 and inaugurated a period of hard times that plagued the state throughout the decade. Charleston cotton prices fell from a high of $0.168 per pound in

---

October 22, 1843, in James Hamilton Papers, SHC; Hammond Diary (LC), March 24, 1842; Hammond to Hamilton, March 14, 1845, Hammond to M. C. M. Hammond, March 9, 1842, both in JHH Papers, SCL. See also Virginia Louise Glenn, "James Hamilton, Jr., of South Carolina: A Biography (Ph.D. dissertation, University of North Carolina, Chapel Hill, 1964), 355, 362.

14. Hammond, "Silver Bluff, Cathwood, Cowden and Redcliffe," June 28, 1859, September 19, 1857.

1836 to $0.129 in 1839, to just $0.084 in 1840. By the middle of the decade, they lingered between six and seven cents per pound. Hammond estimated that he was unable to cultivate cotton profitably for less than ten cents per pound, and thus the 1840s drove him to a searching reassessment of his financial condition and options. "If prices do not improve," he told the Barnwell Agricultural Society in November, 1840, "most of us will become compelled to abandon cotton."[15]

At the same time, Hammond confronted diminishing returns from the wood business that he had pursued since his arrival at the Bluff. His lumber was of poor quality and could not easily be sold in Savannah, and the decline of steamboat traffic with the rise of railroads all but eliminated wood sales at the plantation's river landing. But if wood and cotton were not to yield their former profits, Hammond would find other sources of income. He moved rapidly to adjust to the new situation by diversifying his own production, experimenting with new commodities, such as silkworms, as well as expanding his acreage in food. The Fairfield District plantation had proved insufficiently productive in existing depressed circumstances, and Hammond considered himself fortunate to be able to sell it late in 1840 without incurring a loss. With this capital freed, Hammond turned once again to thoughts of beckoning opportunities in the West. By the end of the year he had again become convinced that investment in virgin land was a necessity. "I shall go West," he declared to his wife. "I must have another plantation & one in the cotton region."[16]

But Hammond could not overcome his reluctance to leave the state in which he was a figure of growing political importance, and he justified these hesitations by translating them into entrepreneurial terms. As the new year opened in 1841, Hammond carefully weighed the alternatives available to him in South Carolina and the West. There could be no further doubt, he concluded, that low cotton prices had rendered it "indispensably necessary for me to make a very material change in my planting operations." In the West yields were high enough, he estimated, that he could profitably cultivate cotton to sell for as little as seven cents a pound, three cents a pound less than the minimum he thought required to make a profit in Carolina. With prices now between eight and nine cents, it no longer made sense to operate a cotton plantation in the East. But

15. Hammond, "Report of the Committee of the Barnwell Agricultural Society on the Culture of Cotton," *Farmer's Register*, IX (October 31, 1841), 600; Hammond Diary (LC), February 9, 1841.
16. Hammond Plantation Diary, May 30, December 11, 1840; Hammond to Catherine Fitzsimons Hammond, December 11, 1840, in JHH Papers, SCL.

Hammond projected an alternative scheme of transforming Silver Bluff into a livestock farm. If he divided the property into three separate sections, the costs of slave management would increase, for he would have to hire three overseers. "For anything but corn & cotton," he believed, "10 to 20 workers are as many as any common white man can attend to." With increased supervision, however, he thought it would be possible to use slaves as animal tenders; the blacks would be thus prevented from the carelessness and abuse of livestock that Hammond, like many southern planters, attributed to his slaves. Hammond made generous estimates of the stock he could produce under such arrangements: as many as seven hundred hogs and seventy steers for slaughter each year, as well as two thousand pounds of butter for market. In addition, he expected the three sections to make small crops of cotton and corn for sale, and he anticipated an overall profit of $245 per slave. In the West, by contrast, his careful calculations led him to expect only enough cotton to average $210 per hand. The difference, he triumphantly concluded, was decisively "in favor of this country."[17]

Hammond's painstaking financial comparison and analysis were convincing to himself at least; he never again seriously considered abandoning Carolina for the West. But the reasons he offered for remaining did not always reflect the equation of profits and losses here so neatly set forth, and he never embarked upon the transformation of the Bluff into a livestock plantation. The one apparent constant in all these financial calculations and manipulations was the conclusion that he would remain in Carolina; it was the particular justifications for this decision that constantly shifted. Less than three months after working out his elaborate comparison of cotton in the West versus stock at the Bluff, Hammond, in a complete turnabout informed his brother that even though he would "make double what I do" by moving West, he did not intend to go. His "negroes would die in becoming acclimatized," he explained, and besides, "Texas is too remote."[18]

But in order to remain in Carolina, he would be compelled to make changes far more dramatic than his efforts during the 1830s to extend the arable portion of his land. As early as 1838, a friend had urged Hammond to consider revivifying his Silver Bluff property rather than abandoning it entirely for Texas. "I am confident," he had written, "you have Marl not far from you & if you have, you

---

17. Hammond Plantation Diary, January 10, 1841; Hammond to Edmund Ruffin, September 26, 1847, in Edmund Ruffin Papers, Virginia Historical Society, Richmond; Hammond Plantation Diary, January 11, 1841.
18. Hammond to M. C. M. Hammond, April 1, 1841, in JHH Papers, SCL.

will do better to get it & improve your old lands." Marl is a kind of clay rich in calcium carbonate that is used even today on acidic soils to increase their friability and their receptivity to the enriching effects of animal manures. Contemporary Soil Survey data indicate that marl would indeed have been an excellent supplement for Hammond's sandy nitrogen- and phosphorus-poor soils. In the third and fourth decades of the nineteenth century, marl was the watchword of the agricultural reform crusade Edmund Ruffin launched in hopes of reversing the declining fertility of Virginia's tired lands. But in the early forties, the "gospel of marl" had only just begun to win converts in the Old Dominion and was almost unknown in South Carolina.[19]

Hammond had long exhibited a casual interest in scientific agriculture, and he subscribed to several of the periodicals that served as the voice of the reform movement, including Ruffin's own *Farmer's Register*. Moreover, Hammond had himself made some half-hearted experiments during his first decade at the Bluff by comparing numbers of cotton bolls produced per acre by different types of cotton seed under varying techniques of cultivation. His deep-seated scepticism led him at first to oppose the ambitious and, he thought, visionary reformist schemes proposed at a Columbia agricultural convention in 1839. But by 1840 he was supporting private efforts to disseminate information, and he actively aided in the formation of an agricultural society in Barnwell District. Yet he remained doubtful about the practicality of Ruffin's bold theories. In an article published in the June, 1840, issue of the *Farmer's Register* under the pseudonym "Middle Country," Hammond inquired about the "propriety" of using marl in South Carolina and about the general applicability of Ruffin's conclusions, drawn from experiments made in Virginia, to areas farther South. But "Middle Country" remained open to persuasion, requesting information rather than rejecting the Virginian's doctrines out of hand. Ruffin responded with confidence about the potential benefits of marl for South Carolina. Hammond carefully read Ruffin's seminal *Essay on Calcareous Manures* during the summer of 1841 and determined to begin marling operations in the fall. In Hammond's mind, these experiments were clearly an alternative to emigration. "Unless marling makes a very great alteration I cannot stand it. This is my last hope." Hard times

19. Elmore to Hammond, April 2, 1838, in JHH Papers, LC. See Avery Craven, *Soil Exhaustion as a Factor in the Agricultural History of Virginia and Maryland, 1606–1860* (1926, reprint; Gloucester, Mass.: Peter Smith, 1965); Avery Craven, *Edmund Ruffin, Southerner: A Study in Secession* (1932, reprint; Baton Rouge: Louisiana State University Press, 1966); Drew Gilpin Faust, "The Rhetoric and Ritual of Agriculture in Antebellum South Carolina," *Journal of Southern History*, XLV (November, 1979), 541–68.

had combined with a reluctance to leave Carolina to make Hammond an agri-cultural innovator.[20]

Twelve miles downriver from his plantation, Hammond located a bluff com-posed largely of marl that he was able to rent for one hundred dollars per year. During the next twelve months, eleven slaves manned a boat that made eighty-five trips to haul nearly a hundred thousand bushels of the fertilizer. Estimating that a prime hand could marl an acre a day, Hammond applied the material in varying proportions to land carefully laid out in experimental squares. "I am en-abled," he explained, "by omitting opening new land, to haul out and spread this marl without interfering with other plantation work or lessening the number of acres planted per hand."[21]

In the first year of his experiment, Hammond recorded increases in produc-tivity as high as 50 percent in cotton and approximately 25 percent in fodder and corn. By the end of 1841 he had become an evangelist for scientific agricul-ture in the South. Invited to deliver the anniversary oration to the State Agri-cultural Society, Hammond publicly announced his conversion. "It will be per-ceived that the means I recommend . . . involve an important change in our system of Agriculture, & a resort to manuring, contracted planting & drainage to an extent which I confess I have not heretofore advocated." As he confided to his diary in early 1842, he was amazed that only a year before he had been con-sidering abandoning Carolina altogether. "Since then," he observed, "impor-tant changes have taken place in consequence of turning my attention to marl & succeeding in procuring it at a reasonable cost. All my calculations are now based on this experiment in which at this time I have the utmost confidence." Given the particular inadequacies of his soils, marl and manure were proper re-medies, although Hammond never fully realized that on his sandy lands, their effects would be all but dissipated within a decade. Hammond's soils required unremitting attention if they were to achieve high levels of productivity. His later complaints about the failures of marling to make permanent improvements indicate that Hammond did not fully understand the best use of the substance he had so wisely chosen to employ.[22]

20. See Hammond Account Book (1838–51); Hammond Plantation Diary, November 29, 1839, January 6, 1840; Middle Country [James Henry Hammond], "Remarks on the Propriety of Using Marl in South Carolina," *Farmer's Register*, VIII (June 30, 1840), 341; Hammond Plantation Diary, March 31, 1841; Hammond Diary (LC), October 19, 1841.
21. Hammond, "Recent and Extensive Marling in South Carolina," *Farmer's Register*, X (No-vember 30, 1842), 519.
22. Hammond Plantation Diary, February 6, 1842.

The adoption of marling, however, marked an important change in Hammond's overall attitude about his agricultural endeavors, one that quickly involved him in a whole series of experimental projects at the Bluff. From his initial days as a planter, he explained to a friend, he had "carried on my business" with "systematic *energy* and *forethought*." But now these analyses and plans would be directed not simply toward maximizing profit. Hammond would begin to regard his plantation activities as part of a wider world of southern agriculture upon which not just the prosperity but the survival of his region and its peculiar institutions depended. Reading voraciously in agricultural literature, Hammond began to generalize, to experiment, to philosophize about the practice of husbandry, and to disseminate his views in essays and orations. Silver Bluff became a source not just of profits but of pride; it would be, he hoped, a kind of plantation on a hill, a beacon guiding agriculturists throughout the South. But Hammond's conversion meant that plantation administration had of necessity to become more complex. He could no longer struggle just for financial gain; now he had to transform agricultural theory into daily practice. As in his management of slaves, Hammond established idealized standards and goals and was inevitably frustrated in his efforts to conduct every detail of plantation operations in accordance with "scientific principles."[23]

Hammond made his new, wider goals explicit, articulating them clearly in the *Carolina Planter* for his fellow agriculturists to read. "My idea of a 'Fine crop,'" he explained, "is, first, an increase of negroes, second, enough made on the plantation, of meat, corn, &c. to feed everything abundantly; third, an improvement, rather than a deterioration, in the productive quality of the lands; fourth, the mules, horses, farming utensils and fences all in first rate order by Christmas, and then, as much cotton as can be made and gathered under these circumstances." Long-term considerations of agricultural improvement had replaced short-term cotton profits as the primary goal of the plantation enterprise. But Hammond would soon discover that the natural increase in slave population for which he called was not the only one of his aims that would prove embarrassingly difficult to realize.[24]

23. Hammond to William Gilmore Simms, January 27, 1841, in JHH Papers, LC. Hammond described to Edmund Ruffin his fear of reading too much and becoming a "Book Planter" who tried "too many new things." Hammond to Ruffin, March 4, 1844, in Ruffin Papers. At various points during the 1840s and 1850s, Hammond subscribed to *Pendleton Farmer, Working Farmer, Farmer and Planter, De Bow's Review, Southern Planter, American Farmer, Ohio Cultivator, Cotton Planter, Rural Register, Southern Agriculturist, Horticulturist, Planter and Soil, Western Farm Journal, Carolina Planter, Farmer's Register,* and *Southwestern Farmer.* See Hammond Account Books (1838–51, 1852–64).

24. Franklin [James Henry Hammond], "Overseers, II," clipping in Edward Spann Hammond

The plantation self-sufficiency Hammond sought was a basic principle of the South's agricultural reform movement. Twentieth-century scholars have argued heatedly about whether or not the antebellum South so concentrated on cotton production as to become dependent on other regions for food. While the balance of historical opinion at present lies on the side of regional self-sufficiency, nineteenth-century southern agricultural writers clearly viewed the situation differently, endlessly berating their compatriots for their dependence on western livestock and grain. "It is the true policy of the cotton planters," a local South Carolina agricultural convention resolved in 1843, "to curtail the cotton crop and increase the provision crop—so as to supply all the breadstuffs and raise all the different kinds of stock . . . which may be necessary for family and plantation use."[25]

Hammond agreed wholeheartedly with this formulation, which fitted neatly with his sectionalist political views. The South must escape the economic as well as the political domination of the free states. Intellectual commitment, however, was not so easily translated into daily reality. Corn posed little difficulty for Hammond, for he produced enough to market a surplus during nearly every year of his management. But meat was another question. Although Hammond fully intended to raise the hogs required to feed his slaves, he found year after year, as he reported in 1833, that he "Did not succeed well with Hogs although I took much pains." Slave theft was one important factor in diminishing Hammond's herds, but his difficulties lay primarily with the hogs themselves. Instead of the expected improvement, Hammond's zealous replacement of Silver Bluff's hardy half-wild sows with Berkshires purchased from the North produced disaster. The purebreds died under the strenuous conditions of southern live-

---

Scrapbook (MS vol. bd., 1844–90, Edward Spann Hammond Papers, SCL). The five installments by Franklin appeared in the Columbia *South Carolinian* in June, 1844, and were then reprinted in the *Carolina Planter*, I (August, 1844), 25–30.

25. "Agricultural Convention, Monticello, Fairfield District, July 5, 1843," clipping in Private Diary of Edmund Ruffin, State Agricultural Surveyor of South Carolina, 1843 (MS in Ruffin Papers). See Robert Gallman, "Self-Sufficiency in the Cotton Economy of the Ante-Bellum South," *Agricultural History*, XLIV (January, 1970), 5–24. For a contradictory nineteenth-century opinion, see R. W. Roper, "Report Before the Agricultural Society of South Carolina," *Southern Agriculturist*, IV (September 1844), 347–50, or Hammond himself, who estimated that South Carolina imported half her flour. *Proceedings of the Agricultural Convention and of the State Agricultural Society of South Carolina from 1834 to 1845 Inclusive* (Columbia: Sumner and Carroll, 1846), 186. See also Gavin Wright, *The Political Economy of the Cotton South: Households, Markets, and Wealth in the Nineteenth Century* (New York: Norton, 1978); James Foust, *The Yeoman Farmer and the Expansion of U.S. Cotton Production* (New York: Arno, 1976); Sam Bowers Hilliard, *Hog Meat and Hoe Cake: Food Supply in the Old South 1840–1860* (Carbondale: Southern Illinois University Press, 1972).

stock husbandry, where even the best-cared-for animals were usually left to run free for much of the year. When Hammond began in desperation to pen his stock, he still seemed unable to reduce their rate of mortality. In 1843 he was compelled for the first time to buy bacon to augment his supply. Two years later he made do by substituting beef for the preferred pork in the slave diet, and by 1847 he was purchasing almost all his plantation meat ration. Between that year and the outbreak of the Civil War, Hammond expended an average of $829 on meat annually, a sum higher than an overseer's salary and higher than any other single plantation expense. A prominent advocate of plantation self-sufficiency, Hammond was himself far from independent of outside food supplies. [26]

Closely related to the goal of self-sufficiency, a second cardinal tenet of the agricultural reform movement in the South was the diversification of plantation production to render the region less dependent upon the fluctuation of the world cotton market. During the 1840s, low prices made this a particularly pressing appeal. In an 1841 address to the State Agricultural Society Hammond himself called for a drastic curtailment of the cotton crop, and his own actions at Silver Bluff indicated his attention to these economic necessities. His plantation records include the details of his crop selection at the Bluff through 1855. Until 1853, when he gathered the first harvest at his newly established Cowden Plantation just downriver from Silver Bluff, these data provide a comprehensive portrait of his decisions about the proper ratio between cotton and corn. Unfortunately, complete acreage and crop records for Cowden seem not to have survived, so that it is impossible to gain an overall view of his decision-making processes after the time that the new plantation began to produce enough corn to influence his actions at the Bluff. Nevertheless, it is possible to reconstruct the logic of his crop choices through a critical period of depression and slow recovery in the cotton market. [27]

Hammond's initial response to what he judged to be a 33 percent drop in prices and values in 1839 was to decrease total acreage planted by nearly half.

26. Hammond Silver Bluff Plantation Book (MS, 1833, in JHH Papers, LC); Hammond to Calhoun, September 26, 1845, in Calhoun Papers; Hammond to Ruffin, August 7, 1845, in Ruffin Papers; Hammond Plantation Diary, December 27, 1845; Coke [James Henry Hammond], "Fencing," *Carolina Planter*, II (June, 1845), 281–83; Hammond Account Books (1838–51, 1852–64). Death of unacclimatized Berkshires was a widespread problem. See James Bonner, *A History of Georgia Agriculture, 1732–1860* (Athens: University of Georgia, 1964), 146. See also on livestock Eugene Genovese, *The Political Economy of Slavery: Studies in the Economy and Society of the Slave South* (New York: Vintage Books, 1965), Chapter 5. See also Coke, "Fencing," 281–83.

27. Hammond, "Anniversary Oration of the State Agricultural Society of South Carolina . . . 25th November, 1841," in *Proceedings*, 175–91.

Yet the next year he increased both cotton and provision crops, possibly to compensate for the drop in price by raising output. In 1842 he shifted toward corn for the first time, but reversed his priorities again in 1843 to return to his concentration on cotton for two more seasons. At last in 1845, when cotton prices had been below an average of eight cents for three consecutive years, he turned decisively toward corn. Through the rest of the decade, Hammond maintained a predominance of corn acreage at the Bluff, but the rise in cotton prices to $0.084 in 1849 seems to have prompted him to shift the balance once again. The South's restored confidence in its economy and its staple crop was reflected in Hammond's own choices, for in 1850, 1851, and 1852 he reestablished the dominance of cotton on his plantation. The pessimism he had expressed in 1841 about the future of cotton was forgotten; Hammond's actions at Silver Bluff seemed to embody the conviction he would later display to the United States Senate when he proclaimed in 1858 that "Cotton is King."[28]

Hammond's decisions appear to have been most directly a function of the changing market price of cotton and his consequent attempts to maximize dollar income per acre. The correlation between market realities and crop choice at Silver Bluff is not perfect, for other influences of course played a part in the annual allocation of acreage. A planter was always anticipating next year's prices when he made crop choices, and his forecasts were at best informed guesses. More tangible agricultural considerations also played a role. The desire to rotate crops and rest certain fields, the need to ensure enough cornmeal for plantation consumption, the particular qualities of certain parcels of land (Hammond feared, for example, that his uplands were too easily exhausted by cotton unless given a great deal of rest and manure) all affected the planter's decisions. Some economic historians have emphasized that corn production was inhibited by the uncertainties of finding buyers in a market far less formally structured than the elaborate web of factors, shippers, and exporters that handled the South's cotton consignments. Hammond never complained of difficulties in the mechanisms of selling corn, and he never developed the pattern of extensive indebtedness that tied many antebellum planters to their cotton factors and thus limited their entrepreneurial flexibility. Nevertheless, the convenience of marketing arrangements for cotton may still have influenced his crop choice. Allocation of workers played a role as well, for cotton, especially the work of picking, was

28. Hammond, *Selections from the Letters and Speeches of the Hon. James H. Hammond of South Carolina* (New York: John F. Trow, 1866), 317.

considerably more labor-intensive than corn. "Ten acres of cotton & ten of corn," Hammond explained, "is as much as I could ever tend to the *full task hand*. 12 of cotton & 4 of corn is about the same thing."[29]

Even with the marginally higher labor costs of cotton, the price structure of the antebellum period made it the more profitable choice, especially given Hammond's fixed labor force. At his average rate of productivity per acre, Hammond would need a market price for corn of $1.23 a bushel to generate as much income from a parcel of land as he could planting cotton to sell at ten cents a pound. If cotton were priced at six cents a pound, however, as it was in the depression year of 1848, Hammond could make more money per acre planting corn to sell for any sum greater than seventy-three cents a bushel. But in 1848, corn had fallen to forty-five to fifty cents a bushel, down from an average of seventy-four cents from 1833 to 1836. The southern market for corn, like the entire regional economy, was dependent upon the demand for cotton. When the price of the South's leading staple changed, so did the value of provision crops. A decade later, when cotton had recovered to $0.122, corn rose to nearly $0.80. Falling cotton prices, therefore, did not in themselves make corn production a more rational economic choice, at least in terms of immediate income maximization. Given Hammond's per-acre productivity, the differential remained with cotton.[30]

Yet in the darkest days of cotton prices during the 1840s, Hammond was induced to change the balance of his acreage to corn. Most likely this decision reflected a desire to decrease his dependence on the widely erratic cotton market. Although corn prices were low, Hammond knew that a provision crop, unlike cotton, was intrinsically valuable to him even if it was entirely held back from the depressed market. Planting corn gave him increased flexibility, for if he grew a surplus, he knew he could store it and use it over several years to feed slaves and livestock. Accumulating extra provisions would also offer him the

29. Hammond to M. C. M. Hammond, February 2, 1843, in JHH Papers, SCL. On cotton marketing, see Harold Woodman, *King Cotton and His Retainers: Financing and Marketing the Cotton Crop of the South, 1800–1925* (Lexington: University of Kentucky, 1968).

30. I made these calculations on the basis of the average per-acre productivity that Hammond calculated for Silver Bluff with an estimated 1:3 ratio of ginned to seed cotton. Corn prices were calculated from "Average Annual Local Prices of Shelled Corn Per Bushel in Virginia, 1801–1860, and Wholesale Prices at New Orleans, 1837–1860," Appendix, in Gray, *History of Agriculture*, II, 1039. Cotton prices are from "Carolina Staples and Cost-of-Living Figures, 1800–1860," Appendix I, in William W. Freehling, *Prelude to Civil War: The Nullification Controversy in South Carolina 1816–1836* (New York: Harper and Row, 1965), 361. See also Smith, *Economic Readjustment*, Chap. III, and Holkham, "Suggestions for Southern Planters."

choice of increasing cotton production in coming years when and if the market improved.[31] Despite his dramatic appeal to fellow Carolinians to liberate themselves from the cotton market, Hammond himself remained largely in its thrall. His behavior of the 1840s, moreover, was strikingly similar to that of planters throughout the region. King Cotton had made the South his vassal, and even Hammond dared not seriously challenge the monarch's sway.[32]

But while he made no effective effort to alter his basic dependence upon cotton, Hammond did make gestures towards the twin ideals of crop diversification and rotation that remained central to his reformist creed. Throughout his planting career, Hammond experimented with new crops, hoping to find a product that could replace cotton as the South's cash staple. In his early years at the Bluff, Hammond tried planting sugarcane. But the yield was inadequate in both quantity and quality, and even the livestock were reluctant to consume it. Hammond had no greater success with the silkworms that were so popular among agricultural reformers in the mid-forties, and his introduction of Bermuda grass into a crop rotation plan left him with tenacious weeds amongst his corn and cotton plants.

Hammond made an even greater error when in the late fifties he confidently set out to make a fortune growing imphee, yet another sort of sugar plant. An entrepreneur named Leonard Wray had promoted this "Chinese sorghum" widely in the agricultural press as a potentially "vast source of wealth." When Hammond read an account of these claims he contacted Wray in hopes of himself introducing sugar as a cash crop. Under Wray's guidance, Hammond planted 109 acres of imphee in 1857 and constructed the necessary refining machinery in expectation of producing thirty thousand gallons of syrup, which he planned to sell for eighteen thousand dollars. Wray, however, provided faulty directions, and the project ended in disaster when the machinery failed, humiliating Ham-

31. Gavin Wright believes that southern agriculturists' recognition of the security and market independence offered by corn served as a primary motivation in crop choice. See Wright, *Political Economy*, Chap. III, and Gavin Wright and Howard Kunreuther, "Cotton, Corn and Risk in the Nineteenth Century," *Journal of Economic History*, XXXV (September, 1975), 526–51; William N. Parker (ed.), *The Structure of the Cotton Economy of the Antebellum South* (Berkeley: University of California, 1970). Discrepancies between Hammond's cotton productivity and sales figures for the early forties indicate that he was indeed holding back a portion of his crop from the market, probably hoping for a better price. This already existing surplus may have also contributed to his increased corn acreage as the decade wore on.

32. Calculated on Gavin Wright's index of cotton/corn (000 bales/ 000,000 bushels), Hammond's index of 25.398 for the 1840s is very close to Wright's statistic for the Deep South region of South Carolina, Alabama, Mississippi, Louisiana, and Georgia in the same period of 26.62. See Wright, *Political Economy*, 166.

mond in front of a crowd of onlookers. Estimating his losses at ten thousand dollars, Hammond dismissed Wray as "an adventurer and imposter" and himself as an "*Ass*" for having been taken in by his claims.[33]

Hammond's other efforts to introduce new cash crops were less dramatic failures, but never produced enough revenue to contribute significantly to his income. His desire to found a winery by importing grape cuttings from the finest French vineyards was thwarted when the vines failed to produce fruit of the same quality in Carolina soil. Nevertheless, Hammond would be grateful for a cellarful of even these inferior domestic wines when the Civil War later cut him off from other supplies. Like many southern agricultural reformers, Hammond experimented as well with orchards, turning to one of the region's most influential experts for advice and assistance. Pomologist Louis Berckmans of nearby Augusta was a central figure in the "horticultural revival" that took place in the South Carolina and Georgia uplands during the 1850s, and his influence on Hammond is still visible in the plantings at Redcliffe. But Hammond's 1856 plan to create commercial apple and pear orchards was as financially unrewarding as his other experiments in crop diversification, and his difficulties in securing experienced supervisors led him to abandon the undertaking. Unskilled slave labor, Hammond believed, was not well suited to the careful management fruit trees requried. No genuine alternative to cotton presented itself, and Hammond's cultivation of small crops of peas or occasional fields of rice, oats, wheat, and rye hardly represented a meaningful departure from prevailing staple agriculture. The Carolinian's major effort at diversification lay in the planting of sizable acreage in corn. Yet because corn prices were so closely tied to the cotton market, and because cotton and corn were similarly exhausting crops, this hardly constituted either a significant movement away from the existing structure of the southern economy or an effective crop rotation plan.[34]

In addition to self-sufficiency and crop diversification, the South's agricul-

33. Silkworms were a widespread response to agricultural depression in the South Carolina and Georgia up-country, as was Bermuda grass. See Bonner, *A History*, 75, 84. On Wray, see Charleston *Courier*, April 16, 1857; Hammond to Leonard Wray, September 29, 1857, in JHH Papers, LC; Hammond to Edward Spann Hammond, September 20, 1857, in JHH Papers, SCL.

34. Hammond Account Book (1852–64), March 3, 1857; Hammond Business Papers, Legal Size (JHH Papers, SCL), March 14, 1860; Hammond to Alexander H. Stephens, April 19, 1860, in Alexander H. Stephens Papers, LC; Redcliffe Orchard Book (MS vol. bd., 1855–64, JHH Papers, SCL). On Berckmans, see Bonner, *A History*. Ruffin objected to Hammond's prescription for crop rotation—"grain—cotton—corn—rest"—and advocated greater crop diversity and more rest. Hammond to Ruffin, December 12, 1846, August 15, 1849, both in Ruffin Papers. Hammond's position was characteristic of up-country planters. See Bonner, *A History*, 186.

tural reform movement preached managerial efficiency. Too many southerners, its advocates warned, were neglectful of the details of plantation administration, if not absent from their lands entirely. Too much of the responsibility for plantation management had been left to overseers, and ignorance had thus been enshrined as the directing force in agricultural affairs.

Hammond himself regarded the upgrading of overseers and their work as central to the advancement of southern agriculture. In the *Carolina Planter*, he bluntly declared that "it would be as much to the interest of planters to improve them, as to improve their lands, stock or manner of planting. In fact, more; for, without improving them, it is very difficult to effect any other improvement." Hammond spoke from direct experience, for overseers at Silver Bluff seemed a constant hindrance to his grand designs. The "first requisite of a *good overseer*" was, in Hammond's view, very like the primary requirement for being a slave: "to OBEY Orders." At times he had to exert considerable self-restraint not to treat his white deputies as if they were indeed his bondsmen. When one overseer especially enraged him, Hammond reported that he could "hardly keep my hands off him." But if blacks were resistant to Hammond's desires for total control, whites, free and equal before the law, were even more unwilling to submit to his demands.[35]

From the first, Hammond's jealousy of his own power created conflicts with white subordinates. This master was, as one of his friends described him to a new overseer at Silver Bluff, "a very particular man," so particular, in fact, that he had a series of six overseers during his first decade of management. Hammond quarreled with his employees not only about their excessive harshness to slaves, their neglect of livestock, and their determination to maximize the size of the crop at whatever cost in abuse of labor and land, but about their drinking habits and family life.[36]

Hammond's conversion to scientific agriculture in the 1840s further increased the demands upon his deputies. One "Smart & . . . high tempered" applicant for the job at Silver Bluff declined at the last moment to take the position. "On reading my rules," Hammond explained, "he said they were to [sic] strict. I told [him] I could not alter them & declined his services." More than once during the forties Hammond dismissed unsatisfactory overseers at the

---

35. Franklin "Overseers," 25, 26; Hammond Plantation Diary, December 15, 1839.
36. Pierce Mason Butler to J. W. Walker, March 18, 1837, in JHH Papers, SCL. On turnover among overseers, see William Kauffman Scarborough, *The Overseer: Plantation Management in the Old South* (Baton Rouge: Louisiana State University Press, 1966) 39.

height of the growing season. In 1845 he explained to fellow reformer Edmund Ruffin that he had fired John Barnes in late July "because he would not weigh measure & attend properly to the details of my affairs—experiments particularly. . . . Damn the overseers." Although Barnes was admittedly "the best I have ever had if left to himself . . . he would not keep the track in *executing* orders, & as I have some dozens of nice experiments in all the branches of farming and stock raising going on, he worried me beyond endurance & continually thwarted all my views in detail. The present race of Overseers are far the greatest curse under which our agriculture labours." Hammond's hierarchical view of the world included a very precise place for these intractable white superintendents who seemed determined to frustrate his resolution to make the plantation as efficient as a factory. "An overseer," he explained, "cant conform to routine more than twice, a piney woods man once & a negro never again."[37]

Hammond understood that difficulty in securing qualified assistants was a far more general problem than his particular dilemma at Silver Bluff. Throughout the South, he recognized, many "persons improperly regard overseeing as a degrading occupation." As a result, only a "limited number" of individuals, characterized by a "want of education generally," were available to fill this role. Most often, Hammond believed, these were poorer whites lacking "better opportunities." This class, Hammond felt, was instilled with an "abhorrence of negroes" that made them almost inevitably cruel to slaves. A number of Hammond's deputies were sons of farmers or small slaveholders in his own neighborhood. The planter may have hoped to engage individuals whose youth, managerial inexperience, and long membership in the network of class and deference around Silver Bluff would make them naturally subservient to him. But ignorance had its disadvantages, and Hammond more often hired professional overseers recommended to him by friends and acquaintances.[38]

Drawn from such backgrounds, Hammond's white supervisors had little understanding or patience for what must often have seemed to them not just intrusions on the legitimate authority of their office, but outrageously harebrained schemes. Untutored in principles of scientific farming, they resisted Hammond's

---

37. Hammond Plantation Diary, January 12, 1840. Hammond threw his overseers off in midseason in 1844, 1847, 1848, and 1849. Hammond Plantation Diary, July 21, 1844, July 8, 1848; Hammond to Ruffin, March 26, 1847, August 7, 1845, both in Ruffin Papers; Hammond to M. C. M. Hammond, September 4, 1849, in JHH Papers, LC; Hammond to Calhoun, August 18, 1845, in Calhoun Papers; Hammond to William Gregg, June 8, 1864, in JHH Papers, LC.
38. Franklin, "Overseers," 29; Hammond to Lewis Tappan, September 6, 1850, in JHH Papers, LC.

deviations from widely accepted plantation practice and routine. It is hard to imagine the reaction of the overseer whom Hammond instructed to collect all slave urine for use as fertilizer on the next year's crop. In some cases overseers were simply intellectually unable to execute Hammond's demands. Mr. Barnes's replacement, for example, became "so utterly confused with my business," Hammond reported, that he did "not half the time know which way the sun rises. Of course the negroes see it & do nothing." Another overseer proved entirely "incapable of keeping . . . accounts of Crops."[39]

Hammond systematically endeavored to improve his overseers' managerial efficiency and to overcome what he described as their lack of "faith" in his agricultural gospel. To encourage careful attention to slave health, he included in some overseers' annual contracts a provision that awarded the employee ten dollars for every slave birth in excess of deaths during the year. Hammond's commitment to increased productivity through closer supervision of work prompted him in 1849 to divide Silver Bluff into two plantations, separating his slave force into two settlements and hiring an additional overseer. He hoped this reduction in work load would improve plantation output, for the laborers could now be more "thoroughly managed." A large-scale operation, he concluded, was not well suited to the practice of scientific agriculture.[40]

Despite difficulties in transforming reformist ideals into reality, Hammond persisted in his improvement efforts. The interest of all Carolinians in scientific farming was noticeably enhanced in 1843 when Edmund Ruffin was invited, largely through Hammond's sponsorship, to make an official agricultural survey of the state. Ruffin's advocacy of the benefits of marl drew statewide attention to Hammond's pioneering efforts, and the two agriculturists developed close personal ties that further reinforced Hammond's commitment to reform. Passing long summer evenings together at Silver Bluff, Hammond and Ruffin analyzed specimens of Carolina soil and shared games of billiards and glasses of port. When Ruffin returned to Virginia, the two planters began an intensive correspondence, with Hammond not just reporting every agricultural idea and experiment but sharing as well his fear that innovation made him an object of ridicule to his conservative neighbors. But the confidence he gained from feeling himself Ruffin's "apostle" enabled Hammond to disregard this mockery and continue in the paths of reform.[41]

39. Hammond to John Fox Hammond, December 31, 1845, in JHH Papers, SCL.
40. Hammond to Ruffin, February 14, July 7, 1844, in Ruffin Papers.
41. On Hammond and Ruffin's relationship, see Drew Gilpin Faust, *A Sacred Circle: The*

U.S. Signal Corps Photo No. 111-BA-1220 (Brady Collection) in the National Archives
Edmund Ruffin, pictured in 1861.

Soon after Ruffin's visit, Hammond wrote to him to announce a whole new series of improvements at Silver Bluff. The "ease with which I have accomplished my marling," he explained, "emboldens me to undertake a great deal. I feel a strong desire to beat the Western planters on my *whole crop*, per *acre* & *per hand* & should think it done at a cheap rate if at no more cost than I should incur in moving, buying, settling & opening a place there." He continued applying marl to new lands into the 1850s and in 1844 began a project to cover already treated lands with animal and vegetable manures, an undertaking that would have maximized the benefits of his original marling. The collection, transportation, and application of these fertilizers demanded an effort as great as shipping marl up the Savannah, and Hammond considered allocating forty hands to this job exclusively, except during the four months of the cotton picking season. Scientific agriculture, Hammond was discovering, was highly labor-intensive.[42]

Before he embarked on wide-scale reform, Hammond had found himself with a surplus of agricultural laborers. In 1838, for example, he had been able to hire out fifteen hands to toil on the railroad near Columbia. But his marling and manuring operations provided more than enough work for his bondsmen. And with slave prices falling along with those for cotton and corn in the early 1840s, Hammond began to expand the size of his force. While he was considering signing a note that would require him to pay for a gang of blacks in four yearly installments, Hammond mused that the slaves "will probably be worth double this before I shall be called upon to pay. The difficulty is that though I could use these negroes now it would be chiefly in making improvements which would not immediately pay a profit." Hammond nevertheless decided to buy and regularly added to his slave force throughout the decade in order to continue his experiments in reform. By 1850 he owned sixty-eight more slaves than he had ten years before; "I have land to work double my force under my new system of marling & manuring," he explained.[43]

Dilemma of the Intellectual in the Old South, 1840–1860 (Baltimore: Johns Hopkins University Press, 1977). Hammond to Ruffin, February 14, 1844, in Ruffin Papers.

42. Hammond to Ruffin, July 7, 1844, in Ruffin Papers. Hammond began to use guano in 1853, another indication of his close attention to the maxims of agricultural reformers. See Bonner, *A History*, 188. On marl, see also [James Henry Hammond] "Marling in South Carolina," *Farmer's Register*, X (July 30, 1842), 366–67. Hammond, *Marl: A Letter Addressed to the Agricultural Society of Jefferson County, Georgia* (Augusta: James McCafferty, 1846).

43. Hammond Diary (LC), August 6, 1842; Hammond to William B. Hodgson, January 1, 1846, in JHH Papers, DU. See also Hammond to Ruffin, June 20, 1845, in Ruffin Papers, Gray, *History of Agriculture*, I, 482–83, Chalmers Gaston Davidson, *The Last Foray: The South Carolina Planters of 1860: A Sociological Study* (Columbia: University of South Carolina, 1971). Note the

Hammond's capital resources and great wealth left him relatively unharmed by the economic depression that raged about him, and he was even able to take advantage of hard times. While most other southerners were suffering from shortages of funds, Hammond had an apparent surplus. Low stock prices prompted him to buy thirteen thousand dollars' worth of railroad shares; yet he still had enough cash to increase his plantation investment. The decreased cost of slaves enabled him to accelerate his plans for improvement. Similarly, he acted to acquire land on favorable terms. In the mid-forties he made a series of purchases that added 337 acres to the Silver Bluff property. And between 1848 and 1852, he at last realized his dream of establishing a second plantation. Through ten judicious purchases—including one bargain of 300 acres for five dollars—he secured 2,789 acres in the Savannah River swamps below Silver Bluff. Wild, marshy, and overgrown, this tract, called Cowden after the live-stock that roamed unbridled through it, stood as the ultimate challenge to Hammond's reformist creed. If he could subdue this land, if he could conquer the vines, brambles, gum, bay, and poplar trees, he would prove himself a most extraordinary agriculturist indeed.[44]

Hammond's interest in Cowden arose from his conviction that Savannah swamp soils contained untold mineral and vegetable riches. From the time of his arrival at Silver Bluff, he had transported what he called "peat" from the marshes to spread on upland soil. On reflection, he decided it would be far more efficient to cultivate the swamps themselves. But the lands of Cowden required a level of preparation, clearing, and draining that would entail a major engineering commitment. In the agricultural literature and in Edmund Ruffin's own efforts on his farm near Richmond, Hammond found the model for his drainage schemes, even though the scale of the operation he contemplated far exceeded that undertaken by Ruffin at Marlbourne. Hammond's bold ambitions were exceeded only by his expectations. His success at Cowden, he was sure, would "revolutionize agriculture in this district at least & quadruple its profits."[45]

In his first attempt, Hammond succeeded in clearing and draining 170 acres of swamp with eighteen hundred man-days of labor. Delighted by the five feet of rich black topsoil he had uncovered, Hammond was certain he could improve

---

consistency of Hammond's behavior with the assertions of Eugene Genovese, *The Political Economy of Slavery*, Chaps. 4 and 6.

44. Hammond Account Book (MS vol. bd., 1834–64, JHH Papers, SCL), 134; Billings, Land Papers, Slave Lists.

45. Hammond to Calhoun, July 20, 1845, in Calhoun Papers.

his rate of reclamation. Because South Carolina contained "hundreds of thousands of acres" of such swamp, Hammond hoped his efforts would serve as a model for transforming the agriculture of his native state. But the project was so enormous Hammond did not think he could complete it even with his expanded slave force, and he feared the effects of the swamp environment on the health of his slaves. Even the limited efforts at reclamation he had already undertaken at Silver Bluff had brought a notable increase in illness among the blacks. In an effort to preserve the health of his slaves, Hammond hired a crew of Irishmen from Augusta, but within three months he had discharged his white workers, declaring the "drunken rascals" entirely unsatisfactory. He replaced them with his own slaves, directed by local whites hired especially to supervise the drainage operations. Installing miles of five-foot ditches with elaborate covered drains, Hammond ultimately reclaimed over seven hundred acres of marsh at a cost, he estimated, of more than twenty thousand dollars.[46]

During the initial years of cultivation, Cowden produced enormous yields. But like most swamp soils, these lands were soon exhausted of the organic matter that had rendered them temporarily so productive. Modern soil scientists estimate that under cultivation swamp topsoil would be depleted at a rate of approximately one to two inches a year in moderate temperatures, and perhaps more rapidly in South Carolina's hot and humid conditions. Hammond's five feet of black Cowden earth would at this rate last less than thirty years. In fact, after the Civil War, Hammond's sons found Cowden almost worthless agriculturally.[47]

During Hammond's lifetime, however, Cowden's yields were often extraordinary. He decided the marsh environment would suit corn better than cotton, and in 1853 he was astounded by the crop's success. One acre produced fifty-one bushels, almost four times the thirteen-bushel-per-acre yield recorded up to that time at Silver Bluff. Throughout the fifties, harvests continued to be highly satisfactory, and in 1857 Hammond noted the statistics for the year's crop with pride. "If anyone can beat that let them try it." The difficulties of the drainage and reclamation project made Hammond all the more delighted with his achievement. As ever, he seemed most comfortable when faced by obstacles others would consider all but insurmountable. His efforts at Cowden, he re-

46. Hammond to Ruffin, March 26, 1847, in Ruffin Papers. Hammond Plantation Diary, February 14, 27, 1851, November 27, December 11, 1850. Note Hammond's report to Ruffin that he failed to keep exact account of costs. Hammond to Ruffin, December 19, 1853, in Ruffin Papers. See also Solon Robinson, "Mr. Robinson's Tour," *American Agriculturist*, IX (February, 1850), 49–51.
47. John Shaw Billings, "Silver Bluff and Cowden" (MS vol. bd., in HBC Papers, SCL). I discussed swamp soils with Arthur Johnson, Department of Geology, University of Pennsylvania.

ported, gave him "all the emotions of a Discoverer & a Conquerer. I am Colum-
bus! Cortez!" he wrote exuberantly. In agricultural reform and improvement lay
a power and a control at least as real as that he exercised over his slaves. Not
only did these activities increase his wealth—and by the 1850s he was reporting
annual profits between thirty and forty thousand dollars—but his attainments
contributed as well to a more general enhancement of his status. "If I have been
active & industrious," he explained in reference to his plantation undertakings,
"it has always been for higher purposes than to accumulate. . . . I delight to
accomplish."[48]

Hammond relished the sense of achievement he derived from extending rational control over operations at Cowden and Silver Bluff. But he thrived too on
the wider influence he knew his role entailed; a master's power had necessarily to
be forged at home, but it then stretched well beyond the immediate boundaries
of his plantation; effective dominance over land and slaves led naturally to authority over other whites in the immediate locality and could even reach
throughout the state and the nation at large. A wealthy and distinguished planter was a natural focus of power in his neighborhood, and it was this local preeminence that served as the foundation and legitimation of wider public ambitions. Through their economic and social functions, plantations were integrated
into a web of social relationships within the surrounding community. Hammond
served variously as banker, doctor, and employer, offering to hold money, prescribe drugs, gin cotton, educate children, and market crops of neighbors fortunate enough to attract his interest and beneficent attention. "Once a year," a
guest at Redcliffe recounted, "like a great feudal landlord," Hammond "gave a
fete or grand dinner to all the country people about, at which . . . every neigh-
bour, poor or rich, for miles about was present." The interactions between the
planter and his less-privileged neighbors had a profound influence upon class relations within the society as a whole. Lacking less-personal structures for social
and economic welfare and education, the South left the relationships of plantation paternalism to fill these institutional roles. Within the microcosm of a plantation and its neighborhood originated the complex ties of interdependence that
assured white solidarity in the antebellum South.[49]

The community around him, Hammond explained, was a "neighbourhood
where there is a small proportion of good land owned by a few men & a vast deal

48. Hammond, "Silver Bluff, Cathwood, Cowden, and Redcliffe," November 12, 1857. Hammond to Simms, May 14, 1852, January 22, 1846, both in JHH Papers, LC.
49. Virginia Clay-Clopton, *A Belle of the Fifties* (New York: Doubleday, Page, 1905), 217–18.

of poor land pretty thickly settled." In fact, Hammond was by far the wealthiest planter and largest slaveholder in his area. In 1850 he owned 30 percent of the improved land in his census tract of forty-one households, and Silver Bluff represented 57 percent of the cash value of the enumerated farms. By 1860 his landholdings were fifteen times as large and twenty-two times as valuable as the average in his census tract of eighty households. This economic preeminence no doubt contributed significantly to the contempt that served as the most salient feature of Hammond's attitude toward his neighbors. They were, he judged, among the "most ignorant, vulgar & I may add most narrow-minded set of people in the world." But Hammond recognized from the first that *noblesse* entailed *oblige* in the Old South, and so he grudgingly accepted certain responsibilities to this "poor set of devils" as an inescapable part of the role to which he aspired. He had "descended low to improve them as in duty bound," he explained. Some of the most respectable neighbors' sons attended the classes held by tutors for Hammond's children, and a few of these local boys later served as overseers at the Bluff. Hammond offered to "School & clothe [one youth] . . . one year for his services another." Some landless whites occasionally worked as extra plantation laborers, as J. Fudge briefly served in the stables before being dismissed for drunkenness. But in Hammond's judgment, white hands "wont stick," and their unreliability disrupted plantation routine. Like many planters Hammond regularly ginned and pressed cotton for small farmers who lived nearby, and permitted the use of his grain mill as well. Lottie Williams was one of several local women to come to the plantation to weave and sew slave clothes, and Hammond agreed to act as a deposit bank for her cash and to market her tiny crop of corn. Ailing neighbors sought Hammond's medical advice, and he often provided drugs for troubling illnesses. Silver Bluff slaves were instructed to help an unfortunate local widow by butchering her hog at killing time and providing her with firewood.[50]

50. Hammond to Tappan, September 6, 1850, in JHH Papers, LC; Manuscript Schedules, Seventh Census of the United States, Agriculture, Barnwell District, South Carolina, 1850, Manuscript Schedules, Eighth Census of the United States, Agriculture, Barnwell and Edgefield Districts, South Carolina, 1860, both in NA. In 1850 Hammond is included in a Barnwell Census tract, in 1860 he appears in both Barnwell and Edgefield agricultural schedules. For 1860 I have used only his Barnwell holdings, for he considered Redcliffe, his Edgefield family seat, a pastoral retreat, not part of his working, productive plantation property. Hammond Diary (LC), July 3, 1841; Hammond Diary (MS in JHH Papers, SCL), September 22, 1848; Hammond Plantation Diary, February 7, November 30, 1832; Hammond, "Silver Bluff, Cathwood, Cowden, and Redcliffe," March 6, 1857; Hammond Plantation Diary, December 12, 1846; Hammond, "Silver Bluff, Cathwood, Cowden, and Redcliffe," August 24, 1858; On relations with neighbors, see also Hammond Account Book

But Hammond often seems to have been somewhat reluctant in his benefactions. He ungraciously grumbled about the "great bother" these services cost him, and his neighbors may have resented this grudging patronage. When Hammond invited a "large party" to Christmas dinner in 1837, only three guests actually came, and the planter raged at the implied rejection of both his hospitality and his preeminence by "these low bred country folk." At times his lack of generosity led to overt conflict, for like the slaves, his neighbors had a keen sense of their rights and his obligations. One nearby resident, who had lived in Barnwell well before Hammond's arrival, had so long used a stream to cross through Silver Bluff that he had come to assume it a form of near-feudal customary right. Hammond was not happy with this presumption on his property rights, and he requested annual rent of ten cents for use of the waterway as a symbolic acknowledgement of his ownership. A series of "coarse & insolent" communications from the neighbor ensued and left Hammond eager to horsewhip their disrespectful author. But he recognized that such behavior would violate widely shared assumptions about the demeanor appropriate to his position as benevolent lord and would draw attention to his failure to extract proper deference from his vassal. Eager for the "personal chastisement" of Mr. Ransey, Hammond explained that the "only thing that deters me is the prospect of the Governorship. This ties my hands." His public image and aspirations could permit no such "affray."[51]

Temperamentally, Hammond found the loosely defined ties of patronage and privilege between himself and his neighbors difficult to manage. As always, he was most comfortable with unchallenged and undiluted omnipotence. But if there existed unspoken limits on his absolute power over blacks, there were even more stringent restrictions on his coercive rights over whites. Indeed, the ambiguities of the master-slave relationship seemed almost simple in comparison to the complexities of power relations among whites in South Carolina's "aristocratical democracy." Yet Hammond was well aware that his culture expected the forms of benevolent paternalism to extend beyond the boundaries of the plantation to encompass a larger "family white and black" within its framework of obligation and manipulative control.[52]

(1852–64), November 3, 1863; Hammond Plantation Diary, December 13, 1831, February 13, 1845, December 12, 1846.

51. Hammond Plantation Diary, September 8, 1842; Hammond Diary (LC), September 10, 1842.

52. Hammond Plantation Diary, December 25, 1837, July 13, 1854.

For James Henry Hammond, the plantation was in one sense a world unto itself, a "little kingdom" in which he could at least seek to satisfy his yearnings for "despotic sway." But the plantation had broader significance as well, for it served at the same time as a foundation upon which to erect his ambitions in the wider world, a base from which to reach out to a more extensive domain of achievement and control. From the first, Hammond recognized that ownership of a plantation and slaves was the surest means of acquiring the status prerequisite to political advancement. Planting, he knew, was "in this country . . . the *only* independent & really honorable occupation. The planters here are essentially what the nobility are in other countries. They stand at the head of society & politics." Yet the ways in which the plantation provided access to power were more complex than simply bestowing the honorific title of "planter" upon the ambitious Hammond. The young Carolinian found at Silver Bluff the financial basis to ensure that "independence" enshrined in republican ideology, as well as funds to support a life-style befitting his aspirations for gentility. In his planting efforts, he discovered a new arena for personal accomplishment and public eminence, and his agricultural leadership encouraged and reinforced his emerging political authority as a defender of the South and its institutions. The assumption of social and economic ascendancy within his Barnwell and Edgefield community served as a first step in the extension of Hammond's dominion beyond Silver Bluff into South Carolina and the nation. The world, he hoped, might become his plantation writ large.[53]

53. Hammond to Simms, April 19, 1847, Hammond to M. C. M. Hammond, May 19, 1848, both in JHH Papers, LC.

Part III

The Hazards of Power

The crisis of my fate personally and politically has arrived.
JAMES HENRY HAMMOND

CHAPTER 7

A More Elevated Ambition

PREOCCUPIED BY NEW RESPONSIBILITIES of marriage and family and by the bitter controversy with the Fitzsimonses over Silver Bluff, Hammond abandoned his accustomed political activism during the spring and summer of 1831. "Absence," he wrote home in August from his honeymoon trip, "without affecting my sentiments has done something towards allaying my passions." No longer did the issues of the tariff and nullification seem so central to either his career or his concerns; the new roles of husband and planter demanded the bulk of his attention. "Moving to Barnwell," he admitted, "may cut off my chance both to be useful or conspicuous but if the interest of my family require it, the sacrafice [sic] must be made."[1]

Yet if Hammond's passions had cooled, those of other states' rights advocates in South Carolina were only intensifying. In July of 1831 Governor James Hamilton had embarked on an all-out organizing campaign designed to evoke a ground swell of popular support for nullification. Hamilton founded the State Rights and Free Trade Association in early July, and before the month was out, Calhoun had at last come out openly for state action against the tariff in his famous Fort Hill letter. When the legislature met in December, Hamilton dem-

1. James Henry Hammond to I. W. Hayne, September 20, 1831, Hammond to Pierce Mason Butler, August 18, 1831, both in Letterpress Book, JHH Papers, SCL. For fuller discussion of nullification see William W. Freehling, *Prelude to Civil War: The Nullification Controversy in South Carolina, 1816–1836* (New York: Harper and Row, 1965), Chauncy Samuel Boucher, *The Nullification Controversy in South Carolina* (Chicago: University of Chicago Press, 1916), David F. Houston, *A Critical Study of Nullification in South Carolina* (New York: Longmans, 1896), and Charles M. Wiltse, *John C. Calhoun, Nullifier, 1829–1839* (Indianapolis: Bobbs-Merrill, 1949).

onstrated his political skills once again by convening a gathering of 112 states' rights delegates in the capital city, where their stirring oratory could not help but make an impression.

During these exciting December days in Columbia, Hammond was far away, fully engaged at Silver Bluff. He had taken possession of the plantation only a month before, and his time was consumed by the demands of establishing his mastery. But his old political allies prevailed upon him not to forget the cause he had so ably supported. "Do us as much service as you can in your solitude," William C. Preston implored from Columbia. Flattered, Hammond responded willingly to requests for advice and aid. Governor Hamilton appointed Hammond a delegate to the State Rights Convention in Charleston scheduled for February, 1832, and early in the new year Hamilton wrote his young protégé, urging that they meet to discuss strategy before the gathering. Recognizing Hammond's preoccupation with personal and plantation affairs, the governor offered to travel up the Savannah to Silver Bluff, hoping to use the meeting as an occasion to lure him from his political retirement.[2]

Hamilton's ploy succeeded, for the convention opened with Hammond in attendance, resplendently attired for his role as governor's aide-de-camp in a new uniform of dark blue coat, lace framed collar, gold epaulettes, red sash, cocked hat with white plume, white gloves, and "State Rights badge." The handsome young officer was well aware of the striking impression he made upon the Carolina gentry, gathered in Charleston for the ritual of race week. Hamilton had cleverly scheduled the political convention to coincide with these festivities, which annually brought the Carolina aristocracy together from every part of the state. Each February, Carolinians flocked to Charleston to display not only the prowess of their horses but the beauty and accomplishments of their daughters, who were presented to society—and to appropriate prospective husbands—during race week's debutante balls. The parties not only served as the premiere event of Carolina social life but also consolidated the ties of personal friendship and loyalty that constituted the strength of the state's master class. The atmosphere in Charleston during these annual celebrations provided a perfect context for consideration of the need to preserve the honor of Carolina against federal encroachment. Hammond himself came away from the convention with renewed radical fervor. Nullification seemed the only possible course of action. "I have myself never fully realized this crisis until now." The en-

2. William Preston to Hammond, January 18, 1832, in JHH Papers, LC; James Hamilton to Hammond, January 16, 1832, in James Hamilton Papers, SHC.

croachments of federal power posed an immediate threat to the survival of republican virtue and independence.[3]

Hammond confronted a direct challenge in the area surrounding his new property, for much of Barnwell and Edgefield was known for its moderate position on the tariff question. Through the spring and summer Hammond pressed states' rights and nullification views on his neighbors in an effort to influence their votes in the upcoming fall elections. Hamilton had identified these contests as crucial, for he hoped to elect enough states' rights delegates to call the convention that the movement's constitutional principles required to pass an ordinance of nullification. Hammond hailed the statewide organizing effort to win control of the legislature as "the chief hope of the Republic." After a brief "furlough," as he described it, Hammond had now returned to the political field of battle, and even the birth on March 30 of his first child, a son named James Henry, could not long distract him from the political turmoil engulfing the state.[4]

Late in May, Hammond gathered with Carolina's nullification leaders at Hamburg, just across the Savannah River from Augusta, for a dinner to honor Governor Hamilton. The participants were enthralled by radical speechmaking that climaxed with the eloquence of the spellbinding William Preston. The "whole affair," Hammond proclaimed delightedly, "went off with great eclat" and succeeded in spreading to the many Georgians in attendance a sense of the sectional grievances they shared with their more militant Carolina neighbors.[5]

In the ensuing weeks, Hammond himself mounted the stump at militia meetings throughout his district, explaining to the common up-country folk the necessity for state action against the tariff. In mid-June he carried the battle over the state line to a public dinner in Augusta honoring a revered local judge. Hammond's appeal to Georgia to support her sister state provoked a lengthy dialogue with his audience over the mechanism for such cooperation. A southern convention, he declared in response to one question, would be "totally inefficient, or unconstitutional and inexpedient" and would produce delays to cool the mounting enthusiasm for the nullifier's cause. With all the unpredictable elements such a pan-southern gathering would entail, a convention was not "as

3. Hammond to J. M. Felder, March 9, 1832, in Letterpress Book, JHH Papers, SCL.
4. Hammond to John Tyler *et al.*, September 13, 1832, in JHH Papers, LC; Hammond to Hamilton, July 28, 1831, in Letterpress Book, JHH Papers, SCL.
5. Hammond to M. C. M. Hammond, May 27, 1832, JHH Papers, LC; Hammond Plantation Diary (MS vol. bd., 1831–55, JHH Papers, SCL), May 26, 1832. See also Augusta *Chronicle*, June 2, 1832.

safe, as expeditious and as sure as Nullification." Hammond believed the movement's success lay in executing a dramatic coup, with South Carolina serving as radical vanguard for the rest of the South. Calm deliberation in a southern convention was too likely to produce compromise or moderation. But if South Carolina could be aroused to act, Hammond was sure her boldness would win others to her support. It was a theory that described the still-distant events of 1861 with striking accuracy but sadly misjudged attitudes of other southern states towards Carolina radicalism in 1832.[6]

July 4 found Hammond on his feet again, addressing Barnwell's Independence Day barbecue. Although heavy rain threatened to interrupt the festivities, Hammond responded to a toast with an impromptu speech lasting over an hour. Ten days later at a local militia muster and public meeting he presented a more formal set of free-trade resolutions, this time in a two-hour oration. The compromises thus far proposed in Congress, he asserted, did not definitively reject the right of the federal government to regulate trade through protective tariffs and failed to make significant reductions in the burden of duties upon the South. It was the responsibility of "State Authorities" to act against "the unconstitutional oppressions of this Government" and to "dictate the measures necessary" for effective relief.[7]

In the few short months since his arrival at Silver Bluff, Hammond had thrust himself into a position of prominence in the region around his new home. Adhering to the advice of his friend Pierce Butler, Hammond had "on every *proper* occasion come out & take[n] the field" and had, despite his professed reluctance, succeeded in keeping himself very much "in public view." His speechmaking had attracted the attention of the press as the nullification movement he represented gained increasing momentum and even inevitability within the state. Old friends from Columbia continued to urge him not to "neglect the duties" his extraordinary gifts had assigned him in public life, but their exhortations seemed increasingly unnecessary.

When the late-summer fever season arrived along the Savannah, Hammond's in-laws insisted that he retreat from Silver Bluff with his wife and baby. But even from the mountains of Pendleton District, Hammond continued to play an active part in the political contest at home. Unable personally to attend

6. Augusta *Chronicle*, June 30, June 23, 1832.
7. Hammond Plantation Diary, July 4, 14, 1832; Hammond, "Preambles and Resolutions" (MS, n.d., JHH Papers, LC); Augusta *Chronicle*, July 21, 1832.

two State Rights party dinners near Silver Bluff, he responded to the invitations with formal statements reiterating the grounds for his nullification position. In mid-August political controversy abruptly called Hammond away from his vacation retreat. The antitariff party had recently established a newspaper in Greenville, an antinullification up-country town. Under the editorship of Turner Bynum, a former Columbia associate of Hammond, the *Southern Sentinel* had sought to attract attention to its cause in this hostile territory by attacking the revered local unionist journal, the Greenville *Mountaineer*. The paper's editor, Benjamin Perry, took personal offense at Bynum's attacks and challenged the interloper to a duel. Hammond agreed to serve as Bynum's second, no doubt remembering similar confrontations during his own editorial career. But this contest had a less happy outcome than Hammond's quarrels. Perry shot his opponent through the hip and groin, and Bynum died the next day. Hammond had been able to take a vacation from the Savannah's fever-ridden banks, but not from the state's political crisis.[8]

Early in October, Hammond returned to Barnwell to make a final speech for nullification and to vote in the all-important legislative election. When news reached Silver Bluff of the results of the contest, Hammond was deeply gratified not only by the triumph of nullification throughout the state but by its sweeping victory in his own home district. In formerly "submissionist" Barnwell, resistance had succeeded by two to one.

Eager to maintain the momentum his organization had created, Governor Hamilton appointed a special session of the legislature for October 22. As expected, it immediately called for the election during the second week in November of a state convention to consider nullification. When the nominating committee of the resistance party in Barnwell chose its convention candidates, Hammond came within a single vote of being selected to represent the area served by his militia battalion. "However proud I might have been to have received such a mark of confidence from my fellow citizens," he confessed to a friend, "I am well aware that from my short residence here I have no claims to it."[9]

Although Hammond's friends in Columbia urged him to come to the capital

---

8. Butler to Hammond, July 10, 1832, I. W. Hayne to Hammond, August 2, 1832, Hammond to Tyler *et al.*, September 13, 1832, all in JHH Papers, LC.

9. Hammond Diary (MS in JHH Papers, LC), February 7, 1841; Hammond to R. A. Gantt, November 7, 1832, in JHH Papers, LC.

during the historic meeting of the convention, Hammond remained at home, eagerly awaiting news from his correspondents on the scene. To no one's surprise, the body approved an ordinance of nullification, written by Hammond's former law teacher, William Harper. In February of the coming year, the document decreed, the federal tariff would become null and void within the state. When the legislature gathered in late November, it provided for implementation of the convention's work and rearranged the leadership of the state to prepare for the coming crisis. Now open in his states' rights advocacy, Calhoun resigned as vice-president and replaced Robert Y. Hayne in the Senate. Hayne in turn became governor, succeeding Hamilton, whose brilliant organizational work was now complete. The state awaited Washington's reaction to its bold stance.

President Jackson left no doubt about his position. In a proclamation of December 10 he emphatically rejected the doctrines of nullification and secession as "contradicted expressly by the letter of the Constitution . . . and destructive of the great object for which it was formed." To the Carolinians, so convinced of the constitutional soundness of their doctrine, Jackson's words seemed harsh and provocative. Hammond himself saw the president's statement as tantamount to a declaration of war, and he wrote at once to volunteer his services to the new governor. The political crisis now clearly took precedence over family and plantation matters. "I shall immediately set about arranging my private affairs for taking the field at an early day," he assured Hayne, "not to quit it until all is settled." Hammond offered to begin recruiting volunteers in Barnwell. "I take it for granted," he informed the governor, "that you will concentrate a large force in Charleston to meet the emergency."[10]

Hayne, too, anticipated some sort of military confrontation. The same day Hammond wrote from Silver Bluff, the governor issued an executive department circular officially assigning him responsibility for "military arrangements in the District of Barnwell." On Christmas Eve, Hammond rode to a neighbor's to plan how to raise a "company of volunteers to meet the crisis," and he himself took the dramatic oath required by the ordinance of nullification, declaring his primary allegiance to his state and her radical constitutional doctrines. In a confidential letter to Hammond and his other aides-de-camp, Hayne elaborated his plans. The governor hoped to gather a force of ten thousand soldiers ready to take up arms at short notice as well as a more elite corps of one hundred minute-

10. James D. Richardson (ed.), *A Compilation of the Messages and Papers of the Presidents, 1789–1902* (11 vols.; Washington, D.C.: Government Printing Office, 1896–99), II, 1160–1162; Hammond to Robert Y. Hayne, December 20, 1832, in JHH Papers, LC.

men in each district. Such arrangements, he believed, would permit the concentration of 2500 of the state's citizens "upon a given point in three or four days." Constitutional principles were to be defended to the death.[11]

In Barnwell, Hammond moved rapidly to execute his commander's orders. In less than two weeks, he gathered two regiments, totaling twelve hundred fighting men, three-fourths of whom were armed with rifles. Even unionists were volunteering to defend the state, and a group of veterans, the "revolutionary remains" of the district, declared themselves ready to fight again, although not one was under fifty years of age. "I made every exertion in my power," Hammond informed the governor, "to stimulate the military spirit of the people & found but little difficulty in succeeding to an extent beyond my expectations."[12]

Hammond did not flag in his efforts at military preparedness. He traveled throughout the district, speaking nearly every day to a different militia gathering—exhorting a company at Ford's Meadow with patriotic fervor, inspiring another at Mrs. Badger's or Cedar Springs or Beauford's Bridge or Colonel Aaron's store with the highest principles of nullification. These dramatic martial assemblies, Hammond hoped, would capture the public eye and sentiment. Urging one of his staff to come dressed in "full feather," Hammond explained, "I wish to make as much display as possible" to impress and excite the country folk.[13]

Too often, however, Hammond was disappointed by his neighbors' lack of either political sophistication or commitment. The people of Barnwell, he reported to his commander-in-chief, "are generally very poor & though staunch yeomanry, not generally . . . public spirited. . . . The fact is that there are not intelligent men enough sprinkled about to stir them up. . . . Whenever they can be collected to-gether I have never failed to produce some ardour among them, but in so large a district, so sparsely populated it is difficult to get them to-gether, & they know so little of the matter that one exhortative does not last long. I mention these things," he continued a bit defensively, "to show you why there has not been as spontaneous a burst of patriotism here as elsewhere." As the effective date for nullification approached, Hammond found that his district fell short of the governor's ambitious plans for defense. He had been unable to gather the requisite number of minutemen or to complete the marching brigade,

11. Hammond Plantation Diary, December 24, 1832; Robert Y. Hayne to Hammond, December 26, 1832, in JHH Papers, LC.
12. Hammond to Robert Y. Hayne, January 8, 1833, in JHH Papers, LC.
13. Preston to Hammond, January 14, 1833, *ibid.*; Hammond Plantation Diary, January 19, 20, 26, February 1, 16, 1833; Hammond to U. M. Robert, February 5, 1833, Hammond to William Erwin, February 5, 1833, both in JHH Papers, SCL.

and in this comparatively poor region, he confronted difficulties in raising money for weapons and supplies as well.[14]

But events in Washington had begun to indicate that military conflict might be averted. On January 16, Jackson had submitted to Congress a request for certain special powers, such as the right to collect customs duties in cash, that he believed could be used to prevent a direct confrontation in South Carolina. Although he also sought enhanced military capabilities, it was becoming clear that his intention was to outmaneuver the Carolinians by placing them in a situation where they, not he, would have to undertake the decisive aggressive act. Calhoun regarded the president's request for military authority as an outrage, but Hammond felt that Jackson had in his January "Force Bill" message in fact retreated somewhat from his "coercive doctrines" of early December. Congress had also begun to consider a new tariff measure that did not fully meet the nullifiers' demands but did promise to cut duties in half by 1834. Hammond himself opposed any such compromise of principle, but he admitted to Preston that he thought most Carolinians would accept it.[15]

Late in January, with tariff revision pending in Congress and with Virginia in the midst of legislative debate on her stance in relationship to the crisis in her sister state, nullifiers gathered in Charleston and agreed to postpone the effective date of their resistance. Hammond supported this delay, and he took advantage of the unexpected reprieve to improve Barnwell's military preparedness. By the end of the first week of February, he could report a total of 552 volunteers, and Hammond himself offered the governor the proceeds of the first hundred bales of his next cotton crop to offset the expense of their required weapons and supplies.

Soon it began to seem that these soldiers would see action after all. Crippled by a series of obstructionist amendments, the tariff reform bill lost momentum in Congress; Virginia declined to offer support; exercise of armed resistance to the encroachments of tyranny seemed to Hammond and his fellow radicals the unavoidable next step. But Calhoun wished no such outcome. Alarmed at the growing threat to the Union, Carolina's senator cooperated with Henry Clay of Kentucky to devise a new compromise tariff that passed Congress by the first of March, and Jackson signed both this measure and the Force Bill on the same day. Although the new tariff gave the nullifiers considerably less than they had originally demanded, they jubilantly proclaimed victory. The Carolina Nullification

14. Hammond to Robert Y. Hayne, January 23, 1833, in JHH Papers, SCL.
15. *Ibid.*; Hammond to Preston, January 27, 1833, *ibid.*

Convention regathered in Columbia, repealed its ordinance, and in a final act of symbolic defiance, nullified the Force Bill.

Hayne had summoned Hammond to Columbia for the dramatic March meeting of the convention, and the young Carolinian reported proudly to his wife, "All the great men of the state are here & I am in constant intercourse with them." He assured Catherine of his preference for the quiet pleasures of home. "But who," he queried pompously, "can disappoint his destiny." Hammond was satisfied with the compromise tariff, regarding it as a "grand concession," but he could not ignore nullification's lesson. After having devoted more than two months to preparing his neighborhood for imminent war, he would not soon forget how close to open violence the struggle had come. "We of the South," he wrote, "are to have no more freedom than we can maintain at the point of the sword & we are determined to be always prepared for that issue whenever it is necessary to make it." The federal government had become a dangerous and permanent adversary.[16]

Given these new realities, Hammond did not wish Barnwell to abandon its growing commitment to military defense. Elected colonel of the regiment of 925 volunteers he had raised, Hammond encouraged his men to retain the sense of urgency about their rights that they had displayed during the crisis. Hammond warned his troops, assembled for review, that although this time "we have substantially carried our point," Carolinians should not "lay down . . . arms until our rights are fully secured," which they could never be so long as "the distilled despotism of the Force Bill is hanging over us." His dignity may have been shaken and his new gilt uniform dirtied when he was unceremoniously thrown from his horse in the midst of his review of the militia unit, but no doubt the fall little diminished Hammond's new importance. Nullification had won him his first elective office in his new home district; it had transformed him into a public figure.[17]

Although the crisis had passed, Hammond was not so quickly to slip from the stage. Invited to deliver Barnwell's Independence Day oration, the young Carolinian offered a display of dazzling oratory. His speech was filled with ominous forebodings, warning that the "slimy deposit of an ancient deluge"— his somewhat unusual metaphor for the growing power of the federal government—"might well produce a monster that will devour our Institutions." The

16. Hammond to Catherine Fitzsimons Hammond, March 13, 1833, in JHH Papers, SCL; Hammond to M. C. M. Hammond, March 27, 1833, in JHH Papers, LC.
17. Hammond, "Fellow Soldiers" (MS, 1833, JHH Papers, LC).

tariff controversy was not the only ground for contention between the nation and the states; Hammond cautioned prophetically that public lands and slavery would before long become equally divisive issues. But for the time being, he concluded on an optimistic note, the Constitution had been "revived from a state almost of atrophy; & greatest of all the efficiency of state interposition to protect the rights of the minority has been placed beyond a doubt."[18]

With "peace declared," as he put it, between the nullifiers and the federal government, Hammond had time at last for his own affairs. Certainly he would not become complacent about public issues; he dutifully accepted appointment as delegate to a board directed to reorganize the militia. As an active advocate of strengthening the system, he urged liberal appropriations and the establishment of a military professorship at South Carolina College. But Hammond was compelled to direct some of his attention to neglected domestic matters. Having "taken a stand against the monopoly of health claimed by . . . the mountains," Hammond dismissed accusations that he was endangering the lives of his family and insisted upon spending the summer of 1833 at Silver Bluff. To emphasize his faith in the salubrity of his plantation, he began construction of a new summer house on one of the property's high and airy sites. Hammond passed July and August watching carefully over his crop and was delighted by the initial cotton prices, which were high enough to seem "something magical."[19]

Hammond's domestic circle was fast expanding. Christopher Fitzsimons, his second son, was born in June, and the household was growing in other ways as well. Upon his father's death in 1829, Hammond had become the head of the family, assuming the special obligations of an eldest son to his widowed mother and younger siblings. Upon his accession to control at Silver Bluff, moreover, he acquired the wherewithal to serve as a genuine patriarch; he could now offer a good deal more than just emotional support, and the tangible opportunities represented by James's new prosperity quickly strengthened frayed family bonds.

Although his sister Caroline Augusta had at twenty-four already grown too old to need much guidance from her brother, Hammond became almost a second father to Marcellus, now nineteen, and John, thirteen. The two proved equally troublesome, each in his particular way. The elder was boisterous, belligerent, and entirely irresponsible; the younger, sullen and lazy. James endeavored to instill in them the ambition and drive his father had imparted to him, but they found it all too easy simply to rely on his social and financial success. In 1832

18. Hammond, "Barnwell Oration" (MS, July 4, 1833, *ibid.*).
19. Hammond to Preston, August 16, 1833, *ibid.*

James had used his political contacts to secure Marcellus an appointment to West Point, despite reservations about the boy's commitment even to acquit himself creditably on the entrance examinations. "I feel very anxious about it," James wrote his brother in a tone reminiscent of the dead Elisha himself, "& would far prefer that you had never got the appointment than to be refused admittance now. . . . You *have not one hour* to lose . . . but must devote yourself night and day." Marcellus qualified for entrance and matriculated at West Point, but James did not relax the pressure of his admonitions. "You have no time to idle. . . . Ten minutes to chat before meals & ten after and an hour at night, & a long letter or two take away a *heap* of time," he cautioned. In October, Marcellus wrote that he had been dropped from the first to the second section in math. James was devastated. "I should have neither eat nor slept but what I would have stuck there."[20]

John's education was equally trying. Hammond had enrolled the boy in Moses Waddel's school at Willington, the alma mater of John C. Calhoun and the most prestigious academy in the state. But John preferred playing the flute to studying, and Hammond complained to the headmaster about his brother's impractical tendencies, "I fear he wants the power of patient investigation, of deep analysis." Just as often, he despaired that John was simply a "rude lazy fellow." Both boys seemed untouched by the drive to excel that had consumed James from his earliest youth. He was bewildered by their lack of motivation, and he responded to Marcellus' attempted explanations with exasperation and an entire lack of understanding. "It is useless for anyone to deny that he is ambitious—we are all so both by nature & education."[21]

Hammond's own ambitions had only been further stimulated by his experiences of 1832 and 1833. His recently acquired plantation offered a whole new arena for achievement, at the same time that the intensification of the nullification agitation had greatly increased his political prominence. Now that the immediate crisis in federal relations had come to an end, Hammond had to think systematically about his goals and priorities in both public and private life. The allure of agricultural entrepreneurship was undeniable. "If I embark on some money making projects my business will become so extended as to require unceasing care and so interesting as to deaden every sentiment of a more elevated

---

20. Hammond to M. C. M. Hammond, March 24, October 13, November 1, 1832, all in JHH Papers, SCL.
21. Hammond to Moses Waddel, April 4, 1833, in JHH Papers, LC; Hammond to M. C. M. Hammond, April 30, 1833, in JHH Papers, SCL.

ambition." Once exposed to the excitement of a political contest, however, Hammond could not easily return to the mundane occupations of everyday life. To "lie upon my oars," he declared, "is . . . impossible." But after the positions of importance he had already held, to run for the state legislature, the logical next step in his advance, "would not excite me." The United States Congress seemed a more inviting challenge. "Upon the whole, therefore," he reported cautiously, "without laying myself out from the beginning for a regular political career I have thought it best 'to try it a session or two' . . . and then go to making . . . money if I liked."[22]

When the state's leaders gathered in the capital late in November, 1833, for the annual legislative session, Hammond left the last responsibilities for packing and shipping the cotton crop to his overseer and rode to Columbia to explore his political future. John M. Felder, staunch states' rights congressman from the district that encompassed both the capital and the outlying district of Barnwell, had decided not to run again, and the nullification party leaders were eager to ensure a successor with appropriate states' rights views.

The widespread public agitation of nullification had been a dramatic departure from Carolina's elite politics, and only the sense of dire emergency that had gripped the state's master class had made the democratic organizational tactics of Hamilton and others acceptable. Now that the moment of crisis had passed, the state's leaders were eager to return to the *status quo ante* and to reassert their control. Having taken advantage of the power of the masses, they were anxious to relegate the people to their accustomed subordinate role. The nullifiers hoped as well to smooth over lingering signs of internal discord by dictating future political arrangements to the defeated Carolina unionists, who were too weakened to protest effectively. Unity would be assured through nullifier control.

Federal law of course required that congressmen be elected by popular vote. Even South Carolina could not manage to construe this choice as the responsibility of the legislature. But the former nullifiers knew they could minimize the people's role in the selection by agreeing among themselves upon a candidate and ensuring that he appear before the voters unopposed. Hammond, whom many radicals considered a plausible choice, found himself "so strongly solicited from various respectable quarters to come out for Congress" that he abandoned any lingering doubts and "consented to run." It was so important for a candidate in South Carolina not to appear to be pressing his own claims, however, that the

22. Hammond to I. W. Hayne, December 17, 1833, in JHH Papers, LC.

public was often left in confusion about a candidate's willingness to stand for office. Too much ambition bespoke a concern with personal, as opposed to public interest; an aspirant was supposed to appear as if the call to public service had been thrust upon him. In the ideal republic of virtue, the best men would be clearly identified by their own excellence; an individual must not push his own claims too vigorously or insistently. Carolina political rhetoric was laced with humble denials of capability from even the most serious of contestants, and Hammond complied readily with these unspoken rules. In December, 1833, he was eager both to be elected to Congress and to avoid seeming a "presumptuous young man seeking office." This simultaneous commitment to two conflicting purposes produced widespread misunderstanding. His calculated diffidence misled some of the leaders of the Carolina oligarchy, who sought and found another willing candidate.[23] When Franklin Harper Elmore announced his intention to run, the nullification party confronted the very situation its leaders had hoped to avoid—two men of sound political principles vying for the same office and threatening to divide radical support.

A lawyer practicing in Walterboro, Elmore had served since 1822 as solicitor for the southern circuit and had proved the soundness of his states' rights principles as a member of the nullification convention. Because Elmore was the more senior, more experienced public servant, many Carolinians expected that Hammond would step aside and lower his sights to the state legislature. Certainly the principles of disinterested virtue would seem to have prescribed such a course. But such assumptions underestimated the force of Hammond's ambition. His appetite for power whetted, he would not so easily withdraw from the contest. His commitment to republican virtue did not extend beyond its usefulness in serving his personal ends.

Leading nullifiers were alarmed at the impending confrontation. "It will harass us beyond measure," David J. McCord declared in exasperation, "if you two oppose each other." Hammond would not listen to advice even from old friends who urged him to step aside. Elmore himself hoped some accommodation might be reached. This "struggle," he wrote to Hammond, "should, if possible, be avoided . . . instead of spending our energies against each other, we should be so arranged that neither be disabled but both reserved for the common cause." Elmore proposed that a convention of delegates from the affected electoral districts meet and decide upon a candidate. Hammond self-righteously greeted this

23. Hammond to Jacob McMichael, December 17, 1833, Hammond to Lewis M. Ayer, December 19, 1833, both *ibid.*

Courtesy of the South Caroliniana Library
Franklin H. Elmore, painted by William Harrison Scarborough.

suggestion as a dangerous introduction of mobocracy; it seemed "the first step towards perpetuating a system of party management." But he offered a counter-proposal, agreeing to abide by the decision of a panel composed of six or seven of their friends in Columbia. "Elmore thinks I will beat him & therefore he flinches," Hammond confided to a friend. But, all in all, he concluded, his opponent was "as cunning as the devil."[24]

24. David J. McCord to Hammond, December 23, 1833, Franklin H. Elmore to Hammond, December 24, 29, 1833, Hammond to Butler, December 29, 1833, all *ibid.*

Amidst such distrust, no compromise was possible, and soon after New Year's Day, 1834, Hammond departed on the first of a series of speaking tours around the district. In the aftermath of nullification, politics in South Carolina exhibited little of the calm unity that the state's veteran leaders desired. Political questions had touched and stirred common citizens, who would not easily be lulled back into their former passivity. And important issues remained unresolved. The test oath passed by the nullifiers required all Carolinians who wished to hold public office to make a pledge of primary allegiance to the state. The derogation of federal sovereignty implicit in this peremptory demand for ideological conformity rankled the unionists and created a continuing source of bitter controversy. Under such conditions, political campaigning assumed a level of contentiousness new to South Carolina, a tone manifested even in the conflict between the two nullifiers Hammond and Elmore. From the start, Hammond recognized that "There will certainly be a contest between Elmore & myself. . . . the canvas will be a warm one," he assured his wife, "& I intend to make it as warm as possible." While his public statements embraced the principles of prevailing republican ideology, with its emphasis on harmony and unity, his own uncontrollable ambition dictated a very different sort of political behavior, one almost as new to Carolina public life as Hammond himself.[25]

The acrimony of the nullification conflict transformed smoldering local resentments into unexpected campaign issues. In the Orangeburg parish of St. Mathews, a political ally warned Hammond, "there has always been an unfriendly feeling between the rich planters on the river & the settlers on the piney land." But now these hostilities were cropping up in new forms as well. The state's formerly partyless and issueless local politics were undergoing remarkable upheaval. In Lexington District, Hammond became embroiled in a controversy over the proper role for the common man in Carolina government. Because he had sat as a member of the general board that had revised the militia laws, he was accused of supporting a provision to remove election of militia generals from the officers to the legislature, a proposal his critics regarded as decidedly antidemocratic. Hammond denied any aristocratical leanings, assuring his antagonists that as the son of a sandhill farmer who had often driven cows through the district, he had himself "sprung up amongst the undistinguished mass of the people." There was no one, he proclaimed boldly, "more thoroughly imbued with the love of democratic institutions than myself." In a direct challenge to the

25. Hammond to Catherine Fitzsimons Hammond, January 24, 1834, in JHH Papers, SHC.

essence of the existing Carolina political system, Hammond asserted his belief that the people should be given the right to elect both president and governor. His so recently voiced fears about the growth of mobocracy seemed all but forgotten under the pressure of enhancing his electoral appeal. In his first general popular election, Hammond was not beyond trading on the humble origins he had struggled so assiduously to escape in order to capture the support of voters rendered newly sensitive to their prerogatives.[26]

Through January, February, and March, Hammond braved Carolina's winter rains to travel the court circuit—not to argue cases as he had as an aspiring lawyer, but to work the court-day crowds. When he had no more pressing appointments, he would stop at every house along his route to make his candidacy known. Some critics accused Hammond of being too eager a campaigner, of seeming "too anxious to force pledges" from potential supporters, of adapting with too much relish to the democratic usages necessitated by the constitutional requirement for popular election of the House of Representatives. Elmore campaigned vigorously as well, but he seemed less comfortable in the role and sought to avoid direct confrontations with his opponent. Sometimes Elmore would wait—hide, Hammond's supporters said—until the young planter had left a town or village before he would himself make an appearance.[27]

In mid-March, Hammond estimated that things were going "pretty fair," but he feared "the contest will be so close that neither of us have any right at this distance of time to be sanguine." Then, abruptly, Elmore withdrew, citing only "bad health." By early April, Hammond held the field alone.[28] With his election virtually assured, Hammond could relax his efforts. He had spent $255 on the contest to that point but would spend only another $75 in the six and a half months remaining before the election. He did not abandon public appearances entirely, for friends and supporters urged him to keep in prominent view until victory was in hand. The political situation remained unstable, and it was important that Hammond continue to remind voters of the soundness of his principles.[29]

---

26. McMichael to Hammond, March 8, 1834, Hammond to H. I. Caughman, December 29, 1833, both in JHH Papers, LC.

27. Paul Quattlebaum to Hammond, March 18, 1834, *ibid.*

28. Hammond to M. C. M. Hammond, March 10, 1834, *ibid.*; Butler to Francis W. Pickens, March 26, 1834, in Francis W. Pickens Papers, SCL.

29. Hammond Account Book (MS vol. bd., 1834–64, JHH Papers, SCL); Robert Y. Hayne to Hammond, June 12, 1834, in JHH Papers, LC.

In June the nullifiers confronted renewed crisis when the state court of appeals struck down the disputed test oath as unconstitutional. Because of the unionist sympathies of two members of the high court, this seemed a political decision. Nullifiers feared the threat it implied to their so recently consolidated power. Did unionist leaders within the state, Governor Hayne wondered, contemplate revolt or civil war? Was the court action just a gesture of defiance? Some extremists counseled an immediate and violent response, beginning with removal of the offending judges by a special session of the state legislature. But calmer heads prevailed. Hammond supported the moderate position adopted by Hayne, who had sought in the aftermath of crisis to follow a conciliatory path. Any precipitate action against the judges, Hammond feared, would result in "trampling the Ermine in the dust" and exaggerating the issue out of all proportion. It seemed the best course to await the regular fall meeting of the legislature and to incorporate the oath's provisions into a constitutional amendment at that time.[30]

But in the interim, Hammond determined, the questions of principle must not be forgotten. On Barnwell's first summer sale day, a time when crowds customarily thronged the district seat to market their produce and greet their neighbors, a revived State Rights and Free Trade Association called for a rally to consider the unionists' latest atrocity. Hammond was chosen to present a series of resolutions to the gathering, and he composed a carefully worded statement of the nullifiers' position on the issue. The court decision, he explained, was partisan rather than judicial, for there were no real grounds for viewing the pledge as a threat to citizens' federal duties. Hammond rested his defense of the oath on a distinction between the concepts of "allegiance" and "obedience" that had been set forth by the nullifiers' caucus during the convention's original discussion of the test oath in March, 1833. A Carolinian, Hammond argued, could owe primary "allegiance" to the state without undermining his duty to the nation, an obligation best described as "obedience." Reproducing the essence of Calhoun's efforts to resolve the problems of dual sovereignty in his nullification theory, Hammond argued that the federal government was an "*agency* not a *sovereignty*." The states had preceded the creation of the Union and retained their rights intact even after joining the national federation. Hammond concluded by recommending that the present crisis be resolved by incorporating the test oath

30. Hammond to Preston, June 12, 1834, in JHH Papers, LC.

into the state constitution, where it would be beyond the reach of the judiciary's interpretive powers.[31]

The semantic distinctions on which Hammond focused were almost certainly above the heads of the majority of rude country folk gathered in Barnwell for the summer sale. But Hammond was appealing beyond his immediate audience. This address was his most studied display thus far of the kind of constitutional theorizing Carolina had come to expect of her leaders. Hammond vested great importance in his intelligence, and he knew he could excel at the intellectual exercises that served as a ritual staple of the state's public life. From the first, Hammond had liked to envision himself in the mold of Calhoun—not an organizer and agitator like Hamilton, nor an orator like Preston or McDuffie, but, above all, an incisive mind leading by means of ideas and principles.

In his campaign for political office, Hammond was not running just for a seat in the House of Representatives but for membership in Carolina's congressional delegation, for inclusion within this informal but all-powerful state leadership group. These men not only planned their actions in Washington as a unit but also served together with state legislative leaders as the caucus that made almost all internal decisions in Carolina politics. Hammond's remarks at Barnwell were thus intended in part to be an announcement to the Carolina leadership of his claim to participation in their exclusive circle. Now that Elmore had been safely dispatched, Hammond began to work to counteract any impression of contentiousness or overly democratic zeal by adopting a solemnly dispassionate and statesmanlike style, by himself emulating the philosophical stance of the revered Calhoun.

When the legislature did gather in December, a constitutional amendment worded so ambiguously as to be acceptable to both unionists and nullifiers at last defused the test oath controversy. But by the time this issue was resolved, Hammond's future was already set. In the October elections, he won decisively, with only a few straggling votes cast for Elmore as a protest against Hammond's unopposed candidacy. Hammond scrutinized the returns from each precinct carefully,

31. Hammond, "Report at a Meeting of the State Rights and Free Trade Party of Barnwell District, South Carolina, Held at Barnwell Court-House, on Monday, July 7, 1834," in Hammond, *Selections from the Letters and Speeches of the Hon. James H. Hammond, of South Carolina* (New York: John F. Trow, 1866), 6–7, 12–14. It is significant that Hammond chose this as the first important statement of his political career when he was considering a collection of his works. In accordance with his wishes, it appears as the first item in the posthumous compilation of his works. For earlier discussion of the issues of "allegiance" and "obedience," see Charleston *Courier*, March 21, 1833.

recording all of the results in detail in the back of his plantation record book. Nearly everywhere, he noted with satisfaction, he had received more votes than any of the candidates for other offices on the ballot. Throughout the state, nullifiers reaped victories, and Hammond could anticipate many allies with whom to share his new life in Washington. [32]

32. Hammond Plantation Diary, October 13 and 14, 1834.

CHAPTER 8

Anticipations of Greatness

HAMMOND'S NEW LIFE in Washington would not begin for over a year. The ambitious young Carolinian had been elected to serve in the Twenty-fourth Congress, and the Twenty-third still remained in active session. Not until March would Hammond be officially commissioned by the new governor, George McDuffie, and not until December, 1835, would he be called to the nation's capital.

The year that intervened might have represented to a different man a time of satisfying rest and anticipation—pleasure in goals accomplished and eager excitement over challenges to come. But Hammond always found it difficult to enjoy his triumphs, for they filled him above all with anxious expectation. Dramatic national developments during the summer and fall of 1835 would only increase his apprehensions. His own personal crisis would be intensified by what seemed an ever more rapidly approaching national calamity over the South's commitment to her peculiar institution.

With the close of the legislative session in December, 1834, however, Hammond's thoughts fled to Silver Bluff. He had come to the state capital as a newly elected federal congressman merely to observe and consult during the final conflict over the test oath. With the enactment of a satisfactory compromise, Hammond's advisory responsibilities were fulfilled, and he hurried to reach home before Christmas. A round of festivities with old college friend Josiah Nott, visiting at the plantation, provided the opportunity for much-needed relaxation. Hammond found time as well to acquaint himself better with young Edward

Spann Hammond, born the previous summer and somewhat ignored by his father during the excitement of the political race.

Hammond's patriarchal obligations seemed steadily to increase. Not only was he producing a new son almost annually, but he demonstrated his responsibility for an ever more extended family by taking in the mysterious "Uncle Turner." Hammond's grandmother's brother, Sterling Edward Turner, had been engaged for years in unspecified business ventures on the coast of Africa. Although Hammond publicly denied that his great-uncle was a slave trader, in private he expressed his certainty that this brutal traffic was the source of Turner's income. When Turner ceased communicating with his Carolina relatives in the summer of 1832, Hammond took advantage of his new wealth to hire a friend of Marcellus to go to Africa and investigate. But Turner had in the meantime begun his return to the United States and arrived in Maine in September, 1833, accompanied, as a cousin reported to Hammond, by a "*goard-headed* awkward—*Warty faced* Crow Black African." Turner was in such wretched physical condition that he was not prosecuted for this obvious violation of laws prohibiting the importation of slaves, but instead was shipped at once to the care of relatives in Carolina. "Poor fellow!" Hammond remarked magnanimously. "He had not a dollar in the world—but shall not want one while I have." For a time the old man moved around amongst his various kin. But one night in the fall of 1834 he arrived for dinner at Silver Bluff, suffered a stroke in the course of the evening and remained there an invalid until he died nearly eight years later.[1]

Although Hammond sympathized with his suffering relative and was gratified to provide him with support, he remained more troubled about his own brothers, who had become his almost exclusive responsibility. "I shall never feel more anxiety for the welfare of my children than I do for that of you & John," he confessed to Marcellus. "Whatever success may attend me I shall always feel it incomplete unless both of you are doing well also." Yet John and Marcellus seemed determined to frustrate and disappoint him. Marcellus' career at West Point continued its downward course until he ranked near the very bottom of his class. As he frittered away his time writing for a literary magazine, Marcellus received letters of ever more desperate exhortation from his elder brother. "Every scientific or historical fact which you *now acquire*," James urged, "is capi-

1. James Henry Hammond Diary (MS in JHH Papers, LC), July 19, 1842; A. R. Latimer to James Henry Hammond, September 24, 1833, Hammond to M. C. M. Hammond, September 17, 1833, Hammond Plantation Diary (MS vol. bd., 1831–55), July 19, 1842, all in JHH Papers, SCL.

tal that will pay heavy interest . . . years hence." Marcellus tried to divert Hammond's attention from his academic failures by reporting his candidacy for class Fourth of July orator. But when the boy wrote that he had lost the election, Hammond did not spare his disdain. "I have never felt more mortified and disappointed. . . . I have felt for you all the trembling anxiety which your opponent felt for himself—and if I really believed you when you say you were indifferent I should at once give you up for lost. . . . reputation is everything & to be compared with nothing but honor."[2] Marcellus continued to amass extraordinary numbers of demerits. At last in the fall of 1835, he behaved badly enough to be dismissed altogether. Only his brother's intervention with the secretary of war restored the cadet to his class and permitted him to graduate the following year.[3]

John's failures were less dramatic. His record at Willington was so poor that James hired a tutor from Charleston to school him at Silver Bluff. Still John would not study. The teacher at last gave up his frustrating task and departed in June, 1835. Hammond determined either to bind John to a trade or place him in a manual training school. The boy had shown no signs of the ambition and energy necessary to achieve the more elevated station his brother had envisioned for him.[4]

But patriarchy had its compensations as well. Since Hammond had acquired Silver Bluff late in 1831, political exigencies had preoccupied him almost constantly, and he had found all too little time to enjoy the perquisites of his new position. Now that he had succeeded in reducing plantation management to a routine, had subdued the initial insubordination of his slaves, and had fairly embarked on his plans for expansion and improvement, Hammond began to direct his attention to some of the southern planter's characteristic pleasures. In December, 1833, he had purchased a part interest in three of his friend Pierce Butler's blooded horses. Since that time the two men had continued to increase their holdings through both purchase and breeding and had acquired as well the

2. Hammond to M. C. M. Hammond, October 17, January 22, March 26, 1835, in JHH Papers, SCL.

3. Hammond to M. C. M. Hammond, October 25, June 20, 1835, in JHH Papers, SCL. Hammond referred to a steward's hall squabble as the cause of Marcellus' expulsion, but his remarks are at odds with family legend as reported by John Shaw Billings, who relates that Marcellus had assaulted a black member of his West Point class for sharing a drinking dipper with a white. I have found no basis for this tale in Hammond's own papers, and there were in fact no black students at West Point during Marcellus' enrollment there. See John Shaw Billings, "The Hammonds" (MS vol. bd., n.d., HBC papers, SCL).

4. See Hammond to M. C. M. Hammond, March 18, 26, July 25, 1835, all in JHH Papers, SCL.

skilled slaves necessary to serve as jockey, groom, and trainer. Fine horses were a traditional interest of the southern gentry, as of their English models. These Thoroughbreds—aristocratic, competitive, assertive—were surrogates for their masters as they exhibited their strength and courage on the track. As a publication of the Carolina Jockey Club acknowledged, the racers were indeed "the impersonation of Carolina chivalry—the *embodied spirit* of Carolina blood and Carolina honor." Within this culture, a victorious horse made a clear statement about the preeminence of his master.[5]

Hammond entered into this new pursuit with characteristic energy, purchasing subscriptions to the *Turf Register* and *English Stud Book*, joining the Augusta Jockey Club, and laying out his own race-course in a field at Silver Bluff. In January of 1835 he and his partner purchased a most distinguished Thoroughbred. Five-year-old Argyle, bred in Virginia, stood fifteen and three-quarters hands high and was so dark brown he appeared almost black except for a small white star on his forehead. The partners paid eight thousand dollars for him but soon began to receive a return on this sizable outlay. At the Charleston race meeting of February 9, Argyle carried Hammond's name to victory before the assembled aristocracy of the state, then easily won a second thousand-dollar purse just a week later.[6]

For the remainder of the spring the horse stood at stud for fees between fifty and seventy-five dollars, and the partners shipped four of their own mares off to Virginia sires in hopes of acquiring more fine Virginia blood. Even though Argyle became sick and was unable to carry out his owners' schemes, Hammond estimated that the horse venture had yielded him $1221.45 for the season. But he could not measure in dollars and cents the satisfaction he had felt in attending the festivities of Charleston's race week as one of the inner circle of triumphant owners.

Despite these successes and despite his continuing responsibilities at Silver Bluff, Hammond began by summer to grow impatient at what he regarded as the interminable postponement of his destiny. After the annual Barnwell militia encampment in May, Hammond invited Governor McDuffie, who had been pres-

---

5. Pierce Mason Butler to Francis W. Pickens, March 12, 1834, in Francis W. Pickens Papers, SCL; Hammond, receipt to Pierce Mason Butler, January 17, 1835, in HBC Papers, SCL; John B. Irving, "Brethren of the Turf," in Irving, *The South Carolina Jockey Club* (Charleston: Russell and Jones, 1857), 177.

6. Hammond, "Journals, Recipes, Expense, &c. of Blood Horses Belonging Wholly or in Part to James H. Hammond" (2 MS vols. bd., 1833–40, JHH Papers, SCL); Hammond Plantation Diary, September 22, 1834.

ent to review the troops, to the plantation. Their lively discussions about public affairs fueled Hammond's impatience. When the governor departed Hammond found himself bored and lonely. He was "tired and sick" of his situation, he complained to his friend I. W. Hayne, and he felt that the "embers" of his ambition would grow "cold for the want of some friendly breeze." Hayne sympathized with Hammond's despondency, explaining, "You are . . . *without an object.*" His election to Congress had left his talent and ambition no outlet. "And you have accustomed yourself," Hayne explained perceptively, "so much . . . to view things so exclusively in regard to their relations to yourself and your schemes that otherwise all is vapid—'weary, stale, flat and *unprofitable.*'" Like the fish that must keep moving and feeding to stay alive, Hammond required constant accomplishment, constant progress in his designs for self-advancement. Waiting to begin his career in Congress, he felt overwhelmed with uncertainty about how he should behave and how he would be received. Idleness only provided more time for worry.[7]

By midsummer, however, the young Carolinian had found a more specific focus for his anxieties about the future. Late in July a seemingly routine shipment of mail arrived in Charleston from New York. As he sorted the letters and packages, however, the postmaster rapidly became aware that the mails were full of antislavery tracts addressed to "a number of respectable gentlemen here." In the preceding three or four years, South Carolinians had learned of an emerging northern movement dedicated to the immediate abolition of slavery. But southerners had assumed that these northern groups were a tiny and unrepresentative radical fringe. Before 1835, abolition agitation, heinous as it might have appeared, had not been felt in any substantial way within the South. The mail campaign of the American Anti-Slavery Society represented a new departure. Although Charleston's postmaster impounded the incendiary publications, the people of the city were outraged by the news of this northern assault, and by evening a mob of three hundred had gathered to seize the offensive documents. The next night an enormous public bonfire destroyed the propaganda, lighting a fire of protest that would spread throughout the state and the South.[8]

Charleston's anger did not quickly subside; the city that vividly remembered the Denmark Vesey slave conspiracy of 1822 had not abandoned its fears of slave insurrection. To Charleston citizens, these abolitionist tracts seemed designed to

7. Hammond to I. W. Hayne, July 4, 1835, I. W. Hayne to Hammond, July, 1835, both in JHH Papers, LC.
8. Charleston *Mercury*, July 30, 31, 1835.

incite a new eruption of black violence. Public meetings convened to condemn the abolitionists and "to advise on the measures to be adopted"; vigilance committees met to protect the city; mobs roamed the streets in search of conspiratorial slaves or abolitionists; free blacks were watched and harassed; an emergency citizens council scrutinized and censored all mail.[9]

The hysteria that gripped Charleston did not penetrate with the same intensity to the up-country neighborhood around Silver Bluff. But like the rest of the state, Barnwell and Edgefield shared a determination to arrest this menace from the North. Hammond was moved to write an angry letter of protest to the editor of the New York *Evening Star* in hopes that this journal might communicate the feelings of the South to sympathetic northerners. "We do not believe," he proclaimed, "that all or perhaps a majority of the Northern people favour the views of these Incendiaries, but what does it boot us if they do not so long as they give them an asylum from which to hurl their murderous missiles." Hammond's solution was extreme: northern states must pass laws, he insisted, yielding the agitators to the southerners whose rights they had violated. "These men can be silenced in but one way—*Terror—death.* . . . This is the *only remedy.*"[10]

In private Hammond was less strident, more reflective about the future course of the South. The abolitionists' petition campaign seemed to him the sign of a new era in sectional relations, an era in which indirect assaults upon southern rights would be replaced by prolonged and direct attack on her most cherished and peculiar of institutions. The tariff had signaled the dangerous growth of federal power; Jackson's Force Bill had provided unmistakable evidence of the perilous increase in the strength of the federal executive; the penetration of abolition into the South by means of the U.S. mails represented only the most recent and alarming example of the threat to the right of the states to determine the nature of their domestic institutions.[11]

As national power steadily increased in relation to that of the states, what had once seemed local concerns began in the eyes of many Americans to appear the responsibility of the nation at large. Proponents of a strong union were coming to consider internal improvements, tariff regulation, and banking facilities as necessary functions of government. This new sense of centralized national power, moreover, was accompanied throughout much of the North by a growing

9. *Ibid.*
10. Hammond to M. M. Noah, August 19, 1835, in JHH Papers, LC.
11. Hammond to I. W. Hayne, September 21, 1835, I. W. Hayne to Hammond, August 13, 1835, both *ibid.*

evangelical zeal, a sweeping revival of religion that concerned itself not just with personal piety but with questions of temporal morality and human benevolence as well. This conjunction of nationalism in politics and evangelicalism in religion did not bode well for the slaveholder, for increasing numbers of Americans were coming to feel that Christian duty required them to act on behalf of the southern slave and that the federal government might offer a vehicle for this intervention. Southerners like Hammond believed that the only way to prevent federal meddling with slavery was to oppose every enhancement of federal power: to battle the tariff, to resist the right of the government to make internal improvements, even to oppose the establishment of a federal museum and research fund with the generous legacy English philanthropist Joseph Smithson had left to the United States. But with the abolitionist mail campaign of 1835, the South was no longer fighting a symbolic enemy; the slavery battle had at last been joined.

If the expansion of federal power could not be curbed, Hammond believed, the South must separate herself from a national union that promised only disaster for her domestic institutions. And in the meantime, the South had to begin systematically exploring the depth and meaning of her commitment to the slave system. Hammond himself had been reading Thomas Roderick Dew's 1832 justification of slavery in the South and had begun to consider the best line of defense for the peculiar institution. Southerners could no longer be just "abject apologists of slavery." The time had come to meet the question "openly, manfully, erect and roll back the misdirected tide of public sentiment. We must argue it somewhere. I have not made up my mind as to the best source for discussion . . . but it must be argued somewhere—& where to my mind is the chief difficulty. I have no doubt of victory but I wish to see such ground selected for the battle as will cover us best both behind and before and make the triumph as bloodless as possible." Hammond would depart for Washington in search of both a means to "distinguish myself" and an opportunity to present a newly assertive defense of slavery. His public career would thenceforth be tied to the escalating struggle over the South's peculiar institution.[12]

As fall arrived in Carolina, Hammond began to make arrangements for his journey north. Francis W. Pickens, a comrade from nullification battles and a colleague-to-be in Congress, invited Hammond and his family to join him and

12. Hammond to I. W. Hayne, September 21, 1835, Hammond to Dear Sir, September 4, 1835, both *ibid.*

Calhoun in a Washington boardinghouse. Pickens apologized that he and Calhoun necessarily lived more frugally than Hammond's fortune might allow, but Pickens suggested that good company and the opportunity for political consultation might compensate. Pickens, too, was ready for some decisive move in the approaching session. "We must strike *a high note & a bold one*. Much will be done in the next five months to decide the fate of this confederacy."[13]

Hammond could not set his date of departure precisely, for Catherine was pregnant again, due to deliver sometime late in October. By the end of November, Hammond was certain, she would be able to travel. William Campbell Preston wrote to invite the Hammonds to embark on a steamer from Charleston to Norfolk with him. The freshman legislator responded ruefully. William Cashel Hammond had arrived on October 30, making a family of four sons—all under the age of 4. This "gang," Hammond feared, behaved so badly as to be "insupportable to any body but myself." He had "had no idea," he reported ingenuously to Preston, "that children would be such a nuisance." His most recent house guests, he warned, had "complained dreadfully of them."[14]

Despite these disavowals, Hammond was eager to spend the three-day passage discussing events to come with the veteran legislator. "I should like for my own satisfaction to know which foot to put down first when I arrive there." Preston, a more experienced father as well as a more seasoned politician, was not easily put off. The two booked passage together on the steamship *South Carolina*.

After his long months of anticipation, Hammond now felt almost numb. "My enthusiasm in politics," he reported to Preston, "has departed from me." But he was quick to explain, "Altho I cannot say I have given up quite yet I am so much overwhelmed by a sense of the difficulties by which we of the South are surrounded that I hate to dwell upon the subject." The situation was indeed a difficult one, for the rising tide of antislavery agitation placed new demands on the South and on her representatives in the national councils. Yet it was not clear to Hammond or to the South more generally how to choose the proper ground on which to stand and fight. On their three-day cruise up the coast Hammond and Preston discussed these threats to their region and its institutions. But as they considered the variety of issues to be addressed by the new Congress,

13. Pickens to Hammond, October 2, 1835, *ibid*. John Boyd Edmunds, "Francis W. Pickens and South Carolina Politics" (M.A. thesis, University of South Carolina, 1964).

14. Hammond to M. C. M. Hammond, October 17, 1835, in JHH Papers, SCL; Hammond to William C. Preston, November 4, 1835, in JHH Papers, DU.

they could have had little inkling that a confrontation on slavery, that most fundamental of all the South's concerns, would come so soon. Nor did Hammond, however "unbounded" his ambition, really expect that as a freshman congressman he would serve as the South's first line of defense.[15]

15. Hammond to Preston, November 4, 1835, in JHH Papers, DU.

CHAPTER 9

Magnificent Intentions

W HEN CHARLES DICKENS visited Washington, D.C., in the 1840s, he
dubbed America's capital the "City of Magnificent Intentions" and
remarked upon "Spacious avenues, that begin in nothing and lead nowhere;
streets, mile long, that only want houses, roads and inhabitants; public buildings
that need but a public to be complete." Dickens was certainly not the first traveler to note the discrepancy between Pierre L'Enfant's monumental design for
the capital city and the reality of the rude town of muddy and rutted streets,
weed-filled vacant lots, and malarial bogs punctuated by a few imposing government buildings. During the early decades of the nineteenth century visitors both
foreign and domestic found Washington an object of mockery. A bleak and
primitive settlement, it lacked culture, commercial life, and even rural salubrity;
the "contaminated vapour" from the city's notorious swamps spread "agues and
other complaints" among its inhabitants.[1]

Yet when Hammond arrived late in 1835, the city was much improved over
the town that had existed only a few years before, not to mention the ruin that
had been left by the British depredations of 1814. Unlike many of his predecessors, Hammond would not have to negotiate the covered boardwalk that had
been the only passage between the House and Senate wings of the Capitol before

1. Charles Dickens, *American Notes, for General Circulation* (New York: Harper, 1842), 97;
John Melish, quoted in James Sterling Young, *The Washington Community, 1800–1828* (New York:
Harcourt, Brace, and World, 1966), 49. See John W. Reps, *Monumental Washington: The Planning
and Development of the Capital Center* (Princeton: Princeton University Press, 1967); Daniel Drake
Reiff, *Washington Architecture, 1791–1861: Problems in Development* (Washington, D.C.: U.S. Com-
mission of Fine Arts, 1971).

a central hall connecting the two chambers was completed in the late twenties. The building was now crowned by a copper-covered dome that attracted even a casual observer's eye to the legislature's newly impressive seat. Hammond enjoyed as well the convenience of the system of piped water installed in the Capitol in 1832 and the advantages of the macadam surface laid the same year over the dirt ruts of Pennsylvania Avenue, the broad boulevard that connected the legislative halls to the president's house, refurbished after the fires of 1814 and open for a seemingly incessant round of levees and balls. Even if a cow pasture and a frog pond stood behind the Capitol to the southeast, before it, along Pennsylvania Avenue, some of the nation's most illustrious citizens promenaded daily, accompanied by ladies arrayed in the most elegant of American and European fashions. Gradually Washington was becoming less isolated from the rest of the nation as the Jackson administration's egalitarian tone helped to create an atmosphere of governmental accessibility. And the completion of Washington's first railroad connection in the summer before Hammond's arrival promised to aid significantly in bringing the capital city into a central place in the nation's social and cultural as well as its political life.[2]

Like most congressmen of his day, Hammond moved into a Capitol Hill boardinghouse. Mrs. Lindenberger's establishment was, in all likelihood, one of the area's characteristic three-story brick houses, described by a contemporary as "decent without being in the least elegant." And like most of his colleagues, Hammond shared lodgings with members of his own state delegation, Senators Calhoun and Preston and Representatives Francis W. Pickens of Edgefield and Waddy Thompson of Greenville. These legislators dined together, passed their leisure time together, and shared political ideas and strategies over dinner or breakfast or before the evening's fire; the "mess" was the basic social and political unit of congressmen's lives.[3]

For the Carolina delegation, this boardinghouse interaction was especially significant, for the conflicts of nullification and the open hostility between Jackson and Calhoun had made these states' rights southerners the core of an emerg-

2. See Margaret Bayard Smith, *The First Forty Years of Washington Society* (New York: Scribner's, 1906); Eli F. Cooley, *A Description of the Etiquette at Washington City* (Philadelphia: L. Clarke, 1829); H. Paul Caemmerer, *Historic Washington: Capital of the Nation* (Washington, D.C.: Columbia History Society, 1948); Casimir Bohn, *Bohn's Handbook of Washington* (Washington, D.C.: C. Bohn, 1956); William Elliot, *The Washington Guide* (Washington, D.C.: Franck Taylor, 1837); Constance McLaughlin Green, *Washington: A History of the Capital, 1800–1950* (Princeton: Princeton University Press, 1962).
3. Young, *Washington Community*, 98–106.

ing opposition party. The Carolinians' antagonism to both the president and Martin Van Buren, Jackson's chosen successor in the approaching fall elections, isolated the residents of Mrs. Lindenberger's socially as well as politically within the capital, for the president was the center of Washington society. Nevertheless, the Carolinians boycotted Jackson's "splendid" Christmas Eve celebration and his New Year's Day reception as well. The southerners did make an appearance at a New Year's Eve reception given by Secretary of War Lewis Cass, whose political views were sufficiently sympathetic to allow the Carolinians to partake freely of the punch, dancing, and late-night supper he provided at his lodgings. But for the most part, the Carolinians' extremism removed them from the society of the many politicians and functionaries who did not clearly distinguish between nullification, secession, and treason.[4]

Catherine Hammond found her life especially circumscribed by these realities. "We Carolinians are in such bad odour here," she explained in a letter home, that she never even saw "a friendly smile." Timid, shy, and just twenty-one years old, she had not the courage to risk rebuff by making the ritual series of morning calls through which young congressional wives developed a circle of acquaintances in the city. Catherine remained at home when her husband could not be at her side to mediate her contacts with the bewildering formalities and animosities of the Washington world. She passed her days occupied with her children, with the other women of the Carolina "mess," and with whatever assistance she could offer James by dutifully copying his letters and compiling lists of constituents prominent enough to receive regular mailings of government documents. But Catherine executed these tedious tasks cheerfully, convinced of her husband's extraordinary talents and promise. "I sometimes fear," she wrote to her brother-in-law, "I feel too much confidence in his success."[5]

Hammond was not nearly so sanguine, and the conflict-charged atmosphere of the capital rendered him increasingly anxious to test his political mettle. But the congressional session seemed interminably slow in getting underway. When the national legislature convened on Monday, December 7, most of Hammond's housemates were not even in residence. After his steamship voyage with the Hammonds, Preston had not come directly to the capital, but had departed on a

4. Charleston *Mercury*, December 28, 1835, January 3, 1836; Cooley, *A Description of the Etiquette*, 11–13; Samuel C. Busey, *Pictures of the City of Washington in the Past* (Washington, D.C.: William Ballantyne and Sons, 1898), 358, 360.

5. Catherine Fitzsimons Hammond to M. C. M. Hammond, April 18, January 25, 1836, both in JHH Papers, SCL; Cooley, *A Description of the Etiquette*, 33.

round of visiting, and Thompson and Calhoun had also not yet arrived. Only Pickens was at hand to introduce his new colleague and to install him in a desk adjoining his own on the House floor.

The legislative chamber was a large semicircular room located on the second story of the Capitol. Twenty-four Corinthian columns spaced around the perimeter supported a gallery that seated one thousand eager spectators, for attendance at congressional sessions was a popular recreation. On the floor, rows of desks marked the places of the 224 members of the Twenty-Fourth House of Representatives. Few of these men had had time to develop any of the personal familiarity that might have created a community of understanding or interest, for the rate of turnover among congressmen was nearly 40 percent from election to election.[6]

The House opened its session by choosing James K. Polk as Speaker, appointing an official printer, filling its committees, and formally adopting its rules. As the legislators wrangled over whether or not they should be permitted to wear hats in the congressional chamber, the tardy members trickled in, one or two presenting credentials each day. By the middle of the month, Calhoun and Preston at last appeared in the Senate, and Congress gradually turned to substantive business.[7]

One day each week was regularly set aside in the House for the receipt of petitions. But December 16 was not like its predecessors. Early in the proceedings, John Fairfield of Maine rose to present two memorials from groups advocating the abolition of slavery in the District of Columbia. This in itself was a fairly routine gesture, for the existence of the peculiar institution in the national capital had long seemed distasteful to many northerners who found themselves forced personally to confront the realities of human bondage in the governmental seat. As abolition had grown in strength over the preceding several years, spokesmen for this movement had begun to direct their attention to the existence of slavery in the District. They reasoned that the abolition of slavery within the capital would appeal even to moderate northerners, and they felt little doubt that Congress, allocated the power to govern Washington, had the right to eliminate slavery within the District's borders. Because the agitation against slavery in Washington ingeniously sidestepped the explosive issue of the right of each state to determine its own domestic institutions, the antislavery

6. Young, *Washington Community*, 89–90.
7. Charleston *Courier*, December 17, 1835.

radicals hoped it would capture the support of many northerners far less militant than themselves. Petitions praying for the elimination of slavery in the District were not new, therefore, but in 1835 they appeared in the changed context of insurgent abolitionism and militant southern resistance.

Before 1835, such antislavery petitions had been customarily either tabled or referred by the House to its Committee on the District of Columbia, where they were ignored. A consensus in Congress that discussion of slavery could only produce threats to national unity prevented any consideration of the substantive contents of these appeals. But on December 16 William Slade of Vermont moved that the memorials Congressman Fairfield had presented be printed for distribution to the members, for he believed that many of his colleagues might be "favorably inclined in regard to the subject" if they were made "distinctly aware of its object." With an impassioned defense of the "respectability" of those submitting the petitions, Slade pressed his case. In face of such vehemence, a representative from New York quickly acted to redirect the discussion of the petitions from substantive to procedural grounds, declaring any futher consideration of the memorials "unprofitable" and moving successfully that the question be dropped.[8]

But the issue was not dead. Two days later William Jackson of Massachusetts presented his constituents' antislavery memorial. Hammond rose immediately and moved that the petition "be not received." This was a novel action as well as an escalation of southern demands, for Hammond was requesting not just that the House table the petition or relegate it to the oblivion of committee but that the legislature refuse to accept the memorial or even acknowledge its submission in the *House Journal*. Hammond intended that the House should testify to its constitutional inability to act in regard to slavery in the District by refusing even to acknowledge petitions on the question. As the *Congressional Globe* reported, Hammond argued that the Representatives' actions had thus far not inhibited citizens from pressing these abolition memorials "upon the House and upon the country," and he thought it "was not requiring too much of the House, to ask it to put a more decided seal of reprobation on them."[9]

The Speaker was confounded by Hammond's action, for he did not know whether such a motion was possible under the House rules of order, or how it should be handled under accepted procedure. While several members offered

8. *Congressional Globe*, 24th Cong., 1st Sess., Vol. III, p. 24.
9. *Ibid.*, 27.

suggestions about how to deal with the novel situation, others rose to address the explosive implications of this ostensibly procedural motion. Tennessee Representative Bailie Peyton regarded Hammond's position as a demand for stronger reassurance that Congress would take no action against slavery; it was an opportunity for the national legislature to eliminate any hint of equivocation. Peyton agreed that he wanted "no evasive votes . . . no propositions to lay on the table." But other southerners misunderstood Hammond's strategy and called for direct discussion of the abolition question. The series of confusing procedural votes that followed left Hammond's original motion, as one Virginia congressman described it, "hopelessly entangled by the rules of the House." Representative Wise of Virginia professed in dismay that he had voted contrary to his intentions because he had not known what question he was voting on, and even Hammond lost track of whether the Speaker had called for a division of the House on his motion to reject or on a motion to discuss the petition's contents. As the correspondent for the Charleston *Mercury* described the afternoon's proceedings, congressmen seemed to be "taking every opportunity to get as far as possible into the merits" of the forbidden topic of slavery. "They were repeatedly called to order, and at times, there was great confusion in the House."[10]

In the midst of this chaos, Hammond rose to defend the purity of his motives in producing such a tumult. He had not, he declared, made the "motion with any reference to party politics. . . . No! His object," read the *Globe*'s summary of his speech, "was a more sacred one. It was to protect the rights of his constituents and his own, and if they could not maintain them by the action of that House, they would maintain them by their own action." To refer the petitions to a committee, Hammond contended, gave the memorials a kind of legitimacy. He "would not treat that petition with so much respect."[11]

Samuel Beardsley of New York was appalled by the extremism of this declaration, studded as it was with implicit references to disunion. He could only conclude, he told his colleagues, that there were "fanatics and incendiaries at the South as well as the North, who hoped to profit by the agitation of this subject." In response to this slur, Pickens stood to defend his fellow Carolinian and with

10. *Ibid.*, 30; Charleston *Mercury*, December 28, 1835.
11. *Congressional Globe*, 24th Cong., 1st Sess., Vol. III, p. 31. See also Hammond's later insistence that he had intended a procedural action and did not mean to open the subject of slavery to direct discussion. Hammond, "Speech on the Justice of Receiving Petitions for the Abolition of Slavery in the District of Columbia," in Hammond, *Selections from the Letters and Speeches of the Hon. James Henry Hammond, of South Carolina* (New York: John F. Trow, 1866), 15.

biting sarcasm offered a militant statement vindicating the South's institutions against the "foul aspersion and calumny thrown upon them."[12]

Hammond's motion had opened a Pandora's box. Northern and southern extremists had both grown dissatisfied with the customary procedural evasion in regard to abolition petitions. The long-standing congressional consensus to exclude all discussion of slavery was disintegrating. Hammond had not intended, he stated on the floor of the House, "to throw a fire-brand" into Congress, but he had in fact done just that. When the House adjourned for the weekend on December 18 with the Carolinian's motion still pending, the legislators knew that the issue would not be easily or quickly laid to rest. The ominously divisive question of slavery had appeared once again on the floor of Congress. It had not been discussed there in any depth since the Missouri debates of 1819, when it had rung out, as Jefferson described it, like a "firebell in the night" threatening the conflagration of the Union.[13]

What were Hammond's motives in introducing this disruptive issue? Whom had he consulted? How did he plan to proceed? Most historians have seen Hammond's motion as an action taken upon instructions from John C. Calhoun, who, embittered by his break with Jackson, sought to destroy Martin Van Buren, the president's heir apparent. The effort to reject abolition petitions in Congress, some historians have argued, was Calhoun's means of forcing Van Buren, straddling the slavery issue in hopes of winning votes both North and South, to take a firm public position on the constitutional powers of Congress in regard to the peculiar institution. Once the issue was raised prominently in Congress, it would be interjected into the campaign, and Van Buren would have to take a stand that, Calhoun assumed, would necessarily displease either North or South and thus divide the Democratic party. Certainly many observers, including the Charleston *Mercury*, saw that flushing out Van Buren could be one beneficial outcome of the petition endeavor. And it might indeed have been a major factor influencing Calhoun's support for the undertaking.[14]

12. *Congressional Globe*, 24th Cong., 1st Sess., Vol. III, p. 33.
13. *ibid.*, 31.
14. Charleston *Mercury*, February 25, 1836; Charles M. Wiltse, *John C. Calhoun, Nullifier, 1829–1839* (Indianapolis: Bobbs-Merrill, 1949), 281. I agree with George Rable that Wiltse overstates Calhoun's influence over Hammond, George C. Rable, "Slavery, Politics, and the South: The Gag Rule as a Case Study," *Capitol Studies*, III (Fall, 1975), 69–88. See also William W. Freehling, *Prelude to Civil War: The Nullification Controversy in South Carolina, 1816–1836* (New York: Harper and Row, 1965), 350; Robert P. Ludlum, "The Antislavery 'Gag-Rule': History and Argument," *Journal of Negro History*, XXVI (January, 1941), 203–43.

But Hammond was not, as Calhoun's biographer Charles Wiltse would have him, simply a lieutenant for the older statesman. Calhoun had only been back in Washington for two days when Hammond took his bold stance, and they had had little time to coordinate a plan of action. Indeed, the confusion that occurred after Hammond's initial motion and his own lack of preparation and knowledge about the procedural rules that were to serve as the vehicle of his assault indicate that Hammond acted, as he later described, "more from impulse than reflection." His speeches, his wife explained to Marcellus, "were short as you remarked" because "they were accidental and unprepared for." It is unlikely, as well, that Hammond acted with Van Buren in mind. With no political experience outside Carolina's "no-party" system, Hammond was still largely innocent about the workings of national parties and even critical of Calhoun's efforts to influence presidential politics on behalf of his own ambitions. Schooled in the public life of Carolina, Hammond tended to view national issues in abstract and constitutional terms. Indeed, Hammond was far more radical than Calhoun. In the days of nullification, he had regarded violent resistance and secession as real and, in many ways, desirable possibilities at a time when Calhoun considered military conflict an outcome to be avoided at almost any cost. Hammond's motion to reject the abolition petitions arose from his belief that the South must immediately either procure adequate constitutional safeguards for slavery or secede. Unlike some southerners, such as Thomas Cooper, who were already unequivocally committed to southern nationalism, Hammond preferred if possible to keep South Carolina in the United States. But not at any price. If the House assumed the right to legislate in regard to slavery, Hammond warned, "I will go home to preach, and if I can to practice disunion, and civil war, if needs be." On the House floor he baldly asserted, "We may have to dissolve the Union." The hostility Hammond had felt directed toward him as a South Carolinian since his arrival in the capital made him all the more reluctant to trust implicit understandings and expressions of goodwill from the North. He insisted simply that the slavery question be directly confronted and settled once and for all.[15]

Hammond's desire to secure congressional acknowledgment of its constitu-

15. Hammond Diary (MS in JHH Papers, LC), February 7, 1841. See also his description of his action as "impromptu." Hammond to M. C. M. Hammond, December 25, 1835, Catherine Fitzsimons Hammond to M. C. M. Hammond, January 25, 1836, both in JHH Papers, SCL; Hammond, *Selections from the Letters and Speeches*, 35. Note that others wrote Hammond about Van Buren, but Hammond himself never mentioned him.

John C. Calhoun, painted by James A. Bogle.

tional inability to act against slavery would have appealed to Calhoun. The senator had sought throughout his career to use the safeguards of the Constitution to keep the South within the Union. But while their goals and perceptions overlapped on the desirability of this measure, Calhoun and Hammond had otherwise separate agendas. While Hammond contemplated secession as a possible ultimate outcome of the congressional confrontation, Calhoun, bitterly opposed to disunion, concentrated on the opportunity to exact vengeance from Van Buren. While Calhoun was attempting to preserve his national political reputation, Hammond had no such need to inhibit his sectional zeal. He initially acted independently of Calhoun in the petition controversy, attracting as a result of his motions a wide spectrum of support. Some of his most zealous backers were in fact Carolina radicals who found Calhoun's political positions too moderate and hoped to have discovered in Hammond a counterweight. During December of 1835 and the early months of 1836, Hammond received a stream of letters from Thomas Cooper, who now believed secession the only remedy, and from Columbia *Telescope* editor Edward William Johnston. The South Carolina journalist urged Hammond to press his states' rights position regardless of Calhoun, whose ambition always seemed to limit the pursuit of southern interests. "Your views about . . . Calhoun," Johnston wrote Hammond in the midst of the petition affair, were "stolen, I think from myself. I have been steadily cursing Calhoun . . . for precisely this thing. We work on . . . and make a doctrine popular. Of a sudden, he comes forward, seizes it . . . ruins the impression which might have been made on the country, by stitching the whole affair to his own political kite-tail." When on January 7 Calhoun requested the Senate to adopt the stance on petitions that Hammond had proposed in the House nearly three weeks before, he was, Johnston's letter suggests, endeavoring to co-opt and control a movement already begun by others whose extremism threatened to undermine the Carolina senator's long-cherished presidential hopes.[16]

Temperamentally unsuited to be a follower, Hammond kept his own counsel in the petition controversy, speaking more moderately than Cooper wished, while at the same time acting with considerable independence from Calhoun. Deeply suspicious of Calhoun and his seemingly self-interested aversion to disunion, Hammond was far from being the older statesman's lieutenant in the congressional battle. The two cooperated as their separate interests coincided, but Hammond acted with his own purposes and ambitions foremost in his mind.

When the House reconvened on Monday, December 21, after its weekend

16. Edward William Johnston to Hammond, February 28, 1836 (see also February 20, March 9, 24, 1836), Thomas Cooper to Hammond, December 15, 17, 1835, January 8, February 6, 12, March 2, 20, 27, 31, April 7, 11, 1836, all in JHH Papers, LC. Unfortunately, the letter from Hammond that prompted Johnston's criticisms of Calhoun seems not to have survived. For another interpretation of Hammond's role in the gag-rule fight, see Lee Benson, "Explanations of American Civil War Causation: A Critical Assessment and a Modest Proposal to Reorient and Reorganize the Social Sciences," in Benson, *Toward the Scientific Study of History: Selected Essays* (Philadelphia: J. B. Lippincott, 1972).

recess, the unresolved issue of the petitions quickly arose again. Over the weekend Wise of Virginia had evidently been briefed by the Carolinians, for he now argued for an explicit acknowledgment of Congress' constitutional inability to legislate on slavery. John Quincy Adams of Massachusetts, sympathetic to the antislavery cause, had also been considering the issues during the two-day adjournment. Now he eloquently argued that Hammond's proposal would deny the constitutional rights of American citizens. In "deference to the right of petition, of freedom of speech, of freedom of the press and freedom of religion," Adams entreated Congress to defeat Hammond's motion. Over the next several days, other business of the House lay unattended as its members wrangled over this threatening question. Even the Christmas recess only postponed the heated debates. On January 18 Adams presented an abolition memorial at the weekly petition day. Hammond once again moved to reject and "gave notice that he would make the same motion in every similar case, until he could procure a direct vote on the subject." From the other end of the political spectrum, Adams warned his colleagues that they were "mistaken if they thought that by putting this question off from week to week they would get rid of it." With each memorial he presented, Adams now delivered an accompanying address on the "sacred right of petition." One exasperated congressman was at last moved to remark that the House seemed to have adopted a new daily order of business: prayers, reading of the *Journal*, and Mr. Adams' speech.[17]

At home in Carolina, Hammond's position was widely praised. As the Charleston *Mercury* explained to its readers, "there is now a prospect of a final decision by Congress as to the extent of its powers regarding slavery." Because of Hammond's actions, the South might succeed in securing explicit assurances of constitutional safeguards for slavery; his motion would make impossible any further "dodging the question."[18]

In reality the situation in the House of Representatives had by late January reached a kind of stalemate, for neither Hammond's nor Adams' tactics had succeeded in forcing the House to shift its traditional policy of evasion. But Hammond had determined to take more decisive action. Heretofore his motions had been essentially procedural, and he had refrained from addressing in depth the substantive issues of slavery and abolition that underlay his crusade. Nor had he had an opportunity fully to display his oratorical and intellectual capabilities; his

17. *Congressional Globe*, 24th Cong. 1st Sess., Vol. III, pp.. 40, 116, 124.
18. Charleston *Mercury*, January 12, 1836.

remarks on the House floor had thus far all been relatively brief contributions to a fast-moving and lively debate.

On February 1, the coldest day yet in an uncommonly snowy Washington winter, Hammond rose from his desk to deliver a two-hour address on the menace of abolitionism. The time had come for him to explain the background of the position he had assumed, to show that the most fundamental issue at hand was not the right of petition, but the South's right to survival. Speaking during much of his address without notes, Hammond presented an impassioned description of his dire apprehensions for the future. To those of his colleagues who had dismissed the abolition movement as the work of a few disreputable fanatics, Hammond conveyed the rapidity of the spread of abolition doctrines and societies, the increasingly wide basis of its acceptance in the North, and the fear these developments engendered in the South. The petitions submitted to the House, he contended, were part of a "systematic plan of operations, intended to subvert the institutions of the South" and could only succeed in dissolving "in blood the bonds of this Confederacy." In a single day that winter, he noted, more petitions had arrived in Washington than had been seen by the previous four sessions of Congress. "A disciplined corps," Hammond concluded, was organizing a conspiracy. For those of his colleagues unfamiliar with the methods of these agitators, Hammond provided a series of exhibits designed to demonstrate abolitionism's dangerous mob appeal. The Carolinian displayed copies of antislavery hymnals, almanacs, and a primer entitled *The Slave's Friend*, as well as such newspapers as the *Emancipator*, *Antislavery Record*, and *Liberator*, from which he read choice incendiary excerpts.

To counter the assertions of antislavery radicals, Hammond embarked on a defense of his region's institutions that marked a new departure in the American Congress. He offered no apologies, but instead delivered the first explicit defense of slavery as a positive good that the national legislature had ever heard. The doctrines elaborated during the previous several years in the proslavery tracts of essayists Thomas Dew and William Harper now appeared in a specifically political context as weapons in the South's defense. Slavery, Hammond declared boldly, "is no evil. On the contrary, I believe it to be the greatest of all the great blessings which a kind Providence has bestowed upon our glorious region." It had produced, he contended, "the highest toned, the purest, best organization of society that has ever existed on the face of the earth." The natural hierarchy within southern society replicated the inequalities of "moral and physical creation." Thus a republican "*Government of the best*," an "aristocracy of talents, of virtue, of generosity, and courage," ruled over an inferior race of blacks, who were, he asserted, as contented a people as existed on earth.[19]

But this admirable society was under attack by irresponsible agitators, just as civilization more generally was under siege by the "Mob," the "ignorant, uneducated, semi-barbarous mass" determined to use the rhetoric of equality to destroy rights of property throughout the world. The North must act to reassure the South by suppressing this threat to southern institutions. Freedom of speech or petition did not include the right to incite violence or destruction. Northern states must pass laws against promulgation of incendiary publications, and the House must discourage agitators by refusing to receive their petitions. Hammond concluded with an acknowledgment that his open discussion of slavery on the floor of the House would inaugurate a new era in national politics.

I have touched on topics to-day which have not heretofore been broached within these walls. In thus departing from the usual silence of the South upon this subject, it may be thought that I have gone too far. But times have changed. . . . We cannot, in my judgment, avoid this danger longer, by closing our eyes upon it, and lulling our people into a false security. Nor can we justify ourselves before the world for the course which we may be compelled to take in order to maintain our rights without boldly declaring what those rights are, defining them and showing that they are inestimable.[20]

Before leaving South Carolina, Hammond had determined to meet the slavery issue "openly" and "manfully erect" in order to "roll back the misdirected tide of public sentiment." The petition issue had simply provided the ground on which he had taken his stand. And it had focused national attention upon him. The Charleston *Courier* declared him "a very promising young man"; the Alexandria, Virginia, *Gazette* proclaimed his "chasteness and elegance of language" to be the mark of "the scholar and the perfect gentleman"; and even the Baltimore *Patriot*, which considered his position too extreme, praised Hammond as a "very talented and unusually agreeable speaker" before condemning his "injudicious and impolitic allusions" certain to "do more harm than good to the cause he was advocating."[21]

Despite its eloquence, Hammond's speech of February 1 brought no solution to the continuing conflict in the House. But three days later, a member of the Carolina delegation introduced a thunderbolt into the proceedings. Henry Lau-

19. *Congressional Globe*, 24th Cong., 1st Sess., Vol. III, Appendix, pp. 565, 566.
20. *Ibid.*, 567.
21. Hammond to I. W. Hayne, September 21, 1835, in JHH Papers, LC. For newspaper reactions, see Charleston *Courier*, February 15, 1836, Hammond Scrapbook (MS vol. bd., 1825–40, JHH Papers, SCL), which includes clippings on the petition fight.

rens Pinckney was a Charlestonian descended from two of the state's most prominent families. A former editor of the *Mercury*, he had been a loyal nullifier and a central figure among Charleston's radicals. Short and heavyset, he did not look the aristocrat and had built up a considerable popular following among the tradesmen and mechanics of his native city. On February 4, he offered a resolution that, he asserted, would solve the conflict over slavery petitions. Pinckney proposed that all such memorials be referred to a select committee instructed to report that Congress had no power over slavery in the states, and that interference with the peculiar institution in the District of Columbia would be "impolitic."[22]

As they listened to these proposals from their Carolina colleague, Hammond and Pickens were aghast. Pinckney had mentioned these ideas to Hammond, who had vehemently discouraged him from taking such a position. Now the Charlestonian was acting in isolation from—even in opposition to—the majority of his state delegation. For the next three days the residents of Mrs. Lindenberger's tried to pressure Pinckney into withdrawing his resolution, for the measure seemed clearly to reject their contention that Congress had no constitutional authority over slavery in the District. Pinckney's proposal merely declared that congressional intervention in slavery in Washington would be "inexpedient."[23]

The Charlestonian's obdurate refusal to yield to Calhoun's pressure convinced Hammond and his messmates that Pinckney was not acting alone. The move seemed inspired by Van Buren, who was seeking a means of escape from the trap in which Calhoun had ensnared him. A compromise solution of the petition crisis would enable Van Buren to retain both southern and northern support and thus prevent a split in the Democratic party that would be fatal to his presidential candidacy. Of greater concern to Hammond, it would allow the slavery issue to be evaded in the approaching election; the South's need for reassurance and security would not be met. Pinckney's action seemed like treason to these angry Carolinians.[24]

When the House turned to the issue once again the following Monday, Pinckney moved to defend his position against the already swelling tide of southern criticism. The petition crisis of the past six weeks, he argued, had been

22. *Congressional Globe*, 24th Cong., 1st Sess., Vol. III, p. 165; Hammond to Editor, Charleston *Courier*, March 21, 1836, in JHH Papers, LC.
23. *Congressional Globe*, 24th Cong., 1st Sess., Vol. III, p. 165.
24. Charleston *Mercury*, February 25, 1836; Hammond Scrapbook.

a means of "wasting and dissipating their strength upon mere abstraction to the extreme excitement of the South and danger to the Union." Pinckney wished to arrest congressional discussion of slavery and put down fanaticism by seeking a "practical" resolution to the controversy. In direct defiance of Calhoun, Pinckney declared that whether his motion was "treason or not, in the opinion of a certain individual," he had acted with the "concurrence of a large number of members from the Southern states." Calhoun and Hammond, he implied, had taken a position far too radical to truly represent their region.[25]

Hammond's response on the House floor reflected both his own feelings and those of his messmates. It was "extremely unpleasant," he declared, "to see gentlemen, coming from the same section of the country, and members of the same delegation, so utterly opposed to each other, as his colleague and himself." Such divisions within the South not only saddened but alarmed Hammond and Calhoun, for they had repeatedly contended that the unity of their section was the first requirement for its defense. How could they hope to impress the North with the dangers of abolitionism when they could not even convince fellow members of their own delegation?[26]

Although Pinckney tried to minimize the significance of the procedural issues Hammond had been pressing for the past month, Hammond insisted that their differences over the "mode of proceeding" involved conflict over the "deepest and most important principles." The report Pinckney was requesting from the House, Hammond argued, would "act as the entering wedge for future legislation" on slavery by Congress. "I can assure this House that a Union based upon the principles of that resolution cannot stand. We cannot give up rights and consent to hold our property at your will."[27]

Despite Hammond's objections, Pinckney's resolution to establish a committee to report on the means of handling antislavery petitions passed overwhelmingly. The abolition issue was now removed from the House floor. Hammond and Pickens had lost their battle, defeated not by a northerner, but by a member of their own delegation. Late in the spring Pinckney's committee would report essentially the same measures he had proposed; the propositions claimed no constitutional prohibition on congressional action in regard to slavery in the District of Columbia. Dubbed the "gag rule" because they provided that all abo-

25. *Congressional Globe*, 24th Cong., 1st Sess., Vol. III, p. 170. See also *Register of Debates in Congress* (Washington, D.C.: Gales and Seaton, 1836), Vol. XII, Pt. 2, pp. 2492–500.
26. *Congressional Globe*, 24th Cong., 1st Sess., Vol. III, p. 171.
27. *Ibid.*; *Register of Debates*, Vol. XII, Pt. 2, p. 2497.

lition petitions should be received but tabled without discussion, the Pinckney resolutions prevented substantive consideration of slavery in the House until they were rescinded in 1844. The overall effect of the measure was damaging to the South but not in the way Hammond had anticipated. At the same time that it yielded the constitutional issue Hammond and Calhoun had regarded as so important, Pinckney's propositions ultimately worked to strengthen abolitionism. The gag rule became an important and effective focus of agitation for the antislavery movement, which claimed that just as southerners denied rights to their slaves, so they were obstructing freedom of speech and petition in the national legislature. The eventual outcome of Hammond's motion of December 18 was thus not to enhance the South's sense of security, but to bring her one step closer to the crisis of fear that would precipitate her out of the Union.[28]

States' rights southerners and Carolinians in particular greeted Pinckney's motion of February 4 with an outburst of bitter condemnation. Even the *Mercury* rebuked its former editor and demanded to know "what was this man thinking about?" The only possible explanation seemed that Pinckney had sold out to Van Buren and had been "swept . . . within the current of that maelstrom of national corruption" represented by the system of political parties and their spoils. But if Pinckney's motivations remained unclear, the import of his action was all too obvious. "He has sacrificed the South," the *Mercury* proclaimed. The Richmond *Whig* was even more blunt: the "abolitionists, through Pinckney's resolution, have obtained a victory which they never dreamed of, and which they never aspired to."[29]

In comparison to this "Mis-Representative," Congressmen Hammond and Pickens appeared especially praiseworthy, "true models of Carolina patriotism and devotion," as a public meeting of Edgefield citizens hailed them. Hammond's constituents in Barnwell held a similar gathering to pass resolutions acclaiming the conduct of their representative. Pinckney's vigorous efforts to defend himself against this ground swell of popular outrage were in vain. The Charlestonian was soundly defeated in the next congressional election.[30]

What Pinckney had lost in Carolina reputation and public support, Hammond had more than gained. Eyes turned to the young congressman as a poten-

---

28. On the long-term effects of the gag rule, see Benson, "Explanations of American Civil War Causation," and Ludlum, "The Antislavery 'Gag-rule.'"

29. Charleston *Mercury*, February 25, 1836; Hammond Scrapbook.

30. Edgefield *Advertiser*, March 10, 1836. Pinckney had some support from the *Courier* and from former unionists in South Carolina. See Robert Y. Hayne to Hammond, February 18, 1836, in JHH Papers, LC.

tial spokesman in the House for the states' rights cause. Some speculated he might eventually be the successor to the aging Calhoun as the voice of the South. But Hammond was not long to occupy this pinnacle of hopes. On February 25, while walking in the Capitol with Samuel Hoar of Massachusetts, he was suddenly struck by a violent "rush of blood to the head & came near going off." Hoar carried Hammond to the congressional post office, just off the second-story corridor. A doctor summoned to the scene bled Hammond and administered half a pint of brandy to revive him. Friends called a hack and sent him home.[31]

Hammond was frightened by the incident, for he feared it marked a new and acute phase of what had previously been a minor chronic complaint. Even as a child he had been plagued by nightmares, and he had long regarded himself as a dyspeptic, one of many in the nineteenth century who suffered throughout life from a vague and protean complex of digestive complaints readily acknowledged to be somehow seated in the nerves. The origins of his latest crisis seemed to Hammond all too clear. "It is anxiety that has been torturing me & undermining my health." The tension created by the petition controversy had become too much for him. But, curiously, his initial response to the dramatic legislative confrontation had been just the opposite. "My husband's health," Catherine had written Marcellus on January 25, "has been better than usual—excitement agrees with him." Only after the February 1 address and the subsequent outpouring of acclaim did Hammond find himself "nervous, melancholy and dreadfully dyspeptic." Nothing was ever more difficult for him than coping with success, for any achievement seemed only to increase the burden of the expectations his father had first fixed upon him. His election as Euphradian orator had filled him with anxiety; his victorious campaign for Congress had left him less jubilant about his triumph than fearful about his future political performance. In the gag-rule controversy, success seemed with even more inevitability to presage failure. After Hammond's impressive debut, he could think of no logical next step. Pinckney's move had left Hammond without any attractive options. This time it was not just irrational anxiety that made him worry that triumph would swiftly be followed by debacle. His subjective fears intensified as he encountered an objective political impasse. Pinckney's propositions appealed to moderate southerners, less inclined to constitutional abstractions than Hammond, as a satis-

31. Hammond to M. C. M. Hammond, February 28, 1836, in JHH Papers, SCL; Hammond Diary (LC), December 5, 1844. There is some confusion about whether the incident took place on February 25 or 26, but Hammond refers to the 25th as the anniversary of his attack. Hammond European Diary (MS vol. bd., 1836–37, JHH Papers, SCL), Vol. I, February 25, 1837.

factory compromise. The erosion of this base of less-radical support pushed Hammond toward the logic of secession. Without constitutional guarantees, he had argued, it was the South's only choice. But Hammond was not yet comfortable advocating out-and-out disunion; he had not embraced the extremism of a Cooper. The South seemed to Hammond too divided to achieve independence without "ruin." Although the failure of his efforts in the House made him fear secession "must take place" before long, he confessed that he looked forward "with deep foreboding" to such an event. Union and disunion seemed equally dangerous. And the broad and gratifying consensus of Carolina support that his ingenious action had initially mobilized was weakening under the pressure of Pinckney's compromise proposals. Already stripped of many moderate supporters, Hammond faced a choice between accepting defeat by surrendering quietly and dropping the petition issue or assuming a position so radical as to guarantee the loss of even more allies, including, in all likelihood, the powerful Calhoun. He had overreached himself. Like Icarus he had flown too high. In his desire for public attention he had provoked a battle that he was not politically able to win but was too proud to lose.[32]

Only illness offered Hammond a means of escaping an impossible dead end. His betrayal by Pinckney in the service of party politics and intersectional harmony had not only blocked the South's achievement of security for slavery but revealed the deep fissures throughout the region and even within South Carolina. It appeared to Hammond not just a traitorous abandonment of principle by a member of his own delegation but an intolerable personal humiliation. Behind it all, Hammond believed, lay the corrupt political culture and the party system that increasingly thrived in the national capital. Hammond would leave Washington with intense "bitterness of feeling" about the circumstances of public life that had made this defeat possible.[33]

As Pinckney's committee deliberated on its report and the House struggled over a contested congressional election in North Carolina, the admission of Arkansas to statehood, and the surplus in the Treasury, Hammond remained confined to his room, taking regular doses of the mercury compound calomel. The medicine quickly had its desired effect, and Hammond started to exhibit

32. Hammond Diary (LC), May 16, 1836; Catherine Fitzsimons Hammond to M. C. M. Hammond, January 25, 1836, in JHH Papers, SCL.
33. Cooper to Hammond, January 8, 1836, Hammond to Tucker, March 11, 1836, in JHH Papers, LC; Hammond Diary (LC), April 18, 1836; Hammond European Diary, II, November 15, 1837.

the state of "salivation" that contemporary physicians regarded as a sign of a positive alteration in the balance of his bodily fluids. In fact he was displaying the first signs of mercury poisoning.

By the beginning of April, however, he felt able to leave his room, even though he remained fearful of another attack. On the eighth of the month he returned to the Capitol, but, as Catherine related, "seemed afraid to venture into the Hall he went only into the Library for a short time." As he later explained to Pickens, "The first time I ever put my foot in the Representative Hall I felt my head swim. I never entered it without a similar sensation." Hammond soon began to doubt whether he would ever go onto the floor of Congress again. Disappointed and frustrated, he described himself with characteristic romantic self-pity as "Broken down at Twenty-Eight . . . one foot in the grave—Dying of decay in the very blossom," and remarked, "Twelve years I have been an invalid."[34]

At last Hammond determined to consult with the most prominent and respected specialists he could find. "If these . . . can do nothing for me—it is all over." Washington possessed only the most rudimentary medical facilities; so in mid-April Hammond traveled to Philadelphia. Previously acquainted with no settlements larger than Columbia, Charleston, or the still-rustic national capital, Hammond was dazzled by his encounter with a real city. For the first time in weeks, he was distracted from introspection about the state of his health. Chestnut Street seemed nothing short of "superb" with its "Houses—Merchandize—People"—all very fine; men could "converse fluently [and] it seems intelligibly about subjects which I . . . cannot fathom." The technological ingenuity of the municipal waterworks astounded him, and he even found that the women were the most beautiful he had ever beheld. "There is no place like Philadelphia that I have seen."[35]

But the magical city promised no certain cure for his complaint. Doctors Granville Pattison and Philip Syng Physick, among the most prominent physicians of their day, could offer little relief for Hammond's acidic stomach, his intermittent pains in intestine and groin, or his digestive difficulties. Physick seemed not even to take Hammond's morbid fears seriously. "To him I am one of

34. Catherine Fitzsimons Hammond to M. C. M. Hammond, March 7, April 8, 1836, in JHH Papers, SCL; Hammond to Francis W. Pickens, May 15, 1839, in JHH Papers, LC; Hammond Diary (LC), April 12, 1836.
35. Hammond Diary (LC), April 17, 15, 1836.

the herd. . . . True he does not laugh at me but—he *doubts* a great deal." The two confirmed Hammond's own conviction that his ailment was chiefly nervous in origin. "Your complaints," Pattison concluded, "are dependent on *Functional* not on organic disease." A trip of a year or two in Europe, Physick advised, was the most likely means to restore his health.[36]

Hammond was uncertain how to react to this advice, uncertain how seriously he wished to take his symptoms or how to weigh them against his commitment to politics and his career. A prolonged absence abroad, he knew, "will throw me entirely out of the line of promotion" in Congress. But, he mused, "I shall hardly be able to fulfil my public duties at this time with increased credit to myself, & I had better resign while my reputation or rather the prospects of a reputation for me are high." Besides, he was disillusioned with Washington. "Talent, virtue, acquirement are all obscured there by overwhelming party intrigue, bluster, blackguardism." The scramble for offices, the widespread corruption, the low level of political discourse all impelled him toward resigning. As he considered the prospect of abandoning "those high purposes of life, for which only . . . existence was worth preserving," he began to feel a growing sense of relief. "In fact to continue in public life now," he concluded after his deliberations, "is for a thousand reasons irksome & disagreeable." He decided he would take the Philadelphia physicians' advice. "Sweet dream of Ambition," he proclaimed in a statement filled with his ambivalence about his public career, "you will be over [and] I shall have seen the end of all my anxieties and toils." Illness could be his means of escape.[37]

Hammond wasted no time. Rejoining his family in Washington, he made immediate preparations to return to South Carolina and settle his affairs. In the fortnight after his May 4 arrival at Silver Bluff, Hammond succeeded in arranging the care of both his business and his family during what he thought might be an absence of two years. Associates in Augusta would help look after plantation matters; Marcellus would be occupied with army service; John was placed as an apprentice in a merchant firm in Charleston; and Pierce Butler took over his racing stock. The most difficult decision, however, was what to do about his own little boys. Taking them seemed impossible, for Catherine could not cope with

36. Hammond Medical Diary (MS vol. bd., 1836–37, JHH Papers, SCL); Hammond Diary (LC), April 14, 1836; Granville Pattison to Hammond, April 19, 1836, in JHH Papers, SCL; Philip Syng Physick to Hammond, April 19, 1836, in JHH Papers, LC.
37. Hammond Diary (LC), April 14, 1836; Hammond to M. C. M. Hammond, August 6, 1839, in JHH Papers, LC; Hammond Diary (LC), April 19, 1836.

them all in unfamiliar lands where servants were sure to be a problem. At last the Hammonds decided that Harry, then four years old, would accompany his parents while his brothers remained behind under the alternating care of James's and Catherine's mothers. Hammond hired a white nurse to assume the day-to-day burdens of the children's management.[38]

On May 18 the travelers took their leave of Silver Bluff. Hammond fearfully contemplated what the uncertain future might bring. Perhaps when he returned from Europe, he would be well enough to enter politics again. In any case, he determined, he would have to look beyond Silver Bluff. "I cannot fix my own & the destiny of my children here. The soil is too thin—the vicinage too poor & ignorant & rude." Perhaps he would move west to plant the rich alluvial cotton lands of Alabama, Mississippi, or Texas. Or perhaps, he worried in morbid self-absorption, it was God's intention that he not return at all.[39]

When an enthusiastic group of his constituents gathered on May 26 in Columbia to pass a resolution regretting "the determination of Hon. James H. Hammond to retire from public life," the young Carolinian was already far away in Washington, collecting his back pay from Congress and acquiring letters of introduction to ease his way in Europe. On June 7 the three Hammonds left the capital to visit Marcellus briefly at West Point and see the sights of Albany, Saratoga, Boston, and New Haven before boarding their ship in New York. Hammond's "sweet dream" of political ambition was, at least temporarily, put aside. In Washington, Hammond's grand designs had fared little better than had those of Pierre L'Enfant. Both sets of plans would long remain unfulfilled, similar tributes to the disappointments so often produced by "magnificent intentions."[40]

38. Hammond to Pierce Mason Butler, May 20, 1836, in Pierce Mason Butler Papers, SCL; Hammond to M. C. M. Hammond, April 10, 23, 25, 1836, Hammond to John Fox Hammond, July 14, 1836, "Instructions from J. H. Hammond on Leaving for Europe, 1836" (MS vol. bd., 1836), all in JHH Papers, SCL.
39. Hammond to Tucker, June 5, 1836, in Tucker-Coleman Papers, Earl Gregg Swem Memorial Library, College of William and Mary, Williamsburg, Va.; Hammond Diary (LC), May 16, 1836.
40. Hammond Travelling Account (MS vol. bd., 1836–37, JHH Papers, SCL).

CHAPTER 10

A Slaveowner in a Free Society

FOR THE ANTEBELLUM AMERICAN, a European journey was an event of far greater moment than it has become in our modern world of rapid, comfortable, and economical travel. The grand tour was usually the occasion of a lifetime. Expected to shape indelibly the voyager's character and attitudes, the journey was an episode recorded, remembered, and widely shared through the popular nineteenth-century genre of the travel account. When on July 16, 1836, James Henry Hammond stood on the deck of the packet ship *England* and sailed out of the "magnificent bay of New York," he entertained an assortment of expectations instilled in him by the writings and firsthand accounts of others who had taken this voyage before him. Although his trip had been prescribed as therapy, Hammond's anticipations of the coming months did not focus exclusively on a restoration of his physical well-being. His decision to undertake the risk and discomfort of travel arose from his social and intellectual aspirations as well as his "search after health." A trip to Europe served as evidence of a voyager's prosperity and as testimony to his cultivation and taste, for the expense was beyond the means of all but a privileged and enlightened few. If Hammond was not to be in Congress pursuing his political ambitions, he could at least be advancing his claims to social and cultural preeminence; he would be improving not just his health, but his mind and his status.[1]

1. James Henry Hammond European Diary, I (MS vol. bd., 1836–37, JHH Papers, SCL), August 7, 1836; Hammond Medical Diary (MS vol. bd., 1836–37, JHH Papers, SCL). On the packet ship Hammond took from New York, two of the other passengers were keeping journals, and one of these was eventually published. Hammond described his own journal as protection lest his shipmates

The first experience of Hammond's therapeutic journey, however, was illness even more debilitating than his previous complaints. On their twenty-day passage to Liverpool, James and Catherine did not once go to the dining room. Rough seas kept them too bilious to leave their beds, and they passed their time "grumbling and repining." From cots placed on the deck they watched Harry, untouched by seasickness, thoroughly enjoying his ocean adventure and winning the favor of the fifteen other passengers aboard.[2]

When the ship docked in Liverpool, the Hammonds disembarked with relief, grateful to be on dry land again. Almost as soon as they acquired clothing warm enough for the unexpectedly chilly English summer, they were off toward London. Uninterested in the busy port city of Liverpool, James was eager to reach Parliament while it was still in session. But on their route through the countryside, they passed by such intriguing sights that Hammond almost forgot this original determination. Even the promise of a certain cure from a specialist Hammond stopped to consult in Leamington Springs seemed less attractive than the castles and monuments Hammond found along his way. He declined to enter the highly recommended three-week therapeutic regime, instead pressing impatiently onward with his sightseeing.

Hammond had arrived abroad with a variety of romantic expectations nurtured by his childhood acquaintance with legends of British knights and kings, of Roman splendour, of chivalric dramas that had nourished the spirits of southern youths of his generation. Throughout his journey, he would be visiting sites so often imagined that he expected an elevation of feeling to transport him, permitting a sympathetic experience of the exciting historic and literary events themselves. When he arrived at Warwick Castle on August 10, its battlements evoked visions of feudal warriors. "This is a realization of those pictures of Romance & Poetry which I have been accustomed to dream of from my infancy. . . . To one coming from the wilds of the New World it looks like enchantment itself."[3]

But Hammond did not see Warwick as simply a vestige of the past. While his

---

try to "caricature me" in theirs. Hammond European Diary, I, August 7, 1836. On Americans on the grand tour, see "American Travelers," *Putnam's Monthly*, V (June, 1858), 561–76; David Donald, *Charles Sumner and the Coming of the Civil War* (New York: Knopf, 1960), Chap. III; Philip Rahv, Introduction, in *Discovery of Europe: the Story of American Experience in the Old World* (Garden City, N.Y.: Doubleday, 1960).

2. Catherine Fitzsimons Hammond to M. C. M. Hammord, October 4, 1836, in JHH Papers, SCL; Hammond Medical Diary, August 13, 1836.

3. Hammond European Diary, I, August 11, 1836.

romantic leanings influenced him to record in minute detail his emotional responses to these historic sights, his political interests and training made him an eager analyst of the contemporary English social order as well. "Is there not," he mused, "a great moral difference between a man, born and nurtured amid these scenes & one bred in the forests of the West? And must he not be less than a man whom it would not elevate and ennoble to have been not only born & nurtured here, but to be the hereditary master of the grand . . . monuments of his illustrious ancestry?" Hammond felt deprived as he confronted the richness of English history and tradition but struggled against his growing infatuation with a hereditary aristocracy to which he had no claim. "Let it not be supposed," he added to his earlier professions of admiration, "that I am dazzled by Warwick Castle & ready to stoop before a titled aristocrat. . . . I am still as proud a freeman as ever, & except in mere outward circumstances feel myself the peer of any nobleman." Yet even as he rejected any notion of his own inferiority, Hammond could not entirely convince himself of his equality with those raised in the traditions of the English aristocracy. "I cannot but believe that I should in many respects have been another being had I passed my life amid the massy battlements of these feudal structures."[4]

In the years since his political debut as an editor, Hammond had been steadily evolving increasingly aristocratic views and had in Congress devoted a significant portion of his most important address to a denunciation of the growing power of the "mob" throughout the western world. His European experiences slowed this evolution in his thought by reminding him that he was no thoroughgoing aristocrat, at least not in the European sense of the term. On his trip abroad, he learned afresh what it meant to dwell in a rigidly hierarchical social order when you were nobody in particular. The combination of his humble origins with his boundless aspirations compelled him to defend as the American ideal a natural aristocracy of talent, in contrast to the English and continental elites of birth. The "inherent difference," he declared, "between a gentleman born & a gentleman only bred . . . is far more obvious among the English than us, & arises from that subserviency to rank which an American never feels & an Englishman never gets over." Himself but a "gentleman bred," Hammond defended the social mobility that his very presence abroad represented.[5]

Hammond approached comtemporary British and European life as a volume

4. *Ibid.*
5. Hammond European Diary, II (MS vol. bd., 1837, JHH Papers, SCL), June 28, 1837.

of social practice waiting to be read and studied. Each new experience promised to open "to an American a new chapter on the social system as it exists all over Europe." For a southerner uncertain not just about the meaning of Americanism but about the degree of his commitment to it as well, these problems of cultural evaluation and definition were rendered especially acute. Each country he visited would serve as a testing ground for social theories still crystallizing in the consciousness of the young Carolinian who had so recently become a spokesman for his section's way of life.[6]

Understandably, Hammond closely observed the white servants and other free workers who filled the positions occupied by slaves in the South. The postilions and domestics along his route seemed to him as stupid and unenlightened as plantation blacks, though the squalor of their villages led him to conclude that their conditions of life and labor were far harsher than those of most southern slaves. These servants certainly appeared far less affable and contented than any slaves he had encountered at home. His initial impressions reinforced his already strong prejudices against the free-labor system.[7]

London intensified both Hammond's positive and negative reactions to English society. Determined from the first not to be intimidated by the sophistication of the Old World and its inhabitants, Hammond moved into four rooms at Fenton's, taking his place in "one of the most fashionable houses in the most fashionable quarter of London." Despite his bold resolutions not to be awed by the city, however, the provincial American, who had only recently encountered a metropolis as large as Philadelphia, was overwhelmed. In an unaccustomed admission of inadequacy, Hammond lamented, "I do not know how to go about finding anything of it. There appears no clue, no beginning, no ending—all is utter confusion to me." In an effort to reassert mastery over a situation out of his control, Hammond fell back on scorn. London dwellings, he proclaimed, were no better than those in Columbia; the House of Lords no more elevated a body than the Carolina Senate, and the English king, whom Hammond glimpsed on a visit to Parliament, a figure of little grandeur. "Dignity," the traveler sneered, "is a thing unknown in England to man or woman." The royal gait seemed more like a "Waddle."[8]

But these condemnations lacked conviction. Hammond's disdain for the king was counterbalanced by an almost childlike delight at the magnificent

6. Hammond European Diary, I, January 12, 1837.
7. *Ibid.*, August 14, 1836.
8. *Ibid.*, August 17, 20, 1836.

pomp of Parliament's ceremonial prorogation, over which the monarch presided only a few days after the Hammonds arrived in the city. Catherine was uncertain whether Harry or his father was more excited by the state coaches and the rows of colorfully uniformed guards. Throughout his voyage, Hammond would display this same sort of ambivalence, vacillating between two logically inconsistent but emotionally compatible attitudes: on the one hand an almost mystical admiration; on the other, arrogant contempt.

Hammond's ambivalence burst forth as active hostility most frequently in his financial transactions with foreigners, for these situations represented a direct and constantly recurring challenge to his *savoir-faire*. Determined that no one should expose him as a foolish rustic, Hammond took pride in refusing to be victimized by merchants or landlords. His morbid fear of being cheated and his determination not to be bettered required him to question and to resist every bill, until his voyage became an ordeal nearly as ego threatening and anxiety provoking as his term in Congress. "I have had a quarrel with every tradesman," he wrote his brother from England soon after his arrival. Bargaining for everything, he confided to his mother, was so stressful that it threatened to undermine those very improvements in health the journey was intended to produce. "I cant help fretting at the little vexations of travelling & the impositions of all sorts of people." The humiliation of being deceived was unbearable. "If ignorance is ever 'bliss,'" he confided to his travel diary, "I think it is so to a certain extent in dealing here that you may not be too much harassed by knowing too well how much you are fleeced." He so resented what he saw as endemic English cupidity that he began to feel an unaccustomed generosity towards New Englanders, whom the staunchly southern Hammond had theretofore regarded as the most avaricious of men. "As to honesty," he admitted, "I have done the Yankees great injustice in supposing them the greatest shavers in the world. The English are far a head."[9]

All in all, life among this "surly, ill-natured set of sharpers" was doing little to improve his health. Hammond responded enthusiastically when a London physician urged a prompt removal to the Continent. A final confrontation stamped his departure with the suspicion and conflict that had characterized so much of his interaction with the English during his seventeen days in their country. As he settled his accounts in preparation for embarking across the

9. James Henry Hammond to M. C. M. Hammond, August 20, 1836, Hammond to Catherine Fox Hammond, November 15, 1836, both in JHH Papers, SCL; Hammond European Diary, II, September 25, 1837; Hammond European Diary, I, August 20, 1836.

Channel, Hammond was infuriated by demands for tips from servants he thought he had already generously compensated. Accustomed to displays of flattering subservience from his slave domestics, the Carolinian found himself at first disconcerted and then angered by the surliness of these whites, who did not even offer him the satisfaction of pretending gratitude. Their presumption provoked him to rage. "I peremptorily refused to pay a penny more to anybody . . . & being now in a passion began to throw out a few damn's at the first of which the Porter fled & saved me the trouble of kicking him down Stairs." Hammond left England, land of "humbuggery and pillage," in disgust. "Although you are the land of my ancestors," he railed, "I hate and detest you."[10]

From the first, France seemed a great improvement—"sunshine after darkness," Hammond wrote home to Francis Pickens. The landscape more closely resembled familiar American scenes, and Paris was as comfortingly intimate as a "*large* Village." Friends from Georgia, also touring the Continent, provided agreeable company and a welcome link with home, and Hammond found himself "employed every moment in the most pleasant occupations." Under these circumstances his health rapidly improved, and only the onset of gloomy fall weather prompted him to make arrangements in "broken French" for a carriage to transport the family southward toward Rome.[11]

The Hammonds passed the month of September on the road, admiring the sights along the route from Paris to Dijon, Geneva, Mont Blanc, and Lausanne. The Alpine scenery was breathtaking, and Hammond's health was good enough to permit him to hike extensively on the glacier athwart Mont Blanc. Voltaire's chateau at Ferney and a house once occupied by Napoleon added a historical dimension to the sightseeing. The magnificent landscapes and monuments were hardly more impressive, however, than the misery so evident everywhere. Beggars surrounded the carriage wherever it stopped, entreating the travelers for the sous Hammond always had ready. Unfamiliar with such displays of want, he felt especially moved by the legions of children who approached him with outstretched hands.

As they crossed into Italy on October 2, Hammond was overcome with "uncommon sensations on putting my foot for the first time on the native soil of the Romans." Italy had been the home of a civilization he had "read, thought &

10. Hammond to Catherine Fox Hammond, September 2, 1836, in JHH Papers, SCL; Hammond European Diary, I, August 24, 1836.
11. Hammond to Francis W. Pickens, September 6, 1836, in JHH Papers, DU; Hammond European Diary, I, August 30, 1836; Hammond to Catherine Fox Hammond, September 2, 1836, in JHH Papers, SCL.

dreamed" about since childhood, a civilization that, like the American South, had once embraced both republicanism and slavery.[12] Their progress south was abruptly halted, however, by an annoying quarantine of fourteen days at Castelfranco, an interruption required before admission to Tuscany and the Roman states. An epidemic of cholera had prompted officials to impose strict regulations in an effort to arrest the spread of the disease. As they crossed the border, the immigration officer took their passports on long tongs and fumigated the documents before he would examine them. When a minor functionary leapt upon a coin Hammond threw him as a tip, the official himself was seized and placed in quarantine.[13]

Hammond had little sympathy with these regulations; he was not accustomed to any restrictions on his freedom of movement. Even the international passport system seemed to him an unwarranted imposition demeaning to his status. As Catherine explained, it was "so like giving a pass to a negro that *we* independent people feel it a degrading thing." To be imprisoned, even for the sake of health, was even worse. Hammond was far away from South Carolina, where a planter's absolute authority served as a fundamental principle of social order. In Europe he had no connections, no choice but to submit to the regulations imposed by the states through which he passed. But he did not yield gracefully. Hammond passed the long days of quarantine complaining and fidgeting, impatient to regain his cherished freedom. Much of the time he aimlessly pitched quoits, and intermittently, he studied Italian. Harry, already bored with traveling, practiced spelling, and Catherine, who had long since begun to wish they had never left home, passed the weeks doing needlework. At last on a cold November day they were permitted to proceed toward the glories of Florence and Rome.[14]

Even in Italy, Hammond could not refrain from belittling many of the attractions he visited, declaring them vastly overrated and in most cases little superior to their American counterparts. Opera at La Scala, for instance, was so dispirited that it was not even as pleasing as a rousing "negro corn shucking song." Rome was initially a disappointment as well, for although he expected to be transported into a rich and vivid past, Hammond found too few antiquities "in any tolerable preservation to excite the imagination even." There was not, he

---

12. Hammond European Diary, I, October 2, 1836.
13. *Ibid.*, October 23, 1836.
14. Catherine Fitzsimons Hammond to M. C. M. Hammond, October 4, 1836, in JHH Papers, SCL.

wrote Marcellus, "enough of Rome left to identify her for one moment with the Rome of antiquity & of our childhood." Instead of classical treasures, the city seemed full of Catholic churches and artifacts that symbolized a sad degeneracy from its former glories. Once the center of the world, Rome was now center of a faith that Hammond, like many Americans of his era, regarded as primitive and spiritually deadening. Even though he probably knew almost no Catholics at home in overwhelmingly Protestant South Carolina and even though he had never even been inside a Catholic church until he visited Notre Dame in Paris, Hammond looked upon the faith as "neither more nor less than pure idolatry," a kind of heathenism that had persisted into modern times. The Christmas mass he attended at Saint Peter's did little to alter his views, for the ceremony seemed a series of magical rites and incantations undertaken with little sincerity or fervor on the part of pope, priests, or congregation.[15]

Hammond's failure to appreciate the Eternal City bespoke an underlying mood of homesickness and melancholy. A rainy and cold birthday in Florence on November 15 had made him feel very far away from family and friends in Carolina, and he had not been able to shake his despondency. Thoughts of classical statesmen and their glories only reminded him of his own ambitions to emulate their deeds and of the piteous "bankruptcy" of his own political career. Like Rome, little remained of it but ruins. Exactly a year before the day of his entry into Rome, he mused, he had taken the congressional oath in Washington, and ten years before that he had graduated in triumph from South Carolina College. On this December 5, however, there was no comparable milestone marking his progress along the road of achievement; he was now on a detour, if not an entirely different route.[16]

Gradually Hammond's depression subsided, and with growing familiarity he began to revise his estimate of the Italian city. Catherine was pregnant once again, and the family decided to stay in Rome until her confinement in February. They succeeded in procuring a large apartment of twelve rooms "of all sorts and sizes with a kitchen in which we make our own breakfast & have our dinner sent to us by a Tratoria." This domesticity provided a welcome relief from the more public accommodations in which they had resided for the past several months. Hammond began to relax and to feel less alienated from his surroundings. The

15. Hammond European Diary, I, October 6, 1836; Hammond to M. C. M. Hammond, December 13, 1836, Hammond to John Fox, December 18, 1836, both in JHH Papers, SCL.
16. Hammond to John Fox, December 18, 1836, in JHH Papers, SCL; Hammond European Diary, I, December 5, 1836.

climate seemed very much like Carolina's, and the American travelers evolved a daily routine to supplant the constant change and movement that had characterized their lives since July. Hammond rose every day between seven and eight, walked for half an hour, breakfasted on bread, butter, tea, and sometimes an egg. From ten until three he toured the city's attractions, climbing stairs, descending into vaults, and generally exerting himself in a manner his health had only recently permitted. At five the family dined, and Hammond then took a walk before returning to the apartment to write or read until he retired at ten. This regimen, combined with his growing enthusiasm for the sights of Rome, seemed remarkably beneficial to his health.[17]

But he continued to be anxious about affairs at home and longed to know about the welfare of his family both black and white. Hammond eagerly awaited each communication from Carolina, especially the letters from his overseer, which he scrutinized for details of crops and workers. In return, he pressed his notions for plantation management and even forwarded a dozen pairs of wooden shoes as an experiment to be tried by "our negroes with good straps around them to keep them on." Christmas was an occasion for especially intense nostalgia, and Hammond thought longingly of the celebration the master provided for his bondsmen each year at that time. Determined that his slaves should remember their owner, Hammond often closed his letters with "howdies" to particular servants. But for Christmas he wished to remind them in more tangible fashion of his continuing concern. Although he was thousands of miles away, Hammond wanted to provide the traditional plantation Christmas gifts, but not the usual frocks and tobacco. Instead he ordered 110 Venetian pipes, some Turkish in design, some of cherry wood decorated in gold, to be shipped home to "shew the people that I do not forget them."[18]

Perhaps Hammond's fond recollections of his absent slaves arose in part from his continuing difficulties with European servants. One valet quit, Hammond reported indignantly, because he was not permitted to have company or sleep past seven. The rapid turnover of household personnel troubled the Carolinian, for he was accustomed to legitimate his role as master by assuring himself of his benevolence and paternalism, notions that remained important to him even in this new European environment. Soon after he arrived in Rome, Hammond dis-

17. Hammond to John Fox, December 18, 1836, in JHH Papers, SCL.
18. Hammond European Diary, I, September 13, 1836; Hammond to Catherine Fox Hammond, January 1, 1837, in JHH Papers, SCL.

charged a valet who had been with him since early September. Yet this "fellow who is rude, unfeeling, faithless, whose stupidity . . . has so often provoked me to abuse him more than I have ever done a slave, this fellow it cost me a severe pang to part with after all." Despite his objective failings as an attendant, Jean might have won reinstatement if only he had indicated that he understood Hammond's emotional expectations of his servants. "Had he exhibited any contrition or shown any feeling of mortification," Hammond admitted, "I believe I should have relented & taken him back." But Jean did not know what it meant to play Sambo.[19]

Despite such difficulties, Hammond found himself each day more involved in the attractions of the city around him. Part of this growing enthusiasm was an increasing interest in the art works he observed everywhere. Since Paris, Hammond had become more and more absorbed by the contents of the museums he toured nearly every day, and he had begun in Florence to acquire some representative objects to ship home. No artist himself, Hammond nevertheless discovered that the purchase of paintings and sculpture was a way to participate in creativity. Moreover, as connoisseur and collector, he could also achieve the more practical and worldly advantages accruing to the upwardly mobile from profitable investment and tasteful conspicuous consumption. "I have become smitten," he confessed in a letter to South Carolina in January, 1837, "with the prevailing mania for the fine arts." In Florence, Hammond had sat for a bust of himself by a sculptor shrewd enough to assure the vain Carolinian that he bore a "striking resemblance" to a statue of Augustus in Rome. When he arrived in the Eternal City, Hammond purchased a picture nearly every other day, frequently commissioning copies of works of the masters, such as Raphael and Titian, that he found especially appealing. He paid a young artist to paint a portrait of Catherine, and acquired a variety of landscapes, classical and biblical scenes, engravings, stone and plaster busts, and some porcelains to complete his collection. As he packed the items for shipment to the United States, he anticipated with pleasure the impression these treasures would make when displayed to his friends in Carolina.[20]

19. Hammond European Diary I, December 4, 1836.
20. Hammond to Milledge Galphin, January 8, 1837, in HBC Papers, SCL; Hammond European Diary, I, November 22, December 20, 1836. See Marion Edmunds, "James H. Hammond's Art Collecting on His European Tour of May 1836–November 1837," in David Moltke-Hansen (ed.), *Art in the Lives of South Carolinians: Nineteenth-Century Chapters* (Charleston: Carolina Art Association, 1978).

By late February, 1837, Hammond had spent two thousand dollars on art work, almost 15 percent of the cost of his seven months abroad. By the time he departed for the United States in October, he had acquired more than forty paintings and about the same number of engravings. Each purchase represented to him the achievement of a new level of artistic sensibility and thus symbolized his continuing progress toward that enlightenment and sophistication his European travels were intended to impart. After his winter in Italy, Hammond reported with new assurance that his ventures in connoisseurship had definitely "improved my taste."[21]

Rome also unexpectedly offered the Hammonds the pleasures and diversions of friendship with another family of traveling Americans, the Morgans of Louisiana. Perhaps because of his erratic health or perhaps because of his lack of fluency in any language but English, Hammond used his numerous letters of introduction only occasionally, and for the most part remained entirely isolated from European society in the cities he visited. But the Hammonds always enjoyed the fellowship of Americans they chanced to encounter. As Catherine's lying-in approached, she was no doubt especially grateful for the company of at least one other woman, for the Morgans were, as she wrote home, "our only acquaintance." When these new friends left Rome, the Hammonds confessed their loneliness and made plans to catch up with the Louisianians after Catherine's confinement. Yet at the same time Hammond sought their companionship, he complained of the Morgans as nouveau riche, as people "vulgar in breeding" with whom he associated only for the "want of better company." Hammond's resentment of European pretensions did not inhibit similar posturing in regard to those he could in any way disdain. Such conflicting egalitarian and hierarchical sentiments were to trouble Hammond all his life—in part, no doubt, because of the social ambiguities created by his own upward mobility. His friends the Morgans could scarcely have been more nouveau riche than he.[22]

On February 3 Catherine delivered another son. "I have not it is true had the comforts of home," she wrote her mother-in-law, "and I have had a very quiet, lonely time, but I have been remarkably fortunate, and so much did I dread it myself, that I can scarcely believe it is all over and I am well again." Hammond was disgruntled not to get a daughter at last and would not give the infant a name. He thought of calling the baby after his brother, but decided he

21. Hammond European Diary, II, April 12, 1837.
22. Catherine Fitzsimons Hammond to Catherine Fox Hammond, February 26, 1837, in JHH Papers, SCL; Hammond European Diary, I, April 2, 1837.

196

could not burden a child with a name so ugly as Marcellus. After having chosen names for four boys already, "I cannot think of any more."[23]

By early March, Catherine was strong enough to travel, and the family departed southwards for Naples. After a fortnight of sightseeing, they packed their carriage aboard a steamer and sailed through a stormy sea to Marseilles. Although slowed by a series of difficulties with customs, immigration, and health authorities and the weather, they at last arrived in Paris. A sheaf of letters chronicling disasters of various sorts at home awaited them. Uncle John Fox, Hammond's one prosperous relative and his mother's financial hope for the future, had died leaving them all out of his will. Far worse, a financial crisis had struck not only the cotton market but the American economy more generally; the Panic of 1837 had begun. Hammond's thoughts had of late already been turning toward home and toward his own future. The latest addition to his family had rekindled his determination to undertake new steps to increase his income. "I feel very uneasy," he had written Marcellus late in January, "& am anxious to get home whence I shall make an immediate trip to the West & get a plantation there—I must have one in the *Cotton Country.*" The financial news that greeted him in Paris only heightened his concern and his sense of helplessness at being so far away.[24]

At the same time he was writing of the West, Hammond's thoughts of America were taking another direction as well; he had begun to plan the resumption of his political career in South Carolina. The governorship seemed a plausible target, and Hammond nervously wrote Marcellus for information and advice. "You have been to Columbia—Write me candidly what you think my standing there & in the State—How high do they rank me? In what class as compared with our other men?" Letters from Calhoun, McDuffie, and Pickens recounted dramatic realignments in Carolina politics, and Hammond chafed at his exile.[25]

Paris had none of its former attraction. "Cannot but wish for a little of the quiet of Rome in the thronged & bustling streets. But I wish for home still

23. Catherine Fitzsimons Hammond to Catherine Fox Hammond, February 26, 1837, Hammond to Catherine Fox Hammond, February 3, 1837, both in JHH Papers, SCL.

24. Hammond to M. C. M. Hammond, January 31, 1837, *ibid.* See also Hammond European Diary, II, April 9, 1837. Hammond and a number of his relatives contested John Fox's decision to leave his property to charity. After a long legal fight, including appeals to higher courts, they succeeded in having the will overturned. Hammond's mother received twenty thousand dollars. Hammond Diary (MS in JHH Papers, LC), June 13, 1842.

25. Hammond to M. C. M. Hammond, January 31, 1837, in JHH Papers, SCL. See John C. Calhoun to Hammond, February 18, 1837, George McDuffie to Hammond, December 19, 1836, Francis W. Pickens to Hammond, November 14, 1836, all in JHH Papers, LC.

more." When Hammond saw a bag of cotton marked with the name of a Carolina producer passing on a cart in the street, homesickness overwhelmed him. Snatching a piece of cotton from a hole in the bag, he "could not refrain from kissing it." Yet Hammond feared his constitution was still not strong enough to permit his return. That elusive "phantom health" seemed "perhaps farther than ever from reach." He complained of giddiness, of pains in his side, of motes before his eyes, and of headaches that prevented him from writing or reading. "Dreadful news from America" of business failures and economic crisis made Hammond all the more eager to return, yet all the more fearful that when at last he did reach home he would find all his affairs a "wreck."[26]

When the doctors summoned to treat Hammond's renewed complaints offered no useful advice, Catherine urged a therapeutic change of scene. In early May, the family took to the road once again for a tour of Germany and the Low Countries, and a steamboat trip down the Rhine. But Hammond was in no mood for sightseeing. "I have never started out with less anticipation of pleasure," he wrote as they left Paris. All the inconveniences of European life that had bothered him for the past ten months began now to seem genuinely unbearable. The Germans were sullen, stupid, and obstinate, "always harassing me in body & in mind." An innkeeper's questions about his name, age, address, and birthplace offended him as unwarranted encroachments. "Of course I only answered a few of them—What Slave in the South is ever questioned so closely."[27]

Worst of all, however, were Hammond's unending difficulties with servants, for his growing impatience with travel made him even more intolerant of what he saw as the peculiarities of the free-labor system. "Servants alone," he proclaimed, "are enough to embitter European life." Accustomed to the attentions of an army of slaves, Hammond demanded a great deal from those in his employ, and was constantly unhappy about the standard of performance rendered. He was appalled that his hirelings should presume to declare limits on his rights over them; he sought in vain for the subservience customarily feigned by all but the most recalcitrant of his slaves. A new European servant, Hammond discovered, "commences cheating . . . in every possible way . . . & screening himself from every bodily service that he can, not . . . [by] laziness like a negro, but by claiming exemption from this, that & the other sort of service."[28]

26. Hammond European Diary, I, April 5, 1837, II, May 18, April 23, 1837.
27. *Ibid.*, II, May 8, 18, 20, 1837.
28. *Ibid.*, April 12, 1837.

The discrepancy between the Carolinian's attitudes and European custom reached a crisis at a Belgian inn. When he suspected his landlady in Charleroi was cheating him, Hammond resolved as usual not to be victimized and ordered his coachman to drive away leaving the disputed charges unpaid. As the coach began to move, a servant of the hotel seized the reins and halted the horses. Although Hammond "warned the servant . . . I would strike him," the Belgian was not easily cowed and surprised the Carolinian by defying him to use physical force. Challenged to defend his claims to authority, Hammond delivered the servant a "severe rap across the hand." But the Belgian still showed no fear of Hammond's power. When the servant "turned upon me," Hammond determined to punish him for his presumption. "He was a sturdy fellow & twice my strength but I held him off untill I wore out my stick on him & then turning the butt gave him several severe blows on the head which sickened him, but the stick was too light to knock him down. . . . The fellow pulled off his hat & his head I was glad to see was in a gore & bled profusely."[29]

Hammond made his next diary entry from the "midst of all the felons" in a local jail. Belgian law imposed on masters restraints unknown to the slave-owners of the American South; an insolent freeman could not be treated in the same manner as an impudent slave. But Hammond could not adjust to these unfamiliar social rules and expectations; he remained unrepentant, insisting he had acted properly to defend his own prerogatives and the foundations of social order by maintaining the proper line of demarcation between the master and the servant class. The true assault in his eyes was not his physical attack upon the Belgian, but the servant's dangerous challenge to the authority Hammond embodied. Under prosecution by Belgian officials, Hammond demanded in return "a process against the servant who assaulted me by seizing my horses." After six hours in a cell "lighted only by two grates," Hammond's anger had subsided enough for him to agree to pay the five-hundred-franc bail required for his release. Although it was officially understood that he was to return for trial in ten days, Hammond forfeited his bond and departed for France.[30]

With this disaster barely averted, misfortune struck again. The very next day, the Hammond baby, sickly from birth, died in his mother's arms as the carriage sped toward the border. The sad parents consigned their "Roman boy" to an oaken box to be shipped to South Carolina for interment. Only in death did

29. *Ibid.*, May 29, 1837.
30. *Ibid.*

Hammond at last name the child, by inscribing Charles Julius on his casket.[31]

Bad news proliferated, and dispatches from America recounted the fall of cotton to a third of its former price and the suspension of specie payments by American banks. These depressing bulletins induced sleepless nights and renewed agitation harmful to Hammond's health. One severe attack of illness, he reported, was undoubtedly occasioned "by reading some dozen American newspapers."[32]

Tired of the Continent, eager at least to hear the English tongue, the Hammonds recrossed the Channel. The comforting similarity of English ways to those of home prompted Hammond to regret "much of the blasphemy" he had "lavished" on England the previous year. His health improved again as he negotiated the omnibus to tour London, attended the opera, laughed through a performance of *The Rivals*, and enjoyed a carriage ride to Windsor Castle. Within a fortnight, however, the novelty of England wore thin, and the vexations of traveling rose again to the fore.[33]

In his homesickness Hammond was beginning to display a growing American chauvinism. When the king died during Hammond's London visit, the Carolinian at first copied those around him wearing badges of mourning. After a day's reflection, he removed the crape, for "I was afraid I should be taken for an Englishman." Hammond's nostalgia and affection for America knew no sectional boundaries; in Sheffield he found himself overcome with warm feelings for a store owner who had been born and bred in Boston and was a "Yankee in every way." Hammond's national loyalties had grown sufficiently intense that he purchased a procelain from the merchant simply "because he was an American." On occasion Hammond's zealous nationalism could become genuinely provocative, for it encompassed a considerable measure of hostility to Old World customs and usages. In a London store Hammond announced that books were far cheaper in the United States. The proprietor responded by explaining "authors were paid higher here—I told him we would send him books—that he said would not do & got mad—said the English cannot furnish brains and books too as cheap as we did—brains he said were much higher here than in America. They must then be scarcer said I." With this parting shot Hammond fled the shop for fear the enraged owner would "cut me up."[34]

31. *Ibid.*, May 30, 1837; Catherine Fitzsimons Hammond to M. C. M. Hammond, September 11, 1837, in JHH Papers, SCL.
32. Hammond Medical Diary, June 27, 1837.
33. Hammond European Diary, II, June 13, 1837.
34. *Ibid.*, June 23, July 2, September 16, June 29, 1837.

A trip through Ireland, Scotland, and Wales provided Hammond with even better opportunities for unfavorable comparisons between British society and his own. Although the Lake District, the Scottish Highlands, and Wales were all strikingly beautiful and parts of Dublin were very fine and although Hammond was especially delighted to visit the grave of his favorite novelist, Sir Walter Scott, the Carolinian was shocked by the deprivation he saw all about him. For a year Hammond had been observing free society. Although he had traveled in the northern United States, he had never before had the opportunity to scrutinize long-established societies with mature and fully developed systems of free labor; nor had he previously had occasion to compare the operation of these systems among people of varying race and character. His difficulties with servants were an important factor in strengthening Hammond's commitment to the southern labor system. But his evaluation of free labor encompassed more general reflections upon the status and condition of the working classes. While he found that European menials exhibited too much independence and too little subservience, the objective realities of their lives seemed to provide small foundation for such claims to autonomy. The actual circumstances of the British and European masses were dependence and deprivation, a situation far worse, he believed, than that of southern slaves. The lot of Europe's "surfs" was one of labor "more constant & unrelieved by far than our negroes from childhood to the grave." And yet they had not the comforts of well-fed plantation bondsmen. Hammond was especially moved by the poverty he saw in Ireland and responded generously to the legions of beggars. "I don't know why it is, but I feel inclined to give & do give five times as much as I did in France & Italy. . . . It makes the heart ache to walk the streets."[35]

Hammond did not soon forget these scenes. For the rest of his life his thinking about slavery would reflect these images of the misery of so-called free laborers. Hammond now argued from the conviction of personal experience that the freedom of free societies was greatly overrated. "Liberty is altogether comparative. The English are crazy about our enslaving the Africans while we regard their much boasted 'British Liberty' as a mere joke."[36]

Hammond was generally disheartened by his Irish tour. "It is very clear," he concluded, "that we have seen too much & ought to go home. . . . It is time to quit sight-seeing." Yet the thought of what awaited him in America brought on "unpleasant symptoms." The Charleston countinghouse in which John had been

35. *Ibid.*, I, September 25, 1836, II, August 14, 23, 1837.
36. Hammond Diary (LC), August 2, 1837.

apprenticed had failed, and each mail brought news of more disasters. "I some-times fear," Hammond confessed, "to go home & meet it all." Catherine had no such reservations. From the first she had doubted the efficacy of traveling, sus-pecting that physicians prescribed European voyages only when they did not know what else to do. And she was certain as well that their idleness exacer-bated his complaints. James's "mind is much more affected than his body," she wrote Marcellus, "and if he had any amusement or occupation I have no doubt he would be much better. . . . But really I feel we are committing sin in the manner in which we now spend our time." Hammond seemed to agree. His life abroad was growing "more & more intolerable," and he, too, recognized the need for "some regular & not too stirring occupation." Although he felt dis-tressed about returning to America without evidence of a marked improvement in his health, he concluded melodramatically that at least it would be better to die at home.[37]

On October 1 the Hammonds embarked from Liverpool for New York. The twenty-seven-day return voyage was even more disagreeable than their original crossing, for this time stormy seas washed unceasingly across the deck. But even seasickness did not dampen Hammond's ebullience. He talked only of America, regaling the many British passengers with accounts of the superiority of the United States to their native land. His contempt for everything English was so pronounced and so offensive to his thirty-one shipmates that "Our intercourse was very unpleasant & in fact nearly ceased before we arrived."[38]

Hammond was undaunted by this hostility, for his mind was wholly preoc-cupied with anticipations of home. But he thought not just of Carolina or of the South. During his months in Europe, Hammond had come to embrace a new identity: he was not just a southerner but an American. The former nullifier and militant sectionalist was aware that this marked a dramatic shift in his loyalties. Profoundly moved by his arrival in New York's magnificent harbor, Hammond thought that even after fifteen months amongst Europe's marvels "I had never seen any thing so fine." He recognized tears in his eyes at the sight of the Ameri-can flag. "I felt that I never loved my country so much. I wondered that I had ever felt otherwise & was conscience stricken for the sin of having at times here-tofore wavered in my affection for her. I mentally renewed my allegiances to our glorious banner, and resolved to live and die beneath its folds." After more than

37. Hammond European Diary, II, August 30, September 10, 9, 26, 1837; Catherine Fitz-simons Hammond to M. C. M. Hammond, September 11, 1837, in JHH Papers, SCL.
38. Hammond European Diary, II, November 1, 1837.

a year of traveling and the enormous expenditure of almost sixteen thousand dollars, Hammond was home at last, his physical health little changed, but his mind greatly altered, expanded, and enriched.[39]

At a time when he sought reassurance about both his personal situation as a newly arrived aristocrat and his philosophical stance as a fledgling defender of southern slavery, Hammond had embarked on a journey to a different world where he could not help but search out emotional and intellectual supports for his positions. Hammond went to Europe to find not just health but a new sense of personal security; he returned a world traveler, art connoisseur, and would-be social philosopher. Certain of his experiences worked at least temporarily to reinforce his national allegiance, but other incidents and perceptions had a countervailing impact, one that in the long run would prevail and come to serve as a pillar of his support for slavery and southern sectionalism. While his reflections about free labor were for the most part less dramatic than his self-conscious conversion experience in the New York harbor, they reinforced his commitment to the South's peculiar institution and provided him with concrete and immediate evidence of the failures—as well as the inconveniences—of free society. He had already encountered comparisons of southern slavery and European labor in his readings; he was certainly familiar with American discussions of European class and privilege. But the force of personal involvement with these realities was to refine his perceptions and provide them with an emotional underpinning that would fix them in his mind and permanently affect his thinking about the nature of social order. For the rest of his life Hammond would refer to his European experiences and the insights they had first impelled him to articulate.

39. *Ibid.*; Hammond Travelling Account (MS vol. bd., 1836–37, JHH Papers, SCL).

CHAPTER 11

The Sound of the Trumpet

HAMMOND'S LONG-ANTICIPATED RETURN was every bit as gratifying as he had dreamed. Carolinians and former congressional colleagues visiting in New York provided an enthusiastic welcome, as well as company for a round of homecoming celebrations, excursions to the races, and shopping expeditions. But Hammond did not tarry long in the North. By steamboat and carriage he passed through Philadelphia and Washington to Columbia, arriving in time to observe his thirtieth birthday on November 15 "among *friends*." A military band serenaded the travelers on the night of their arrival in the state capital, and they found themselves the objects of excited and flattering attention. Even the Fitz-simonses seemed to have forgotten past hostilities in their pleasure to have their family reunited again. Wade Hampton II, husband of Catherine's elder sister Ann, demonstrated this new amity by providing his sister and brother-in-law with a coach-and-five to transport them in speed and style from Columbia to Silver Bluff. By the eighteenth, they were home at last with their tribe of sons, grown and changed nearly beyond recognition but, their parents noted grate-fully, in good spirits and fine health.[1]

The thrill of homecoming was soon replaced by the difficulties of resuming life in circumstances quite different from those that had prevailed when Ham-mond had left Carolina for Washington two years before. The nationwide Panic of 1837 had depressed the cotton economy generally, but the less-productive lands of the old seaboard states had been far more harshly affected than those of

1. James Henry Hammond European Diary, II (MS vol. bd., 1837, JHH Papers, SCL), Novem-ber 15, 1837.

the new Southwest. In these changed conditions, Hammond felt even more strongly than before his departure that western cotton land was a necessity. Silver Bluff seemed in many ways a marginal enterprise; it had to be supplemented by other investments. The land company Hammond had bought into in Texas had failed in the panic, so the acquisition of another tract in the Southwest and the further rationalization of operations at the Bluff stood at the top of Hammond's agenda as he began to organize his business affairs. But his dissatisfaction was not simply economic. After exposure to sophisticated continental taste, Hammond found the area around Silver Bluff culturally and socially inadequate as well. Each new contact with his neighbors—their rudeness in not answering his invitations, their indifference to his European treasures—intensified Hammond's determination to escape "from the woods into the world."[2]

Despite this resolution, Hammond remained uncertain about where his destiny lay. Because of the trip's failure to relieve his physical complaints, Hammond now regarded himself as a chronic invalid, one whose dyspeptic constitution would always prevent him from executing too active a public role. Yet the limitations imposed by his health seem not to have been entirely fixed in Hammond's mind and largely reflected his own changing inclinations and ambitions. For the rest of his life, the invocation of illness would serve to moderate that political ambition he had always found it so difficult either to banish or to restrain; it would mediate his successes and excuse his failures. Dyspepsia functioned for Hammond as a means of evading the overwhelming burden of responsibility inherent in power and achievement.

His reentry into the political arena was complicated as well by the drastically altered contours of Carolina public life. As one former political associate had written Hammond in Europe, "you won't know your state when you return." The economic issues the panic had inserted into public life had destroyed the tenuous alliance of Calhoun and the Whigs, united briefly by their common resistance to Jackson's executive "usurpations." Political forces had regrouped and were now aligned around the issue of the national bank. Antagonistic to all enhancement of federal power, Calhoun opposed reestablishment of a central bank, while the nationalist Whigs supported the financial institution. In his advocacy of the subtreasury as an alternative system, Calhoun demonstrated an antipathy for the national bank that attracted the support of many traditionally antibank Jacksonians. Calhoun now found himself in the camp of his old enemy,

2. Hammond Diary (MS in JHH Papers, LC), February 6, 1841.

Jackson's successor in the White House, Martin Van Buren. This reversal of loyalties, first displayed in a special congressional session in September, 1837, was so dramatic as to baffle Calhoun's constituents, who could not initially comprehend the reasons or the justification for such a shift in allegiances. But, more significantly, it split the Carolina congressional delegation even more fatally than had the Pinckney resolutions of 1836. Preston, his earlier disunionist nullifier days forgotten, embraced the centralized national bank and the Whig party. Calhoun was able to hold only Francis Pickens and the radical sectionalist Robert Barnwell Rhett, a freshman in the national legislature, to the support of his position. Calhoun's continuing effort to unite the South in sound states' rights principles faltered as he failed even to forge a consensus within his own delegation. But the senator was not easily daunted. After the special session ended in October, he rushed home to organize the state against the bank before the imminent legislative elections. A series of public statements to his constituents explained the reasons for his bewildering change of position, and Calhoun's efforts produced an overwhelming victory for the prosubtreasury candidates.[3]

When Hammond returned to Carolina in the fall of 1837, he found himself in a difficult position in regard to these developments. His personal ties to Preston were strong, and had been reinforced by a series of marriages cementing an alliance among the Fitzsimons, Hampton, Preston, and Manning families, all of whom were now Hammond's cousins. His old friends P. M. Butler and James Hamilton had endorsed the bank as well. Yet Hammond's own states' rights political philosophy clearly prescribed a pro-Calhoun, antibank stance. "There is no argument in favor of a national bank," he succinctly summarized in his diary, "that may not be used in favour of a despotism."[4]

The bitterness of the legislative session that began in Columbia almost immediately upon Hammond's return convinced him that he had little to gain from any explicit public statement of his views on the bank. His more general political future remained similarly uncertain. Even before his return from Europe, Hammond had received letters from Carolina urging him to run for governor, state senator, and high militia office. Elmore, his replacement in Congress, generously offered Hammond his old seat back again. But Hammond declared that both his "health and inclination" prohibited him from taking "any part in

---

3. See Charles M. Wiltse, *John C. Calhoun, Sectionalist, 1840–1850* (Indianapolis: Bobbs-Merrill, 1951), and Virginia Louise Glenn, "James Hamilton, Jr., of South Carolina: A Biography" (Ph.D. dissertation, University of North Carolina, Chapel Hill, 1964).
4. Hammond Diary (LC), November 2, 1837.

public life beyond the limits of the state." The idea of a brigadiership in the militia attracted him, but his long absence disqualified him. Over the New Year's holidays, Hammond caucused with local leaders in Barnwell and decided he should not try for the South Carolina Senate. Although he continued publicly to deny any interest in returning to political office, he deceived few of those who knew him well. In response to a communication from Hammond detailing his reasons for opposing the bank, Elmore responded from Washington with thanks for "your very welcome letter in which you most eloquently eschew all politics & immediately give me a most convincing proof of how little it engages your attention, by telling me all that passes here with a running commentary. . . . The old war horse loves the sound of the trumpet & it is just as impossible for you to forget the aspirations & hopes of early years."[5]

Yet Hammond had little idea how best to realize these hopes. Increasingly outspoken attacks on slavery on the floor of Congress during the late winter of 1838 called for a forceful southern response. But this time it was Barnwell Rhett, not Hammond, who took the lead in the defense of southern institutions in the House. Hammond recognized all too clearly that he was no longer a figure of central importance in the struggle over southern rights. Divisions within the Union and divisions within Carolina were challenging him to act on behalf of his ambitions and his principles. The situation was rife with both dangers and opportunities, for Hammond as well as for the South.

Hammond postponed taking any decisive action. The battle between Calhoun and Preston gripped the state, as the senior senator pressed for unquestioning loyalty from his subordinates. Calhoun transformed a special session of the legislature called in May to aid victims of a Charleston fire into an instrument in his drive for control by pressuring it to instruct all members of Carolina's congressional delegation to support the subtreasury. This humiliation for the Preston forces was followed by a vitriolic campaign against all probank candidates standing for office in the fall elections. Although Calhoun's triumph in these contests was not complete, he was by late 1838, as his biographer Charles Wiltse described, "almost absolute master" of South Carolina.[6]

Troubled with personal matters that had accumulated during his long ab-

5. James L. Clark to James Henry Hammond, August 3, 1837, in JHH Papers, LC; Pierce Mason Butler to Hammond, October 13, 1837, in JHH Papers, SCL; Hammond to S. W. Trotti, in JHH Papers, LC; Hammond to M. C. M. Hammond, January 3, 1838, in JHH Papers, SCL; Franklin H. Elmore to Hammond, April 2, 1838, in JHH Papers, LC.
6. Charles M. Wiltse, *John C. Calhoun, Nullifier, 1829–1839* (Indianapolis: Bobbs-Merrill, 1949), 394.

sence, Hammond had a convenient excuse for not publicly taking sides in this bitter political strife. Instead he reorganized Silver Bluff, renting a section of the plantation to a neighbor and offering a considerable portion of the remainder for sale to any buyer who would meet his price. In March and April he traveled south to examine lands in Georgia and Florida as part of his search for attractive investments.

Family matters required attention as well, for although Marcellus was established in an army post, John was at loose ends again. When the youth's efforts to secure a military appointment failed, James encouraged John's expressed interest in studying medicine at the University of Virginia. Hammond's own sons were now old enough to require instruction, and the planter hired a tutor to begin regular schooling at the Bluff. On March 27 another prospective pupil arrived when Catherine delivered a sixth son. This time, however, Hammond had no difficulty choosing a name for the child. Paul Fitzsimons Hammond, named for Catherine's brother, constituted living testimony to the rapprochement between James and his wife's kin.

In the fall of 1838, with the cotton crop nearly ready for harvest, with John settled in Charlottesville, with the remainder of the family rested and healthy after an extended trip to the mountains, Hammond took his first tentative steps back into public life. On October 15 he joined a commercial convention in Augusta as an official representative of Barnwell District. When the bank issue threatened to divide the gathering, Hammond staved off confrontation by moving that the question be dropped and that the meeting restrict itself to consideration of other means for the South to improve her economic position within the nation. Once again he avoided embroiling himself in dangerously divisive issues. He would wait until he could identify a victor in order not to risk his share of the spoils. But his allegiances were deeply divided and the situation was a continual trial for him. "I am with Calhoun & Co in principle—But my private relations are more agreeable on the other side," he confided to his diary. "I have not been so happy since I began to take an interest in these political questions as I was before."[7]

By the end of 1838 public affairs had not yet entirely succeeded in luring Hammond away from what he described as his "objectless existence" as a private citizen: he filled his time with family and plantation matters and found his chief

7. Hammond Diary (MS in JHH Papers, SCL), January 6, 1839.

source of excitement in construction of a new house in Columbia. At last he had decided to move his family from the Bluff to town, where his boys could procure a better education than that provided by the succession of unsatisfactory tutors at the plantation. Hammond himself looked forward to living in a community where he could display the taste he had acquired in Europe to neighbors more appreciative than the "low-bred country folk" of Barnwell. The Columbia house was intended as a monument to his new sophistication, a demonstration that he not only could accumulate money but had the refinement to spend it well. Hammond purchased a two-acre lot adjoining the house in which he had been married on Bull Street, one of Columbia's main thoroughfares. In December, 1838, two slaves sent from the Bluff began to build. Hammond took the plan from a structure he had seen in Rome; the dwelling was to have a piazza on all four sides supported by thirty-six white columns with arches in between. With thirteeen-foot ceilings and twenty-by-twenty-four-foot rooms, the building was designed to be the finest in Columbia. Hammond himself supervised much of the construction, ordering nails and lumber, marble for the steps, wrought-iron railings, and wallpaper for the downstairs rooms. During its erection, the mansion became a focus of interest and attention in the provincial capital and prompted considerable comment from wondering observers who had never seen its like before. To one onlooker, the structure resembled a Catholic church; another thought it a copy of the United States Bank. But all agreed, Pierce Butler reassured Hammond, that it would be "splendid." By the time it was completed in June, 1841, it had cost nearly thirty thousand dollars.[8]

In April, 1839, Hammond temporarily abandoned his personal concerns to attend a second session of the commercial convention, this time in Charleston. But his friends failed to elicit more than this minimal reengagement in public life. "You owe it to yourself & to your state," Pickens insisted, urging his friend to consider Congress or the state legislature. "I tell you," Pierce Butler added, "you ought to be ambitious of political elevation & distinction." Although Hammond responded to these entreaties with pleas of ill health, a week's militia encampment in late May began to change his mind. In their capacities as officers, the leaders of Barnwell District gathered annually for military exercises

---

8. Hammond Plantation Diary, (MS vol. bd., 1831–55), December 25, 1837, Hammond Journal of Building a House in Columbia (MS vol. bd., 1838–41), both in JHH Papers, SCL; Butler to Hammond, November 10, 1839, in JHH Papers, LC. See also Nell S. Graydon, *Tales of Columbia* (Columbia: R. L. Bryan, 1964), 238.

and informal political discussion. To Hammond's surprise, he discovered in these exchanges widespread concern about resurgence of the old Union party. Although he had thought the "hatchet fairly buried" and the nullifiers' triumph conceded by all, he now found that the political upheavals of recent months had stirred up old hostilities from 1831–1833 as well. The "old Union Party is perhaps more thoroughly organized than ever, & are not only insinuating themselves into office, but combining on all occasions to keep nullifiers out."[9]

For Hammond, as for many Carolinians, nullification had become part of a mythic past, a golden and triumphal era for states' rights principles and for South Carolina. To abandon these ideals and allegiances seemed to Hammond unthinkable. He urged a district rally in Barnwell to "get out a ticket of nullifiers so strong that it cannot be beaten easily." When discussion arose about the composition of this slate, it became clear that Hammond was a logical gubernatorial choice. With the governorship as lure, and the principles of nullification as legitimation, Hammond would at last be able to abandon his reservations about a return to politics. The three honors he most desired in public life, he confessed to his diary, were a militia brigadiership, the gubernatorial chair, and a U.S. Senate seat. To his friends, he more cautiously allowed that he would not "object to being Governor."[10]

Almost as soon as he returned from the encampment, Hammond began to regret that he had agreed to enter the race. Those Carolinians closest to him personally were all on the "wrong side of the question now most prominent": the subtreasury. To have such men as his leading supporters would be "fatal." Hammond worried that since his return from Europe he had not even consulted with Calhoun. "I ought to have been cultivating my interest more." Calhoun was now surrounded by a new clique of supporters Hammond would have to win over to his side. Barnwell Rhett and Franklin H. Elmore in Congress and their brothers Alfred Rhett and Benjamin F. Elmore in the state legislature struck Hammond as "third-rate men" devoted to enhancing their own power. A natural jealousy of him would render it difficult for Hammond to win their trust. But he

9. Francis W. Pickens to Hammond, May 9, 1839 [miscatalogued as 1835], Butler to Hammond, April 20, 1839, Hammond to Pickens, May 15, 1839, all in JHH Papers, LC; Hammond Diary (LC), May 26, 1839. See also *Proceedings of the Fourth Convention of Merchants and Others, Held in Charleston, S.C., April 15, 1839, for the Promotion of the Direct Trade* (Charleston: A. E. Miller, 1839). Note Hammond's comments on the general political situation, made under cover of pseudonym in "Upcountry," Charleston *Courier*, May 9, 1839. Hammond identifies himself as author in Hammond to Pickens, May 15, 1839, JHH Papers, LC.
10. Hammond Diary (LC), June 1, May 26, 1839.

recognized that he must soon place himself before the public if he ever intended to be politically active again. The truth is, he wrote, "I must go back I fear into the arena. There is no class of independent, well-informed gentlemen, distinct from politicians, office-holders & hunters, as well as from mere money speculators, in which I can take my stand. I am therefore in danger of having no *caste* whatever, which will not do unless my position were above all *castes*."[11]

In antebellum South Carolina, politics provided the most manifest distinctions among men. Hammond had sought to show he had money, taste, and intelligence. Each of these was implicitly a kind of superiority in itself. But, more important, the possession of these attributes could entitle a Carolinian to an even more explicit sort of power. Public office was bestowed largely in recognition of these other accomplishments. The competitions in horses and houses were in a sense all preliminary skirmishes; politics was the battle. Amidst the insecurity and uncertainty of Carolina's aristocratical democracy, political—as contrasted with social—rank was clear. Public affairs was the "arena," as Hammond put it, where success was most directly and widely acknowledged; this was where the audience of his contemporaries could indicate it accepted the claims to preeminence Hammond made through economic achievement and tasteful consumption. Lacking family background, Hammond regarded political endorsement as a critically important ratification of his arrival in the Carolina elite. To abandon his political career was impossible. From boyhood, Hammond explained, "My whole training has been with a view to public life & no one has a keener sense . . . of its honours."[12]

Hammond transformed his annual late-summer trip to the mountains into a political survey of the state leadership, many of whom lived or vacationed in the up-country area. He began with his old friend and colleague, Francis Pickens of Edgefield. Although Hammond felt him too calculating to be entirely reliable, Pickens was a cousin of Calhoun and was believed by some to "control" the senator "in all practical matters." Not wishing to display unseemly eagerness for advancement, Hammond subtly left the congressman with the "impression" he was not averse to being governor, indeed "was perhaps desirous of the office but would wait to be pressed a little." From Pickens, Hammond proceeded to the great man himself. On August 17 he made a long-overdue visit to Calhoun in his Pendleton District home. But Hammond was frustrated to find the senator

11. Hammond Diary (SCL), October 6, 1839.
12. Hammond to Pickens, May 15, 1839, in JHH Papers, LC.

and all his family confined to bed by a summer fever. "This is a very great disappointment to me," Hammond complained to his diary. "I have come here chiefly
to see him, to ascertain his views of political affairs & to disclose mine to him."
Two days later Calhoun was at last well enough to receive visitors. Hammond
managed to elicit the senator's views on the issues at hand, to confirm Calhoun's
anger with Preston and his growing devotion to the Rhetts. But Hammond de-
tected as well a certain coolness that made him uneasy about the position Calhoun might take towards his gubernatorial candidacy. Undaunted, Hammond
continued his round of visits with former governor George McDuffie and then
with Calhoun's arch enemy, Waddy Thompson of Greenville. In mid-September, Hammond arrived for several weeks' stay at Limestone Springs, a resort
"where all the good company of the State is assembled now." As the Elmores and
their friends played whist together, Hammond found himself excluded—from
their political intrigues and their card games alike. "The relation of these men
towards me here," he feared, "is distinctively that of men opposed but willing to
keep up the forms of society."[13]

When he returned home Hammond was still uncertain whether to continue
in his ambitions for the governorship or to try for the legislature from either
Columbia or Barnwell. He knew the choice was crucial, for "I would not like to
risk a defeat" that would injure both position and pride. Some Barnwell citizens
reportedly resented his projected move to the capital; others differed with his
stand on contested local issues, making his success in a local campaign nearly as
problematical as a victory for statewide office. Escalating strife among Carolina's
leadership further complicated Hammond's difficulties in determining where his
best opportunity lay. Amidst such conflict, political life was becoming increasingly unpredictable and easy victories almost impossible to guarantee. For the
past decade gubernatorial candidates had all run unopposed, but it seemed unlikely that such a consensus would emerge for the 1840 contest. Nearly every
issue in the 1839 fall legislative session in Columbia evoked acrimonious debate,
and the Carolina delegation in Washington seemed equally factious. Barnwell
Rhett, eager to eliminate all rivals for Calhoun's favor, posed as an ally of Francis Pickens at a Democratic caucus and withdrew Pickens' name from consideration for Speaker of the House while he was still en route to Washington. Upon
his discovery of Rhett's unauthorized action, Pickens became enraged at what he

13. Hammond Diary (LC), August 17, 18, 1839; Hammond to John Fox Hammond, August
27, 1839, in JHH Papers, SCL; Hammond Diary (LC), September 24, 1839.

considered the "vilest intrigue ever known," and determined to crush the Rhett clique. Now the division in the state was not limited to Calhounites and Prestonites; the pro-Calhoun faction had split bitterly as well.[14]

Hammond chafed at the uncertainties of the situation and at his inability to make accurate calculations about the future. He feared that as a gubernatorial candidate he would confront "pretty strong opposition," for he knew he tended to take his "grounds too strongly against men & measures & thereby incur enmity. . . . I should either cease to do anything or do more I prefer the former—but cannot—& dread the latter—I expect I shall therefore just go on the same way & destroy my prospects entirely." An admitted prisoner of his ambition, Hammond had begun to regard a gubernatorial race as inevitable. Pickens was eager to use him as a weapon of retribution against the Rhetts; the old nullifiers saw him as a sound states' rights candidate who could suppress resurgent unionism. His aspirations conveniently coincided with their needs.[15]

Hammond was a candidate peculiarly ill-suited to the situation. Always contentious, he was not likely to smooth over the widening divisions within the state and build a broad consensus around his candidacy. He did indeed, as he himself recognized, tend to "incur enmity," and within the already factious Carolina politics, his campaign exacerbated existing conflicts. "One would think," he once remarked of himself, "I was conceived in discord and brought forth in passion, so thrifty am I in the accumulation of troubles. I appear only in my element when in a storm." Yet this flash of insight was not entirely characteristic. More often, Hammond's lack of awareness of his abrasiveness left him unable to moderate his effect upon others; he was ignorant of how disputatious he seemed.[16]

For example, late in the fall of 1839, just as he was beginning self-consciously to establish his position in regard to the gubernatorial race, Hammond participated in a convention in Columbia to create a state agricultural society. Appointed to the committee to prepare business for the meeting, Hammond became the outspoken opponent of state aid for agriculture. Until farmers and planters themselves adopted reformist attitudes, he argued, action by the state could have little effect. A geological and agricultural survey of South Carolina, a measure Calhoun strongly supported, would be, Hammond insisted, a waste.

14. Hammond Diary (LC), November 7, 1839; Pickens to Hammond, December 15, 1839, in JHH Papers, LC. See "Gubernatorial Controversy, 1840" (scrapbook in JHH Papers, LC).
15. Hammond Diary (SCL), December 31, 1839.
16. Hammond to I. W. Hayne, July 21, 1831, in Letterpress Book, JHH Papers, SCL.

"We are not yet prepared to make use of the results . . . —nor do I think we can get the right sort of man." Hammond was pleased by his performance at the gathering. "On the whole I think I have gained," he reported, "having pressed no point bitterly & kept my temper well." But others saw him differently. To the "friends of Agriculture," his course appeared "*ultra,*" so extreme as to risk the ruin of the state. Instead of gaining allies, Hammond had created an "agricultural party," a new source of division in Carolina and a basis of opposition to his candidacy.[17]

Despite the mounting tempest surrounding the gubernatorial succession, Hammond was not discouraged; by the first of the new year he had almost definitely decided to run. The chief magistracy would serve as the vehicle of his reentry into public life. Yet within the structure of Carolina politics, this decision was in many ways curious, for in the Palmetto State, the governor played an almost purely ceremonial role; he had no power to introduce or to veto legislation, and no right to succeed himself. His presence at the capital was required only during the three- or four-week legislative session that began in late November each year. One of Hammond's friends declared bluntly that the governor's office was "powerless, uninfluential insipid unenviable." A writer in the Charleston *Courier* explained more delicately that the office was "not of great executive power," although it did impart a degree of prestige to its occupant. Here Hammond perhaps recognized a means of enhancing his status and political visibility without unduly taxing his delicate health or undermining his entrepreneurial pursuits at Silver Bluff. Service as governor would entail far less of the day-to-day "political drudgery" Hammond had found so distasteful a part of his earlier foray into public life.[18]

The ceremonial nature of the post attracted Hammond's gubernatorial opponents as well. Calhoun had been regarding South Carolina's growing factionalism with alarm. Conflict was undermining the state's traditional deferential politics and threatening the unity of opinion Calhoun felt necessary for the defense of southern institutions and of his own position in national councils. Opposed on principle to party politics, Calhoun was troubled by the tenaciousness of the party identities of the nullification period. Robert Barnwell Rhett, sharing a

17. Hammond Diary (SCL), November 29, 1839; W. S. Reynolds to John Peter Richardson, September 20, 1840, in John Peter Richardson Papers, U.S. Department of Agriculture Library, Beltsville, Md.

18. Angus Patterson to Hammond, January 17, 1840, in JHH Papers, LC; Charleston *Courier,* July 2, 1840 (see also Charleston *Mercury,* July 31, 1840); Hammond Diary (SCL), January 6, 1840.

mess with the senator in Washington, was well aware of Calhoun's concerns and undertook to offer his assistance in healing breaches within the state. At meetings during the 1839 legislative session in Columbia and during a brief visit he made to Columbia early the following month, Rhett joined with the Elmores and their followers to devise a plan that would both win Calhoun's favor and work to enhance Rhett's own power within the state. Former nullifiers, they decided, would woo the loyalty of the old unionists by supporting one of their number for prominent political office. Because the governorship offered considerable political prestige, yet little substantive power, it could safely be offered to one of the enemy camp. On January 10, the Charleston *Mercury*, a staunch nullification organ edited by Rhett's brother-in-law, announced the nomination by "consultation" in Columbia of former unionist John Peter Richardson for governor on the basis of the plan of reconciliation Rhett had devised.[19]

How much Calhoun knew in advance and how much he approved is unclear; he chose to remain silent. Pickens, already deeply distrustful of the Rhetts, was sure the senator was at heart opposed to their movement, and he urged Hammond to continue his plans to run, assuring him Calhoun's support would eventually be his. Others of Hammond's friends approached the young Carolinian from a very different political position. Determined to overthrow Calhoun's domination of Carolina politics, they saw Hammond as a potential instrument of the senator's demise. T. T. Player cautioned Hammond that he must never expect support from Calhoun for "the simple reason that you act upon an independent judgment about all things, & I warn you of it, because you can not be too vigilant of treacherous demogogues." Player advised Hammond to oppose Calhoun openly, for, he prophesied, "the dynasty is falling."[20]

Emotionally committed to the race, Hammond would for the rest of the campaign heed that advice most favorable to his continuing candidacy. Yet in his effort to accommodate all those who offered support, he often found himself in the company of strange political bedfellows. Already he was receiving simultaneous overtures from Calhoun's bitterest opponents and from Francis Pickens, who regarded himself as Calhoun's truest ally. "It is difficult," Hammond acknowledged, "for me to act however purely under these circumstances without incurring the hostility & what is worse the suspicion of one side." Despite warn-

19. Charleston *Mercury*, January 10, 1840. See also Wiltse, *John C. Calhoun, Sectionalist*, 53–59, and the Franklin H. Elmore Papers, LC.

20. T. T. Player to Hammond, January 1, 1840, in JHH Papers, LC; Hammond Diary (SCL), January 6, 1840.

ings from friends of his duplicity, Hammond wanted to trust Pickens' assurances completely, for he saw the anticipated support of Calhoun as the guarantee of his ultimate success.[21]

By mid-February almost every paper of significance in the state had responded enthusiastically to the Richardson nomination, presenting a "most formidable array" of opposition to Hammond's aspirations. Awaiting the appearance of his own friends' letters bringing his name into nomination, Hammond became agitated and melancholy, longing for "one to whom I could unfold all my feelings." The "excitement of politics is very distressing to me," he concluded. "I give up to it too much." Because, as the Edgefield *Advertiser* explained, the office of governor was customarily "bestowed (rather than solicited . . .)," it was important that Hammond not show too much eagerness for the post. But Hammond felt paralyzed and frustrated by these constraints and chafed at surrendering control of his political fate to others—even his own partisans. He was not accustomed to such dependence. "There is no concert or management among my friends," he worried, "& I cannot without doing what I think wrong produce it. I cannot electioneer for myself nor correspond with everybody about it."[22]

But he did correspond actively with Calhoun throughout the winter and spring, eagerly seeking some indication of the senator's support. In letters that alternated between fawning obsequiousness—"I acknowledge my inexperience in politics and my inability to grapple with such subtle and important questions as these"—and a scarcely hidden resentment of Calhoun's tacit acceptance of the Richardson movement—"It is hard to force a man at once upon both parties & call it a measure of conciliation"—Hammond endeavored to curry favor. Unmoved, Calhoun continued to profess his "strict neutrality" as well as his regret that the contest was becoming so heated and divisive. "My strength here," he wrote Hammond from Washington, "depends on the union at home."[23]

With Hammond's nomination in the *Courier* and the Edgefield *Advertiser* in mid-February, the governor's race began openly to manifest those very characteristics of bitter factiousness that Richardson supporters had hoped it would permanently dissipate. The day after "Charleston" put forth Hammond's name in a letter printed in the February 13 *Courier*, the *Mercury* replied with an attack

21. Hammond Diary (SCL), January 6, 1840.
22. Hammond Diary (SCL), January 20, February 12, 1840. See Pickens' warning in Pickens to Hammond, February 18, 1840, JHH Papers, LC.
23. Hammond to John C. Calhoun, March 10, 1840, Calhoun to Hammond, February 23, 1840, both in JHH Papers, LC.

upon the motives behind his candidacy. "If Col. HAMMOND is a Sub-Treasury man and a friend of Mr. CALHOUN, we do not see how he can allow himself to be brought forward," thereby, the *Mercury* insinuated, preventing the unification of the state under Richardson. Throughout the campaign, Hammond would confront these same charges of traitorous Whig allegiance, probank and anti-Calhoun sympathies, despite his friends' explicit denials that he held such views.[24]

Accustomed to one gubernatorial candidate, South Carolina soon had three. The revered judge David Johnson, an old unionist and a subtreasury man, had considerable support in his own up-country region of the state and among the former antinullification forces and their traditional organ, the Charleston *Courier*. Some of Hammond's friends applauded Johnson's entry into the race since it promised to divide the unionists, but because of his age, few considered him a serious candidate. Hammond was certain he would withdraw before the election in December.

Although even the local Edgefield *Advertiser* opposed Hammond's candidacy, the young planter felt his prospects were still viable. Many Carolinians, he believed, resented the political manipulation that Richardson's candidacy represented. On a trip to Charleston in late February, Hammond secured the support of former governor James Hamilton and several other low-country politicians, and Hamilton secretly promised to organize all former nullifiers on Hammond's behalf. Early in March a large public meeting in Barnwell gave Hammond further encouragement by endorsing his candidacy and disproving the *Advertiser*'s assertion that the "*entire section*" supported Richardson.[25]

Hammond's hopes for success rested on a calculation that the cynical and dictatorial maneuverings of Rhett, Elmore, and other Richardson supporters would alienate those legislators responsible for choosing the governor in the fall. Yet because Hammond was willing to accept the support as well of a variety of disaffected groups whose views he did not share, his campaign became tainted by identification with the anti-Calhoun, pro-Preston, pro-Whig, and antisubtreasury forces within the state. While he accepted their aid, Hammond sought to dissociate himself from their unpopular views. His only purpose in running, he assured Calhoun, was "to give the Nullifiers an opportunity to say openly if they were willing to . . . throw the power of the state into the hands of their old

24. Charleston *Courier*, Febraury 13, 1840; Charleston *Mercury*, February 14, 1840. See Maxcy Gregg's reminiscences of the way suspicions of Hammond's Whig sympathies defeated him in 1840. Maxcy Gregg to Hammond, March 29, 1852, in JHH Papers, LC.
25. James Hamilton to Hammond, March 3, 1840, in JHH Papers, LC; Charleston *Courier*, March 9, 1840.

opponents—& to give the people or their representatives a fair chance to arrest the formation of a spoils party in So. Ca." His friends pressed the same argument upon the public in the columns of those newspapers that would print their communications. On July 16 a correspondent in the *Advertiser* proclaimed that a Hammond victory would be a "triumph of candor, ingenuousness and disinterested patriotism over the intrigue, double dealing, and machinations" of the Rhett clique. Hammond portrayed himself as the representative of a traditional Carolina politics of republican virtue against the incursions of a new system of parties, logrolling, and corruption.[26]

But Hammond's partisans raised more substantive issues as well, stressing the dangers of having a former unionist as governor when the tariff issue reappeared, for soon Congress would be called upon to effect the reductions promised for 1842 by the postnullification compromise in the national legislature, and there was some uncertainty that protariff forces would carry out the bargain. Hammond's clearly articulated opposition to protection indicated he would be much more likely than Richardson to stand firm against unfair duties. His "brief but brilliant" career in the House, another supporter emphasized, ensured that no Carolinian could forget his devotion to states' rights principles. His proslavery speech in the 1836 Congress had "fixed our opinions, and rendered firm our faith in the justice of our cause."[27]

Hammond's opponents charged him with an array of shortcomings. His insistence upon running in itself warranted suspicion about his loyalties to Carolina, for, his rivals alleged, Hammond's candidacy threatened Richardson's efforts "to collect together the broke [sic] fragments of our strength, which has been severely paralyzed by internal dissensions and to consolidate it into one undivided and unbroken phalanx." Hammond was also too young, his opponents objected, and too many recent governors had come from the Savannah River area. His old friendship with Preston bespoke Whig leanings that Hammond's long failure to openly commit himself to the subtreasury only confirmed. Hammond's efforts of the previous year to remain aloof from this controversy had backfired. His credentials as a nullifier seemed to matter less than his position on the bank question, for as the editor of the *Advertiser* emphasized, "Nullification is not now the question at issue, and . . . the Sub-treasury is." By June allegations of his Whig leanings had become so widespread that Hammond felt

26. Hammond to Calhoun, March 10, 1840, in JHH Papers, LC; Edgefield *Advertiser*, July 16, 1840; Charleston *Mercury*, May 20, 1840.
27. Charleston *Courier*, February 13, June 2, 1840.

compelled to abandon his previous reliance on friends and to present his views personally. On June 18 he published a statement in the *Advertiser* supporting the subtreasury and expressing his preference for Democrat Martin Van Buren against his Whig opponent William Henry Harrison in the fall presidential contest. But even this unequivocal declaration did not relieve Hammond of the suspicion of harboring secret Whig sympathies. Because of the support Hammond received from those few unpopular Whigs who did exist in Carolina, his opponents found continuing accusations against Hammond almost irresistible.[28]

Richardson's supporters regarded Hammond as foolishly obstinate. No previous gubernatorial canvass had ever aroused such bitterness, but neither appeals to patriotism nor invocations of self-interest could persuade Hammond to withdraw. He scorned a promise from the Rhett faction that he would be awarded the governorship in 1842 or possibly a seat in the U.S. Senate and self-righteously proclaimed this offer to be just another evidence of the partisan dictation of Carolina politics that he was determined to oppose. Hammond expressed his tenacious ambition, his unwillingness to acknowledge defeat, as a principled defense of republican political ideals against a new demagogic order.[29]

Hammond remained convinced, despite the flagging confidence of his friends, the defection of most of his Charleston supporters, and the continuing silence of Calhoun, that he had a fair chance to win the state by relying on the "incorruptible firmness of the old nullification party." And even if he lost, he declared, it "would perhaps give me more prominence to be made a martyr in the cause than even to be elected." Hammond had begun to suspect that despite his avowed neutrality Calhoun and not Rhett was the mastermind behind the Richardson conciliation strategy. But even Calhoun's request, conveyed through Pickens, that Hammond withdraw had little effect upon the determination of the young Carolinian to persist in his candidacy. Hammond seemed, for at least brief periods, to thrive on a level of discord others found intolerable.[30]

By summer hostilities had escalated almost to the point of violence. When a writer in the *Mercury* intimated that Hammond had himself penned a pseu-

28. Edgefield *Advertiser*, July 16, February 27, July 2, March 6, June 18, July 30, 1840; Charleston *Mercury*, July 30, December 8, 1840. There were some grounds for these suspicions. Hammond was not an enthusiastic Democrat—or party man of any sort. He confessed to his intimates that he was "only a lukewarm V[an] B[uren] man." Hammond to M. C. M. Hammond, July 12, 1840, in JHH Papers, SCL.

29. Hammond Diary (SCL), April 4, 25, 1840. See A. J. Pemberton to Hammond, April 29, 1840, in JHH Papers, LC.

30. Hammond Diary (SCL), April 8, 1840; Hammond to M. C. M. Hammond, April 30, 1840, in JHH Papers, LC; Clark to Hammond, April 19, 1840, in JHH Papers, SCL.

donymous attack upon Richardson in the *Courier*, Hammond was ready for a duel. But the author of the article denied he had intended to allude to Hammond, and the editor published a disclaimer to settle the conflict. In Edgefield several duels did occur between Richardson supporter Louis Wigfall and a series of Hammond sympathizers, one of whom was ultimately killed in an exchange of fire.[31]

August brought a respite from conflict when Hammond, ignoring the advice of those who urged him to canvass the up-country resorts, departed for New York to acquire the furniture and accessories necessary for his new Columbia house. Catherine, who was again awaiting confinement, was not able to travel; so Hammond was compelled to make his choices without her aid. He felt lonely and indecisive and wrote affectionately to his wife that he missed "some one to scratch my head and make much of me," as well as to guide his purchases. At last he settled upon four marble mantels, two dozen stained maple arm chairs for the dining room and another dozen for the bedchambers. He worried most about bedsteads, for Catherine had requested the French style, but they had become unfashionable, and Hammond discovered that they were decidedly "not the thing." Even at several hundred miles' remove from Carolina, however, Hammond could not dismiss the governor's race from his thoughts, and he urged Catherine to save all the relevant newspapers for his return.[32]

When he reached home, Hammond found little optimistic news about the progress of his candidacy. The up-country districts of York, Union, and Spartanburg evinced little sympathy for Hammond; the last Charleston supporters had faded away; and Calhoun's neutrality had become but a thin disguise for his true preference for Richardson. Recognizing the senator's real sentiments at last, Pickens had become cool and distant, and Hammond lost a mainstay of support.

But the young planter continued to hope. When returns from the legislative

---

31. Charleston *Mercury*, June 11, 1840. Thompson T. Player was actually the author of "A Sub-Treasury Nullifier," which appeared in the Charleston *Courier* on June 10, 1840. See James Rose to Hammond, July 10, 1840, Hammond to T. Lynch Hamilton, June 16, 18, 22, 1840, John Stuart to T. Lynch Hamilton, June 19, 29, 1840, Hammond to Stuart, June 22, 1840, all in JHH Papers, LC. On the Edgefield duels see A. P. Burt to Hammond, July 8, 1840, in JHH Papers, LC. Wigfall fought Preston Brooks and James P. Carroll, and killed Thomas Bird. See Whitfield Brooks to Hammond, July 2, 1840, Butler to Hammond, July 2, 6, 8, 18, 1840, Player to Hammond, July 6, 26, 1840, all in JHH Papers, LC; Hammond to M. C. M. Hammond, July 12, 1840, in JHH Papers, SCL. See also Alvy L. King, *Louis T. Wigfall: Southern Fire-Eater* (Baton Rouge: Louisiana State University Press, 1970), 25.

32. Hammond to Catherine Fitzsimons Hammond, August 25, 1840, in JHH Papers, SHC.

balloting came in, Hammond reported to Marcellus that "it is thought a re-action is taking place in the State in my favour," and he evaluated his prospects as "fair." As the legislative session approached, Hammond made plans to leave Silver Bluff, grateful that he would be able to occupy himself in Columbia with the details of unpacking and arranging furniture in the nearly completed house. Late in September, Catherine had delivered another child—a girl at last—and mother and daughter were not yet ready to travel. From the capital Hammond reported regularly on his progress both with the house and with the election. Harriet and Catty Hampton, teenage daughters of Wade Hampton and Cather-ine's sister Ann, offered to assist their uncle in hanging pictures, and Hammond pleased himself supplying his almost nightly political entertainments with sup-pers of turkey, duck, corned beef, ham, wine, and cigars.[33]

But these housekeeping distractions did little to allay his worries about the gubernatorial contest and about his political future more generally. Unable to resist political involvement, Hammond was at the same time unable to enjoy it; politics seemed to consume him entirely. "I often ask myself," he wrote reflec-tively to his wife, "how it is that I am here giving up everything to a contest which I loathe, where I am . . . afraid of success at the very moment I am obliged to appear most anxious for it."[34]

When the legislature convened, conflict arose almost immediately about when the gubernatorial decision should be made. Hammond believed he was gaining ground every day, and he regarded a move to hasten the election as part of a general and long-standing conspiracy against him. His opponents, on the other hand, saw efforts to postpone the election as a cynical maneuver on the part of Hammond's forces to gain time for base electioneering, to change dele-gates' minds and to win over former supporters of Judge Johnson, who had at last withdrawn from the race. The representatives from Richland District, which in-cluded the capital, had been refused seats in a credentials fight, and Hammond's lieutenants, certain of the Columbia delegates' votes, won a postponement until these places were filled. But these tactical efforts made little difference. When at last the roll was called on the gubernatorial question on December 9, Rich-ardson won an overwhelming victory, 104 votes to Hammond's 47. All but three of the seventy former unionists in the legislature supported Richardson, who

33. Hammond to M. C. M. Hammond, October 28, 1840, in JHH Papers, LC; Hammond Diary (SCL), November 7, 1840.
34. Hammond to Catherine Fitzsimons Hammond, December 4, 1840, in JHH Papers, SHC.

also, according to Hammond's calculations, managed to win the votes of thirty-four nullifiers. Hammond took Barnwell and Lexington and the votes of some staunch states' rights advocates and personal friends.[35]

Although by the last weeks of the canvass he had come to expect defeat, Hammond remained bitter about the campaign. Three times, he noted, he had been offered bribes of high office if he would withdraw his opposition to Richardson. But he had declined to become a tool of the Rhett-Elmore faction, the "Regency" that now ruled South Carolina. His refusal had produced hostility and conflict unknown in any previous governor's election. "The strangest objections have been made to me," he remarked in early December. "One objects to my house—another to my pictures—another to my drinking too much wine with the Whigs & I am called the aristocratic candidate &c &c." A new political culture was emerging in South Carolina, and it was clear to Hammond that "the school in which I had trained myself was . . . extinguished." Nullification, dependent upon the grass-roots organizing techniques of James Hamilton, had introduced a new politics of mass participation into the state, bringing South Carolina ever closer to the party contests and machinations that were becoming the norm in the democratizing politics of the rest of the nation.[36]

But political rhetoric had not changed as dramatically as had behavior. Almost all factions within the state professed allegiance to an older tradition of republicanism, to a consensual political order that acclaimed as leaders the best and most virtuous of its citizens. The sanctions against seeming too eager for office and the decrying of demagoguery, of party, and of spoils all represented the persistence of these older values. In the gubernatorial campaign of 1840 both Hammond and his opponents sought to identify themselves as heirs of the true

35. *Ibid.*, December 6, 1840. For Hammond's analysis of the roll-call vote, see Hammond Diary (LC), February 7, 1841.
36. Hammond to Catherine Fitzsimons Hammond, December 6, 1840, in JHH Papers, SHC. Hammond to William Gilmore Simms, February 2, 1851, in JHH Papers, LC. The press repeatedly noted the unusual factiousness of this gubernatorial campaign. See Charleston *Mercury*, July 30, 1840; Edgefield *Advertiser*, July 2, March 26, 1840. On the persistence of republicanism in South Carolina politics, see Kenneth S. Greenberg, "The Second American Revolution: South Carolina Politics, Society, and Secession, 1776–1860" (Ph.D. dissertation, University of Wisconsin, Madison, 1976); Kenneth S. Greenberg, "Representation and the Isolation of South Carolina, 1776–1860," *Journal of American History*, LXIV (December, 1977), 723–43. Greenberg emphasizes continuity a bit more than I would, for while I see rhetorical consistency, I think much of political behavior was changing. See also, Robert M. Weir, "'The Harmony We Were Famous For': An Interpretation of Pre-Revolutionary South Carolina Politics," *William and Mary Quarterly*, XXVI (October, 1969) 473–501, for the best exposition of what I have called traditional political values of South Carolina.

republicanism—Hammond through his attacks on Rhett's "dictation" and "management"; the Richardson forces through their appeals to unity and consensus. Indeed, Calhoun's overarching goal within the state was to restore the politics of deference that the agitations of nullification had undermined. Having all but eliminated Preston and the Whig opposition in 1838–1839, Calhoun needed only to reconcile the old unionists and nullifiers in order to align the state behind him in cherished unity. But while this might have achieved the form of the old politics, it could not restore its substance. The world of republican elitism was irretrievable. To be a leader in the new political world of Carolina, one had to be a manager—or have a henchman like Rhett to undertake the necessary but distasteful political maneuvers. Discipline, not deference, was becoming the new foundation of political power.

Without the interference of Hammond, Calhoun's followers might have been better able to realize the senator's goals without departing so markedly from traditional Carolina style. Calhoun's "neutrality" enabled him to retain at least a semblance of the older virtues. But in the 1840 campaign both sides departed significantly from prevailing ideals. The personal ambitions of Calhoun and of Hammond were the true motive forces within the canvass; it was as important to Calhoun's power to retain Carolina unity as it was to Hammond's aspirations to shatter it. A politics of partisan oppositions and interests replaced the traditional world of deference and harmony. Even though the rhetoric bespoke an earlier era, even though the lingering aristocratic structures of Carolina government dictated that the legislature and not the people make the final gubernatorial choice, Carolina was slowly entering a new political world. And even though he overtly espoused traditional republican political values, Hammond contributed significantly to accelerating the changes already underway.

Although his supporters urged him to continue the noble battle against "Regency" domination, Hammond's commitment to reform would fall victim to ambition. Because Calhoun had ostensibly remained aloof from the contest, his hand could bear the olive branch. The Regency Hammond had denounced in 1840 would in 1842 serve as the vehicle of his advancement to the governor's chair.

CHAPTER 12

The Crisis of My Fate

For James Henry Hammond, as for most South Carolinians in the early 1840s, times were hard. Nationwide depression had struck so deeply in the seaboard cotton states that even many masters of five hundred slaves, Hammond reported, found difficulty procuring the cash to "pay their negroes for chickens." The expenses of his lavish new Columbia house and the neglect of plantation business during the gubernatorial campaign had reduced Hammond's liquid resources, and he was compelled to borrow to meet daily expenses. Although he estimated his worth at nearly $200,000, the cost of maintaining the style of life befitting his growing prominence had him scrambling to pay his bills.[1]

Yet this unsettling situation seemed to disturb Hammond less than did a cluster of other anxieties produced by his recent political campaign. He was in the grip of emotional as well as financial depression. The hostility surrounding the recent election had not only shattered any lingering idealism about public life but had raised profound doubts about the depth of his commitment to a political career. Hammond's experiences as a candidate had left him "morbidly melancholy" and had reinforced a longstanding ambivalence about his ambitions. The attacks to which he had been repeatedly subjected had created in Hammond a sense of deep personal as well as political isolation. During 1840 and 1841, he began to seek a remedy for these intensified feelings of loneliness and to look beyond politics for the fulfillment of his drive for fame. Hammond's dissatisfac-

1. James Henry Hammond to M. C. M. Hammond, June 8, 1841, March 19, 1840, in JHH Papers, SCL.

tion was at once personal and more broadly social; he wanted adoration and validation from intimates, as well as from the world at large. Indeed, each of these needs continually stimulated and enhanced the other, ultimately producing by the middle of the decade a crisis in both his private and his public life.[2]

A difficult and contentious man, Hammond appeared to most of those around him as hard, cold, aggressive, even unfeeling—"a shrewd calculator," as he himself described his public image. Yet, he insisted in characteristically self-pitying introspection, these were misperceptions by those who did not see the reality behind his mask. The "world judging by appearances my bearing & conversation have been wholly deceived in my character." Hammond maintained that he had "always been a shy & sensitive person. . . . The very excess of my sensitiveness has led me to assume as much as possible of the reverse in order to conceal it." Far from hard, Hammond explained, he simply could not "bear that others should see my emotions & even those which might be honestly exposed I shrink from exhibiting." By withdrawing, Hammond feared he conveyed an arrogant and supercilious impression. Yet he felt incapable of overturning this image by reaching out to those around him. Imprisoned within himself by a pride that inhibited him from risking rebuff and by a desire for power that made him resist emotional dependence as strongly as he did financial or social subservience, Hammond not surprisingly longed for meaningful human contact. In early 1841 he began a new diary with the explanation, "I want a friend . . . to whose sympathetic bosom I could confide *anything*—To whom I could speak of myself as I *am*. . . . Such a friend," he concluded sadly, "I can now only find in this book."[3] Yet he would continue to look elsewhere for the emotional sustenance he knew he required. Nurtured on Byron and Shelley, on romantic notions of spiritual exile as well as visions of friendships that "link *soul* to *soul*," Hammond craved that intensity of feeling and intimacy of human relationship that his outward coldness and his judgmental defensiveness made all but impossible to achieve.[4]

During the height of the gubernatorial strife, Hammond had sought comfort in personal ties. But no one could "understand, sympathise, console me." Catherine, though a "good soul," would only be threatened by any revelation of his deepest thoughts, for he was certain she would not understand him. Under the

2. James Henry Hammond Diary (MS in JHH Papers, SCL), February 16, 1840.
3. *Ibid.*, December 16, 1849; Hammond Diary (MS in JHH Papers, LC), December 12, 1844, April 17, 1836, February 6, 1841.
4. Hammond to I. W. Hayne, January 21, 1841, in JHH Papers, LC.

pressure of politics, he had found himself seeking consolation in the image of a "dear sweet girl whom I think of twice where I do so once of this gov. matter." Cryptic references to "the beloved" in his diary for 1840 are never explained, but it seems Hammond found in infatuation a relief from campaign tensions that, he reported, made him long to read poetry and cry all day.[5]

"The hearty support of my friends" provided another important source of comfort in this period of stress. Since his marriage and his removal to Silver Bluff, Hammond had been out of touch with many of his old Columbia ac-quaintances, and the hard times in Carolina had since prompted many of his youthful intimates, men such as I. W. Hayne and Josiah C. Nott, to depart for the more prosperous Southwest. Hammond hoped his return to Columbia would place him in a more congenial social environment than Barnwell, where he had found "not a soul to whom I can converse of any thing save neighbourhood news & crops." But more significant than any new Columbia ties was Hammond's growing intimacy with poet and novelist William Gilmore Simms. After the two had jointly participated in the founding of the state agricultural society in the fall of 1839, they struck up a correspondence about plantation affairs. Simms lived only fifty miles from Silver Bluff in Barnwell District near Orangeburg. As their letters became more frequent, the two men discovered that their views were uncannily similar on a variety of topics ranging from local politics to the condition of southern literature and the decline of their native state. Soon Simms and Hammond sought each other's company regularly. Simms was a gruff, yet imposing figure, his portly body crowned by a disproportionately large head covered in an unruly mass of curls. He was a delightful companion—"a most incessant talker," Hammond immediately observed—jovial and witty, a well-known raconteur. Exchanging visits between Silver Bluff and Simms's Wood-lands, the two men spent many hours during the next two and a half decades playing billiards, sipping port, cracking walnuts, and discussing their personal, professional and political frustrations in the South.[6]

Like Hammond, Simms had an introspective and morbid streak and felt sim-ilarly alienated and isolated from the society around him. Although he was un-questionably the most popular author of the region, Simms believed his gifts were insufficiently appreciated; the South, he feared, was fundamentally hostile

---

5. Hammond Diary (SCL), February 16, January 29, February 24, 1840.

6. *Ibid.*; Hammond Diary (LC), February 6, July 3, March 30, 1841. For descriptions of Simms, see Paul Hamilton Hayne, "Ante-Bellum Charleston," *Southern Bivouac*, I (1885), 257–68, and Hammond Diary (LC), March 30, 1841.

Courtesy of the South Caroliniana Library
William Gilmore Simms, *circa* 1859.

to the life of the mind. Since Hammond also felt his intellectual talents were unrecognized in Carolina, the two formed a bond based upon their shared sense of rejection and neglect—upon what they regarded, within the terms of the prevailing romantic outlook, as their inevitable alienation as men of genius from a society insensitive to their special gifts. As Simms recalled more than two decades later, Hammond became his "most confidential friend. . . . Never were thoughts more intimate than his and mine. . . . I felt that there was something kindred in our intellectual nature. Certainly there was much, very much in common between us. Never did man more thoroughly appreciate his genius—its grasp—its subtlety—its superiority of aim. And most deeply did I sympathize with him under the denial of his aim and the exercise of his powers."[7]

As, in Hammond's words, the "most distinguished literary character of the South," Simms interacted with a multitude of intellectually inclined southerners, and he began to introduce Hammond into a "sacred circle" of men of mind determined to establish a place for intellect and intellectuals in the Old South. Simms had from the first a profound impact upon Hammond, broadening his aspirations beyond the narrow political world upon which they had previously focused and providing him with a vocabulary and a framework of explanation in which to express his growing frustration and discontent. Continually stressing Hammond's "great mental superiority," Simms urged him to contribute to regional periodicals, to undertake speculations on metaphysics and critical essays on contemporary philosophical issues. Reawakening Hammond's early interest in intellectual achievement, the novelist encouraged his new friend to identify himself primarily as a man of mind and to organize his understanding of the world around this assumption. The "peculiarly intellectual individual," Simms insisted, possessed a "peculiar moral constitution," which often doomed him to both "eminent solitude in the world of fame" and "corresponding solitude in the world of the affections." The description seemed to Hammond an all too insightful portrayal of his plight.[8]

Hammond hoped that his move to Columbia early in 1841 would resolve many of the dilemmas that had been troubling him and, at the very least, would end the isolation he had felt at Silver Bluff. The greetings of neighbors, who welcomed the Hammonds with a stream of visits and generous tributes of wine and food, were highly flattering, and the newcomers reciprocated with a housewarming party. But almost at once Hammond was disappointed. Many of his guests seemed unappreciative of his house—they were jealous he was sure. And when he displayed his European art treasures, they "gazed at them with the apa-

---

7. William Gilmore Simms to Edward Spann Hammond, November 20, 1864, in Mary C. Simms Oliphant, Alfred Taylor Odell, and T. C. Duncan Eaves (eds.), *The Letters of William Gilmore Simms* (5 vols.; Columbia: University of South Carolina Press, 1952–56), IV, 469–70.

8. Hammond to James Polk, September 4, 1847, *ibid.*; William Gilmore Simms, "Southern Literature," *Magnolia*, III (February, 1841), 72–73; Simms to Hammond, December 25, 1846, in JHH Papers, LC; William Gilmore Simms, "Fanny Kemble: A Year of Consolation," *Southern Quarterly Review*, XII (July, 1847), 200; William Gilmore Simms, "A New Spirit of the Age," *Southern Quarterly Review*, VII (April, 1845), 314. For more on Hammond's literary productions, see Chapter 13.

thy of Indians." The Columbians' taste appeared hardly more elevated than that of his rural Barnwell neighbors. Even these town dwellers, Hammond concluded, had neither "intellect nor information," and they whiled away their time smoking, drinking, and playing backgammon. Within weeks, Hammond was thoroughly bored by the triviality of capital society and impatient at the idleness that had replaced his daily plantation responsibilities. Life had become little more than a dull "round of frivolities."[9]

Yet Hammond retained hopes of discovering other satisfactions in Columbia. A pleasant dinner with eight professors and writers at the home of South Carolina College political economist Francis Lieber left Hammond determined to make a place for himself in the world of letters. Unlike the others with whom he supped on turkey, tongue, and truffled pheasant, Hammond recognized that as yet he possessed no intellectual stature. "I have never written a book, nor even an Essay or critique. I am therefore at the beginning in that line." Increasingly he found himself preoccupied—"persecuted"—by the notion of a substantial literary undertaking.[10]

In part, this diversification in Hammond's interests arose directly out of his disillusionment with politics. The doubts he had always expressed about public life and the ambivalence that had led to his resignation from Congress in 1836 had been significantly intensified by his unpleasant experiences during the gubernatorial campaign. Hammond reported to I. W. Hayne a "great change" in his attitudes, a "most thoro' contempt" for public office. Even the presidency, he observed, made a man hardly more famous than a well-known murderer. "Political honors," he confided to Simms, "are the most ephemeral of all earthly distinctions." For the first time, Hammond began to couple his complaints about public life with explicit recognition that there existed alternative means of satisfying his longing for fame. Simms's literary labors seemed to Hammond "far more honorable pursuits" than the race for political office.[11]

While part of Hammond wished to transfer his aspirations to a different sphere of endeavor, another part sought to deal with his dissatisfactions by rejecting ambition altogether. As he enrolled his four eldest sons in school in Columbia, Hammond reflected on their futures and on the means of saving them from his own fate. Even as a child, he remembered, he had felt driven, always

---

9. Hammond Diary (LC), February 28, 1841, June 21, 1842, May 12, 1841.

10. *Ibid.*, February 7, August 28, 1841.

11. Hammond to I. W. Hayne, January 21, 1841, Hammond to Simms, January 27, 1841, all in JHH Papers, LC.

"looking to the future. . . . On! on! has been the cry with me from the first. . . . My poor dear boys . . . ," he vowed, "I shall be careful not to make you too ambitious or too anxious." In spite of this determination, Hammond was soon complaining that the children's schools were insufficiently demanding to meet the standards of achievement he could not help but hold out for his sons. The teachers held classes only until three o'clock in the afternoon and then permitted the boys to "run wild." Evidently the young Hammonds ran wild before three as well, for their tuition bill included a substantial charge for damage to desks and chairs. Hammond was disgusted, for he had of course abandoned none of his hopes for the success of his offspring. The establishment of a southern dynasty would serve as one avenue to the posterity he sought. Hammond's sons would join their father as victims of his unbounded ambition.[12]

Hammond's dynastic goals were evident as well in the nature of the advice he provided his brothers. Marcellus and John were now adults, yet James continued to supply them with a stream of exhortations that accompanied his undoubtedly more welcome financial assistance. John had completed his medical training at the University of Pennsylvania and in the spring of 1841 returned to Silver Bluff with the intention of practicing at nearby Beech Island. Marcellus was stationed in Arkansas, and eagerly anticipated promotion to captain or perhaps, through his brother's influence, transfer to a prestigious post in Washington. In 1841, however, James seemed less concerned with their professional careers than with the interest both youths had expressed in matrimony. The dissatisfaction Hammond had begun to express at the lack of emotional intimacy in his own marriage had little apparent effect upon his prescriptions for Marcellus and John. Marriage, he declared, was above all an instrument of self-advancement; love a mere "rigmerole." To wed a woman "with less than $20,000 *in present possession*," he believed, was "an act of insanity." An orphan with a fortune, he remarked, was his idea of a perfect match. To Hammond's immense relief, Marcellus had just broken off a highly irregular liaison with an Indian woman in Arkansas, and James urged him to seek a mate with wealth and status. In the spring of 1842 the young soldier announced his engagement to Harriet Davis of Augusta whom James had specifically identified as the richest and most eligible of the maidens of local society. Hammond could scarcely contain his delight.[13]

12. Hammond Diary (LC), February 14–15, March 1, September 18, 1841; Hammond, Business Papers (JHH Papers, SCL), December 16, 1843.
13. Hammond to John Fox Hammond, May 2, 1841, July 29, 1842, Hammond to M. C. M. Hammond, April 29, June 24, 1842, all in JHH Papers, SCL; Hammond Diary (LC), July 13, 1842.

But Hammond communicated contradictory messages to his brothers and sons, and taken as a whole, his admonitions reflected the confusions and uncertainties that plagued his own life. At the same time that he drove himself into a state of intense "anxiety created by the idea that the 'main chance' depends on having every screw tight & the whole machinery moving on clock-work principles," he had begun to question those aspirations upon which his life had been built. And while he explicitly warned his brothers and sons that ambition was a "species of madness" that produced only "misery," he simultaneously urged them ever onward in the race for power and prominence. The madness of ambition held Hammond firmly in its grasp.[14]

Despite reservations about his political future and despite the growing distractions of intellectual pursuits, Hammond's public career seemed during 1841 to progress almost of its own accord. The militia vacancy Hammond had awaited since his return from Europe appeared early in the year. For "many small reasons," he decided to run for the brigadiership. Almost apologetic for seeking office once again, Hammond explained to his diary that he was "fond" of the military and would appreciate the opportunity to travel about the state on reviews. His show of indifference was hardly convincing; he remained eager for every possible enhancement in status. Even though military titles were of "no consequence," he decided that since they were the forms of address regularly used in social intercourse, "we had as well have the highest." After his successful election in May, Hammond became "the General," a title he used for the remainder of his life.[15]

In June, Hammond received another acknowledgment of his growing prominence when he was chosen a director of a branch of the state bank; in November he was invited to be a trustee of South Carolina College; and late in the fall he made a "decided hit" as the anniversary orator of the state agricultural society. Hammond's address expounded the insights he had acquired in his past few years' ventures into scientific agriculture. His experiments with marl, diversified crops, drainage, and manure took on broader significance as he prescribed them as the most rational and effective response for all Carolinians to make to the "impending failure of our Great Staple." Economic difficulties, the leveling off of British demand for cotton, and the higher productivity of the Southwest all foretold, he warned, the end of Carolina's nearly exclusive dependence on staple

14. Hammond to William B. Hodgson, January 1, 1846, in JHH Papers, DU; Hammond to John Fox Hammond, January 29, 1841, in JHH Papers, SCL.
15. Hammond Diary (LC), February 8, 1841.

production. In the future, farmers must grow a wider variety of crops, and Carolinians should begin to seek economic self-sufficiency by developing manufactures. Agricultural reform, careful attention to the methods of scientific planting, would be the state's only redemption. If the planter were to be saved, he must abandon his prejudice against "book farming" and begin to apply intellect and reason to plantation practice. Hammond presented the crisis of Carolina's economy in terms of his emerging concern about the role of thought and of the man of mind within southern culture. In South Carolina, Hammond told the state agricultural society, the planter must henceforth be a scientist and an intellectual.[16]

Hammond's oration, he reported, was "as highly complimented as anything I ever did." Many in Columbia were certain it had guaranteed his success in the next governor's race. Hammond professed to be "indifferent" to his political fortunes, but he could not have helped but notice an emerging consensus around his candidacy; the 1842 election seemed to promise little of the acrimony that had plagued the 1840 campaign. In the months immediately following his December, 1840, defeat, however, Hammond had remained bitter and had vowed vengeance. Although compelled at last to acknowledge that nullification "*per se*" was dead, he had been still determined to "annihilate those who have betrayed it" through their support of Richardson and unionism. Even in his disenchantment with politics, Hammond could not dismiss a desire to vindicate himself through a resounding electoral triumph. To be elected governor in 1842 in spite of the opposition of the Rhett clique, he at first thought, would be the "most satisfactory compensation" for his humiliating defeat in the legislature. How, he tentatively inquired of Francis Pickens early in 1841, did Calhoun view the situation?[17]

Calhoun astutely recognized that Hammond, despite his resolution to "annihilate" the Regency, was ripe for co-option. However disillusioned he might claim to have become with public life, Hammond remained transparently susceptible to its enticements. An award of the governorship would transform Hammond's attitude towards his enemies and help forge the unity Calhoun had so long sought in Carolina.

16. Hammond to John Fox Hammond, December 5, 1841, in JHH Papers, SCL; Hammond, "Anniversary Oration of the State Agricultural Society of South Carolina . . . 25th November, 1841," in the *Proceedings of the Agricultural Convention and of the State Agricultural Society of South Carolina from 1839 to 1845 Inclusive* (Columbia: Sumner and Carroll, 1846), 190.

17. Hammond to John Fox Hammond, December 5, 1841, in JHH Papers, SCL; Hammond to

In mid-February, 1841, at Calhoun's urging, the Rhett faction approached Hammond indirectly, by means of a henchman authorized to assess Hammond's position. Opposition to Hammond's candidacy in 1840, the intermediary reiterated, had arisen from a desire to reunite the unionists with the rest of the state. But now, he explained, Calhoun, the Rhetts, and their followers "would be pleased to have you for the next Governor." The letter offered Hammond the support of old unionists, old nullifiers, and the Charleston *Mercury* and promised a "unanimous vote" in the 1842 legislature. The Rhett clique believed that it wielded sufficient control in Carolina to pledge delivery of every vote of the governing body nearly two years before it was even elected.[18]

Hammond's reply was cautious, but he displayed none of the settled hostility to the Rhetts he had expressed only weeks before. The "support of Mr Rhett & his friends," he responded, would be "highly gratifying," and the prospect of healing divisions "which I have perhaps had some agency in causing" would in itself be "a great inducement to me to become a candidate." But Hammond coupled these conciliatory remarks with an entirely inconsistent profession of his continuing loyalty to those anti-Rhett forces that had supported him in the last election. If Rhett was trying to "seduce" him away from his friends, Hammond declared self-righteously, he could regard this overture with nothing but "scorn." Reassuring some of his followers who had heard rumors of his rapprochement with the Regency, Hammond vowed he would not leave them "in the lurch."[19]

Rhett was displeased by Hammond's ingratitude and disturbed by his stubborn independence. But committed to reconciliation, he sent assurances that Hammond still had his support. Hammond feared he had wounded Rhett's pride by his unappreciative response to the congressman's advances, yet he could not help but wonder about the broader motivations behind these conciliatory gestures. The best course of action seemed not to alienate the powerful clique but, at the same time, to maintain a safe independence from them. Not surprisingly, it proved almost impossible to keep his own followers on this tightrope. An attack upon the Regency that appeared in the press under the pseudonym "Wardlaw" was widely attributed to Hammond, who was distressed to find it had in fact been penned by one of his lieutenants from the 1840 campaign. The suspicion

---

I. W. Hayne, January 21, 1841, Hammond to Francis W. Pickens, January 27, 1841, both in JHH Papers, LC.

18. M. E. Carn to Hammond, February 15, 1841, in JHH Papers, LC.

19. Hammond to Carn, March 18, 1841, *ibid.*; Hammond Diary (LC), March 25, 1841.

that he had himself authorized the attack might well destroy any possibility of cooperation with the Rhetts. An alliance with the Regency, he emphasized to his supporters in a complete turnabout from his earlier vows of unyielding opposition to the ruling clique, was not only an avenue to power but the only way to overcome continuing accusations of disloyalty to the Democratic party, to Calhoun, and to the South. Hammond was becoming a political realist.[20]

By late 1841, Rhett was less concerned about the activities of Hammond's followers than about the loyalty of his own. Many former unionists in the Richardson party were objecting to Hammond as strongly as Hammond himself had protested Richardson's nomination two years before. Rhett was beginning to doubt "whether they can now be managed." He promised to push Hammond's candidacy at a caucus during the next session of the legislature, but he could not ensure success.[21]

There was indeed much opposition to Hammond in the meeting of Rhett's followers that gathered at Columbia in December. But the dissenters had no plausible alternative candidate and decided Hammond had too much strength to be defeated without creating irreparable divisions in their own faction. Hammond chose to regard the eventual consensus in the group not as a triumph of management by the Regency, but as evidence of its surrender to him and his supporters. Declining to view himself as a tool of the Rhetts or of Calhoun's larger designs, Hammond declared his nomination to be a vindication of his efforts in 1840 against the "vile combination" represented by the powerful clique. After the legislature adjourned in late December, Hammond wrote exultingly to Marcellus, "All parties have concurred to nominate me for next Governor & I am to have no opposition." Calhoun quickly communicated his good wishes to the candidate. "It is the glory of our little state," he reminded Hammond and congratulated himself, "to act with a spirit of liberality and patriotism unknown to the other states."[22]

The difficulties Hammond had encountered in his earlier campaign seemed entirely absent this time. The *Mercury*, controlled by the Rhetts, enthusiastically endorsed his candidacy on February 10, and the press throughout the state supported him with the unanimity they had offered Richardson two years

20. Hammond to Charles Carroll, August 31, 1841, Carroll to Hammond, August 23, 1841, both in JHH Papers, LC.
21. Carn to Hammond, November 18, 1841, *ibid.*
22. Albert Rhett to George McDuffie, August 3, 1842, in Robert Barnwell Rhett Papers, SHC; Hammond to M. C. M. Hammond, December 22, 1841, in JHH Papers, SCL; John C. Calhoun to Hammond, December 31, 1841, in JHH Papers, LC.

before. The newspapers contained none of the controversial correspondence that had filled their columns in 1840. But this harmony was not as deep-seated as it appeared. Richardson confided to Rhett his reservations about Hammond's nomination and found it as difficult to manage the dissatisfaction of his followers as to control "an unbroken and indomitable Bucephalus." Rhett informed Hammond about some of the objections among those who had not been included in the Columbia caucus, and he urged the candidate to aid his own efforts at reconciliation by "muzzling some of your more impetuous friends."[23]

By the time the legislature met late in November, 1842, Hammond could hardly contain his impatience to have the gubernatorial question settled. But a sudden burst of eleventh-hour opposition nearly snatched the prize from his hands. A group of legislators, some resentful of Rhett's management, others directly hostile to Hammond, decided to advance low-country rice planter Robert F. W. Allston as the opponent of "caucus dictation and nomination." As a correspondent in the Charleston *Courier* explained, "They saw that a few aspiring men were assuming to act as dictators." Ironically, the resistance to "management" and "dictation" that Hammond had hoped would carry him to victory in 1840 nearly brought his defeat in 1842. He won eighty-three votes to Allston's seventy-six and would probably have lost the election had not Allston announced publicly that he did not consider himself a candidate. The efforts of Calhoun and Rhett to manage two gubernatorial contests in the service of state unity had succeeded in electing their chosen candidates, but at the cost of dividing rather than harmonizing Carolina.[24]

Hammond had little time to dwell upon the humiliation he felt at this unexpectedly narrow victory. The day after the election he was inaugurated governor in the chamber of the house of representatives before a gallery filled with the "beauty and fashion of Columbia" and "many of the most distinguished of our fellow-citizens from other portions of the state." His inaugural address adopted a conciliatory tone, and the new governor swore fealty to the federal Constitution in an effort to reduce anxieties about his disunionist past. Hammond deplored the economic condition of Carolina; warned against the dangerously expanding strength of political parties, which had "sometimes forgotten right, in the pur-

23. Charleston *Mercury*, February 10, 1842; John P. Richardson to Robert Barnwell Rhett, January 21, 1842, in Rhett Papers; Albert Rhett to Hammond, February 6, 26, 1842, both in JHH Papers, LC; Hammond to Calhoun, September 10, 1842, in John C. Calhoun Papers, Clemson University, Clemson, S.C.
24. Charleston *Courier*, December 10, 17, 1842.

suit of power"; and extolled the Carolina constitution for its conservative tendencies and its success in "preserving every feature of republicanism" while giving "due influence to intelligence and wealth."[25]

Hammond's term began in the atmosphere of harmony his inaugural address had been designed to foster. The legislature, charged with the selection of two United States senators to replace Calhoun and Preston, who had resigned, settled even-handedly upon the revered up-country states' rights champion George McDuffie and the respected low-country unionist Daniel Huger. And the delegates formally expressed as well the "unanimous wish of the people of South Carolina" for the election of John C. Calhoun to the presidency. Even if Calhoun's efforts to reconcile the parties within the state had not been entirely successful, he had managed to achieve what many believed to be his deeper purpose: he had won support from all factions for his own ambitions.[26]

Hammond's responsibilities during this first legislative session of his term were minimal, for his predecessor had already delivered a message to the representatives that served as the agenda for discussion in the governing body. Richardson had addressed a number of issues that would in the future require Hammond's attention, including the condition of public education and the 1842 passage by Congress of a high regulatory tariff, directly contravening the compromise that had ended the nullification controversy. But Hammond's most immediate concern proved to be the establishment of the Agricultural and Geological Survey, recommended by Richardson and enthusiastically passed by the legislature soon after the new governor entered office. Hammond had abandoned earlier opposition to the undertaking because of his own conversion to what he called the "gospel of marl." Having discovered the possibility for agricultural improvement in deposits of calcareous manures in the soils around Silver Bluff, Hammond was eager to identify similar riches throughout the state and to encourage their use in the salvation of Carolina's planting economy. His growing interest in scientific farming had generated increasing admiration for Edmund Ruffin, the pioneer of agricultural reform in Virginia, and Hammond welcomed the allocations of funds to hire a surveyor as an opportunity to bring Ruffin to Carolina. The possibility of attracting the eminent and knowledgeable

25. Charleston *Mercury*, December 14, 1842; Hammond to Calhoun, November 17, 1842, in Calhoun Papers; Charleston *Mercury*, December 14, 1842.
26. Committee on Federal Relations, *Reports and Resolutions of the General Assembly of South Carolina Passed at Its Regular Session of 1842* (Columbia: A. H. Pemberton, 1843), December 19, 1842, p. 83.

Courtesy of the South Caroliniana Library

James Henry Hammond in the uniform of the governor of the State of South Carolina.

Virginian and of enlightening Carolina planters in the use of marl had, Hammond reported, "disarmed my opposition & that of many others" to a survey.[27]

The great bulk of Hammond's gubernatorial duties, however, lay not in administering substantive programs, but in making ceremonial appearances. During January, 1843, the new chief executive traveled throughout Carolina on mil-

27. Hammond to Edmund Ruffin, January 11, February 5, 1843, both in Edmund Ruffin Papers, Virginia Historical Society, Richmond.

itary reviews intended to impress a dispersed rural population with the meaning and majesty of state power. Hammond's old brigadier's uniform was hardly adequate for this new role; he outfitted himself in the elaborate costume prescribed by militia law for Carolina's commander-in-chief. His uniform alone cost $150, his gold epaulettes $40 more, and he sported as well silver embroidered stars, gold shoulder straps, buff gantlets, and a cap with a large white plume. The handsome young governor cut an impressive figure.[28]

Hammond's military tour culminated early in February at Charleston's race week, where a grand parade, part of the annual festivities, capped the smaller militia exhibitions the governor had reviewed throughout the state. Because of the hostility so recently expressed by the many low-country planters who had supported Allston against him, Hammond complained of feeling uncomfortable in Charleston. He was grateful for a torrential rainstorm that provided an excuse for not attending the Jockey Club ball, but even freed from this obligation, he still grumbled of being "overwhelmed with pomp and circumstance." The governorship seemed not to provide the satisfaction Hammond had anticipated.[29]

In spite of his feelings of alienation, Hammond's suite at Stewart's Hotel became an official reception chamber where the elite of the state called in a steady stream. The governor persuaded Edmund Ruffin, just arrived to assume his post as surveyor, to share his quarters in order to meet as many of Carolina's planters as possible. Ruffin's brilliance soon distracted Hammond from his social discomfort in Charleston, and the governor delighted in accompanying the new surveyor on many of his visits to plantations, marl beds, and agricultural societies.

The interest these two men shared in agricultural reform and uplift in many ways paralleled the concerns Hammond had begun to explore with his friend Simms. Like Simms and Hammond in Carolina, Ruffin had felt his labors were "little appreciated" in Virginia. The South treated the man of mind—be he poet or scientific agriculturist—as a prophet without honor. Hammond and Ruffin agreed that the wasting of the southern soil was a manifestation of the growing barrenness of the southern mind and erosion of the southern character. But with Ruffin, as with Simms before him, Hammond began to develop a friendship that was more than simply intellectual or professional. Their feelings of intellectual futility were accompanied by a profound sense of isolation and personal loneli-

28. Bill of William Glaze, 1843, Bill of Stevenson & Walker, March 23, 1843, both in Hammond, Business Papers. Hammond's uniform is on display in the Museum of the College of the Citadel, Charleston.
29. Hammond to M. C. M. Hammond, February 24, 1843, in JHH Papers, SCL.

ness that seemed the inescapable lot of the scientist, the thinker or reformer in the Old South. "I have no assistant, no sympathizer, no consoler," Hammond confided to Ruffin as he described his own agricultural experiments. "If it be of any consolation to you to know of others suffering like yourself," Ruffin reassured him, "I can afford you some of it." Before Ruffin returned to Virignia, the two men had developed a friendship that would last the rest of their lives. Although Hammond urged Ruffin to settle permanently in South Carolina after his wife died in 1846, the Virginian could not bring himself to leave his family and his native state. But he and Hammond maintained their friendship through letters and occasional visits. Their lively correspondence not only encompassed a variety of personal, political, and agricultural topics but included exchanges of books, pamphlets, and even hybrid peas. A vine that grew from a seed Hammond sent his friend still flourishes outside Ruffin's house.[30]

The consolation Hammond found in his intensifying intimacy with Ruffin sharply contrasted with the mounting tribulations of his gubernatorial term. In spite of the very limited power vested in the governor by the Carolina constitution, Hammond was determined to be more than a ceremonial figure. His first systematic presentation of his policies, the governor's official message to the legislature of November, 1843, directly addressed a number of the most divisive questions of the day. Hammond decried the newly enacted federal tariff as unjust and oppressive, advocated prompt annexation of Texas, and called for curtailment of the state bank's powers and the overthrow of the existing system of free schools. In a second communication to the representatives, Hammond revived an issue that had produced difficulties between Carolina and Washington more than two decades before and had served as a prelude to the open hostilities of nullification. Since the twenties, Carolina law had required that free colored seamen entering Charleston be confined to city jails to prevent the "moral contagion" that would arise from their interaction with local blacks. Hoping to eliminate their dangerous influence altogether, Hammond called for a statute restricting the sailors to the vessels on which they served.[31]

---

30. Hammond to Ruffin, July 7, 1844, in Ruffin Papers; Ruffin to Hammond, July 6, 1845, in JHH Papers, LC. See Private Diary of Edmund Ruffin, State Agricultural Surveyor of South Carolina, 1843 (MS in Ruffin Papers), June 10, 1843.

31. Hammond, "Message to the Senate and House of Representatives of the State of South Carolina, November 28, 1843," in Hammond, *Selections from the Letters and Speeches of the Hon. James H. Hammond, of South Carolina* (New York: John F. Trow, 1866), 51–79; Report of the Committee on Federal Relations, December 13, 1843, in Governors' Messages, Legislative Papers, 1831–59. SCA. The official name of the state bank referred to throughout was the Bank of the State; it should not be confused with the State Bank in Charleston.

The program of action Hammond proposed for the state faithfully reflected his emerging social and political philosophy. The militant insistence on southern rights—represented in the issues of the tariff, Texas, and colored seamen—embodied an outlook Hammond had espoused since his youthful days as a nullification editor. But his call for improved educational opportunities within the state marked a new departure in his understanding of the bases for southern sectionalism. Not only must Carolina defend herself from outside aggressions; she must reform and uplift her people as well. The "only hope we can have of the . . . lasting duration of our institutions," he proclaimed to the legislature, "is by resting them on the solid foundation of a people imbued with lofty sentiments, and deeply versed in all the lore of learning." Carolina should defend herself "not less by power of intellect than by force of arms." In the past quarter-century, he lamented, education had not advanced but deteriorated within the state, largely, he believed, because of inadequate secondary-school facilities. Instead of devoting its resources to free schools for paupers—schools that most citizens were too proud to use—the state should employ "every dollar which can be spared" to establish a system of district academies. The graduates of these institutions would serve as a force for enlightenment throughout the state and would provide a steady supply of teachers for both primary and secondary pupils. Attention to the intellectual development of her citizens, the governor asserted, was the "first duty" of the state and an all-important aspect of her self-defense.[32]

Few Carolinians understood their governor's insistence on the "power of intellect." Hammond's suggestions for an academy system generated little support in the legislature, where the Committee on the College, Education, and Religion called for the continuation of the free-school system under a new plan of "judicious economy" and "strict accountability." The legislature was far more concerned about the attack on the state bank that Hammond had made a central feature of his message. In part, his call for the bank to employ its capital to retire the state debt reflected his general fiscal conservatism. But his views were politically motivated as well. If paying off the debt would weaken or destroy the bank, so much the better, he proclaimed. Banks were instruments of tyranny, for they gave governments dangerous economic power. In South Carolina, the bank, under the presidency of F. H. Elmore, had served as the tool of the hated Regency. By an assault on the bank, Hammond could direct a suitably principled

32. James Henry Hammond, "Message . . . 1843," 71, 73. It was during Hammond's governorship that the Citadel became a military college.

rhetoric against his old political enemies. Bank failures and suspensions during the financial crises of the early forties had created a popular legacy of resentment that Hammond could manipulate for his own ends.[33]

Elmore parried Hammond's opening thrust by compiling a lengthy report defending the bank's fiscal soundness and by claiming that several of Hammond's proposals—the speedy discharge of the public debt, in particular—were the avowed policy of the bank. "We *gained* a complete victory," the governor wrote in his diary; "the Bank attempted to claim one." Nevertheless, Hammond's hostility to the financial institution remained undiminished; he would not be satisfied until it was destroyed.[34]

Although he complained of the favorable press given Elmore's defenses of the bank, Hammond was for the most part satisfied by his performance during the first full legislative session of his term. But his pleasure was all but obliterated by the concern he felt about a personal conflict that threatened to end his career and reputation, if not his life. "Fear, anxiety, & bitter grief are my hourly companions—the fruits of my own wickedness and folly," he wrote in his annual birthday prayer. "A crisis has arrived."[35]

On the first of November, 1843, Hammond had received a letter from his brother-in-law Wade Hampton II, denouncing him for the attempted seduction of Hampton's daughter Catherine on the preceding thirteenth of April. Hammond remembered the incident well, for it was the culmination of an evolving intimacy between Hammond and his four nieces, Harriet, aged twenty; Catherine, nineteen; Ann, seventeen; and Caroline, fifteen. Since his return from Europe and the subsequent rapprochement with the Hamptons and Fitzsimonses and particularly since his move to Columbia, Hammond had naturally come into more frequent contact with the Hampton children. Young Wade III liked to visit his tribe of Hammond cousins at Silver Bluff; Harriet and Catherine had helped their uncle decorate his new town house during their aunt's confinement. But about 1840—Hammond was himself uncertain of the exact date—the relationship between the four Hampton daughters and their uncle began to evolve in an extraordinary way. Their devotion to Hammond, their sisterly contests for his attention and affection encompassed an ever-increasing degree of physical

33. Report of the Committee on the College, Education, and Religion, 1843, in Governor's Messages, Legislative Papers, 1831–59, SCA.
34. Hammond Diary (LC), January 31, 1844.
35. Hammond, "Birthday Prayer, November 15, 1843" (MS in HBC Papers, SCL).

intimacy, with "all of them rushing on every occasion into my arms & covering me with kisses—lolling in my lap—pressing their bodies almost into mine wreathing their limbs with mine, encountering warmly every part of my frame, & permitting my hands to stray unchecked over every part of theirs & to rest without the slightest shrinking from it, on the most secret and sacred regions— & all this for a period of more than two years continuously. Is it," he pleaded in self defense, "in flesh and blood to withstand this?"[36]

Certainly Hammond had lacked the capacity to resist, and he confessed in his diary to "every thing short of direct sexual intercourse." His relationship with the girls had begun to intensify at a time when he was most avidly searching for affection, when he had begun to recognize his alienation and loneliness in Carolina society and to acknowledge the limitations of his marriage, when he had started to seek out the consoling friendship of men like Simms and Ruffin. Hammond did make feeble attempts to resist the Hamptons, and even considered flight from Columbia, where he reported in August, 1841, that he found himself "beset by temptations of no ordinary character." But his political career brought him always back to the capital and the adoring embraces of his lovely nieces.[37]

Within a society that prescribed rigid standards of purity for ladies of their social position, the girls' behavior was perhaps even more unorthodox than that of their uncle. Certainly innocence must serve as a partial explanation, for since Ann Hampton had died in 1833, these girls had lacked a mother's instruction— as well as her close supervision. The Hampton daughters had, for example, been permitted to give "unmatronized" parties that aroused comment among some of the Carolina elite. But whatever may have motivated the girls, Hammond knew that his behavior had been unpardonable. Their "loose manners" and "ardent temperaments" could neither excuse nor explain his response to these "pure and innocent young girls," Hammond admitted. "I have been wrong in the matter." But, he explained, his transgressions were the "result of impulse not design." For once, he had acted in an unplanned manner. While nearly every venture in his life was calculated, considered, undertaken "on clock work principles," he found himself ultimately unable to regulate himself, his needs and emotions so completely. The incident with the Hampton girls arose, as Hammond himself understood, "from trying to control myself in every particular." His design for self-

36. Hammond Diary (LC), January 31, 1844.
37. *Ibid.*, July 2, 1844; Hammond Diary (SCL), December, 1846; Hammond to M. C. M. Hammond, June 4, 1844, in JHH Papers, LC; Hammond Diary (LC), August 4, 1841.

advancement had left no space for a human being within its rigid confines. His "morbid and solitary habits" engendered a need for love that the unquestioning devotion of these young girls provided. It was a temptation this desperately lonely and emotionally needy man could not resist. Hammond would pay a high price for this brief relaxation of control, this temporary obliviousness to the dictates of ambition and self-advancement.[38]

When on April 13, 1843, Catherine Hampton took offense at a familiarity, her uncle was surprised by the girl's apparent shift in attitude, but he apologized and decided to halt his intimacies with his nieces entirely. For the eight weeks that remained before he left Columbia for the summer, Hammond maintained his usual cordiality with all the Hampton family. But in the fall, Catherine evidently reported the incident to her father, and Wade Hampton wrote to break off relations with his brother-in-law. Hammond at first hoped he might mend the breach through the intercession of another of Hampton's kin, John Preston, who had treated Hammond warmly in the past. "I knew he was acquainted with the ways of the girls, & to him I could give a full statement of every thing." So as not to arouse his wife's suspicions, Hammond paid a neighbor's servant to carry a letter to Preston requesting an interview. From the piazza of his Columbia house Hammond watched the messenger ride down Bull Street. Within an hour, one of Preston's servants appeared at Hammond's door with a note that declared "atonement & oblivion were impossible" and severed all ties. The Hamptons and their kin had determined that Hammond must be destroyed.[39]

How they would destroy him was not yet clear. Hammond was certain that Hampton regarded his actions as too disgraceful to merit a challenge on the field of honor. The code of chivalry prescribed that duels could take place only between gentlemen, and Hammond was sure Hampton no longer regarded him as such. More likely, Hampton or one of his henchmen would simply confront Hammond and attempt either to shoot or horsewhip him. But, Hammond speculated, his official status was certain to complicate the process of retribution. Any attack upon the governor would harm the reputation of the state as well as the personal standing of the incumbent. Besides, Hampton was well known as an opponent of the southern traditions of dueling and personal violence.[40]

38. Hammond Diary (SCL), December, 1846; Hammond Diary (LC), January 31, 1844; Hammond to William B. Hodgson, January 1, 1846, in JHH Papers, DU; Hammond to Simms, July 8, 1848, in JHH Papers, LC. See letter of John Manning to Mrs. Manning, n.d., in Williams-Chesnut-Manning Papers, SCL, for discussion of the "unmatronized party."
39. Hammond Diary (SCL), December, 1846; Hammond Diary (LC), January 31, 1844.
40. Nell S. Graydon, *Tales of Columbia* (Columbia: R. L. Bryan, 1964), 121.

Courtesy of the South Caroliniana Library
Wade Hampton II

Arming himself with pocket pistols, Hammond awaited Hampton's revenge almost impatiently, for he was eager to have the troubling issue settled once and for all. He determined himself to say nothing of the matter, for he wished, he said, to protect the Hampton girls and his still unsuspecting wife. But the rupture did not remain secret for long. By the time the legislature gathered in late November, 1843, Hammond realized that news of a "blow up" had spread throughout Columbia. Yet Hampton still made no move to contact Hammond.

His vengeance would not be swift. Instead he would seek a punishment of slow torture, destroying Hammond's reputation and career rather than simply taking his life. By December it was clear to the young governor that Hampton's plan was "to black ball me & to mortify me & mine by keeping us out of Society & all respectable persons from coming to our House." Hampton waged a war of rumor and innuendo, a campaign against which Hammond could mount no easy defense.[41]

Throughout the social season that accompanied the legislative session in Columbia, Hammond tried to prevent the scandal from spreading. To avoid public humiliation, he tried to select guests carefully for each official occasion at which he was required to preside. But he could not keep his wife from sending invitations to the governor's ball to all her Hampton relatives, and he was forced to make light of their failure to attend. As soon as his obligations in Columbia were fulfilled Hammond withdrew with his family to Silver Bluff.

Yet he could not entirely retreat from the pressing public issues of the day. There could scarcely have been a more awkward time for Hammond to find himself so nearly paralyzed by his fear of the Hampton affair's repercussions. The presidential contest of 1844, fast gaining momentum, was crucial to the destiny of the South, to the fate of South Carolina, to the ambition of John C. Calhoun, and thus to the fortunes of James Henry Hammond. A rising tide of antislavery sentiment in the North threatened to prevent the proposed annexation of Texas on the grounds that it would extend the boundaries of slavery within the nation, and John Quincy Adams seemed so close to victory in his battle against the gag rule that congressional meddling with the South's domestic institutions appeared an imminent and alarming possibility.

Hammond himself was directly affected by the growing hostility towards slavery when a Carolina slave-stealing case attracted international attention. In the fall of 1842 a dissolute white resident of Fairfield District named John Brown had been tried and convicted for aiding a slave in escaping her master. Brown was sentenced to hang, but when Hammond received additional information convincing him that Brown had had no "criminal design," he commuted the felon's sentence to thirty-nine lashes. "I pardoned Brown," Hammond explained, "simply because I was satisfied of his *innocence* & for no other reason whatever." But while the matter had aroused no particular interest in Carolina, elsewhere it quickly became a *cause célèbre*. Abolitionists regarded Brown—who in actuality

41. Hammond Diary (SCL), December, 1846.

was stealing his mistress—as a bold liberator sacrificing his life on behalf of freedom. Hammond received a deluge of letters from the North, and even the British House of Lords expressed concern about the unfortunate thief. At last, Hammond decided he had to reply to this outburst of antislavery fervor. In June he penned a long and carefully considered response to a letter written him in Brown's behalf by the moderator of the Free Church of Glasgow. Published in the Charleston *Mercury* and in the Charleston *Courier* during December of 1844 and then reprinted in pamphlet form, Hammond's defense of the system of human bondage became a proslavery classic.[42]

The governor began his letter by complaining of the invasion of his and Carolina's prerogatives represented by the foreign efforts on Brown's behalf. But he passed quickly from this issue, for he wished to base his arguments not on questions of right and power, but on considerations of morality and justice, on a general evaluation of slavery as a system of labor and of social relations. The South's peculiar institution, he asserted, was not only ordained by God in both Old and New Testaments, but was a far more benevolent arrangement than existed between workers and industrialists in Britain. Hammond had not forgotten the "squalid misery" he had himself seen in England and Ireland, and he wrote with feeling of the deprivation of so-called free laborers. Their liberty, he proclaimed, was no more than a choice of whether to beg or steal, to starve or go to prison. Slaves, by contrast, were well-fed, their families rarely separated, their race in general uplifted from African barbarism to Christianity and civilization in the South. Glaswegians should cease to look at the issues in abstract terms. Instead of thinking about rarefied conceptions of freedom and bondage, about chimerical notions of reform, they should observe actual conditions of life. The objective circumstances of slavery in South Carolina were in fact superior to the conditions of freedom in the British Isles. The peculiar institution, he concluded even more affirmatively than he had in his inaugural proslavery statement in Congress in 1836, was a benevolent system ordained by God and a blessing to blacks and whites alike.[43] Hammond felt a moment of crisis had arrived for the South, a moment when she must boldly assert her rights and aggressively defend her labor system as a positive good.

42. Hammond to Calhoun, June 7, 1844, in Calhoun Papers. See also Hammond to John Fox Hammond, April 2, 1843, in JHH Papers, SCL; Hammond, *Letter of His Excellency Governor Hammond to the Free Church of Glasgow on the Subject of Slavery* (Columbia: A. H. Pemberton, 1844). See also Charleston *Courier* and Charleston *Mercury*, December 9, 1844.

43. Hammond, "Letter to the Free Church of Glasgow on the Subject of Slavery," in Hammond, *Selections from the Letters and Speeches*, 108, 112.

While Hammond viewed the national political situation as a disaster, Calhoun saw it as an opportunity. Van Buren's open opposition to the annexation of Texas made him unacceptable to the South and all but disqualified him for the presidency. The field lay open for a candidate of more genuine southern sympathies. Even in the days of their alliance around the subtreasury, Calhoun had never trusted the New York politician and was relieved not to have to pretend friendship any longer. Aware that his own recent proslavery statements in his new post as secretary of state had destroyed the possibility of his own candidacy by alienating the North, Calhoun hoped to invoke his old strategy of uniting South and West behind the standard of James K. Polk, whose platform called for the annexation of both Oregon and Texas. A new Democratic party, friendly to the South, supportive of slavery and free trade was in the offing. Calhoun was certain that the Jacksonian era of executive usurpations and expanding federal power was at an end. "A revolution in our politicks of a highly salutary character" was imminent. There was now "a better prospect" for the Union, he declared, "than there has been since the election of Genl. Jackson in 1828."[44]

Hammond viewed the situation rather differently. The nomination of Polk seemed to him to signal the incipient end of the Union. Whigs and Democrats would both be split into warring sectional camps, and the nation would soon follow. Already southern Democrats were insisting on Texas, although their northern counterparts vociferously opposed annexation. The fissure in the Methodist church over the slavery issue in May, 1844, seemed to Hammond prophetic. "If Christians are compelled to divide on account of Slavery how can unbelievers hold together," he warned. Hammond could find no grounds for optimism in Polk's candidacy.[45]

In Congress, Robert Barnwell Rhett agreed; there seemed no basis for Calhoun's faith in an imminent reversal of northern hostility towards southern interests. By late spring, after Congress had rejected the Texas annexation treaty and had refused to adjust the tariff, Rhett had had enough. In a Washington speech, the Carolina representative called for a southern convention to demand the annexation of Texas, and for a South Carolina meeting in April, 1845, to nullify the tariff if it had not yet been repealed. Anxious for Polk's electoral success, Calhoun was alarmed by this defection; it seemed to him "the worst moment that could be selected" to talk of separate state action. Such agitation

---

44. Calhoun to Henry W. Conner, July 3, 1844, in Henry W. Conner Papers, LC.
45. Hammond to Calhoun, June 7, 1844, Hammond to Simms, June 18, 1844, in JHH Papers, LC.

would strengthen Whig prospects for the presidency and perhaps force Polk to move towards the northern—Van Buren—wing of the Democratic party. But Rhett's radical cry, reiterated in a speech at Bluffton, South Carolina, on July 31, won Hammond's enthusiastic endorsement and launched an organized campaign known as the Bluffton movement against Calhoun's moderation.[46]

Hammond believed that Calhoun was *"faltering"* in his responsibilities to Carolina because his own desire for the presidency did not permit him to risk disunion. "I cannot doubt," Hammond observed, "that at this moment he is endeavoring to sacrifice the South . . . on the altar of his ambition." It was too late to reform the federal government in the South's interest, as Calhoun allegedly intended; a president sympathetic to the region could do little to stem the tide of northern hostility. The opposition to the Texas treaty had been led by Thomas H. Benton, a prominent member of Calhoun's own party. There could be no hope of safety for Carolina either in the Democratic party or the Union. Hammond wholly concurred with the venerable George McDuffie that the moment was at hand when "the fate of the South must be decided forever." Always resentful of Calhoun's preeminence in Carolina politics, and still bitter about his actions in the gubernatorial campaign of 1840, Hammond welcomed the appearance of a movement against Calhoun's domination.[47]

Unable to act in his own behalf against the Hamptons, Hammond was undoubtedly grateful as well for a stirring political battle to engage his energies. Hampton had refused to provide his brother-in-law the relief a direct confrontation would have offered; Hammond felt himself agonizingly and "utterly powerless" in the matter. But during the stressful year of 1844, Hammond turned to a series of other conflicts, almost as if to distract himself from anxious contemplation of his own transgressions. The struggle with Calhoun and the Glasgow proslavery tract were logical outgrowths of positions the Carolinian had assumed earlier. But at least one of the battles Hammond joined in the course of the year seems to have been entirely avoidable and suggests that he may have been searching for the sense of competence and self-assurance he found only in action, in the assertion of power and prerogative that confrontation always entailed.[48]

46. Calhoun to Conner, July 3, 1844, in Conner Papers; Robert Barnwell Rhett to Armistead Burt, September 9, 1844, in Armistead Burt Papers, DU; Columbia *South Carolinian* August 22, 1844. On Bluffton, see Chauncy Boucher, "The Annexation of Texas and the Bluffton Movement in South Carolina," *Mississippi Valley Historical Review*, VI (June, 1919), 3–33; and Charles M. Wiltse, *John C. Calhoun, Sectionalist, 1840–1850* (Indianapolis: Bobbs-Merrill, 1951), 190–95.
47. Hammond to M. C. M. Hammond, August 25, 1844, in JHH Papers, LC; Hammond Diary (LC), October 25, 1844; McDuffie to Hammond, September 1844, in JHH Papers, LC.
48. Hammond to M. C. M. Hammond, June 4, 1844, in JHH Papers, LC.

Early in September, Hammond issued a gubernatorial proclamation naming the first Thursday of October a day of Thanksgiving to "God the Creator, and his son Jesus Christ, the Redeemer of the World." To his surprise he received in response to this announcement a complaint from a group of Charleston Jews who found his allusion to Christ offensive and requested an apology. Hammond's political friends urged the governor to be conciliatory, for the Charleston Jewish community was wealthy and influential. Hammond himself admitted to being "not a professor of Religion," nor a "fit and proper defender of the Christian Faith." He had not even thought of the Israelites, he confessed, when he had issued his original announcement. But he would not amend his remarks or make a public apology.[49]

To demonstrate their dissatisfaction, the synagogues ignored his appointed day of thanksgiving, and more than one hundred Charleston Jews composed a memorial and protest to the governor. His mention of Christ, they complained, was "exclusive, arbitrary & sectarian," and they again requested an apology. However indifferent to religion, Hammond was far from unmindful of any threat to his authority. Eagerly he rose to respond to what he considered the Israelites' insolence. Their petition, he declared, was "impertinent"; South Carolina was a "Christian community" as its Sabbath laws unmistakably indicated. Refusing to make amends, Hammond demanded that the low-country Jews cease "fulminating your wrath at me." This sarcastic and intemperate declaration provoked yet another outcry from the Jews, who protested the unfortunate tone of the gubernatorial pronouncement and asserted that the Carolina constitution promised them not just toleration but equal rights. Hammond remained unmoved, and added Carolina's Jews to his growing list of enemies.[50]

On the political front, the battle continued. Calhoun had been working energetically through the late summer and early fall to prevent Rhett's defection from becoming a full-scale revolt against his leadership. By extracting public promises from Polk about Texas and the tariff, Calhoun managed to retain the support of his first lieutenant, Francis Pickens, and to quiet the protests of Rhett and McDuffie until Polk's victory was assured. But Hammond remained unreconciled. As the date for the November meeting of the legislature approached, Hammond never wavered in his certainty that Polk neither would nor could al-

<hr />

49. Charleston *Mercury*, September 13, 1844; William Yeadon to Hammond, October 14, 1844, Hammond to A. Moise *et al.*, November 4, 1844, Hammond to R. Pinckney, September 28, 1844, all in JHH Papers, LC; Hammond Diary (LC), November 17, 21, 1844.
50. Hammond to Moise, November 4, 1844, in JHH Papers, LC.

leviate the grievances of the South. Despite the urging of Pickens, James Hamilton, and other old political associates that Hammond avoid alienating Calhoun by at least giving Polk a chance to act in his new presidential capacity, the governor would not abandon his radicalism. Even if the rest of the state had been paralyzed by the force of Calhoun's will, Hammond was determined not to bow to the older statesman's dictation. Driven by motives as much personal as political, he would fashion his official governor's message into a call for southern resistance to northern aggressions and Carolinian resistance to the all-powerful Calhoun. As he left Silver Bluff to return to the capital, Hammond expected to encounter not only the hostility of Hampton and his henchmen but the animosity of Carolina's Jews and the enmity of Calhoun's "understrappers," who were undoubtedly "already instructed to hunt me down." It seemed to the young governor that the "crisis of my fate personally and politically has arrived."[51]

Hammond's intemperate behavior, his propensity for generating conflict, coexisted with a dispassionately rational intellect that displayed itself most favorably under the pressure of controversy. Hammond's supreme gift was his incisive and relentlessly logical mind, his ability to weave fact, detail, and principle into forceful argument. In his all-important governor's message, he would use these resources to the utmost, forging a position he hoped would prove unassailable. As Calhoun's biographer Charles Wiltse noted, Hammond's communication to the legislature in 1844 exhibited a "cold detachment that made it far more effective—and more dangerous—than Rhett's impassioned outburst" at Bluffton in July. Hammond began by evoking the spectre of economic distress that had gripped the state since 1837, and laid the blame for hard times squarely upon the federal system. The tariff of 1842 was higher than the law South Carolina had declared null and void a decade before; the Democratic Congress had failed for two years to repeal it; the South had been betrayed. But the wrongs against the South, he continued, were more than economic. An abolitionist conspiracy was seeking to destroy the region's rights and her domestic institutions. The rejection of the Texas annexation treaty, he asserted, was evidence of the "deep seated hostility of every portion, and almost every individual, of the North, to our system of Slavery, and their fixed determination to eradicate it." The South's security had been trampled by the North's "fanatical zeal to uproot an institution

---

51. James Hamilton to Hammond, November 12, 1844, Ker Boyce to Hammond, November 4, 1844, both *ibid.*; Hamilton to Calhoun, November 24, 1844, in Calhoun Papers; Hammond Diary (LC), November 17, 1844. Hammond showed a draft of his message to Rhett, who was delighted with it. Robert Barnwell Rhett to Hammond, November 3, 1844, in JHH Papers, LC.

with which is linked forever, and inseparably, the welfare, and almost the existence, of five millions of their fellow citizens." Hammond had insisted upon confronting the slavery question directly in the House in 1836; now once again he was forcing the issue when other southerners—including many staunch sectionalists—preferred to shy away. Compromise seemed to Hammond impossible. He urged Carolina's lawmakers to adopt "any measures, however startling they may appear, that will place your rights and property exclusively under your own control, and enable you to repel all interference with them, whatever shape it may assume." The Union, he reminded them, was "a compact for justice, liberty, and security. When these fail," he warned, "its living principles are gone."[52]

But the legislature did not share these disunionist views. In the state senate, F. W. Pickens, acting as a spokesman for Calhoun, rose to his feet as soon as the governor's message was delivered to offer resolutions against Hammond's position and to affirm Carolina's confidence that Polk would act in the South's interest on both the tariff and Texas questions. Although Pickens' proposals passed the upper house with a rapidity and unanimity that Hammond regarded as personally "mortifying," the measures faltered in the lower chamber. Simms, serving his only legislative term, and other Hammond supporters struggled to keep the resolutions under the aegis of the pro-Bluffton Committee on Federal Relations. But Calhoun's henchmen succeeded in removing the measures to a Committee of the Whole where they were debated intermittently throughout the session.[53]

Meanwhile events elsewhere encouraged Hammond to hope the legislature might yet be radicalized. The North was perpetrating yet another outrage. Massachusetts had sent an agent to Charleston to commence federal court action on behalf of colored seamen from the Bay State who had been imprisoned in Charleston under the controversial Carolina law. Once again, outsiders were meddling with the South's domestic institutions. Samuel Hoar—the very man who had been at Hammond's side at the time of his seizure in the Capitol in 1836—officially informed the governor of his intention to sue for the release of

52. Wiltse, *John C. Calhoun, Sectionalist*, 193. Hammond, "Message to the Senate and House of Representatives of the State of South Carolina, November 26, 1844," in Hammond, *Selections from the Letters and Speeches*, 100, 101, 103–104.
53. Hammond Diary (LC), November 28, 1844. See Charleston *Courier*, December 9, 19, 21, 1844; *Niles National Register*, January 5, 1845. See Pickens' obsequious letters to Calhoun, November 2, 15, December 18, 27, 28, 1844, all in Calhoun Papers. Robert F. W. Allston wrote his wife that the message was "flatly opposed." Robert F. W. Allston to Mrs. Allston, November 26, 1844, in Robert F. W. Allston Papers, South Carolina Historical Society, Charleston.

the incarcerated sailors, and Hammond transmitted the letter to the legislature to alert them to this latest danger as well as to solicit their instructions about a response. In accordance with their wish that Hoar be at once returned to his native state, Hammond dispatched his aide-de-camp Preston Brooks to Charleston to escort the northern agitator to the first available boat for Boston. But the citizens of the port city had already forced Hoar to leave the state by the time Brooks arrived.[54]

Although the incident created a stir throughout the state, it failed to have the dramatic political effect for which Hammond had hoped; it did not seem to engender many doubts among the legislators about the conciliatory policies Calhoun had prescribed to settle sectional differences. But when news reached South Carolina that the U.S. House had on December 3 repealed the gag rule, Hammond fully expected his radicalism to be vindicated. Calhoun had advised Carolinians to wait and see. Surely by now, Hammond thought, they had seen enough. It seemed to him unthinkable that after such a blow as the defeat of the gag rule Carolina could continue to trust her rights to the national government. Surely her legislators would be moved to decisive action and to recognition of the perils they confronted within the Union.

The obvious volatility of the situation prompted Pickens to immediate action. To deflect Carolina's anger over gag-rule repeal and to dissociate this issue from Calhoun's support for Polk, he offered a second series of resolutions denouncing this congressional outrage. The House had betrayed the South, Pickens' measures admitted, but with a chief executive like Polk, they simultaneously implied, the region still had reason to vest its hopes in the federal government. Passed immediately by the South Carolina Senate, Pickens' second set of proposals did not signal any change of sentiment or strategy by Calhoun; Hammond was badly mistaken when he at first regarded them as a sign Calhoun was moving toward his own position. Pickens' resolutions on the gag rule were a limited and gentle rebuke.

Just before the adjournment of the Columbia legislature, Pickens' original motions condemning Hammond's message passed the house by a vote of fifty-seven to thirty-nine. At the same time, the members of the lower chamber,

---

54. Samuel Hoar to Hammond, November 28, 1844, Governor's Message November 30, 1844, both in Governors' Messages, Legislative Papers, 1831–59, SCA; "Samuel Hoar's Expulsion from Charleston," Senate Document #4, Commonwealth of Massachusetts, 1845, *Old South Leaflets*, VI, #6, 126–50 (Boston: Directors of the Old South Work, Old South Meeting House, n.d.); "Mr. Hoar's Mission," *Southern Quarterly Review*, VII (April, 1845), 455–78; David Duncan Wallace, *History of South Carolina* (New York: American Historical Society, 1934), II, 497.

eager to be home for Christmas and unwilling to agree upon even a mild criticism of the federal government, indefinitely postponed action on the gag-rule question. Despite the governor's stirring call to action, the Carolina house had decided "patiently to await the measures of the new administration, and to take no separate action, which may embarrass their progress in carrying out the policy to which they stand pledged."[55]

Hammond ended his gubernatorial term, he lamented, "repudiated" by the legislature. Until the last moment, he had endeavored to regard Pickens' second set of resolutions as a vindication of his own position. But when the house chose to table these relatively moderate criticisms of the national government and to pass Pickens' original proposals expressing faith in federal action, Hammond could only acknowledge defeat. Calhoun's ultimate control over Carolina politics was confirmed. Principles seemed to have fallen victim to the dictates of power, and in this contest of force, Hammond had come off second best. With the encouragement of McDuffie and others of his radical supporters, Hammond comforted himself with his unstinting devotion to the gospel of states' rights. But for one who found failure so painful, it was small consolation. He noted that in the campaign to choose his successor, candidates for the first time made no attempt to disguise their electioneering, and the election of a unionist only compounded his sense of rejection. Governor William Aiken, who had defeated pro-Bluffton candidate Whitemarsh Seabrook, issued a proclamation of thanks-

---

55. *South Carolina House Journal*, 1844, pp. 20–31. Pickens saw Hammond "and his clique"— in much the same way Hammond regarded Calhoun and his followers—as engaged in a power play for political control. See Pickens to J. Edward Calhoun, December 7, 1844, in Francis W. Pickens Papers, SCL. On Hammond's optimistic and misguided view of Pickens' gag-rule resolutions as a triumph for his own radical views, see Hammond to John Fox Hammond, December 20, 1844, in JHH Papers, SCL, and Hammond Diary (LC), December 22, 1844. The roll call on Pickens' first set of resolutions reveals a basic low-country–up-country division. The low-country legislators were most likely to vote against Pickens and against Calhoun's faith in federal generosity to the South. Legislators from Greenville, York, and Spartanburg—in a traditional unionist stronghold—voted unanimously against Hammond, as did four out of five legislators from Edgefield, part of his home turf. But all of Barnwell was with Hammond. Charleston, as at the time of nullification, was divided, and there, two of his newly won enemies—Henry L. Pinckney, his 1836 gag-rule opponent, and M. C. Mordecai, a Charleston Jew—voted against him. On Pickens' second set of resolutions, those condemning gag-rule repeal, fourteen of the legislators who had supported Hammond on the first vote turned against him and voted to table the resolutions. This is evidence of the lack of a disciplined "governor's party" in the house as well as the radicals' suspicion of Pickens' second proposals. John Boyd Edmunds has argued that the resolutions attacking the repeal of the gag rule were too radical for the moderates and not radical enough for most Blufftonites. Hammond saw these resolutions as sufficiently radical, perhaps thus revealing himself as somewhat more moderate than some of his fellow Blufftonites. John Boyd Edmunds, "Francis W. Pickens and South Carolina Politics" (M. S. thesis, University of South Carolina, 1964), 117–18. See also *South Carolina House Journal*, 1844, pp. 162–64.

giving carefully worded to conciliate the Jews and to sound as if the most conspicuous cause for state gratitude was the defeat of Hammond and the Bluffton movement.[56]

But Hammond ended his term troubled by more than political misfortunes. His personal anxieties intensified in the last days of his term as well, for he feared that the surrender of his official mantle might leave him open to either a challenge or an attack from the Hamptons. At the inauguration of the new governor, Hammond could see both Hampton and Manning prominent in the audience. He was nearly certain they planned to waylay him after the ceremony, to claim their vengeance now that he was a private citizen once again. After the proceedings, Hammond accompanied Aiken to his lodgings for a congratulatory glass of wine, then returned to his own house, all the while apprehensive that each step might be his last. When no confrontation came, Hammond decided to remain in Columbia for a day to provide Hampton every opportunity to act and thereby to prevent any intimations that he had ignominiously fled as soon as he had surrendered the protection of the governor's office. The following morning Hammond rode down Main Street to the statehouse so that every citizen could see he was still in town. But Hampton made no move. The course of his retribution would be less direct, but more excruciating.[57]

Hammond did not yet know what that revenge would be. As he left Columbia he dared to hope the issue had been dropped. But he feared its continuing repercussions, his wife's discovery of the reasons behind the coolness of her Hampton kin, and the impact upon his public ambitions. Already he had decided to move from Columbia altogether. But he could have had little idea that the events of the past few months would sentence him to a thirteen-year exile at Silver Bluff.

56. Hammond Diary (LC), December 26, 12, 1844; McDuffie to Hammond, December 12, 1844, in JHH Papers, LC.
57. Hammond Diary (SCL), December, 1846; Hammond Diary (LC), December 10, 1844.

Part IV

In a Different Sphere

Power . . . no man can have, but at home *writing on topics of deep interest*
with unsuspected motives.
JAMES HENRY HAMMOND

CHAPTER 13

A More Virtuous Energy
Hammond and the Works of Mind

A FTER HIS REBUFF by the legislature, his quarrel with the Hamptons, and his unsuccessful rebellion against Calhoun, Hammond retained few illusions about his immediate political prospects. Although he could not yet assess the impact of these recent crises on his long-range opportunities, Hammond recognized that for the near future the pursuit of public office would be futile. The interruption of his political career, distressing in its implications of failure and defeat, nevertheless held its compensations. For one as ambivalent as Hammond had always been about the demands of political ambition, this enforced withdrawal was in many ways a relief. "I rejoice at my release from public cares," he exclaimed to a former member of his gubernatorial staff. Indeed, Hammond found so many positive justifications for his retirement to Silver Bluff that he was almost able to convince himself that the move was voluntary. "I am not soured in the least," he bravely insisted; "I have no disappointment to complain of whatever." At last he could abandon the vexations politics had always represented. His early ambition, he explained, had not been truly his own, but had arisen from "shame & gratitude to my father." His more recent efforts to achieve fame and position had "been prompted by any thing but permanent feelings of my own—evil spirits I think have overcome my constitutional abhorrence of the public gaze." Now he was determined to break away from these unsettling and unprofitable preoccupations. Public affairs had "ceased to be either an useful or agreeable avocation."[1]

1. James Henry Hammond to Beaufort T. Watts, June 27, November 24, 1845, in Beaufort T. Watts Papers, SCL; Hammond to William Gilmore Simms, June 3, 1845, in JHH Papers, LC; Ham-

But this retreat would bring no escape from ambition. Hammond would not "let my mind run fallow." His political retirement would serve as the opportunity to embark upon those intellectual undertakings that had begun increasingly to attract his interest. Hammond simply transferred his struggles to a new arena, one, he reassured himself, at once more elevated and more meaningful than the sordid world of political aspirations. "People cannot conceive that one may be ambitious of *Power* & despise empty offices." He admitted to Simms that he was "ambitious of power." But he was not, he insisted, "ambitious of further *office*. *Power* . . . no man can have, but *at home* writing on topics of deep interest with unsuspected motives." For the next five years, Hammond would wield influence through the power of his pen. From his library at Silver Bluff, Hammond produced a steady stream of writings on an extraordinary variety of topics, from marl to metaphysics. Because, as he explained, his "habits of thought" had previously been directed almost exclusively toward politics, many of his efforts had obvious and direct public import, as, for example, his defenses of slavery and his continuing attacks upon the state bank. But Hammond sought to place these issues in the broadest possible philosophical context and to examine them in light of the most pressing social and intellectual issues of his day. With an unaccustomed leisure to read and study, Hammond undertook as well a series of more abstract explorations designed to relate the immediate crises of the South to more transcendent issues of religion, morality, and philosophy. He sought to move beyond the domain of contention and controversy in which he had been so long immersed into a more permanent truth. Perhaps by transforming the mind of the South, he might ultimately succeed in altering and uplifting her politics and character.[2]

Almost as soon as he returned to Silver Bluff from Columbia at the end of his gubernatorial term, Hammond began inscribing passages of the Bible that seemed to have particular personal relevance into a manuscript notebook he labeled "Untitled Thoughts." He soon added to the volume more systematic and ambitious speculations upon the nature of religion, morality, and the immortality of the soul. Simultaneously, Hammond was elsewhere addressing somewhat more mundane issues in essays on agriculture and addresses on such subjects as fencing, overseers, turnips, and marl. In the late spring of 1845, he completed a

---

mond to Nathaniel Beverley Tucker, January 24, 1847, in Tucker-Coleman Papers, Earl Gregg Swem Memorial Library, College of William and Mary, Williamsburg, Va.

2. Hammond to M. C. M. Hammond, January 27, 1845, Hammond to Simms, July 14, 1845, James Henry Hammond Diary, July 14, 1845, all in JHH Papers, LC.

longer and more philosophical defense of slavery than the earlier Glasgow essay. This new tract, presented as two letters to the English abolitionist Thomas Clarkson, attracted widespread attention and—in the South—acclaim. In the months that followed, Hammond produced timely articles on the boundary dispute with Great Britain over Oregon, the popular vote for presidential electors, and late in 1847, more than twenty newspaper essays on publicly supported railroads and banks. A piece in the *Southern Quarterly Review* in 1849 assessed the fundamental nature of northern and southern societies, the orations delivered in December of the same year at the South Carolina Institute in Charleston and before the two student societies of South Carolina College placed in more abstract terms the concerns that lay at the foundation of all his considerations of contemporary politics and society.[3]

Although Hammond wrote and published throughout his life, the period between the close of his governorship and the end of the decade was by far the most intensely productive. It constituted an interval of comparative calm in a life of hectic public activity. Yet it was a period when his demands upon himself were transformed rather than diminished. Hammond devoted these years to a combination of the practical agricultural management necessary at Silver Bluff with an equally energetic commitment to intellectual inquiry; he divided his time, as he explained, "between business, books, cursing & fiddling." Hammond usually spent his mornings on the plantation and his afternoons "stretched out on a sofa" reading and writing for, by his estimate, four to six hours each day.[4]

3. Hammond, "Untitled Thoughts" (MS vol. bd., 1844–55, JHH Papers, SCL); Coke [James Henry Hammond], "Fencing," *Carolina Planter*, II (June, 1845), 281–83; Franklin [James Henry Hammond], "Overseers," *Carolina Planter*, I (August, 1844), 25–30; Hammond to Edmund Ruffin, June 20, 1845, in Edmund Ruffin Papers, Virginia Historical Society, Richmond; Hammond, *Marl: A Letter Addressed to the Agricultural Society of Jefferson County, Georgia* (Augusta: James McCafferty, 1846); Hammond, *Two Letters on Slavery in the United States, Addressed to Thomas Clarkson, Esq.* (Columbia: Allen, McCarter, 1845); Phocion [James Henry Hammond], "Oregon—War—Notice," Augusta *Constitutionalist*, n.d. [1846], clipping in Edward Spann Hammond Scrapbook (MS vol. bd., 1844–90, Edward Spann Hammond Papers, SCL); Falkland [James Henry Hammond], "The Appointment of Electors," Charleston *Mercury*, October 6, 7, 1846; Anti-Debt [James Henry Hammond], *The Railroad Mania: And Review of the Bank of the State of South Carolina* (Charleston: Burges, James, and Paxton, 1848); Hammond, *The North and the South: A Review of the Lecture on the Same Subject, Delivered by Mr. Elwood Fisher Before the Young Men's Mercantile Association of Cincinnati, Ohio* (Charleston: James S. Burges, 1849); Hammond, *An Address Delivered Before the South Carolina Institute, at Its First Annual Fair, on the 20th November, 1849* (Charleston: Walker and James, 1849); Hammond, *An Oration, Delivered Before the Two Societies of the South Carolina College, on the Fourth of December, 1849* (Charleston: Walker and James, 1850).

4. Hammond to Simms, April 1, 1845, in JHH Papers, LC; Hammond to Ruffin, June 20, 1845, June 16, 1846, both in Ruffin Papers; Hammond Diary (MS in JHH Papers, SCL), January 29, 1848.

While the bulk of Hammond's published work dealt with topics of immediate concern to the South, it would be a mistake to ignore his more abstract thought, represented chiefly in his unpublished notebooks and journals. Acutely aware of the South's lack of sympathy for pure intellectual speculation, Hammond presented most of his more transcendent concerns to the public within the context of particular and immediate problems. To discuss philosophical abstractions in the public press of the South, he once observed, would be as inappropriate as "dancing in church." But he was nonetheless concerned with "the Philosophers from Pythagoras to Whewell," with the difficult problems of epistemology and theology that lay behind the establishment of any plausible theory of social arrangements or action. Logically, therefore, such issues precede his more specifically political views and provide an intellectual framework intended to justify both these particular ideas and his role in advancing them. The Carolinian intended to make his position unassailable.[5]

Like many other Americans of his day and many southerners especially, Hammond was alarmed by what seemed to him an unprecedented rate of progress in the modern world. Change had attained a momentum that was transforming not just technologies and economies but also long-cherished social and political arrangements as well as traditional systems of belief and morality. These disruptions had created seemingly irreconcilable differences among men about the proper course of action in this "new era of civilization." Both religious and political factionalism abounded, for there was little agreement about the essential nature of either truth or virtue. Without such consensus, there could be no firm basis for social order. The rise of "superfluous benevolence," of misguided philosophies from abolitionism to socialism and feminism, Hammond believed, derived from this wider failure to evaluate the impact of intellectual and moral, as well as material change.[6]

Behind this confusion lay the rapid advance of science. Since the rationalist revolution of the seventeenth century, the inductive methods identified with the axioms of Sir Francis Bacon had provided a new degree of rigor and certitude in the study of the natural world. Spiritual insights and aspirations had been, Hammond feared, all but eclipsed in the consequent growth of materialism

5. Hammond to Simms, June 26, 1848, in JHH Papers, LC; Hammond to David J. McCord, February 25, 1848, in David J. McCord Papers, Alderman Library, University of Virginia, Charlottesville.

6. Anti-Debt, *Railroad Mania*, 14; Hammond, "Two Letters on the Subject of Slavery in the United States, Addressed to Thomas Clarkson, Esq.," in Hammond *Selections from the Letters and Speeches of the Hon. James H. Hammond, of South Carolina* (New York: John F. Trow, 1866), 130.

founded in man's expanding ability to know and master the world around him. This "is a Practical Age," Hammond announced, "An age of action fact & common sense," an age in which the traditional truths of religion and morality derived from revelation rather than inductive experiment appeared to have no place. The seeming conflict between reason and revelation had undermined the legitimacy of all religious truth, and men had accordingly neglected its spiritual precepts to pursue those material benefits science could promise them in the terrestrial world. The achievement of "wealth & public Office" became ultimate goals, obscuring the more transcendent, less practical pursuit of the good and true. Men of the nineteenth century seemed all too often to believe that "the highest objects of life, the most important duties to posterity are fulfilled by constructing steam engines, and railroads, and electric telegraphs." Increasingly, the ideal and the real, the moral and the practical, the religious and the scientific seemed separated, if not inherently opposed. Prevailing utilitarian philosophy openly rationalized this amorality and sought to enshrine it as a secular replacement for those systems of meaning that had governed men's actions in the past. But there could be no hope of social order, Hammond maintained, in such a "gospel of enlightened selfishness." Only through general agreement on the basis of ultimate truth, only through reconciliation of reason and revelation could the social ills of the day be relieved. A science of society and morality had to be erected on as convincing and legitimate a foundation as the emerging sciences of the physical world.[7]

Like most other thinkers of his day, Hammond never doubted that the essential principles of religion would ultimately prove consistent with reason. Men had simply to apply the Baconian system to moral problems in order to show that the truths of revelation and the traditional conceptions of virtue could be affirmed through empirical methods. A "foundation might be erected apart from Revelation, on which *all men* would agree to place themselves. . . . And . . . from these truths thus universally conceded," traditional principles of religion "might be so clearly and logically deduced, that no man could refuse his assent. And all this . . . apart from & without any aid from what is called Revelation." From the first, Hammond argued, Bacon had intended his Great Instauration to transform the study of the social as well as the physical world. But his followers had been so preoccupied with the materialistic implications of his philosophy that they had

7. Hammond, "South Carolina College Oration, June 5, 1849," (MS in JHH Papers, LC); Hammond, "An Oration Delivered Before the Two Societies of the South Carolina College, on the 4th of December, 1849," in Hammond, *Selections from the Letters and Speeches*, 207.

failed to recognize its idealist components. Now, at last, the time had arrived for a new "Baconian era in moral science and in morals."[8]

Hammond did not expect to find inductive proof for the Immaculate Conception, the divinity of Christ, or the existence of the Holy Ghost. These details of Christian theology he dismissed as "mysteries" as absurd as the superstitions of any other religion or sect. But the more general "*precepts*" of Christianity, by which he meant its moral imperatives, made it in his view the "most perfect of all systems of religion" and one that his new moral science would place on a firm foundation for the ages to come.[9]

Hammond's confidence that reason and revelation could be easily reconciled and his casual dismissal of the central tenets of Christian doctrine may have arisen in part from the aridity of his own spiritual nature. "When so many believe & are happy why can I not do the same?" he complained. "I desire to believe," he confessed plaintively on another occasion. But his soul seemed insensible to the religious feelings that affected others. Even as an impressionable young man at a camp meeting he had discovered that there "was a void within me." The evangelical message "fell upon me like dew upon the desert sands." During the early 1850s his continued longing for faith led him to Spiritualism, for he thought that "Spiritual Intercourse" might provide irrefutable empirical evidence of supernatural power. "I am much inclined to believe in the spirits & am very anxious to do it *if I can*," he wrote to Simms. The two South Carolinians both became involved in the highly popular Spiritualist movement, and on a trip to New York, Simms visited a spirit medium with a list of questions that he and Hammond had jointly compiled. Spiritualism appealed to Hammond because it promised a kind of proof for the existence of a "future life for men" that obviated the need for the faith he could not feel. But he worried that public knowledge of his interest in the movement might lead to mockery. And he concluded as well that the "common mind" was not yet ready for Spiritualism's truths. Traditional religion was still needed among the masses to hold the "'hangman's whip to keep the world in order' . . . let Priests reign a while yet over those who require hell & devils to restrain them."

Hammond's own religious doubts did not weaken his commitment to the institutional utility of the church. His understanding of the social influence of religion generated a concern for its theological and epistemological validity. "Some-

8. Hammond, "Untitled Thoughts," February 13, 1848.
9. Hammond, "Christianity, October 10, 1839," (MS in JHH Papers, LC).

thing supernatural," he conceded, ". . . appears to be indispensable in the government of man in all his relations." The overthrow of the tenets of biblical revelation would produce "endless revolutions in the political & social systems." In spite of his sense of alienation from its more emotional center, Hammond nevertheless supported organized religion actively and generously. Not surprisingly, denominational identity struck him as essentially meaningless; for many years he paid pew rents to the Episcopal church in Columbia, but attended Baptist and Methodist services as well. He established two churches on his plantation, and made enthusiastic contributions to the Southern Methodists after their 1844 secession from the national denomination over the issue of slavery.[10]

But Hammond did not doubt that religion could and must be justified apart from its contribution to social control. Baconian induction could, he hoped, validate the principles of religion by creating a new social science that would illuminate moral and social laws, truths that would both predict and prescribe the future course of society. Instead of conducting experiments in a laboratory, the analyst of society would scrutinize the evidence of human interrelationships embodied in the past. All "history," Hammond believed, "is but a description of Experiment" awaiting Baconian perusal for the revelation of its general truths. The scientific study of former societies would elucidate principles of social arrangements and human behavior, revealing moral laws relevant to troubling nineteenth-century crises. Only "when we have conquered, sacked, and seized possession of the Past," Hammond asserted, would men "have real knowledge, and . . . then . . . comprehend ourselves—our civilization and our mission."[11]

Hammond's faith in a positivistic social science that would allay conflict by eliminating all bases for philosophical and thus social and political discord was strikingly Comtean. Through the European and American reviews to which he subscribed, Hammond was undoubtedly exposed to the French thinker's prescription for solving social dilemmas by means of the would-be science of sociology. But he was in all probability more familiar with these questions from the

10. Hammond Diary (LC), December 10, 1844; Hammond Diary (SCL), January 29, 1849; Hammond to My Dear Friend, August 29, 1828, in JHH Papers, SCL; Hammond to Simms, December 17, 1853, in JHH Papers, LC; Hammond Diary (SCL), December 15, 1853; Hammond to Simms, June 1, March 20, 1857, Simms to Hammond, December 8, 1856, Hammond to Simms, May 28, August 31, 1854, all in JHH Papers, SCL; Hammond, "Untitled Thoughts," April 15, 1845. See Hammond Account Book (MS vol. bd., 1852–64, JHH Papers, SCL), October 1, 24, November 10, 25, 1855, for examples of his ecumenism in church donations. On the popularity of Spiritualism in this period, see R. Laurence Moore, In Search of White Crows: Spiritualism, Parapsychology, and American Culture (New York: Oxford University Press, 1977).
11. Hammond, "An Oration Delivered Before the Two Societies," 206–207.

discussions of Simms and the circle of young southern intellectuals with whom the novelist surrounded himself. Since the early 1840s, for example, a transplanted British scholar named George Frederick Holmes had been urged by Simms to become one of his "Brotherhood of the Quill." The two authors lived near Orangeburg and were able to meet often to "crack a bottle together" at Simms's plantation and to exchange views on the state of southern letters and the condition of moral philosophy in the modern world. In the *Southern Quarterly Review* and the *Southern Literary Messenger*, Holmes published a series of essays dealing with contemporary philosophical dilemmas and addressing many of the abstract issues that Hammond also found troubling. In 1845 Hammond discovered Holmes's work and became an enthusiastic supporter of the young writer, even aiding him in securing a professorial post at the College of William and Mary. Unlike Hammond and Simms, Holmes was an authentic scholar, formally trained in classics and philosophy. His specialized knowledge provided his intellectual associates with a depth of learning they themselves lacked.

The similarities between Holmes's positions and the more philosophically oriented of Hammond's writings are striking. Holmes too was concerned with discovering the "true laws of social organization, with the design of thence descending to the amelioration of the social distemper of the times." He too saw confusion surrounding the criteria for knowledge and the relationship of scientific and religious truth as the source of these terrestrial disorders, and he called for "an intellectual reformation analogous to the Instauration Magna of Lord Bacon." The Baconian inspiration, he argued, offered the possibility of a systematic means of understanding the social world—one that paralleled the methods and boasted the same legitimacy as natural science. Like Hammond, Holmes argued that in its restriction to "things sensible and material" Baconianism had been sadly perverted by the nineteenth century. Thus "shrunk and withered," the inductive philosophy had contributed significantly to the prevailing preoccupation with "man, matter, and money" and the neglect of more eternal verities. A "renovation of knowledge," the establishment of new foundations for religious and secular truth, had necessarily to precede any social improvement. Morality must be given a convincing scientific basis through an examination of the "direct parallelism" between past and present. History would become the science of society.[12]

12. David F. Jamison to George Frederick Holmes, August 28, 1845, in George Frederick Holmes Papers, LC. See also Tucker to Hammond, March 13, October 13, 1847, Hammond to

Holmes's yearning for an objective social philosophy attracted him to the work of Auguste Comte and to the French thinker's advocacy of a credible science of society. But Holmes could not accept Comte's dismissal of religion as an outmoded conceptual system that would soon be replaced in the march of progress. Both Hammond and Holmes sought to retain the legitimacy of the divine. Yet they concentrated their investigations not on the particular substance of religious truth, but on the means of arriving at it. Any inconsistencies between scientific and sacred precepts, they confidently asserted, arose from inadequate methods of religious and moral inquiry, methods they were committed to improve through the new Baconian science of morality they prescribed. Any conflict between science and religion was more apparent than real, they concluded with ingenuous optimism.

The intractable philosophical dilemmas of the day not surprisingly proved more than Hammond could easily handle. Even with his wide reading and with Holmes's substantial assistance, his writings remained derivative and even naïve. Acknowledging the conflict of idealism and empiricism, of reason and revelation, Hammond was compelled to fall back upon a kind of old-fashioned faith that new methods of inquiry would prove them ultimately reconcilable. Perhaps, he asserted hopefully, man might gain knowledge through action, faith through works, and thus prove the unity of spiritual and material truth.

In Hammond's view, these issues assumed much more than abstract importance. As he explained the nagging philosophical quandaries of his age, he began to regard them with characteristic solipsism as mirrors of his own personal difficulties; he saw the nineteenth-century dilemmas of reason versus faith, of idealism versus empiricism embodied in the conflict between thought and action that characterized his own life. Who knew better about the preoccupation of the era with the pursuit of wealth and office to the neglect of the more transcendent achievements of mind and spirit? He too had long felt himself torn between material and more spiritual goals. And now, condemned by circumstance at least temporarily to abandon his more immediate mundane ambitions, he could justify both the legitimacy and superiority of his new intellectual preoccupations.

Tucker, November 12, 1847, all in JHH Papers, LC. Holmes is quoted in Drew Gilpin Faust, *A Sacred Circle: The Dilemma of the Intellectual in the Old South, 1840–1860* (Baltimore: Johns Hopkins University Press, 1977), 63, 70, 71. Hammond listed subscriptions to "4 English Reviews"—the *Spectator* and the *Eclectic Magazine*, among others. See Hammond, Business Papers (JHH Papers, SCL), January 1, 1855, July 1, 1858.

"Mere wealth," declared this adventurer and agricultural entrepreneur, "confers no valuable or real power on its possessor. Over men of enlightened minds & true hearts it neither increases or diminishes his influence. . . . for all great & good & noble purposes knowledge alone is power." Intellectual endeavors, he concluded in a phrase borrowed from Aristotle, represented "a *more* 'virtuous energy.'"[13]

Hammond had found a rationalization for his new career as essayist and thinker. Social questions could be profitably and validly explored through the use of Baconian methods; men of mind could offer to the world around them truths as irrefutable as the amazing discoveries of natural science during the past century. "Men of Learning," Hammond declared, would and must "lead with noiseless step the vanguard of civilization," and "mark out the road over which . . . posterity marches." These individuals, not the ordinary run of sordid politicians, would be the true "guides & guardians" of the human race. Hammond's intellectual efforts represented a higher and more immodest ambition; he had simply redefined the boundaries of the domain within which he sought power and control. His abstract speculations did not constitute a retreat to an ethereal world unconnected with the realities of everyday existence. Knowledge was just the ultimate power, with the potential to subsume political, social, and economic authority within it. The relevance of thought to immediate social issues had admittedly to be demonstrated and explored; the preeminence of the man of mind had similarly to be generally established. But Hammond did not doubt that those beings who have "received from heaven an extraordinary endowment of intellect and virtue" should be "adored" by the lesser members of the human race.[14]

Throughout the 1840s Hammond grew increasingly aware of the existence of these "great minds" around him. Hammond's generalizations about the intellectual's role emerged from his interaction with others who regarded themselves as men of mind and shared his frustration at their treatment within the South. But they determined to supply one another with the sustenance the South did not

13. Hammond, "South Carolina College Oration"; Hammond to Tucker, January 24, 1847, in Tucker-Coleman Papers. On the influence of Comte in America, see Richmond Laurin Hawkins, *Auguste Comte and the United States, 1816–1853* (Cambridge, Mass.: Harvard University Press, 1936).

14. Hammond, "An Oration Delivered Before the Two Societies," 227; Hammond, "South Carolina College Oration"; Hammond, "An Oration on the Life, Character, and Services of John Caldwell Calhoun, Delivered on the 21st November, 1850, in Charleston, S.C., at the Request of the City Council," in Hammond, *Selections from the Letters and Speeches*, 231.

provide. As Simms explained, "in a guild like ours, which the world never welcomes to its love . . . there should be much love among ourselves! We, at least, will try to love one another at once as men and authors."[15]

Hammond's friendship with Simms was soon supplemented, as we have seen, by his growing intimacy with Edmund Ruffin, by a widening intellectual interchange with thinkers like George Frederick Holmes, and toward the end of the decade, by a deepening bond with Nathaniel Beverley Tucker, a William and Mary professor of impeccable states' rights credentials who had inaugurated an intensive correspondence with Hammond after reading his Clarkson letters. Under the influence of his half brother John Randolph of Roanoke, Tucker had been a southern nationalist since at least the time of the Missouri Compromise debates of 1819–1820, and he enthusiastically embraced Hammond's call for the moral and political uplift of the South. The correspondence he had opened with Hammond during the gag-rule controversy ended when Hammond went to Europe. Tucker wrote again in 1846, and the two were soon exchanging letters on natural rights, the evils of banking, the benefits of slavery, and the future of moral philosophy. Hammond presented Simms to Tucker through the mail as another pupil "with myself under your tuition," and provided Holmes with an introduction to his senior faculty colleague when the young Englishman moved from South Carolina to William and Mary in 1847. Tucker found that he and Holmes "harmonize perfectly in everything," and the Virginian was delighted as well by his correspondence with Simms and Hammond. "How pleasing it is," he wrote Hammond, "when one who has been led to distrust his own deepest convictions by observing that they seem absurd to those around him, discovers that some other whom he never saw . . . has arrived at the same conclusions." Hammond confided to Simms his amazement at how similar their perceptions were. Tucker seemed to express "in every point my own views so much better than I can do it myself." Hammond accordingly offered to finance publication of Tucker's works, just as he had frequently offered monetary assistance to the impecunious Simms. He submitted drafts of his political writings to the venerable professor, just as he sent agricultural compositions to Ruffin and his more literary ventures to Simms. This network of men of mind gratified Hammond's deeply felt need for "some one to test ideas with—some flint for my steel." But their

15. Simms to John Esten Cooke, July 26, 1859, in Mary C. Simms Oliphant, Alfred Taylor Odell, and T. C. Duncan Eaves (eds.), *The Letters of William Gilmore Simms* (5 vols.; Columbia: University of South Carolina Press, 1952–56), IV, 164–65.

A portrait of Nathaniel Beverly Tucker painted about 1847 by William G. Brown.

interaction was as much emotional as intellectual. "Your letters," Hammond declared to Tucker, "are a part of my sustenance." Tucker responded in kind, "yours
are meat, drink and clothing to me."[16]

A shared sense of alienation within the South cast these men together in a

16. Hammond to Tucker, May 12, 1847, in Tucker-Coleman Papers; Tucker to Hammond,
March 13, October 13, 1847, Tucker to Hammond, February 6, 1847, Hammond to Simms, April 1,

common search for a role for the intellectual in their region, and this quest would inform all of Hammond's thought and writing. If their ideas could just be made relevant to the dilemmas of their fellow men, Hammond emphasized, the world would be compelled to heed their wisdom. Intellectuals would not only resolve the troubling fissure between ideas and action but occupy the place in society they had so long sought. When Simms complained of his neglect, Hammond assured his friend that no prophet was ever honored in his own country. He comforted Ruffin with similar words, explaining that "instantaneous general appreciation" could never be expected for the works of mind. But Hammond and the other members of his intellectual network hoped to be able to change the distressing realities that had made each of them feel so isolated and rejected within the South. A reform of knowledge to give learning a firm scientific foundation and a distinct social applicability would transform both the South and their place within it.[17]

Hammond's more abstract speculations were thus all directed at creating a new philosophy of social action that combined the transcendent legitimacy of eternal truth with a popularly attractive pragmatism. Together with those other southern thinkers who formed the circle of his most intimate associates, Hammond embraced a vision of conservative reform based in a new understanding of the social change that defined their era. "I would much prefer," Hammond reflected, "to be regarded as one who grappled with the evils & follies of his day & resting on established principles & facts resisted the rash spirit of universal change, than to be classed among those who spread their sails to every novel breeze, plunged wildly into every visionary scheme of improvement whose advocates raised the maudlin shouts of Onward! Onward! Progress! Progress!" Every proposed change, Hammond believed, every human intervention into existing social arrangements had to be carefully assessed in light of the truths of history. While many fanatical nineteenth-century reformers believed "nothing is venerable in antiquity," Hammond insisted that the past be the measure and guide of the future. A false notion of progress had arisen, urging the enthusiastic embrace of everything new; the world was threatened by a "wild and reckless

---

1847, all in JHH Papers, LC; Hammond to Tucker, March 4, 1847, in Tucker-Coleman Papers; Hammond to Simms, July 25, 1847, February 5, 1849, in JHH Papers, LC; Hammond to Ruffin, February 6, 1846, in Ruffin Papers; Hammond to M. C. M. Hammond, May 12, 1849, in JHH Papers, SCL. See also Hammond to Tucker, November 12, 1847, Hammond to Tucker, April 29, 1850, both in Tucker-Coleman Papers; Tucker to Hammond, May 7, 1850, in JHH Papers, LC.

17. Hammond to Ruffin, July 22, 1846, in Ruffin Papers.

spirit of innovation wh. delights to break up established forms merely because they are old."[18]

Any careful observer of human history, Hammond believed, would soon see the erroneous assumptions upon which the utopian schemes of northern and European reformers were based. Men were not naturally good, but selfish and corrupt. Any efforts to uplift society by changing institutional arrangements were bound to fail as long as these limitations of human nature were not acknowledged. Real improvement could come about only through changes in men's hearts and minds. Social amelioration would not result from the increase or redistribution of wealth, that chimerical goal of so many misguided contemporary reformers. True progress, Hammond argued, was spiritual and moral; the "facilities of the intellect" and the "sentiment of the heart" were the "springs which finally sustain and move all political, social, & industrial institutions."[19]

Hammond's evocation of history as the source of the standards by which to resolve social dilemmas guaranteed that the resulting social guidelines would be highly conservative. Past reality not only prescribed future action; inescapable historical facts established limitations on the possibilities for change that could not be safely ignored. Intrusive reform efforts aimed at immediate social amelioration were bound to fail, he warned, for the power of tradition was inevitably stronger than the power of mere men.

Society was in Hammond's view an intricate system of customs and interrelationships that had evolved over centuries to produce the particular arrangements of his own era. Because it appeared as the work of the ages, society had a sort of natural transcendence; because of the determining force of the past, man's ability to intervene positively in social processes was severely limited. And it was limited most specifically to the intellectually gifted, the "men of learning" within the human race. Hammond had devised a social philosophy that legitimated his own and his region's anxieties about the threat of change at the same time it called for men like himself to monitor the floodgates of progress. But to attract the attention of fellow southerners whose deference and acclaim could alone place him in the position he desired, Hammond had to translate these theories into the particular social contexts and conflicts that were of immediate

18. Hammond to Lewis Tappan, August 1, 1845, in JHH Papers, LC; Hammond, "An Oration Delivered Before the Two Societies," 199, 223; Hammond to Tucker, January 26, 1847, in Tucker-Coleman Papers.

19. Hammond, "South Carolina Institute Address, June 30, 1849" (MS in JHH Papers, LC).

interest to his region. His thought had to be embodied in existing social issues.[20]

Within Hammond's conception of reform, the first step in uplifting the South was education. Southerners had to develop the spiritual and intellectual resources necessary to understand and defend themselves. Because the problems Carolina faced were at base "wholly of a moral character," reform had to begin with an attack upon "Ignorance and prejudice . . . petty interests, false reasoning, unsound calculations & above all traditional forms of thought & habits of action." Education was thus central to individual human and wider social improvement. To Hammond it seemed "by far the most important matter of Temporal concern." Yet improved opportunities for formal schooling were but a small part of Hammond's prescription; in his view the education his section required included far more than classroom instruction. Southerners, he feared, had little comprehension of themselves, their regional assets and liabilities, the purposes of their political, social, and economic institutions.[21]

Hammond recognized that the political goals for which he had been struggling would remain impossible to achieve as long as such ignorance persisted. Even though it was "important that the North and South should fully comprehend their respective strength and weakness before the threatened and apparently impending breach is made," the South still remained the intellectual vassal of the North, depending upon the "Yankee press" for knowledge of the world, attending northern schools and colleges, and far too often thinking northern thoughts. Within the all-important realm of politics, Hammond found that the insidious perils of party constituted an even greater threat than these more obvious dangers of northern dominance. This growing factionalism, Hammond argued, also arose from ignorance. "Our peculiar institutions," he feared, would count "nothing in the scale against party ties." Faction required men to place the desire for power above the pursuit of principle; the resultant greed and self-interest would destroy those constitutional guarantees that served as the South's only certain defense. In this era of expanding popular control, it seemed to Hammond that "demagogues . . . are corrupting the people & . . . the only radical cure is by education." Political power must rest with those who understood

20. Hammond, "An Oration Delivered Before the Two Societies," 227; On this conservative, historicist conception of change in the Old South, see Theodore Dwight Bozeman, "Joseph Le-Conte: Organic Science and a 'Sociology for the South,'" *Journal of Southern History*, XXXIX (November, 1973), 565–82.
21. Hammond, "South Carolina Institute Address"; Hammond, "Education, 1848" (MS in JHH Papers, LC).

the implications of their actions. In the *Mercury* of October, 1846, Hammond spoke out against transferring the election of president and governor from the state legislature to the people, for he believed that Carolina's citizens were not yet sufficiently enlightened to act responsibly. "Corrupt them with the constant exercise of political power with its excitements the false lights that will from every quarter be made to shine & delude them—the permanent party lines— the miserable factions that must speedily arise & what confidence can we place in their decisions," he asked Simms. It was the moral and intellectual shortcomings of the masses that Hammond emphasized publicly, but he worried perhaps even more about the dangerous susceptibility of the ignorant to the lure and promise of "progress" and social change. Slavery, for example, would be "weakened by every accession of administrative & executive power to the masses *even here.*"[22]

Hammond's philosophy of reform thus vindicated Carolina's traditional elite politics. Because of its moral and intellectual superiority, Hammond argued, the existing leadership class must retain its institutional political control until the masses had been successfully indoctrinated about the dangers of precipitous social change. Before Hammond was willing to cede any of the planters' social and political advantages, he wanted the ideological hegemony of the master class to be absolute.

All change and progress had therefore to be undertaken cautiously, but certain new "forms of thought and habits of action" were necessary to preserve the contours of Carolina's social order. The decline of planters' profits and productivity, for example, made agricultural reform a necessity. But, as with politics, agricultural progress was to consist chiefly in education and enlightenment under the guidance of the mentally and morally gifted.

South Carolinians, Hammond declared in his agricultural essays and orations, had shamefully exploited their land, exhausting their soil and diminishing their profits to a point where they could no longer compete with the Southwest. The income from cotton would certainly continue to fall, and the "swelling tide of emigration" from the state would not abate. "It is time," Hammond called, "to stop all this—to rally upon the land we love, & uniting our minds & energies rejuvenate it—reclaim its worn out fields." The mind of the scientist would

22. Hammond, "The North and the South," *Southern Quarterly Review*, XVI (July, 1849), 311; Hammond to Tucker, July 3, 1849, in Tucker-Coleman Papers, EGSWM; Falkland, "The Appointment of Electors"; Hammond to Tucker, September 22, 1848, in Tucker-Coleman Papers; Hammond to Simms, November 10, January 1, 1846, July 23, 1847, all in JHH Papers, LC.

be joined to the energy of the planter as Carolina embraced a new scientific agriculture; the reputation of "book farmers" would be rehabilitated along with the soil; prejudice would be abandoned "against those who affect to read as well as plough."[23]

Hammond derived his agricultural recommendations from those two sources of knowledge his understanding of the Baconian system prescribed: rational experimentation and historical investigation. His exhortation in favor of marl, published as a pamphlet in 1846, began with an account of the fertilizer's antiquity; Hammond cited references to it in the works of Varro and Pliny. "Marling . . . ," Hammond insisted, "is certainly no novelty—no untried experiment that can for a moment be classed among modern humbugs." The persistence of marling over the centuries, he argued, was one sure demonstration of its efficacy. Its chemistry was of equal importance with its history. Even though Hammond feared he might bewilder the untutored farmer, he provided a lengthy explanation of the action of lime on the soil, the role of silica and iron, and the proper proportions of marl for each acre. His essay on the fertilizer represented an embodiment of his philosophy of improvement: reformers need not be seduced by "modern humbugs," but could turn to science and history for truths that would enable them to better themselves and their condition.[24]

Although marl was perhaps Hammond's favorite remedy for agricultural decline in Carolina, he advocated a number of other measures equally consistent with his concept of reform. He contemplated publishing his own agricultural journal to spread the gospel of enlightenment throughout the South, and urged Ruffin, who had undertaken a similar venture in Virginia, to locate a small printing press for him. When this plan failed, Hammond concocted another even more "visionary scheme"—the establishment of "a *College* for Agricultural Sciences" at Silver Bluff with a laboratory, a resident professor, and students from all over the state. "We could turn out annually 50 young men . . . able to think, reason & act in farming as professional men in their callings." At present, he complained, "not one Agriculturist in 100,000 knows the least thing of Botany, Geology, minerology [sic] or chemistry, all of which sciences are essential to his knowing what he is about every day of his life." This plan, too, remained no

23. Hammond, "South Carolina Institute Address"; Hammond, "Address to the Agricultural Club of Matlock, South Carolina, July 3, 1847" (MS in JHH Papers, LC).

24. Hammond, "Marl: A Letter Addressed to the Agricultural Society of Jefferson County, Georgia," in *Proceedings of the Agricultural Convention and of the State Agricultural Society of South Carolina from 1839 to 1845 Inclusive* (Columbia: Sumner and Carroll, 1846), 394; Hammond to Ruffin, January 2, 1846, in Ruffin Papers.

more than a vision, but Hammond did succeed in a somewhat more modest endeavor with the founding in 1846 of a local farmers club to serve as a dissemina-
tor of up-to-date agricultural theory and practice. The ABC Farmers Club of
Beech Island required each member to subscribe to one agricultural paper and
undertake one experiment annually. Hammond himself, by far the largest land-
holder in the area, dominated the proceedings, regaling his neighbors with
Cato's views on manure, as well as with the results of his own undertakings at
Silver Bluff.[25]

Hammond's concern with agricultural change grew out of his conviction
that economic decline threatened the stability of the Carolina social order. If
the plantation system were to prove unprofitable, the peculiar institution and
the society erected upon it would be endangered as well. Without dramatic
change, Carolina "must soon become utterly impoverished. . . . One of the first
results would be the loss of our Slaves & the total subversion here of an institution from which we have heretofore reaped the greatest benefits." Agricultural
change and improvement, therefore, were essentially conservative undertakings: alterations in farm practice could ensure the perpetuation of existing social
arrangements. But Hammond did not justify reform simply in terms of its material and social benefits. Hammond liked to think of his own agricultural work as
directed toward more transcendent ends than mere profit. To replenish the land
was to exercise the religious responsibility of stewardship; human beings were
"accountable" to heaven for the productive use of the "infinite variety of gifts
which it has pleased God to bestow upon man." Husbanding the divine bounty
was ultimately a spiritual endeavor of "great moral effects." In planting, Hammond believed, man could thus resolve the troubling dilemma of thought and
action by combining mind and energy in tilling the soil; scientific and religious
purposes would be joined; the planter could satisfy his own pecuniary desires at
the same time that he executed God's commands.[26]

Husbanding God's bounty, however, encompassed more than just tilling the
soil. Planting, Hammond believed, could not possibly "absorb all the genius &
draw out all the energies of our people." Nor could the South prosper without
some diversification of her economy away from its exclusive preoccupation with

25. Hammond to Ruffin, July 22, February 6, 1846, both in Ruffin Papers. "Record of the Proceedings of the Beech Island Agricultural Club, 1846–1862" (typescript in SCL). The ABC Club
later became the Beech Island Agricultural Society.
26. Hammond, "South Carolina Institute Address"; Hammond, "Anniversary Oration of the
State Agricultural Society of South Carolina . . . 25th November, 1841," in *Proceedings*, 183.

agriculture. History had shown that "purely agricultural people have been in all ages the victims of rapacious tyrants grinding them down." As long as the South remained dependent on the North for manufactures, so long would she remain economically oppressed by tariffs and high prices. Therefore, he argued, the South must undertake new ventures, experiment with cotton manufacturing, with the production of its own slave shoes and cloth, with establishing a degree of self-sufficiency. Hammond himself considered purchasing an up-country cotton factory from William Gregg, the successful entrepreneur who had founded the mill town of Graniteville only a few miles from Silver Bluff. With Hammond's encouragement, the members of the ABC Farmers Club discussed jointly sponsoring a factory of about four thousand spindles. Although the plan was never realized, it serves as testimony to the close connection between agricultural improvement and economic diversification: both fit neatly within the framework of conservative reform and southern redemption Hammond had articulated.[27]

Hammond's most explicit advocacy of industrial development appeared in an 1849 address to the South Carolina Institute in Charleston, an organization founded just a year before to "aid in lifting the Mechanic Arts from the low condition they have hitherto occupied in the South." Even though his audience was composed of Carolinians particularly sympathetic to the idea of industrial development, Hammond felt obliged to devote much of his address to dismissing stereotyped doubts about the effects of manufacturing. Industry would not, he insisted, corrupt the people's morals, undermine the region's dedication to free trade, or weaken the institution of slavery. In fact, he argued, cotton manufacturing could cement nonslaveholders' allegiance to the South by providing them profitable employment in an industry directly dependent upon the plantation system. In their determination to avoid the disruptions that industrialism had caused in the North, southerners must not reject development altogether. Carefully monitored diversification of the southern economy, he urged, could serve as the means of averting more drastic change. "It must not be supposed that in thus advocating the encouragement of the mechanic arts & extensive manufacturing among us . . . that I look upon them in any other light than as means— not ends." The "preponderating" influence within the South must remain with

27. Hammond, "South Carolina Institute Address"; Hammond to M. C. M. Hammond, May 7, 1849, in JHH Papers, LC. See also "Proceedings of the Beech Island Agricultural Club," and Thomas P. Martin (ed.), "The Advent of William Gregg and the Graniteville Company," *Journal of Southern History*, XI (August, 1945), 389–423.

the agricultural class. "The thing is," Hammond explained to Tucker, "to reconcile industry with free trade, slave labour, agricultural advancement & Southern tone."[28]

In his call for industrial development, as in all his proposed reforms, Hammond was urging minor adjustments and improvements designed to stave off wider social upheaval. And the ultimate purpose of all change should, he contended, always be the enlightenment and consequent moral uplift of the people of the South. Industry, like scientific agriculture, would contribute to the "training of the mind" in the region; reform would conveniently yield both monetary and spiritual profits. Through economic improvement and diversification, Carolina would ensure the survival of her social order and the vitality of her mind and spirit, both now so threatened by northern oppressions.[29]

Hammond's intensified concern with philosophical and intellectual undertakings thus did not require him to abandon his deeply ingrained interest in public affairs. He continued to champion the political positions he had so long espoused, changing the arena but not the substance of the controversy, seeking his goals not in the electoral or legislative process, but through the pen. Yet as he recast the problems of slavery, southern economic development, and sectional strength in terms of his legitimating ideology of intellectual values, the issues themselves were necessarily somewhat altered to fit within his newly articulated philosophy of reform.

His long-standing opposition to the Bank of the State of South Carolina became an embodiment of his social vision; the bank itself and the "Railroad Mania" its speculations supported stood in Hammond's mind as examples of the false "spirit of progress" he deplored. In a series of articles published in the fall of 1847 in the Charleston *Mercury* and in a second group that appeared in the Hamburg *Journal* the following spring, Hammond elevated his old enmity to the Elmore faction to a war of economic and moral principles. Under a succession of pseudonyms—"File Closer," "A Voter," "A Farmer," and most tellingly, "Anti-Debt," Hammond attacked the bank and its president, Elmore, for failing to move more rapidly to retire the state debt. Financial liability, he argued, represented a certain loss of virtue, as well as a threat to social order. The bank

28. Hammond, "South Carolina Institute Address"; Hammond to Tucker, July 3, 1849, in Tucker-Coleman Papers. See also Hammond, "Progress of Southern Industry," *De Bow's Review*, VIII (1850), 501–522.
29. Hammond, "South Carolina Institute Address."

had consistently urged Carolina to "squander money" in wasteful and profligate schemes that threatened the state with eventual bankruptcy. In encouraging speculation, the institution had contributed to dangerously misguided notions of progress. Every community, Hammond acknowledged, should "judiciously and zealously apply their industry and means to secure and improve all the natural advantages they possess. . . . But," he urged in a summary of his case against the Bank, "an artificial . . . system of forcing nature . . . becomes unwise, dangerous, and destructive." The Bank of the State represented to Hammond a part of the "tendency of the present age . . . to *over do*."[30]

As with so many other evils of the era, the bank existed, Hammond complained to Simms, "solely in consequence of the ignorance of the people." But Hammond's efforts to edify produced little more than a heated pamphlet controversy and ultimate frustration. All but forgetting the detached and disinterested posture his new role of essayist and intellectual prescribed, Hammond reverted to the near-total absorption that had characterized his earlier political involvement. His antibank and antirailroad essays poured forth with such volume and rapidity that his brother Marcellus purchased the Hamburg *Journal* in the spring of 1848 to provide a sure outlet for this torrent of words. In pursuit of a political goal, Hammond was like a man possessed; his "Anti-Debt" outburst occurred almost in spite of himself. To Simms, Hammond confessed himself full of "repentence for having wasted my time in writing about Rail Roads & Banks." Under the excitement of politics, he had written the articles too "hastily" to give them what he had come to view as appropriate erudition.[31]

Even though a proposal to float additional railroad bonds was defeated by the legislature in December, 1847, Hammond felt he had failed both himself and his cause. His articles had not really been understood "by the body of the people." But more importantly, he had fallen prey to "temporary invasions of old feelings," sentiments he now deemed beneath him. Forgetting his resolution to transcend political squabbles, the old war-horse had once again responded to the

30. Anti-Debt, *Railroad Mania*, 5, 9, 13, 14–15. See F. H. Elmore Scrapbook (MS dated 1848–50, in Franklin Harper Elmore Papers, LC), in which Elmore includes and identifies a number of Hammond's articles from this period, including many from the Hamburg (S.C.) *Journal*. For general background on the bank controversy, see J. Mauldin Lesesne, *The Bank of the State of South Carolina: A General and Political History* (Columbia: University of South Carolina, 1970).

31. Hammond to Simms, December 31, 1847, January 14, 1848, November 17, 1847, all in JHH Papers, LC. On the distinction between a reviewer or essayist and a controversialist, see Hammond to M. C. M. Hammond, March 5, 1849, in JHH Papers, SCL, and Hammond to Simms, December 22, 1848, in JHH Papers, LC.

sound of the trumpet. "I see the folly of it now that the thing is over & the excitement gone," he admitted to Simms. "You'll not catch me in such a scrape soon again. Cui bono?"[32]

To whose good indeed? The bank simply did not mean enough to most Carolinians to attract the audience Hammond sought for himself and for the dissemination of his larger message of uplift and reform. It was the issues connected with southern sectionalism that could secure widest attention. Into his discussion of these conflicts, therefore, Hammond incorporated his particular concerns about the role of mind and of the thinker in the Old South. Hammond's defenses of slavery and of southern rights became a vehicle for presenting his philosophy of society, government, and progress, as well as a means of convincing the region of the importance of his role as critic, thinker, and intellectual.

Hammond's proslavery tracts, especially his two letters to English abolitionist Thomas Clarkson, published in pamphlet form in the spring of 1845, won him greater acclaim than he had ever before enjoyed. "They have exalted my reputation," Hammond noted with satisfaction in his diary. One friend wrote exuberantly of the reaction throughout Carolina. "If to be toasted is to be happy," he reported, "then you are the happiest man in the State. 4th July 1845 seems to have been kept only to celebrate your praises." Even the usually reticent Calhoun was generous with tributes. "You are now so fairly enlisted & with so much eclat as the defender of the South against the assaults of the abolitionists that you will not be permitted to sheath your sword."[33]

Hammond's active support for slavery was in no sense a new departure. "The opinions I formed at an early period," he explained, "have constantly gained strength." But the argument he presented in his Clarkson letters represented a new level of sophistication for Hammond. In the leisure available after the close of his governorship, Hammond had determined to read "everything I could lay my hand on upon both sides of the question." He secured a list of titles on race from his old college friend Josiah Nott, now a Mobile physician with a growing reputation in ethnology, the emerging "science" of racial differences. From the New York antislavery spokesman Lewis Tappan, Hammond requested a subscription to "the newspaper considered the ablest & most in the confidence of the

---

32. Hammond to Simms, December 31, 1847, January 14, 1848, both in JHH Papers, LC; Hammond to McCord, in McCord Papers.

33. Hammond Diary (LC), July 3, 1845; James Walker to Hammond, August 1, 1845, John C. Calhoun to Hammond, August 1, 1845, both in JHH Papers, LC. On proslavery thought see Faust, *A Sacred Circle*, Chap. VI, and Drew Gilpin Faust, *The Ideology of Slavery: Proslavery Thought in the Antebellum South, 1830–1860* (Baton Rouge: Louisiana State University Press, 1981).

abolition party." He was committed to developing an argument for slavery based on the widest possible knowledge of fact and opinion, for Hammond was "firmly convinced that the more it is discussed, the stronger we shall become everywhere."[34]

But to be both effective and legitimate, the defense of human bondage had to be raised above the sordid realm of sectional politics into a domain of timeless values and irrefutable truth. The proslavery argument represented Hammond's most determined and successful effort to reconcile moral and spiritual principles with practical mundane matters, to make his intellectual concerns immediately relevant. Hammond would justify slavery in terms of a hierarchical ideology that called not only for the dominance of white over black but for the preeminence among whites of men of intellectual endowments like his own. In the proslavery argument Hammond united his own ambition with the cause of the South. His case for human bondage invoked his system of disinterested and transcendent values and identified his world view with the South's most distinctive institution. Hammond hoped simultaneously to elicit a regional affirmation of slavery and of himself and his place in this slave society.[35]

If the proslavery argument was to represent the works of mind, it had in tone and scholarly rigor to meet those standards Hammond had acknowledged as the criteria of truth; it must not be partisan or polemical but offer facts and principles derived from religion and the scientific examination of history, nature, and society. Hammond agreed with Simms that nothing could be more "inauspicious and evil than that we should convert the slave question into political capital for any object." Hammond deplored Calhoun's plan for a proslavery newspaper in Washington, for he feared the publication would be devoted primarily to sordid political agitation and to the advancement of Calhoun's presidential ambitions. Such a project would demean rather than exalt the slavery cause.[36]

Hammond's justifications of slavery began in a realm far removed from politics. The "first question we have to ask ourselves," he asserted in the Clarkson letters, was whether slavery was consistent with the will of God. "Our only safety against the torrent of abolition," with its evangelical crusade against the

34. Hammond to Tappan, April 8, 1845, Hammond to Josiah C. Nott, August 3, 1845, Hammond to Tappan, March 25, 1845, all in JHH Papers, LC. Hammond subscribed to the *Emancipator* and the London *Anti-Slavery Reporter*. Hammond to Dear Sir, May 24, 1845, in JHH Papers, LC.

35. William Gilmore Simms, in "Gen. Hammond's Letters on Slavery," *Southern and Western Monthly Magazine*, II (July, 1845), 72, argues that his defense of slavery makes Hammond too valuable a spokesman to leave out of South Carolina's councils.

36. Simms to Hammond, October 20, 1847, Hammond to Nott, August 3, 1845, both in JHH Papers, LC.

immorality of slavery "is to drive our piling to the rock—'the rock of ages'—the Bible." Hammond's examination of scripture revealed God's express prohibition of interference with another's property, his sanction of slavery among the Chosen People. No "visionary notions of piety or philanthropy" had prompted Christ or the apostles to speak out against the system of human bondage that had thrived around them, and Paul had even apprehended a runaway slave and returned him to his master. An array of biblical quotations supported Hammond's contention that "American slavery is not only not a sin, but especially commanded by God through Moses and approved by Christ through His Apostles."[37]

Since Revelation seemed in no way to prohibit slavery, Hammond turned to the inductive examination of the social experiments of history to serve as a second prop for his case. The experience of Rome, Athens, and Sparta, perhaps the greatest civilizations the world had ever known, appeared to Hammond certain evidence that slavery's opponents were entirely "ignorant of the essential principles of human association revealed in history." But Hammond was less interested in comparing the South with societies of the past than with other communities of his own day. Once again he evoked the scenes of poverty and deprivation he had witnessed abroad. "If my slaves could see precisely what I have myself seen of the condition of the labourers both in Europe & America & could know as I do & as every one must know that freedom would entail the same fate on them, I would not hesitate a moment," he boldly declared to Lewis Tappan, "to give them their choice between slavery & emancipation believing they would as myself prefer to be slaves rather than *such free men.*" Hammond's letters to Clarkson contained lengthy excerpts from parliamentary reports demonstrating the misery of the British working class. "Your *fellow-citizens,*" he contended, "are more miserable and degraded, morally and physically, than our slaves; to be elevated to the actual condition of whom, would be to your *fellow-citizens* a most glorious act of *emancipation.*"[38]

It was not just the wondrous achievements of societies like Greece and Rome that Hammond cited as evidence of the superiority of slave to free labor. Human bondage, he argued, created the social order that accorded most perfectly with Christian moral precepts. The exploitation of "free" laborers, who had in reality liberty only to starve, represented the soulless materialism of England and the North. While "free society" cared only about the labor it could extract from its

37. Hammond to Calhoun, July 20, 1845, in John C. Calhoun Papers, Clemson University, Clemson, S.C.; Hammond, "Two Letters," 123, 124.
38. Hammond, "Two Letters," 176; Hammond to Tappan, April 8, 1845, in JHH Papers, LC.

workers, southerners assumed responsibility for every aspect of the lives of the human beings God had "entrusted" to them.[39]

Consistent with Christianity, southern slavery accorded with the precepts of nature as well. Objective verification of black inferiority through the researches of ethnology would soon demonstrate that the subordination of Negroes was justified by modern science as well as by scripture and history. Although the field had not yet advanced to the point of absolute reliability, Hammond did not doubt that ethnological data would soon provide another source of firm support in the defense of the South's social order, for it would confirm that men were differentially endowed and thus providentially suited for social inequality.

In the idealized system of human bondage Hammond described, duty and responsibility, not greed, tied master and worker together. Slaves, he contended, were kindly treated, well fed, and well housed; families were rarely separated. The peculiar institution served to lift up heathen Africans into the enlightenment of Christian civilization. The naturally weak and inferior were protected by an institutionalized system of dependence; the seemingly objective criteria of race structured society; men of superior mind exercised power and authority. As one of southern society's sharpest native critics, Hammond knew such perfect arrangements did not actually exist. But the only way to legitimate slavery, his argument implicitly warned, was to transform the South and its peculiar institution into the paradise of his essays. The proslavery argument thus became as much a call to reform as a justification of the status quo. The benevolent ties of stewardship would not only be perfected between master and slave, but would serve as a model for all other social relationships. Beings of inferior intellect and endowment would be subservient to their superiors. Slavery truly served as the "cornerstone" of southern society, Hammond explained, for it ensured that social authority would be vested in those "both educated and independent in their circumstances." Hammond's social creed was, as he later described it, based in "the great fundamental principle of the subordination of the inferior to the superior man—as made by God." Just as intellect was the attribute that most clearly differentiated the Caucasian from the African, so it, not the claims of hereditary aristocracy, should serve as the criterion of social differentiation among whites. Hammond's ideology of subordination simultaneously guaranteed that the black would be on the bottom and Hammond himself on top. Yet by founding this doctrine in religion, history, and science, he portrayed it as more than simply

39. Hammond, "Two Letters," 143.

self-serving. The unity of truth exemplified in the defense of slavery affirmed the ultimate consistency of science and religion and demonstrated the existence of a valid moral philosophy—and thus the need for moral philosophers—in the modern world. For Hammond and many of his associates—men like Simms, Ruffin, Tucker, and Holmes, who also wrote proslavery essays—the defense of human bondage was in an important sense an effort to revitalize southern society, to provide a system of beliefs that would impart meaning to the regional way of life and, in so doing, establish an essential role for their particular talents in the South.[40]

Yet the acclaim that greeted Hammond and other southern defenders of slavery did not represent that wider shift in intellectual and moral outlook for which the Carolinian had hoped. Southerners were glad to have plausible arguments with which to justify their peculiar institution and even grateful to those thinkers who had formulated and promulgated them. But the people of the South did not embrace what Hammond had hoped was the inescapable logical consequence of the premises of his proslavery tracts. Most southerners saw only the immediate utility of the defense of slavery in the growing controversy with the North; they did not look beyond the specific terms of Hammond's arguments to the social philosophy that provided a wider framework for the essays.

Feeling as solitary at Silver Bluff "as if I were in the great Sahara," Hammond was frustrated by the failure of his writings to win him the understanding and recognition he craved. He could neither suppress his ambition nor decide how best to achieve his goals. Even Caesar and Bonaparte, he was convinced, would have been hard pressed to attain greatness as "pine land cotton planters" in the Old South. "Certain I am," he mused to Simms, "that . . . I was born out of my true place, & have always been playing a part not my own. . . . In some spheres I believe I might have shone." But in Carolina, there were no adequate libraries to consult, no publishers to offer support and encouragement, no audience to provide appreciation. Writing for reviews seemed "lost time. No fame, no pleasure, no effect." Simms articulated his friend's difficulties perhaps even better than Hammond himself, "Your ambition only suffers you to work in the sight of the public. . . . Your love of approbation is a larger development than you will allow, or perhaps believe yourself."[41]

40. *Ibid.*, 126–27; Hammond, "Speech Delivered at Barnwell C. H., S.C., October 29, 1858," in Hammond, *Selections from the Letters and Speeches*, 345.
41. Hammond to Simms, February 10, 1849, February 19, 1846, June 3, 1845, all in JHH Papers, LC; Hammond to McCord, February 25, 1848, in McCord Papers; Simms to Hammond, May 10, 1845, in JHH Papers, LC.

Each of Hammond's intellectual efforts left him more convinced that in the South, as he complained to Tucker, "the idea is universal that not to reach high official rank is to accomplish nothing." The lure of politics would not die. But the anxieties it had always engendered were equally persistent. If Hammond even for a moment admitted the power of his true aspirations, the pressure of achievement became almost unbearable. "Now what afflicts me," he wrote in his diary, "is my perfect conviction that I can never meet any such expectations. It is painful to know that one *must fail.* This feeling makes me look with absolute horror at the idea of reentering public life." It was far easier to hide behind a veil of illness than to struggle with ambition. "The fact is," as Hammond repeatedly complained to Simms during these years at Silver Bluff, "I have not & never had any physical constitution. And whatever I might be, this effectively prevents my *being.*" Headaches, dyspepsia, and dizziness plagued Hammond, although he admitted he "could not pass for an invalid with any but the closest observers."[42]

Yet Hammond would not entirely succeed in escaping into illness, nor in repressing his political ambitions. Even though many Carolinians had opposed the positions he had taken as governor and even though many of Hampton's circle had been permanently alienated, Hammond's unusual talents had not been entirely forgotten, and the publication of the Clarkson letters had prompted renewed discussion of a possible place for him in the United States Senate. A loyal band of supporters continued to press his name for office, keeping his insatiable political ambition alive despite his professed determination to extinguish it completely. Hammond would never be happy out of "sight of the public," nor would he ever be able to free himself from the political aspirations that held him in their sway.

42. Hammond to Tucker, December 1, 1848, in Tucker-Coleman Papers; Hammond Diary (SCL), February 21, 1847; Hammond to Simms, February 19, 1846, in JHH Papers, LC.

CHAPTER 14

To Enlighten and Warn the South

DESPITE HIS RESOLUTION to abandon public affairs, Hammond could not easily slip into a life of rural contentment. He had been trained, as he described it, to regard politics as the arena of highest mortal achievement, and he could relinquish neither his need nor his "delight to accomplish." The political "treachery" he had experienced during his term as governor had engendered the wish but not the will to escape from public life. The late 1840s, moreover, were an era of escalating crisis for the South, a time when the Texas question, the Wilmot Proviso, the Mexican War, and the emerging conflict over the status of slavery in the newly conquered territories made complacency almost impossible. In threatening to exclude the peculiar institution from America's western lands, the North was not only challenging the balance between free and slave states that had been scrupulously maintained since Missouri and Maine were admitted together in 1820; the Free-Soil movement seemed to many southerners an effort to impugn their way of life. A slaveholder could hardly stand aloof from the intensifying controversy.[1]

But Hammond's pride had been deeply wounded by the defeat of his measures in the Carolina legislature in 1844, and he was torn between a bitter rejection of the South and its spirited defense. The acclaim that greeted his Clarkson letters contributed significantly toward resolving this conflict. Despite the stormy Hampton incident and the failure of the Bluffton movement, the enthusiastic reception of the Clarkson letters seemed to demonstrate that Hammond had, as

1. James Henry Hammond to William Gilmore Simms, January 22, 1846, in JHH Papers, LC.

a friend remarked, proved "seaworthy" in Carolina's turbulent political ocean. His brilliant defense of slavery even launched a movement for his prompt return to office as a successor to the ailing George McDuffie in the United States Senate. Late in 1844 the notion of Hammond in federal service would have been almost unthinkable; his opposition to the national tariff had bordered on overt— some would have said treasonous—secessionism. But in the course of the next two years, dramatic realignments had transformed politics both within Carolina and throughout the nation.[2]

At first Hammond had felt vindicated in his strident sectionalism; the mistrust of Polk that had fueled the Bluffton movement seemed at first entirely justified, for the new president passed over the South in his executive appointments and made no move toward the tariff reform Carolinians viewed as essential. Calhoun's apparent failure to influence Polk emboldened his enemies at home, and by the summer of 1845, Blufftonites Rhett and McDuffie began to call once again for decisive state action. From his solitude at Silver Bluff, Hammond enjoyed the spectacle of the discomfited Calhoun, disappointed in his hopes for a cabinet post and compelled to accept Daniel Huger's long-standing offer to resign from the U.S. Senate in his favor just to be able to remain in public life.

Calhoun's nearly unanimous reelection to Congress by the legislature did not mark an end to his difficulties at home. In the effort to create an alliance of South and West to check the growing power of the North and perhaps serve as a firm basis for his presidential ambitions, Calhoun had in the fall of 1845 declared his support for federally funded internal improvements on the Mississippi River. Always a favorite measure with westerners, internal improvements had long appeared to Calhoun and to most states' rights southerners as unconstitutional, vesting unwarranted power in the central government. To those who had consistently opposed any national aid for such projects, Calhoun's new stance, which he justified by designating the Mississippi an "inland sea," seemed opportunistic and potentially dangerous. Even Francis Pickens, theretofore Calhoun's staunchest and most docile lieutenant, openly objected to this new departure.

The relations between Calhoun and his henchmen became even more strained over the Mexican War, declared in May of 1846 and opposed by the senator as unnecessary. While Calhoun feared the centralizing tendencies that were naturally associated with any national conflict, Pickens began to speak openly against the senator's position and to appeal to the state's martial spirit. Ham-

2. Paul Quattlebaum to Hammond, August 28, 1845, *ibid.*

mond himself understood Calhoun's anxieties and wished to avert any situation that would enhance federal power. But at the same time he and many other Carolinians were almost delighted by the prospect of a real war, a diversion from the dreary experiences of economic depression and political conflict that had filled the past decade. Hammond lent his enthusiastic support to a volunteer unit from his neighborhood that named itself the "Hammond Guards."[3]

Although he dissented from Calhoun's position on Mississippi improvements and from his extreme opposition to the War, Hammond did not speak out, for after his experiences of 1840 and 1844, he had begun to recognize that there was little he could gain from direct opposition to the senator. "Mr. Calhoun overshadows us," he wrote resignedly to Tucker. "He is the King in our game whom we cannot abandon & cannot protect. If we shield him from 'check', he immediately throws himself into a 'stale-mate' & blocks every movement." Temperamentally unable to serve as one of Calhoun's henchmen, Hammond had long premised his own future in Carolina upon successful opposition to the senior statesman. But now, at last, Hammond was beginning to regard Calhoun as a kind of unavoidable political given, who could be dealt with even if not entirely mastered or controlled. And Pickens' recent insubordination had made Hammond's past transgressions fade in significance. When passage of a compromise tariff early in the summer of 1846 at last eliminated the major justification for the Bluffton revolt, Hammond saw that the conjunction of circumstances had made a degree of reconciliation and a new relationship with Calhoun possible. In spite of their other differences, Hammond and the Senator did share similar anxieties about a war with Britain over the Oregon boundary, and Hammond sought to capitalize on this harmony of views. Military confrontation with England, both Carolinians knew, would damage the cotton trade, so Hammond wrote Calhoun a deferential letter offering "warm & cordial approbation" of the senator's course on the issue. In Calhoun's Oregon stance, Hammond discovered a new "firmness & lofty purpose" that made reconciliation with the senior statesman seem both principled and palatable.[4]

---

3. On the divisions in South Carolina in regard to the Mexican War, see Ernest M. Lander, Jr., *Reluctant Imperialists: Calhoun, the South Carolinians, and the Mexican War* (Baton Rouge: Louisiana State University Press, 1980), and James W. Gettys, Jr., "'To Conquer a Peace': South Carolina and the Mexican War" (Ph.D. dissertation, University of South Carolina, 1974).

4. Hammond to Nathaniel Beverley Tucker, January 24, 1847, in Tucker-Coleman Papers, Earl Gregg Swem Memorial Library, College of William and Mary, Williamsburg, Va.; Phocion [James Henry Hammond], "Oregon—War—Notice," Augusta *Constitutionalist*, n.d. [1846], clipping in Edward Spann Hammond Scrapbook (MS vol. bd., 1844–90, Edward Spann Hammond Papers, SCL);

This rapprochement reflected as well Hammond's growing willingness to accept Calhoun's unwavering commitment to the Union. Throughout his public life, the Carolina senator's devotion to southern rights had always reflected his desire to preserve national bonds; Calhoun had dedicated his career to making the South and her peculiar institutions secure within the framework of the United States government. After the successful negotiation of an Oregon treaty and the reduction of the tariff, Hammond's hostility towards the federal government likewise began to abate. These shifts in national policy, combined with the military triumphs of the Mexican War, left him feeling, he confessed in astonishment, "*truly patriotic.*" By midsummer, 1846, he announced himself "At last . . . a 'Union Man' . . . a *full citizen* of the Republic," and he began to listen with growing interest to talk of his election to the Senate. Unable to beat Calhoun, Hammond began to contemplate joining him in Washington.[5]

As always, Hammond was anxious that no one should detect in him any unseemly zeal for political office. "I may be fastidious," he wrote to Simms, "but . . . thought there was no particle of *honor* conferred by an office obtained by coaxing & begging & intriguing." Yet he still displayed guarded enthusiasm about the notion of a return to public life. "I should certainly regard it as a very high compliment to be elected to the Senate," he admitted. In mid-August, his hopes were further excited by the formal announcement of McDuffie's impending retirement. Now there was a certain vacancy.[6]

Although Hammond declared it his intention to "merely let events take their course," he was by mid-fall delivering impromptu speeches in his neighborhood and following political intrigues with the avidity of a committed candidate. When his old rival F. H. Elmore's name was brought forward, Hammond began to construe his own candidacy as a "duty I owe the State . . . to afford a rallying point" to the opposition forces. Hammond knew well that if he were elected senator the "calumnies" produced by the Hampton incident would be put "to rest forever." Under such circumstances, the lure of office was irresistible.[7]

The results of the contests for legislative seats in mid-October further strengthened his resolve and encouraged him to articulate his philosophy of political reform. The defeat of those he viewed as the most intelligent and best-

---

John C. Calhoun to Hammond, January 23, 1846, James Henry Hammond Diary, February 14, 1846, both in JHH Papers, LC.

5. Hammond to William B. Hodgson, January 24, 1847, August 23, 1846, both in JHH Papers, DU.

6. Hammond to Simms, September 18, 1846, in JHH Papers, LC.

7. Hammond to Simms, October 4, 1846, *ibid.*

qualified candidates—including Simms—appeared to Hammond as the clearest evidence yet produced that a *"revolution* is going on" that threatened to "make us openly what . . . we virtually almost are—a mobocracy." Even South Carolina seemed to be falling prey to the rising forces of democracy. Some of the new legislators were talking of giving the choice of governor and presidential electors to the people; others even went so far as to advocate an elected judiciary. "Something" Hammond urged, "must be done to arrest the tendency of things." He convinced himself that the crisis was so acute he could not refuse if called upon to serve. But he simultaneously recorded in his diary anxieties that made him daily "more averse to mingling openly in public affairs."[8]

The legislature regarded Elmore as the most prominent candidate for the senatorial vacancy. Hammond was certain his opponent had the tacit support of Calhoun, and he knew that a friend writing from Columbia was correct when he said that Hammond was generally regarded as "not quite pliant enough," "not *clique* enough," not "exactly one of those who would 'sneeze every time Mr. C. might choose to take snuff.'" Even McDuffie felt Hammond had little chance, although he assured the younger man that he wished it were otherwise. Hammond held a tight rein on his aspirations, not even permitting himself to think that Elmore might be defeated. Insisting that he was "no candidate," he declared to Simms that Elmore seemed entirely "suitable" for the vacancy. Above all, Hammond wanted to avoid a situation in which he would again experience open political defeat, for he feared this would produce the impression that he was a "fallen public character." If he was to retire from politics forever, he wished to maintain at least an appearance of having chosen such a course, rather than having had it too obviously thrust upon him.[9]

But when Elmore unexpectedly abandoned the race just days before the legislative vote, Hammond found himself and his reputation on trial before the state. Hammond's supporters at once brought his name forward, and the legislature responded in an encouraging manner. It was then that Wade Hampton moved to exact his long-awaited revenge. To Hammond's friends and foes alike, Hampton privately announced that he intended to make available certain documents that proved the former governor's unfitness for high office. The exposures,

8. Hammond to Simms, October 15, 1846, *ibid.*; William DeSaussure to Hammond, October 31, 1846, Hammond Diary, October 21, 1846, both in JHH Papers, SCL.
9. Quattlebaum to Hammond, November 6, 1846, Hammond to Simms, November 23, 1846, both in JHH Papers, LC; Hammond Diary (SCL), November 25, 1846. See George McDuffie to Hammond, in JHH Papers, LC.

he assured the legislators, would "prostrate" Hammond forever. "If anyone who sees that correspondence and knows how Hammond has acted towards me can then support him it will be a condemnation of me," Hampton reportedly declared to one intimate. Hammond's old friend A. P. Aldrich, now a member of the state senate, set out immediately from Columbia to Silver Bluff to plan a response to this looming scandal. Hammond provided Aldrich with the details of his rupture with his Hampton relatives, but instructed the senator to leave any public revelations to Hampton himself. Although some of Hammond's supporters urged him to come at once to Columbia and meet Hampton's charges, Hammond desired no such confrontation. "I cannot call him to account," he confessed. Hammond had to maintain a defensive posture. "It is highly important to me that Col Hampton should herald his own infamy." His own position, Hammond emphasized, must be one of silence—both to quiet the storm of gossip and to protect the ladies involved. "I have often told you," he wrote Simms, "that the strength of my position was firm & patient sufferance." The former governor composed a careful letter for Aldrich to take to Columbia and show to his supporters. Admitting that he had "committed a great indiscretion," Hammond stated as well his resolution not to disclose any of the causes of his break with Colonel Hampton and to trust to the "verdict of my fellow citizens" upon the contents of the letters Hampton was planning to release. But Hammond could not believe that Hampton would himself risk his daughters' reputations by making such matters public.[10]

Hampton had enough power to block Hammond's election. Even though few legislators lowered themselves sufficiently to read the incriminating documents, the clouds of innuendo had their effect. After leading on the first two ballots, Hammond faltered and lost the Senate seat to A. P. Butler, an Edgefield neighbor and long-time acquaintance, the brother of Hammond's old racing partner. Although Hammond declared he "rejoiced as events have turned out in regard to everything" and professed relief at not having to tax his precarious health with a move to Washington, it was evident from his anger toward Butler that he was not quite so sanguine about this defeat. Butler's victory, he stated bluntly, had "ruptured our ties." Yet Hammond was gratified by the loyalty of so

10. David F. Jamison to George Frederick Holmes, December 13, 1846, in George Frederick Holmes Papers, DU; Hammond to M. C. M. Hammond, December 4, 1846, Jamison to Hammond, December 24, 1846, both in JHH Papers, LC; Hammond Diary (SCL), December 26, December 4, 1846; Hammond to Simms, December 8, 1846, in JHH Papers, LC; Hammond Diary (SCL), December 4, 2, 1846. See A. H. Pemberton to Hammond, December 4, 1846, in JHH Papers, SCL.

many of his followers and by the widespread criticism of Hampton for having called upon the legislature to settle a personal quarrel. "My friends both in & out of the Legislature assure me," Hammond wrote Ruffin, "that I stand now much better in consequence of that mountain having at length given birth to its mole." Hammond believed that at last his "penance is accomplished."[11]

Hampton had sought to place Hammond's baseness beyond doubt. But out of either allegiance to the former governor or more general feelings of delicacy, most legislators had declined to examine the materials Hampton had made available. Hammond's reputation remained clouded in mystery, but his enmity with the Hamptons emerged into public view, and the four young women became objects of scandal. Their father had won a victory of sorts, for he had made clear that any support for Hammond would be regarded as a direct challenge to the authority and substantial power of Wade Hampton, a man one contemporary described as the Warwick, the kingmaker, of South Carolina. But the father triumphed at his children's expense: Harriet, Catherine, Ann, and Caroline were far more vulnerable than their uncle. One state legislator remarked that "after all the fuss made no man who valued his standing could marry one of the Hampton girls." The four in fact remained single all their lives.[12]

Hammond anticipated no such lasting damage to his own status. At a post-election conference at Silver Bluff in mid-January, his friends McDuffie, David F. Jamison, Simms, and Aldrich left the unsuccessful candidate confident that the Hampton business "will never again injure me in the least." His supporters remained eager to run him for the Senate at the very next opportunity, and a circle centered around Simms identified Hammond as potential founder of a new party in Carolina that would oppose the politics of vested interest and would instead dedicate itself to the unwavering pursuit of principle. A friendly editor in nearby Hamburg begged permission to reveal all the facts behind the Columbia gossip in order to destroy Wade Hampton's reputation and show Hammond as the man of superior honor. But Hammond restrained him in the certainty that discretion remained the best policy.[13]

11. Hammond Diary (SCL), December 9, 1846; Hammond to Edmund Ruffin, December 21, 1846, in Edmund Ruffin Papers, Virginia Historical Society, Richmond; Hammond to Simms, December 8, 1846, in JHH Papers, LC; Hammond to Hodgson, December 8, 1846, in JHH Papers, DU.

12. Jamison to Holmes, December 13, 1846, in Holmes Papers; Hammond Diary (SCL), January 23, 1847. See Benjamin F. Perry, *Reminiscences of Public Men, with Speeches and Addresses*, Second Series (Greenville, S.C.: Shannon, 1889), 110.

13. Hammond to William Bobo, February 12, 1847, in JHH Papers, LC; Hammond Diary (SCL), April 4, 1847.

Yet the issue seemed doggedly to refuse to die. On a late summer trip to New York designed to "rouse myself from the dull habits contracted in my seclusion," Hammond was unexpectedly confronted by the scandal. Encountering an acquaintance from Carolina, Hammond was bewildered by the gentleman's chilly response to his own enthusiastic greeting. After hastening upon his way, the unfriendly Carolinian suddenly stopped, returned to where Hammond was standing, and delivered a nervous condemnation of the former governor's conduct toward the Hampton girls. Almost too surprised to respond, Hammond reported the incident in his diary in tones of combined bewilderment and rage. While he denounced his accoster as a mere "lickspittle" of the Hamptons, he was at the same time alarmed by this evidence that the whole issue was less moribund than he had believed. It did not bode well for the political hopes Hammond could not seem to relinquish.[14]

At home by mid-September, Hammond kept a close watch on political developments. Calhoun, he soon recognized, was assuming a newly aggressive posture in anticipation of a bitter struggle over the status of the territories about to be annexed by the treaty ending the Mexican War. The South, Calhoun contended, could not defend her interests in these new lands through existing political parties, but must unite into a single southern front to preserve her domestic institutions and to extend them to the West. Basically satisfied with what he regarded as a "bonafide Free Trade & anti Internal improvements administration," Hammond deplored Calhoun's attacks upon Polk and his party and suspected that the senator was acting chiefly for "political and selfish purposes" intended to advance his progress towards the presidency. Calhoun's policy of encouraging the South to focus its anger on the Wilmot Proviso, a measure that proclaimed all new territories off limits to slavery, seemed to Hammond an unfortunate tactic. Not only was he certain that the Proviso would never pass the Senate and therefore posed no real threat, but he also preferred to have the battle for slavery take place within a different context. Human bondage should be defended, he believed, not so much through the assertion of power—in the political realm of spoils and interests—as through the demonstration of its rightness and virtue in proslavery treatises. Calhoun's introduction of open discussion of human bondage in Congress seemed to Hammond a contraversion of those principles he himself had struggled to establish in the gag-rule debates of

14. Hammond to Simms, September 26, 1847, in JHH Papers, LC; Hammond, Memorandum of a Conversation, September 6, 1847, in HBC Papers, SCL.

the mid-thirties. The slavery question, it seemed, was becoming a tool of Calhoun's ambition.[15]

But even if Hammond was able to follow national events with intense interest and to present his opinions in detailed letters to his friends and epistles to the public press, the planter believed he "cut no figure" in Carolina public life. Isolated at Silver Bluff, he maintained his official posture of political retirement, even convincing himself at times of its authenticity. Many of Hammond's friends doubted the wisdom of his reticence, for they believed it fueled rather than dampened speculation about his alleged improprieties. His avoidance of Columbia, Simms reported, produced the "impression with many that you dare not show yourself and this opinion is the only thing (almost) that confirms the belief in the evil tales at your expense."[16]

Hammond nevertheless insisted upon his cautious course, remaining away from Columbia and the Hamptons and staying out of the political limelight. But growing frustration with his projected career in letters edged him ever closer to the political arena. A general lack of public response to his 1847 essays against the Bank of the State of South Carolina reinforced his intensifying sense of painful irrelevance. "I have neither health nor books, nor any stimulant to systematic intellectual exertion," he complained. "I am surrounded & hemmed in by people entirely incapable of appreciating me. Who carp at what is not in conformity with their narrow minds, & have no conception of mine." The escalating presidential campaign seemed of far greater interest than the solitary literary endeavors with which he was engaged, and by late January, 1848, Hammond had begun to address political barbecues in his neighborhood.[17]

Hammond's interest in the presidential canvass arose in large measure from his enthusiasm for Zachary Taylor. A Mexican War hero and Louisiana slaveholder publicly affiliated with neither Whigs nor Democrats, Taylor seemed to Hammond to represent an opportunity to unite the South and circumvent existing parties and factions. But Calhoun, despite his own similar commitment to southern unity, did not see Taylor as an effective vehicle for achieving this end,

15. Hammond to M. C. M. Hammond, February 26, 1847, Hammond to Simms, March 27, 1847, both in JHH Papers, LC. It was at this time that Hammond was so vocally opposed to Calhoun's establishing a proslavery paper in Washington. See discussion of this issue in Chapter 13.

16. Hammond to Simms, September 26, 1847 in JHH Papers, LC; Simms to Hammond, November 30, 1847, in Mary C. Simms Oliphant, Alfred Taylor Odell, and T. C. Duncan Eaves (eds.), *The Letters of William Gilmore Simms* (5 vols.; Columbia: University of South Carolina Press, 1952–56), II, 378.

17. Hammond Diary (SCL), January 29, 1848. See A. Magrath to Armistead Burt, January 30, 1848, in Armistead Burt Papers, DU.

for the senator was less confident about the soundness of Taylor's states' rights views. When Taylor agreed to run as a Whig, Hammond admitted a few doubts, but remained generally confident that no slaveholder could at bottom truly support the centralizing measures long associated with the Whig party. And Hammond enjoyed displaying his own superiority to faction, represented, he alleged, by his support for the best candidate, irrespective of official party identity or ties.[18]

Between 1844 and 1848 Hammond and Calhoun had nearly reversed their positions in regard to the office of the presidency and its relevance to southern rights. In the earlier election Calhoun had insisted that the salvation of the South lay in the victory of the slaveholding candidate Polk, while Hammond had declared the grievances of the South beyond such simple remedy. But in the ensuing four years Hammond's growing confidence in the federal government— as well as his renewed interest in federal office—had convinced him that the South had much to gain within the Union. Calhoun, by contrast, rebuffed in his own hopes for the presidency, alienated by Polk's war policy, and alarmed by the mounting controversy over the territories, now stood aloof from the canvass, arguing that the differences between Taylor and his Democratic opponent Lewis Cass were insignificant in their bearing upon the South's problems. More radical, constitutional and not simply electoral changes had to be sought. As Calhoun became more extreme, Hammond assumed increasingly moderate positions. But the two retained their near-polar opposition. It was as if Calhoun and Hammond could never occupy the same political or ideological space. "Calhoun's long reign here," the younger Carolinian observed, "has overshadowed & dwarfed everything," including, Hammond believed, his own career. Given the choice of being Calhoun's minion or his adversary, Hammond chose autonomy and opposition.[19]

But like Calhoun's support for Polk, Hammond's enthusiasm for Taylor was short-lived. Even before the election, the Louisiana general had all but repudiated the Democrats among his supporters by declaring himself a sound and committed Whig. Yet if Hammond had come to feel "indifferent" by the time of Taylor's victory, he was soon to express greater vehemence in his sentiments towards the new chief executive. Despite his southern heritage, Taylor appeared as

---

18. Hammond to Tucker, May 12, 1848, in Tucker-Coleman Papers. See Charles M. Wiltse, *John C. Calhoun, Sectionalist, 1840–1850* (Indianapolis: Bobbs-Merrill, 1951), and Jon L. Wakelyn, "Party Issues and Political Strategy of the Charleston Taylor Democrats of 1848," *South Carolina Historical Magazine*, LXXIII (April, 1972), 72–86.
19. Hammond to Tucker, June 8, 1849, in Tucker-Coleman Papers.

president to be "'sectional' in favour of the North," blithely disregarded south-ern claims for a right to slavery in the territories as he set about establishing free states in California and New Mexico. Calhoun, more alarmed than ever, ap-pealed for a display of unity by the South's delegates in Congress and presented for their adoption a "Southern Address" enumerating the region's grievances and calling for immediate relief. Within South Carolina, vigilante committees gathered to defend sectional rights, and an assembly met in Columbia in May to consider Carolina's official stance in regard to the territories. At Calhoun's urg-ing, the body called for a pan-southern meeting but left to Mississippi, a state less tarnished than South Carolina with the image of political extremism, the responsibility for choosing a place and a date. Mississippians, this time as out-raged as the leaders of their sister state, scheduled a southern convention for Nashville the following June, and South Carolina promptly indicated her willing-ness to attend.[20]

In private correspondence Hammond had long argued that the territorial question was misleading, for he believed that slavery would not prosper in the arid wastes of the far Southwest. But once the South had fixed upon the ques-tion of slavery's expansion and had transformed it into a contest of power and an issue of constitutional rights, he recognized that she could not back down. The South must, he wrote to Calhoun, ensure that the division of territories preserve her parity in the Senate. "Our only safety is in *equality* of *power*." Sympathetic from the first to a southern convention, Hammond found himself for the mo-ment in Calhoun's camp. The confrontation between North and South had be-come so direct and inescapable that hardly any ground remained for difference among loyal southerners. States' rights Carolinians could ill afford the luxury of disagreement over style and tactics. Northern aggressions had forged agreement between Hammond and Calhoun.[21]

Unlike Calhoun, however, Hammond was reluctant to press hard for a pan-southern meeting. Such a gathering, he wrote Marcellus, was unquestionably his "favourite measure, but to *agitate* it in So. Ca. would be injurious." Carolina's reputation for radicalism, he feared, might taint the meeting in the eyes of the more conservative states of the South. As the movement for a convention

20. Hammond to M. C. M. Hammond, September 18, 1848, Hammond to Simms, March 9, 1849, both in JHH Papers, LC. See Thelma Jennings, *The Nashville Convention: Southern Movement for Unity, 1848–1850* (Memphis: Memphis State University Press, 1980).

21. Hammond to M. C. M. Hammond, November 16, 1849, Hammond to Calhoun, March 5, 1850, both in JHH Papers, LC.

gained popularity, Hammond continued to press other, less directly political dimensions of southern independence upon the Carolina public, publishing a review essay on the economic conditions of North and South in the summer number of the *Southern Quarterly Review* and completing his two erudite and philosophical orations for presentation to the South Carolina Institute and the students of South Carolina College in December. The college address marked Hammond's first public appearance in Columbia since the close of his governorship. Although the oration itself was well attended and well received, William C. Preston, now college president, did all he could to diminish Hammond's success. "The social cordon," Hammond reported, "was drawn stringently." Only two of his oldest friends dared call upon him, and he visited no one. Clearly the scandal had not blown over as Hammond had trusted and hoped.[22]

But at least Hammond's rehabilitation had begun. Meeting in the capitol at the time of Hammond's Columbia visit, the legislature chose the former governor as one of four delegates to the proposed Nashville meeting. Yet far from honored, Hammond found his election "truly mortifying," for he had received the fewest ballots of any of the victorious four candidates, winning "less than *one third* of the votes of the whole Legislature—Can I feel," he worried, "that I represent the state?" His friends in Columbia assured him that his low total was simply a result of the absence of many of his friends at the time of the balloting. Undoubtedly they knew too that Hammond had won because Hampton was indifferent to the convention movement and did not regard the post of Nashville delegate as honorific enough to warrant his attention. Even without Hampton's intervention, Hammond had not fared well. "What perhaps gives me most pain," Hammond explained, "is to see how stern the opposition to me still continues." This brief foray back into the political world left him feeling bitter and betrayed, disillusioned again about public life. "Damn politics so far as elections are concerned," he wrote Simms. "I can do more for my own reputation through the press, at infinite less cost."[23]

Although Hammond had initially announced his intention to decline the Nashville appointment, the entreaties of Calhoun and other prominent Carolinians soothed his bruised ego. The Carolina senator was persuasive in his insis-

22. Hammond to M. C. M. Hammond, November 16, 1849, *ibid.*; Hammond, "The North and the South," *Southern Quarterly Review*, XVI (July, 1849), 273–311; Hammond to Simms, December 13, 1849, in JHH Papers, LC.
23. Hammond to Simms, December 20, 1849, Quattlebaum to Hammond, December 18, 1849, both in JHH Papers, LC; Hammond Diary (SCL), December 17, 1849.

tence that "If the South is to be saved now is the time." Hammond repeated this urgency in his own declaration to Marcellus that disunion seemed inevitable and "*now* is the *best* time." His brief phase of patriotic unionism had entirely passed; the possibility that the North might succeed in excluding slavery from the Mexican territories as well as in abolishing the slave trade in the District of Columbia revived Hammond's secessionist sentiments. But his renewed radicalism, he recognized, had to remain covert. The "greatest danger" to the South, he believed, arose from "the *fears* of our own people." "Take care," he wrote Beverley Tucker, who had been chosen as a Nashville delegate from Virginia, "not to *alarm* too much." In general, this caution characterized Hammond's public behavior throughout the months of the crisis of 1850. The Bluffton failure of 1844 had made him wary of assuming more extreme stands than public opinion in Carolina was ready to support, and Carolina's isolation in the crisis of 1833 had taught him that his native state must be similarly careful not to move too far ahead of the rest of the South. In 1850 Hammond aspired to be a statesman, not a revolutionary. He did not expect that the Nashville Convention would achieve what he still regarded as the ultimate goal of disunion. But he hoped the gathering would serve to advance the cause of southern independence by bringing pressing sectionalist issues into more prominent public view both within Carolina and throughout the region as a whole. It was not yet a time for secession, but it was a critical opportunity "to enlighten and warn the South."[24]

Although Hammond feared throughout the spring that congressional efforts to achieve a compromise on the territorial questions might render the Nashville gathering irrelevant, June arrived with the Great Compromiser Henry Clay still lacking the legislative majority he sought for his conciliatory measures. And for the South the political landscape had gravely altered. On March 4 Calhoun had listened, too ill even to speak, as his last call for southern rights and final warnings of impending crisis were read on the Senate floor. Before the month was out,

---

24. Calhoun to Hammond, January 4, 1850, Hammond to M. C. M. Hammond, February 1, 1850, both in JHH Papers, LC; Hammond to Tucker, February 7, 1850, in Tucker-Coleman Papers; Hammond to Simms, March 26, 1850, in JHH Papers, LC. Philip M. Hamer, *The Secession Movement in South Carolina, 1847–1852* (Allentown, Pa.: H. Ray Haas, 1918); Chauncy S. Boucher, "The Secession and Cooperation Movements in South Carolina, 1848–1852," *Washington University Studies*, V (St. Louis: Washington University, 1918), 65–138; Laura A. White, *Robert Barnwell Rhett: Father of Secession* (New York: Century, 1931). Hammond composed a set of resolutions to present at Nashville if he found the climate radical enough to sustain them. These proposals called for conventions in all the slave states to send delegates to a general southern congress, empowered to dissolve the union and form a new government and constitution. Hammond Diary (SCL), March 17, 1850.

the venerable Carolinian was dead, leaving a leadership vacuum both within his state and throughout the South. With a confidence born of their mutual devotion, Simms assured Hammond he would be acknowledged as Calhoun's natural successor. Governor Whitemarsh Seabrook, charged with appointing a temporary replacement to Calhoun's Senate seat, thought otherwise, however, and found several Carolinians he preferred to Hammond. First choosing James Hamilton, the governor then shifted his support to Langdon Cheves, who declined the honor. F. H. Elmore at last accepted the post but died in just over a month, and the office fell to Robert Barnwell. In spite of being so ignominiously passed over in these appointments, Hammond did not abandon his own conviction that Calhoun's position as the intellectual and political leader of the South was now rightfully his own, and he began to display what he viewed as an appropriately statesmanlike dignity.

The most immediate impact of the senator's death was to reinforce Hammond's posture of moderation. Released at last from that political version of the Oedipal battle that had so long characterized his relationship with Calhoun, Hammond sought to re-create himself in the dead father's image—to abandon his youthful extremism for the caution and sobriety of the mature statesman. With Calhoun's death ended Hammond's political adolescence. No more, he determined, would he feel compelled to "enact Hotspur."[25]

When the Nashville meeting assembled in June, 175 delegates representing nine southern states joined to voice their concerns about the future of the South within the nation. The Clay compromise measures, supported by an alarming number of southern as well as northern congressmen, seemed to concede so much and had so "lowered southern tone" that Hammond feared even discussion of decisive southern action would be impossible. Appointed one of Carolina's two representatives to the Resolutions Committee, Hammond struggled to ensure the inclusion in the final report of a call for another meeting—one that could gather, he hoped, after Congress had passed what he was sure would be its outrageous solutions to the territorial question. At that time some more radical action or at least discussion might be possible. Perhaps then the southern people could be aroused to rise up against the concessions their representatives seemed to be so willingly making in Washington. On the other questions debated in the Resolutions Committee, Hammond said little, passively accepting the convention's major demand—the extension of the Missouri Compromise

25. Hammond to Hodgson, April 2, 1850, in JHH Papers. DU.

line to the Pacific. "Finding early that no remedies requiring separate action of the South could be even suggested, I resolved to be silent, as I did not care to discuss what I had no faith in, though compelled to support it."[26]

The one manifestation of true radicalism at the meeting was an address written by Robert Barnwell Rhett and approved by the Resolutions Committee at Hammond's urging. Attacking the Clay compromise measures under debate in Washington, Rhett provoked a storm of protest from the more conservative delegates and most especially from the convention's president, Judge William Sharkey of Mississippi. Unable to resist this challenge and eager to prevent the intemperate Rhett from displaying the full force of his extremism on the convention floor, Hammond rose to his feet and, as he reported, "demolished" the judge's arguments. His cool and forceful rhetoric secured the ratification of the address by the convention as a whole.[27]

Despite this brief display of his true sentiments, the overall posture adopted by Hammond—and indeed by all of South Carolina's representatives—was of calculated caution. This restraint achieved its intended impression, for the southern press reported the surprising reasonableness of the Carolina delegation with no little amazement and with new respect. What Hammond said, one correspondent noted, was "moderate and conservative; and what particularly surprised me throughout the nine days' sitting of the Convention, was the calm, dignified . . . attitude taken and held by the South Carolina delegation." Clearly Hammond himself succeeded in conveying the statesman's mien—appearing, in the view of at least one newspaperman, to embody the intimations of immortality of the classical sculptured bust. "Mr. Hammond's head," this journalist reported, "struck me as very fine. He is of a pale intellectual aspect, with a high forehead, white and polished as marble; indeed his whole face was almost as colorless as alabaster, and seemed chiselled out of marble."[28]

Disappointed at the conservatism of many of his fellow delegates, Hammond nevertheless left Nashville pleased at least that the "South has *met*, has acted with great harmony . . . & above *all has agreed to meet again*." Union within the

26. Hammond Diary (SCL), May 26, 1850; Hammond to Simms, June 16, 1850, in JHH Papers, LC. See Robert C. Tucker, "James H. Hammond and the Southern Convention," *Proceedings of the South Carolina Historical Association*, XXX (1960), 4–14.

27. Hammond Diary (SCL), August 10, 1850.

28. "The South Carolina Delegation," "Southern Convention" and untitled clippings from unidentified newspapers, in Edward Spann Hammond Scrapbook. See also Robert F. W. Allston, "Nashville Convention, May-June, 1850" (MS in Robert F. W. Allston Papers, from the collections of South Carolina Historical Society, Charleston); [William Gilmore Simms], "Southern Convention: A Review of Its Events," *Southern Quarterly Review*, n.s., II (September, 1850), 191–232.

region seemed all-important and, at this juncture, the best that could be expected. And whatever their differences, leaders from nine southern states had exchanged views and begun to establish a measure of solidarity.[29]

Hammond's satisfaction about these germs of southern unity proved short-lived. Rhett's extremism, controlled only with difficulty during the convention proceedings, burst forth upon his return in a Charleston speech that demanded immediate separate state action by Carolina. "Altho' I concur in every sentiment of Rhett's," Hammond wrote to Simms, "I regret extremely that he gave utterance to them just now. We succeeded at Nashville in overcoming the prejudices of the South against us as 'Hotspurs &c' This speech will destroy all the effect of our policy."[30]

Rhett's decision to pursue such a sharply divergent course underscored dramatic contrasts between him and Hammond. Since the public eye had already begun to focus on the two Carolinians as the leading contenders in the fall election for a permanent Senate replacement for Calhoun, the differences between them grew all the more significant. Rhett and Hammond had both been requested to deliver public eulogies for Calhoun, establishing a symmetry Hammond found most distasteful, for it appeared to him too much as if the heirs apparent were engaged in an oratorical joust over the dead senator's remains. But even if the contest seemed too blatant and overwrought to fit Hammond's cherished fantasy of being called from contemplative retirement by public acclaim, he was not about to withdraw.

By fall, Hammond had decided that the Nashville Convention ought not to meet again. In early September, Congress had passed the measures known as the Compromise of 1850, closing California to slavery, eliminating the slave trade in the District of Columbia, and offering the South in return only a strengthened law providing for the return of fugitive slaves by the North. Bad as these measures appeared, with their implicit acknowledgment of Congress' right to legislate on the slavery question, Hammond found the acquiescence of so many moderate southerners to be even more alarming. Instead of being radicalized by these northern outrages, their desire for peace at any price had led them to betray their region's true interests. A second convention seemed to have little purpose. With even South Carolina badly divided on issues of cooperation and secession, Hammond feared another meeting would only emphasize and publicize the South's disunity and weakness.

29. Hammond to Simms, June 16, 1850, in JHH Papers, LC.
30. Hammond to Simms, June 27, 1850, *ibid.*

Hammond wrote the governor requesting that he be replaced as a delegate. But the personal and family illness he cited as the cause of his resignation deceived no one. To his friends, Hammond's withdrawal seemed a gesture of political self-destruction. "Nothing but the most *serious cause* ought to prevent you going," one loyal follower ominously warned. Another frankly declared that Hammond's stance made his election to the Senate all but impossible. These objections seemed only to encourage Hammond in his obstinacy. He was absent from Nashville when the convention regrouped on November 11, he explained to his diary, "because I wished to shew that I was not seeking political offices." Because the South had not yet been sufficiently awakened to hear a disunionist message, Hammond was certain the meeting could accomplish little of use. His earlier belief that "now is the time" had been replaced by a conviction that "the true crisis is not yet, & . . . he who husbands his strength now can expend it to much more effect a few years hence." The substance of Hammond's politics had not changed since Bluffton days, but his style and tactics were vastly altered. Instead of preaching disunion to an unreceptive South, he decided to remain at Silver Bluff, nursing his ailing children and slaves and working on his eulogy of Calhoun.[31]

The oration Hammond delivered in Charleston on November 21 represented the final resolution of his long and awkward relationship with the man who had in effect controlled South Carolina politics for Hammond's entire adult life. The name of Calhoun had so long prevailed in the state that, "Few of us," Hammond remarked to his audience, ". . . can remember the era when we heard it first. We have grown up since childhood under its mighty influence." Like the archetypal parent, Calhoun seemed to have "had no youth." His death was thus all the more disturbing, for Carolinians had come to regard him as nearly immortal. Freed at last from the senator's domination, Hammond could undertake to "analyze his life with the strict impartiality of a distant posterity." While in private Hammond could still complain that Calhoun's "towering genius" had served to divide the South, he began in public to demonstrate an admiration for Calhoun that his feelings of rivalry had not permitted while the elder statesman remained alive. In the past Hammond had often complained that the senator was "too prudent," a "stumbling block" to secession, a man driven by his single-minded desire for the presidency. But with Calhoun's demise, the younger Carolinian

31. Hammond to Governor Whitemarsh Seabrook, October 18, 1850, Maxcy Gregg to Hammond, November 4, 1850, Hammond to Simms, November 11, 1850, all *ibid.*; Hammond Diary (SCL), November 29, 30, 1850.

was ready to forgive him these transgressions, to admit that the South would have supported no more radical policies than those the senator had espoused. When Calhoun's writings on government were posthumously issued in 1851, Hammond acclaimed them as the most brilliant intellectual productions ever penned by an American.[32]

From resentment of Calhoun, Hammond moved slowly toward identification with the goals and style of the dead statesman, attributing to Calhoun many of the dilemmas Hammond had himself experienced in the course of his own career. His eulogy became yet another call for the South to acknowledge and honor "those great Minds that have been appointed to shed light and truth upon the world." Like every such genius, Calhoun had had to contend with the force of ambition, the lust for achievement with which Hammond had so long struggled. "Mr. Calhoun's enemies," like Hammond's own, believed that ambition "infected him to an extraordinary and dangerous degree." But Hammond excused him: "the enemies of every distinguished man have said the same." And Calhoun, Hammond found in another striking instance of similarity to his own plight, was victimized by Carolina, which through its failure to reward intellectual preeminence compelled him to tarnish his essentially abstract and contemplative mind in the corrupting struggle for political office. With the senator removed from the scene, Hammond no longer felt driven to play *enfant terrible* to Calhoun's senior statesman. At last he could afford to sympathize with the older Carolinian and to admit his brilliance, for at last it seemed possible that Hammond might assume his mantle.[33]

But the senatorial election that took place in Columbia only days after Hammond delivered his Charleston oration proved yet another crushing disappointment. Hammond was resolute in his opposition to Rhett's radical strategy, for he was certain that in the existing climate of southern conservatism it could come to little more than "ridiculous vapouring." To elect Rhett would be for the legislature to give its "approbation to abortive violence," instead of to the careful preparation required for successful independent action at some future date. "I do not think there ever was a time calling for so much caution and mature delibera-

32. Hammond, "An Oration on the Life, Character, and Services of John Caldwell Calhoun, Delivered on the 21st November, 1850, in Charleston, S.C., at the Request of the City Council," in Hammond, *Selections from the Letters and Speeches of the Hon. James H. Hammond of South Carolina* (New York: John F. Trow, 1866), 232, 294, 233; Hammond Diary (SCL), April 7, 1850; Hammond to Tucker, April 28, January 23, 1850, both in Tucker-Coleman Papers; Hammond to Ruffin, September 30, 1851, in Ruffin Papers.

33. Hammond, "An Oration on . . . Calhoun," 231–32, 190–91; Hammond, "Thoughts and Recollections" (MS vol. bd., 1852–53, JHH Papers, SCL), March 28, 1852.

tion." From his new vantage point of maturity, Hammond regarded the radicals as "puerile." Only his conservative policy would permit South Carolina ultimately to "effect our purpose not only without conflict in arms, but without violent change of any sort." Rhett, he feared, was likely to produce an internal revolution through his agitation for an external one. [34]

Hammond's enemies in Columbia gleefully seized upon these views, declaring him a submissionist who had demonstrated his support for the humiliating Compromise of 1850 by refusing to attend the second Nashville meeting. Hampton and his supporters once again brought forth the intimations of sexual scandal and gossiped as well about Hammond's recent quarrels with his brother Marcellus and son Spann. These rumors, Hammond feared, succeeded in creating the "impression . . . very extensively that I was a *Monster*. My talents could not be denied but that was my sole qualification for any position in life, & these, deprived of all moral support were rather to be feared & suppressed than to be cherished." Hammond felt so anxious about the election that the days of waiting for a decision seemed "more painful than any I ever encountered." Yet his fears were coupled with confidence. "I have heard it from a hundred sources that the almost unanimous opinion of the State is that I am now the first man in SoCa—that is as a Statesman & man of intellect." [35]

Evidently the legislature did not share this view. After trailing Rhett by only six votes on the first ballot, Hammond lost ninety-seven to forty-six on the fourth, when Rhett at last achieved a majority. "Your not going to Nashville defeated your election," a friend in the legislature bluntly reported. "This blow," Hammond wrote to Simms, "is fatal." His career as a public man, he declared in his diary, was over; he was "annihilated forever." South Carolina had humiliated him; he would counter by in turn rejecting Carolina, moving across the Savannah to dwell in Augusta, sending Spann and Willie to the University of Georgia and Paul to school in Augusta. While the legislature, swept up in a wave of extremism, raised taxes by half to provide arms for the state and called for another southern convention to discuss secession, Hammond complained in solitary despair to his diary. The Rhett clique had defeated him in his initial gubernatorial race exactly a decade before. Now they had crushed him again with demagogic and irresponsible calls for revolution. [36]

34. Hammond Diary (SCL), November 30, 1850; Hammond to W. H. Gist, December 2, 1850, in JHH Papers, LC; Hammond Diary (SCL), December 27, 1850.

35. Hammond Diary (SCL), December 14, 1850; A. P. Aldrich to Hammond, January 7, 1851, in JHH Papers, LC.

36. Lewis M. Ayer to Hammond, December 18, 1850, Quattlebaum to Hammond, December

But Hammond's sense of catastrophe reflected more than simply the destruction of his public life. His private world had simultaneously disintegrated as well. "Difficulties betwixt my wife & me" had prompted Catherine Hammond in early December to take her two young daughters and flee Silver Bluff for the consolations of her own family in Charleston. Her husband did not expect her back before spring at the earliest, and perhaps not at all. Hammond had proved unsuccessful in two of the roles the Old South valued most highly. He had failed as both patriarch and politician.[37]

17, 1850, Hammond to Simms, December 23, 1850, all in JHH Papers, LC; Hammond Diary (SCL), December 21, 1850. Hammond wrote his determination to reject South Carolina on the back of a check drawn to Harry which, when redeemed, made his sentiments public and caused quite a stir. Hammond to Harry Hammond, January 24, 1851, in JHH Papers, SCL.

37. Hammond Diary (SCL), December 15, 1850.

Part V

The Irony of Success

Thou reap'st no fruit tho' thou did'st sow the seed.
WILLIAM GILMORE SIMMS

CHAPTER 15

A Predominant Family of Our Name

J AMES HENRY HAMMOND found personal relationships difficult. Both his own temperament and the values of his culture demanded that he always dominate those around him; southern planters, he once explained, "are accustomed . . . to control and scorn to be controlled." Yet Hammond was a man of almost boundless emotional needs, endowed with what he himself described as an "excess of . . . sensitiveness" and with a yearning for human closeness. His continuing search for the solace of satisfying personal ties was a shaping force in his life, producing both his formative interaction with a "sacred circle" of southern thinkers and the Hampton incident that all but destroyed his political career. Hammond's simultaneous desire for the emotional distance and safety of dominance and the equality of intimacy created an unresolvable paradox that plagued him all his life. Unable to "bear that others should see my emotions," fearful to admit to the vulnerability inseparable from all feeling, Hammond blamed others for failing to understand him; unable to doff his "garb of indifference," he suffered in lonely isolation. "Ah how much oftener would I give," he lamented to his diary, "but that I know not how."[1]

In its encouragement of pride, of mastery, of aggression and control, the Old South did little to imbue its planter class with human skills. Those very charac-

1. James Henry Hammond, "Anniversary Oration of the State Agricultural Society of South Carolina . . . 25th November, 1841," in *Proceedings of the Agricultural Convention and of the State Agricultural Society of South Carolina from 1839 to 1845 Inclusive* (Columbia: Sumner and Carroll, 1846), 183; Hammond Diary (MS in JHH Papers, LC), December 12, 1844, April 17, 1836, February 6, 1841.

teristics that had enabled Hammond to succeed in his society worked at the same time to undermine much of his happiness. His mind, he explained, "teaches me to suspect rather than confide—to hate rather than love." As he strived to exercise "despotic sway," he found himself too often resented rather than loved by his subjects.[2]

In the confined circle of family life, these difficulties were only intensified. With his own parents and siblings, Hammond had from an early age been accorded a position of privilege. His father had identified his first son as a genius, and the rest of the family had thenceforth granted James the homage appropriate to such abilities. But his special status produced difficulties as well as rewards. From at least the time of his father's death in 1829, young James wielded his superiority over the rest of the family in unrelenting and intrusive efforts to direct their lives. And while his mother, sister, and brothers grew increasingly dependent upon him as he achieved wealth and success, they demonstrated their growing resentment by refusing to acquiesce in his control. The "yoke" of Hammond's oppression, as John once explained, was a "dreadful burden."[3]

Assuming a paternal role with his two younger brothers, James sought to fill them with his own ambition, to repress those tendencies to "prodigality" that Elisha had flogged out of his oldest son. But the younger Hammonds never satisfied James's expectations. Marcellus had a brief and lackluster military career before, as we have seen, delighting his elder brother by marrying a wealthy Georgian who provided him with a plantation that could serve as both occupation and support. His preeminent accomplishment, however, lay in the realm of what James called "swinish swilling," and his reputation for drunkenness became legendary in the community where he lived. James never abandoned his hopes that Marcellus might reform and make better use of his talents. "You can easily be the next Gov.," he wrote his brother in 1857, "if you will not allow any man to *see* you *noticeably in liquor* between now & then." Although Marcellus made it to the state legislature, he never advanced further, and James always lamented "how he had *squandered* capacity and opportunity."[4]

Occasionally Marcellus' resentment of his brother's imperiousness burst into

---

2. Hammond Diary (LC), April 17, 1836; James Henry Hammond to William Gilmore Simms, April 19, 1847, in JHH Papers, LC.

3. John Fox Hammond to M. C. M. Hammond, June 5, 1855, in JHH Papers, SCL.

4. Hammond to M. C. M. Hammond, February 5, 1849, in JHH Papers, LC; Hammond to M. C. M. Hammond, January 20, 1857, in JHH Papers, SCL; Hammond to Harry Hammond, November 23, 1855, in HBC Papers, SCL.

Courtesy of the South Caroliniana Library
Marcus Claudius Marcellus Hammond, James's brother.

open hostility, but for the most part the two siblings demonstrated considerable fondness for one another. As James summed it up in one of his efforts to convince Marcellus to give up the bottle, drinkers could "be loved, but are neither admired, respected or trusted in anything of importance." Despite his exasperation at Marcellus' intractability, James maintained close and affectionate ties with his brother. After his marriage in 1842, Marcellus settled not far from Silver Bluff, and the two Hammonds shared political and agricultural discussions,

John Fox Hammond, James's brother.

exchanged frequent letters and visits, and claimed many friends in common.[5]

Hammond never had such warm feelings for John. After a difficult adolescence during which he showed little aptitude for any employment, the youth succeeded in acquiring a medical degree. But his "rude defying manners" prevented him from building a successful practice either in Beech Island or Augusta. He at last joined the army as a surgeon and served in a series of posts in

5. Hammond to M. C. M. Hammond, May 15, 1852, in JHH Papers, SCL.

the West before becoming a Union officer during the Civil War. Hammond speculated in 1853 that John might well be the "most disagreeable man" in the United States army, and John, for his part, felt that James had treated him like "a son disowned." Having fled to California to escape his brother's control, John committed a final act of defiance in his military service against James's beloved South.[6]

James's sister Caroline possessed fewer means of demonstrating her independence. Because opportunities for women lay almost exclusively in marriage, Caroline's education mattered far less than that of her brothers, and Hammond had few reasons to intervene in the young girl's life, which he left largely to the direction of their mother. Yet on the one question of importance to James, Caroline managed to defy her brother's will. She selected for a husband an itinerant Bible salesman whom James despised. Bemoaning the "spiteful temper" Caroline had demonstrated in so opposing his wishes, Hammond cut off all relations with his sister and refused even to attend her funeral when she died suddenly two years later.[7]

Elevated from his earliest years to a position of dominance within his family, invested after his father's death with responsibility for their welfare, Hammond assumed as well the patriarchal right to their control. His mother, a querulous, pipe-smoking woman, seemed to understand that at least the appearance of submission to her son's dominance was the price of his much-needed support. During her life, which ended only months before Hammond's own, she largely surrendered the management of family affairs to his direction. Because he regarded his siblings' successes as almost inseparable from his own, Hammond sought to bully them into behavior appropriate to the position and prominence he sought. Marcellus' drinking, John's rudeness, and Caroline's unfortunate marriage threatened Hammond's pretensions; he could not establish a dynasty alone. In the family-centered social hierarchy of the Old South, his siblings became objects to be manipulated in his design for self-advancement.

Trained in such relationships within his family of origin, Hammond instinctively reacted in similar ways with his own wife and children. As we have seen, Hammond married for power rather than for love; his wife, like his brothers and

6. Hammond to M. C. M. Hammond, September 18, 1846, in JHH Papers, SCL; Hammond to Simms, September 30, 1853, in JHH Papers, LC; John Fox Hammond to M. C. M. Hammond, July 3, 1853, in JHH Papers, SCL. On John's army career, see Edgar Erskine Hume, *Ornithologists of the United States Army Medical Corps* (Baltimore: Johns Hopkins Univesity Press, 1942).

7. Hammond to John Fox Hammond, April 11, 1844, Hammond to M. C. M. Hammond, November 10, 1847, both in JHH Papers, SCL.

Catherine Fox Hammond, James's mother.

sister, was to be part of his larger purpose. His alliance with Catherine Fitz-simons was calculated to secure him a plantation and a place within Carolina society; he explicitly urged his younger brothers and sons to choose their part-ners on similar grounds. These attitudes toward marriage and towards his own wife reflected Hammond's more general views about women, their capabilities, and their place in the world. He accepted without question the prevailing ideol-ogy of female inferiority, for it was entirely consistent with the hierarchical assumptions that prescribed the subjugation of blacks and the subordination of lesser whites. Women, as he explained to his son Harry, were made "to breed," to serve as "toy[s] for recreation," or to bring men "wealth and position."[8]

For the most part, Catherine Hammond meekly accepted this view of her own incapacity. Overawed by her dashing fiancé, she herself was hardly more than a child when she surrendered her hand and fortune to him in 1831. As a young wife in Washington in the 1830s, she feared to venture out alone; she was always ready to assure those around her that her husband was "a great man," and she vowed never to "complain that God had seen good to limit my natural abilities."[9]

But at the same time that Catherine's subservience flattered his ego, Hammond's very sense of superiority to his wife troubled him as well. Only "one woman in ten thousand—not one more," he warned Harry, "has mind enough to be a true 'help-meet' to a man of mind." And Catherine was sadly unfit for this role. Although she admired, she had not the intelligence truly to appreciate the intellectual qualities that were so important to his self-image. She "has no art of administering any real comfort," Hammond repeatedly complained. He esteemed and revered her, he declared, but he could not love her. Yearning for a marriage of companionship and affection, Hammond's ideology and ambition helped to imprison him in a relationship that could never satisfy these needs. Although his alliance with Catherine succeeded in extricating him from poverty, he soon recognized that marrying without love created "still greater ultimate difficulties."[10]

In the first years of his marriage, however, Hammond's feelings of emotional and intellectual distance apparently did not inhibit an active sexual relationship with his young wife. Harry was born just nine months after their wedding, and their next five sons were spaced fifteen, twelve, sixteen, fifteen, and fourteen months apart. Such short intervals indicate that Catherine was in all likelihood putting her children out to wet nurses, for lactating mothers do not ordinarily conceive again so rapidly. But after Cattie's birth in 1840, the Hammonds' pattern of procreation changed markedly. Perhaps after at last producing the daugh-

8. Hammond to John Fox Hammond, May 2, 1841, *ibid.*; Hammond to Harry Hammond, December 20, 1852, in HBC Papers, SCL.

9. Catherine Fitzsimons Hammond to M. C. M. Hammond, June 8, 1858, in JHH Papers, LC; Hammond to Catherine Fitzsimons Hammond, August 8, 1845, in JHH Papers, SHC.

10. Hammond to Harry Hammond, December 20, 1852, in HBC Papers, SCL; Hammond Diary (LC), August 30, 1842; Hammond Diary (SCL), February 22, 1853.

ter they had longed for, the couple began to practice some form of birth control.[11] Certainly James complained often enough in the hard financial times after 1840 of the enormous expense of so many offspring. As the couple grew older, their fertility would have naturally declined, and this too may have had its effects. Or the abrupt halt in Catherine's pregnancies after 1840 may have marked a deterioration in their relationship, an interpretation made plausible by the occurrence soon after this time of the Hampton imbroglio, the first evidence of the "ultimate difficulties" produced by this loveless marriage.

Hammond clearly regarded the liaison with his nieces as the result of having tried too completely to rationalize his life, of having left no space for human feeling in his drive for fame and fortune. At first he successfully concealed the affair from his wife, but the hostility of her Hampton relatives eventually required explanation and disclosure. Whether she initially discovered the scandal from others or whether Hammond himself confessed his misdeeds is not clear, and Catherine left no record of her feelings about her husband's transgressions. But Hammond reported his wife's reaction to be less of anger than injury. Their failure to produce more children in the years that immediately followed the scandal may indicate the emergence of a greater sexual distance between them, but as Hammond described Catherine's conduct, she seemed less to withdraw than to cling to him with a newly intense possessiveness that "watched [him] with lynx eyes & harassed [him] with suspicions." While such behavior represented in part a desire to punish her erring husband, Catherine's jealousy and the anxiety that underlay it bespoke those feelings of inadequacy and dependence that seem generally to have characterized her relationship with James.[12]

In October, 1849, Catherine produced another daughter, Elizabeth, whose sunny disposition made her from the moment of her birth the delight of the Hammond household and of her father's middle age. The appearance of a child after a nine-year interval might perhaps be seen as a reaffirmation of familial and marital ties after the long and difficult years that had followed the Hampton scandal. But just a year later a new issue of contention disturbed domestic peace at Silver Bluff. In the Hampton affair Catherine had apparently not aggressively asserted her displeasure, but she did not always feel so constrained in regard to her wifely rights. In the fall of 1850 an unspecified "want of caution" on Hammond's part led Catherine to discover his liaison with two female slaves. Ham-

11. See Norman E. Himes, *The Medical History of Contraception* (Baltimore: Williams and Wilkins, 1936).
12. Hammond Diary (SCL), December 15, 1850.

mond was indeed sexually involved with both Sally and Louisa Johnson. Although it is not clear whether he maintained relationships with both women simultaneously or if the younger at some point succeeded the older as the object of his attentions, he acknowledged that he might have sired children by both Louisa and her mother.[13]

Catherine was outraged. Far from passive in response to this discovery, she demanded from her husband "concessions . . . to which," Hammond confessed, "I am averse, because they involve injustice and cruelty to others." In all probability, she insisted that Sally and Louisa be sold. When her husband refused, Catherine took her two young daughters and departed to relatives in Charleston. Hammond resolutely refused to yield to her demands. Catherine's absence stretched from days to weeks until at last he began to fear that their separation might be permanent. With Harry off at college in Columbia, Spann and Willie at the University of Georgia in Athens, and Paul away in school, Hammond passed a solitary winter at Silver Bluff. On his wedding anniversary in June, Hammond sent his wife a peace offering of a carriage horse "that you stand very much in need of," but the gift failed to work its desired effect. Catherine was by this time residing with other relatives outside Augusta, and James made brief but frequent visits from Silver Bluff, explaining publicly that his family had moved to Georgia because of his disgust with South Carolina politics. But Hammond had little hope of a full and permanent reconciliation with his wife. "Peace and happiness are gone, I fear forever," he despaired in the fall of 1851.[14]

Hammond readily admitted that the causes of his domestic crisis lay in his own character, in the "great craving of my nature" that his wife left unfulfilled. This need for love, the same yearning that had led to the Hampton incident, seemed to him now undeniable and irrepressible, and he defended its expression in sexual infidelity as preferable to emotional unfaithfulness. "I do not love any other," he wrote, "But I have not been immaculate. I could not be—I tried it— Oh, I tried it fully—fully & failed wholly. I should fail were I to try it again. Shall I pretend to do it, knowing I cannot succeed? If not, what then?"[15]

By the winter of 1851–1852, James and Catherine had arrived at a kind of standoff, and even the unexpected death of their sixteen-year-old son Willie

13. Hammond Plantation Diary (MS vol. bd., 1831–55, JHH Papers, SCL), January 8, 1838. See also Hammond to Harry Hammond, February 19, 1856, in JHH Papers, SCL.
14. Hammond Diary (SCL), December 15, 1851; Hammond to Catherine Fitzsimons Hammond, June 24, 1851, in HBC Papers, SCL; Catherine Fitzsimons Hammond to William Cashel Hammond, July 2, 1851, in JHH Papers, SCL; Hammond Diary (SCL), September 7, 1851.
15. Hammond Diary (SCL), December 15, 1850.

from typhoid failed to unite the estranged couple. Their interaction declined, and by spring Hammond was complaining that his wife never even sent him a message "unless it is something to annoy." But the situation deteriorated still further when late in May, 1852, Hammond discovered that the Fitzsimonses had begun to publicize his domestic difficulties. It seemed to him the logical culmination of the hatred and resentment his wife's family had held toward him since the early days of their courtship.[16]

The torment Hammond had endured for nearly two years intensified as friends requested explanations that Hammond declined to provide. On a summer visit to a Charleston resort, Hammond found himself shunned, and he feared that he had "entirely lost social caste." But the price of reconciliation still seemed far too high. "Nothing will satisfy," he wrote Marcellus, "but that I shall surrender captive & be a *pardoned convict*—slave & prisoner day & night & execute her vengeance on my accomplices. This is too much."[17]

By fall, however, indications of a compromise began at last to appear. Still refusing to sell Louisa, Hammond agreed to send her away from Silver Bluff to Charleston, where she would work as a maidservant in the Fitzsimons family. But he insisted he would not allow her to go until the first frost had ended the sickly season in the low country, and he required that she not "be put in the backyard among the negroes—in other words turned loose in the town. Mrs. Fitzsimons must take her—as she deserves to be taken—as her own maid & look after her." Yet by December, Catherine had still not returned to live at Silver Bluff, although Hammond had written Simms that he hoped she would be home for Christmas dinner. In April of 1853, Catherine set up housekeeping in a rented dwelling in Aiken, then moved to another house in Augusta in January of 1854.[18]

Throughout this period Hammond recorded in his diary brief sojourns by his wife at the Bluff as well as his own frequent visits to her, and in the summer of 1854 he noted a vacation of several weeks with his family in the mountains. Publicly Hammond explained their unusual living arrangements by citing his

16. *Ibid.*, June 7, May 21, 1852.
17. *Ibid.*, July 29, 1852; Hammond to M. C. M. Hammond, August 11, 1852, in JHH Papers, SCL.
18. Hammond to M. C. M. Hammond, September 25, 1852, in JHH Papers, SCL. See Christopher Fitzsimons to Hammond, November 17, 1852, in JHH Papers, SCL; Hammond to Simms, December 15, 1852, in JHH Papers, LC; Hammond to M. C. M. Hammond, April 15, 1853, in JHH Papers, SCL.

wife's desire for the sociability of town, Cattie's need for a good school, and his own unrelenting responsibilities at Silver Bluff. However real these factors may have been, Catherine's continuing displeasure with her husband played its part as well. Hammond had not broken all ties with Louisa when she departed for Charleston in the fall of 1852, for he recorded occasional cash gifts forwarded to her, and in March of 1853 she returned to the plantation. Either Hammond managed to keep Sally and her daughter hidden by quartering them away from the main house, or Catherine slowly resigned herself to the situation, for by 1855 James and Catherine were living together again. But they were not yet entirely reconciled, and John described an arrangement in which Hammond and his family would regularly "seperate [sic] for part of the year."[19]

The details of how this domestic crisis was ultimately resolved remain unclear. After 1856 both Catherine and James were apparently in full-time residence at the new property Hammond had purchased in Beech Island, and they set about constructing the mansion in which they would live together until Hammond's death. Sally and Louisa Johnson remained on the plantation too, though in the field quarters far away from the main house, until at least the end of the war. Hammond continued to take an interest in them and their activities, noting in his diary, for example, every time they moved from one quarter to another at Cowden or Silver Bluff.[20]

Hammond's special treatment of the Johnsons extended to at least some of their offspring as well. When Henderson—whom his mother Sally identified as Hammond's son—grew old enough to work, his owner did not send him to the fields with the other slave children his age. After briefly employing him in the household, Hammond arranged for Henderson to work for a horticulturist in Augusta. Two years later, the planter made more formal provisions to ensure that the boy would acquire skills that could always guarantee him a position of privilege within the slave system. This time Hammond drew up a bond of apprenticeship for the fourteen-year-old youth, binding Henderson to Charles Axt, an immigrant German viticulturist living in Georgia. Under the terms of the agreement, Hammond required Axt to give Henderson four years of training

19. Hammond Plantation Diary, August 8, January 2, 5, 10, 12, 1854; Hammond Account Book (MS vol. bd., 1852–64, JHH Papers, SCL), March 1, 1853; Hammond Plantation Diary, March 5, 1853; John Fox Hammond to M. C. M. Hammond, June 5, 1855, in JHH Papers, SCL.
20. Hammond Plantation Book (MS in JHH Papers, LC), March 1, 1856; Hammond Redcliffe Journal (MS vol. bd., 1861–64, JHH Papers, SCL), November 24, 1861, January 25, 1862.

in the wine trade, and to demand no other sort of work from him. Hammond wished to ensure from the start that his young slave would not be compelled to perform demeaning household or personal chores for his new master.[21]

Hammond's interest in the boy did not end with the signing of the contract. In March of 1860, six months after the beginning of Henderson's term, Hammond received at his Senate post in Washington an anonymous letter from Augusta describing Axt's "brutal treatment" of his slave apprentice. "Many German Citizens" concerned about the behavior and reputation of their fellow countryman described to Hammond a scene in an Augusta bar in which Axt punished Henderson for running away by tying the youth's hands and legs and suspending him from the ceiling. From the distance of the national capital, Hammond had limited ability even to evaluate the truth of the letter. But he wrote at once to Alexander Stephens, a political associate and former fellow congressman from Georgia, and asked him to investigate. If Henderson had been treated badly, Hammond wrote Stephens, he should be retrieved from Axt at once.[22]

Stephens undertook his commission with great earnestness. After his own black carriage driver confirmed that a "mulatto boy" hired by Axt had run away several weeks before, Stephens arranged an appointment to question the German. Axt denied beating or mistreating Henderson, and offered to send the slave for Stephens' inspection. Alone with the boy, the Georgian interrogated him about the reports Hammond had received. Henderson related that he had in fact run away because he had neglected his work and feared a whipping. After his capture, Axt had tied him to prevent his escaping again. When the German had gone out and left his apprentice lying on his side, his hands bound behind his back and his foot elevated and fastened to a ceiling joist, Henderson had "cried and hollered" to protest his discomfort and fear. Upon his return, Axt flogged the boy with willow switches for raising such a commotion, but Stephens found no scars of a "severe whipping" on Henderson's back. Stephens concluded that Henderson's story and the marks on his arm from the switches constituted no condemnation of Axt's masterhood, especially since the boy seemed "very cheerful" and professed to be well pleased with his situation.[23]

Hammond accepted Stephens' judgment, in part, it seems, because he did

21. Hammond, "Silver Bluff, Cathwood, Cowden, and Redcliffe" (MS vol. bd., 1856–87, JHH Papers, SCL), August 15, 1856.
22. Many German Citizens to Hammond, March 20, 1860, Hammond to Alexander H. Stephens, March 31, 1860, both in Alexander H. Stephens Papers, LC.
23. Stephens to Hammond, April 8, 14, 1860, both in JHH Papers, LC.

not know what else to do with Henderson. The young slave, his owner reported, was a "very bad boy" with a "wild & daring spirit" and a "propensity for petty theft" that had defeated Hammond's attempts to make him into a house servant. But Hammond anxiously urged Stephens to keep Axt and Henderson under surveillance, and if he learned of any brutality to send the young slave home immediately.[24]

Many southern planters refused to recognize that a sexual liaison with a slave should involve any obligations or ties beyond the moment of physical encounter, and they often tended to ignore the obvious derivation of mixed-blooded slave offspring. But Hammond did not reject his black family in this way, and he readily admitted feelings of obligation toward his black kin. Even though, as he once explained to Harry, he was not entirely convinced Henderson was his child, he preferred to act on Sally's professed certainty; he did not want to risk leaving a son unacknowledged. He singled Henderson out for special treatment and opportunities; he refused to have Louisa or Sally mistreated, even to appease his enraged wife; he demonstrated an anxious concern about the Johnsons' health and welfare and would not countenance any risk of exposing Louisa to low-country fever.[25]

But at the same time, he took no action that would pose a direct challenge to the foundations of the slavery system he had so articulately defended. Hammond never considered freeing any of his black family or sending them outside the South. The best life for them, he remained convinced, lay within the bounds of the paternalism he idealized, and he bowed without hesitation to the usages of the peculiar institution. For his black kin, Hammond sought slavery at its best, nothing more and nothing less.

In the case of Henderson's alleged mistreatment, Hammond controlled an initial impulse to bring Henderson home at once. Instead he sought the judgment of a respected fellow slaveholder, who determined that the whipping the boy had received lay within the acceptable limits of a master's prerogative. Stephens could offer the objectivity of an outsider ignorant of any special relationship between Henderson and his owner. And if the Georgian had any suspicions about the origins of this "mulatto boy," he never voiced them. Stephens' intervention enabled Hammond to be certain that his concern about the slave youth would not exceed the limits appropriate to its expression; Hammond knew Ste-

24. Hammond to Stephens, May 18, 1860, in Stephens Papers.
25. See Chapter 5 for further discussion of this issue.

phens would advise action consistent with their culture's norms, even if not with Hammond's emotions.

Hammond's references to his black family demonstrate much sincere feeling even within relationships that were by their very structure exploitive. But these emotions were always carefully regulated by the constraints of the system in which Hammond lived, constraints he was unwilling in any way to oppose. Here, as in so much of the rest of his affective existence, Hammond felt compelled to keep his inner life under the tight regulation that left him frustrated, lonely, and unfulfilled.

With his legitimate offspring, Hammond's relationships were hardly more rewarding. As in nearly all his personal associations, Hammond's drive for domination produced a framework of interaction in which he and his children, particularly his sons, struggled incessantly for mastery. As the boys reached adolescence, their relationship with their father grew ever more difficult, for their petitions to be treated as adult equals appeared to Hammond as intolerable affronts to his jealously guarded prerogative. Issues of property and inheritance became the vehicles for these battles of will, and the bonds of familial affection seemed all too frequently forgotten. Wealth assumed an instrumental role within family relationships as Hammond employed his financial authority to reinforce his psychological dominance. Once again he sacrificed the rewards of love in his struggle for the satisfactions of power.

Although Hammond nowhere explicitly set forth his child-rearing notions, he embraced a philosophy of human nature that portrayed every individual as a battleground for the forces of good and evil. The maturation process in his view consisted in repressing the evil and encouraging the good through careful training and discipline. Control was the watchword of development. In Hammond's case, this discipline had been largely physical; Elisha had believed in frequent applications of the rod. But in his own role as father Hammond seems to have relied less on physical than on psychological punishment. Even if he rejected Elisha's harsh methods, however, he passed on many of the elder Hammond's precepts about the overarching importance of systematic self-regulation. In exhortations to his adolescent brother John about masturbation, in insistence that each of his children carefully oversee the operations of his bowels, in castigations of his sons for their financial extravagance, Hammond presented his dependents with unrelenting demands to exert mastery over any disorder or irregularity. And he greeted their failures with devastating rebuke. John's anxious disclosure of his nocturnal emissions evoked withering censure. "The infirmity

320

to which you are subject passes belief. I never knew or read of such a case. . . . If the thing is as you say it can only arise from excessive weakness." A decade later Hammond responded to Harry's confession that he had overspent his allowance at college with an equally biting reprimand. Elevating his son's minor financial embarrassments to the level of "Bankruptcy," Hammond declared, "I have always apprehended that you would prove incapable of handling money. And if so it would be absurd to entertain any hope of your ever becoming a useful man."[26]

Hammond endeavored to rule his sons with sarcasm and scorn, weapons they perceived as symbols of rejection by their otherwise all too "undemonstrative" father. In the longing for his little boys he expressed in his diary during his months in Europe in 1836–1837, in the utter misery he felt upon the deaths of fifteen-year-old Kit in 1848 and sixteen-year-old Willie in 1852, the strength of his paternal feeling is unmistakable. But in day-to-day interchange with his sons, these emotions were not easily expressed. His disapproval appeared much more frequently. As Catherine understood well, "Mr. H. is very much concerned about the boys. . . . & it is only in words & manners that he seems harsh—for there never was at heart a kinder Parent." She knew "Mr. H. is . . . the most liberal of fathers—but when he is irritated he does not spare words not of reproof but of sarcasm and abuse. He does not . . . consider how very serious his words are."[27]

Understanding James's behavior did not necessarily make Catherine's domestic life any easier. In 1850 she was distraught when her husband so upset Spann that the sixteen-year-old ran away from home and decided in a dramatic rejection of his father's dynastic aspirations to change his name. The causes of this quarrel are not clear, for in later life Spann tore the relevant pages from his father's diary. Apparently, however, it revolved around Spann's refusal to study and Hammond's complaint that the boy was always ready to "do any thing rather than what was expected or required of him." With his uncle Marcellus' encouragement, Spann publicly accused his father of "harshness & unkindness," creating a minor local scandal. Hammond recognized the sources of the contretemps in his own natural aloofness, and explained that "because I did not flatter him as

26. Hammond to John Fox Hammond, June 25, 1841, in JHH Papers, SCL. See also Hammond to John Fox Hammond, n.d., in School Papers, JHH Papers, SCL; Hammond to Harry Hammond, March 14, 1851, in HBC Papers, SCL.

27. Loula Comer Hammond to Virginia Clay-Clopton, September 21, 1911, in Clement Claiborne Clay Papers, DU; Hammond to M. C. M. Hammond, October 4, 1848, Catherine Fitzsimons Hammond to M. C. M. Hammond, July 26, September 2, 1858, all in JHH Papers, SCL.

others did, he took up the idea that I did not like him." Despite the "appearance of indifference" that he assumed "before the world," Catherine knew her husband was deeply injured by Spann's behavior and mortified by the widespread knowledge of their rift. Even though the father fully expected the break to remain permanent and made plans to provide Spann with a diminished inheritance, Catherine intervened to encourage her son to relent. His father's feelings for him, she reassured the boy, were profound. "Oh Spann you have acted with the greatest injustice & ingratitude to the kindest of Parents." Her role was to convey to her children the love their father could not express.[28]

Unable even with his children to reveal deep-felt emotion, Hammond compensated by spoiling them, coupling his rigid demands with indulgences that could not but have confused his sons about their father's expectations. As young children they seem to have been subjected to minimal control, for Hammond ruefully reported that as toddlers in the mid-1830s, Harry, Spann, Kit, and Willie made so much noise as to drive visitors from the house. Their unruly behavior persisted into their first years at school, when, as we have seen, Hammond was compelled to pay special charges for the damage they inflicted on their classroom. By 1848, little had changed, for Kit and Spann, then fifteen and fourteen years old, engaged their tutor in a fistfight that led their father to exclaim in disgust, "I don't know what to do with my boys." When Spann entered college three years later, he remained unsubdued and almost immediately succeeded in getting himself suspended for throwing several classmates down a flight of stairs. One victim protested by imbedding a knife in his assailant's arm, and Spann returned to Silver Bluff to nurse his wounds. Harry tended less toward violence than more pacific forms of self-indulgence. "Somebody has imbued him," Hammond complained in 1847, "with the Epicurean philosophy, & he thinks life was given him solely for 'pleasure!'" Harry appeared to his father "disgustingly foppish in his dress," too inclined to bloat himself with overeating and other extravagances.[29]

28. Hammond Diary (SCL), May 18, 1850; Catherine Fitzsimons Hammond to Edward Spann Hammond, May 17, 1850, in Edward Spann Hammond Papers, SCL; Hammond Diary (SCL), May 18, 1850; Catherine Fitzsimons Hammond to Edward Spann Hammond, May 17, 1850, in Edward Spann Hammond Papers; Catherine Fitzsimons Hammond to M. C. M. Hammond, July 26, 1858, in JHH Papers, SCL.

29. Hammond to William C. Preston, November 4, 1835, in JHH Papers, DU; Hammond, Business Papers (JHH Papers, SCL), December 16, 1843; Hammond to M. C. M. Hammond, August 6, 1848, in JHH Papers, LC; Hammond to Harry Hammond, March 14, 1851, in HBC Papers, SCL; Hammond to M. C. M. Hammond, December 30, 1847, Hammond to William Cashel Hammond, n.d., both in JHH Papers, SCL.

Hammond's sons manifested the shortcomings of the young rich, of heirs apparent, too assured of their own prerogatives and too well supplied with money. Yet even if he deplored such propensities, Hammond himself encouraged this behavior by instilling a pride of position in the boys and providing them with generous sums with which to indulge their elevated tastes. The year he turned eighteen Harry received an annual allowance of six hundred dollars—20 percent more than Hammond paid his overseer the same year—and it was at this time that Harry fell into his "Bankruptcy" at South Carolina College. When Spann and Paul reached a similar age, they were given equivalent amounts, and the sums placed at their disposal continued to rise. According to family legend, Spann went off to the medical college in Charleston in 1853 with two race horses and three slaves. But these patterns of indulgence did not signify any relaxation in Hammond's ultimate expectations of his sons. Although he had vowed to shield them from the ambition that had rendered his own life so difficult, he could not help but regard their accomplishments as an extension of his own. Hammond's contributions to their lack of self-discipline did not prevent him from complaining constantly about his sons' inadequacies. "Boys fit for nothing but to spend money," he declared in 1858 in despair.[30]

Although spending money well, Hammond readily admitted, was an "essential part of every gentleman's education," it could hardly substitute for those social and intellectual accomplishments that had provided the basis for his own success. Because education had served as the foundation for Hammond's own advancement, he regarded his sons' schooling as critically important. As he so often remarked, knowledge was synonymous with power.[31]

But satisfactory schools were not easily found in South Carolina, where there was no system of public education before the Civil War. One of Hammond's stated reasons for moving to Columbia in the early 1840s was to procure instruction for his children, and the boys attended nursery and grade schools in the capital. After Hammond's return to Silver Bluff he himself had to hire and board teachers, for there were no educational institutions nearby. A succession of tutors instructed the children over the next several years, and Hammond found each more trying than the last: Mr. Blake and Mr. White had no disci-

30. John Shaw Billings, "The Spann Family" (MS vol. bd., HBC Papers, SCL); Hammond Diary (LC), February 15, 1841; Hammond, "Silver Bluff, Cathwood, Cowden, and Redcliffe," June 26, 1858. On sums distributed to his sons, see Hammond Account Book (MS vol. bd., 1834–64, JHH Papers, SCL), and Edward Spann Hammond Account Book, 1859–63, Edward Spann Hammond Papers.

31. Hammond to Harry Hammond, December 20, 1852, in HBC Papers, SCL.

pline; Mr. O'Brien drank; Mr. Hough taught them nothing. "I can't keep a teacher up to the mark," he despaired. The boys must have learned in spite of these instructors, however, for Harry went off to South Carolina College in 1849, Willie and Spann to the University of Georgia, and Paul to the College of Charleston and the University of Virginia a few years later.[32]

Yet education was only a beginning. As Hammond knew from his own experience, it was a prerequisite, but certainly not an assurance of success in the Carolina social order. An appropriate marital alliance was equally necessary. Forgetting that he had vowed not to poison his sons with ambition, forgetting his regrets about his own marriage, Hammond gave his offspring the same advice he had received from his father and had already passed on to his brothers Marcellus and John. He did his utmost to protect his sons from the folly of marrying women without fortunes. "Somehow—God forgive me," he wrote Harry, "I never could bear poor girls. . . . Even the sweetest pills should be gilded." After Spann became engaged to his distant cousin Clara in 1856, Hammond discovered her wealth to be less than Spann had initially reported. Without telling his son, Hammond wrote directly to Clara demanding she break their betrothal. "Do you know that Clara's fortune was only $20,000," he exclaimed to Marcellus, who had encouraged the match. Spann resentfully acquiesced, and six years later wed a Virginian of good family named Marcella Morris. But the couple was not happy, and one day after the end of the Civil War, Marcella boarded a train for home and never returned. Spann divorced her and married again but would always blame his father for destroying his chance for personal happiness.[33]

Hammond, in turn, felt his peace of mind continually imperiled by the behavior of his sons. Because his need to control was so great, any act of independence by one of the boys seemed a gesture of defiance; because his expectations were so high, the youths' modest accomplishments almost escaped his notice. Part of Hammond's tendency to disparage their achievements undoubtedly arose from the father's sense of competition with his sons, from a desire to retain do-

32. Hammond to Simms, December 13, 1849, in JHH Papers, LC; Hammond Diary (LC), February 15, 1841; Bill of Jane Bryce, May 5, 1841, Bill of William Irving, both in Hammond Business Papers; Hammond Plantation Diary, August 27, 1849; Hammond to Catherine Spann Hammond, December 11, 1843, in JHH Papers, SCL; Hammond to Edmund Ruffin, August 23, 1846, in Edmund Ruffin Papers, Virginia Historical Society, Richmond; Hammond Plantation Diary, October 26, 1846; Hammond to Simms, July 26, September 22, 1848, both in JHH Papers, LC.

33. Hammond to Harry Hammond, December 20, 1852, in HBC Papers, SCL; Hammond to Simms, January 20, 1857, Hammond to M. C. M. Hammond, November 12, 1860, both in JHH Papers, LC; Edward Spann Hammond, notebook (MS vol. bd., 1861–1909, Edward Spann Hammond Papers, SCL).

minion over them by refusing to acknowledge them as equals. When Harry and Spann graduated from medical school at the University of Pennsylvania in 1855, their father, recently turned homeopath, belittled their therapeutic abilities. When Harry three years later requested support for a term at Harvard that would qualify him to fill a vacant chair in natural science at the University of Georgia, Hammond was entirely unsympathetic. Harry fled to Cambridge without saying good-bye, and Hammond remained more impressed by this evidence of what he regarded as the youth's ingratitude and bad temper than by his son's serious academic ambitions. "Let him be defeated" for the professorship, Hammond declared peevishly to Marcellus. "It will do him great good. . . . You don't know how he overrode all *my* plans here."[34]

Harry, like his brothers, suffered under his father's disapproval. All his twenty-seven years, he wrote from Massachusetts, "I have accomplished nothing . . . not one single undertaking has resulted in success." He believed himself the "living, walking realization of utter incompetency, patent to every eye." He had left, he explained, because he could no longer bear the onus of failure; he felt compelled to discover an area in which he might succeed. With Spann, too, shortcomings seemed to attract more paternal attention than success. When the youth decided to run for the legislature in 1858, his father signaled his approval—and perhaps his regrets over the recent incident with Clara—by advancing his son the land necessary to qualify him for membership in the Carolina legislature. But throughout Spann's energetic campaign, Hammond complained incessantly about the youth's absence from plantation responsibilities. Perhaps there was no room for two politicians in the family.[35]

Harry's academic success, Spann's electoral triumph, all seemed to count for nought. Eager to please their father, the boys felt themselves incapable of winning his approval or meeting his extravagant expectations. "Your danger is," Simms wrote Hammond perceptively, "that you overawe your boys, overwhelm them, and make them halt & hesitate, if not fear, so that they become distrustful of themselves." Yet part of Hammond sought this very goal, for in their doubts about themselves lay the foundation of their father's continuing control over them. In his behavior towards his sons, as in his choice of women—his very

34. Hammond, "Silver Bluff, Cathwood, Cowden, and Redcliffe," September 1, 1859; Hammond to M. C. M. Hammond, August 10, 25, 1858, both in JHH Papers, LC; Hammond to M. C. M. Hammond, October 1, 1858, in JHH Papers, SCL.

35. Harry Hammond to Hammond, October 1858, in HBC Papers, SCL; Hammond Account Book (1852–64); Hammond to M. C. M. Hammond, September 22, 1858, in JHH Papers, SCL.

much younger wife, his teenage nieces, and two slaves—Hammond displayed a desire to shield himself from the impact of deeper emotion by insisting upon a position of dominance that necessarily distanced him from those he might most naturally love. Through a posture of disapproval toward his sons, Hammond attempted to regulate his own feelings to inhibit any expression of affection that might leave him vulnerable before these young men he so fervently desired to keep dependent upon him.[36]

Hammond's disgust at what he viewed as the "incompetency of the boys" appeared most forcefully in the realm of plantation affairs, for here his sons' performance affected his own ambitions most directly. His drive for achievement encompassed a desire to establish a "rich, educated, well bred & predominant family here . . . of our name." As patriarch, he wished to extend the power he claimed within his own society across generations, to control the future as well as the present, to mold his sons in accordance with his own design.[37]

In the mid-1850s Hammond began self-consciously to consolidate the traditional accouterments of dynastic rule. Having apparently forgotten the "undistinguished" nature of his origins, he hired a British genealogist to demonstrate his direct descent from English nobility. When the researcher insisted that the family came from "good honest yeomen," Hammond threw the letter in the fire and refused to pay the bill. The modest plantation house he had built in the 1830s no longer seemed adequate to his elevated self-conception, and Hammond purchased a new tract of land with a symbolically commanding view of the surrounding countryside on which to erect a suitable dwelling. Redcliffe, completed in 1858 at a cost of twenty-two thousand dollars exclusive of labor, was intended as both "family mansion" and family monument.[38]

But these dynastic aspirations ultimately depended upon his sons' capabilities as plantation administrators, for land and slaves provided the necessary foundation for family position and wealth. And Hammond despaired that his boys had "no management." Reluctant to yield his control of plantation affairs, Hammond constantly found fault with his sons' execution of the responsibilities he had assigned them. When Spann ran Cowden in 1857, when Harry, Spann, and Paul took charge during their father's senatorial term in Washington, Hammond

36. Simms to Hammond, November 10, 1857, in JHH Papers, LC.
37. Hammond to M. C. M. Hammond, August 10, 1858, *ibid.*
38. H.G. Somerby to J. C. Barber, January 29, March 19, 1856, in JHH Papers, SCL; Hammond Diary (SCL), May 12, 1855.

declared the results disastrous. In 1859 he scornfully judged Spann's crop yield to be just a quarter of what he himself would have achieved. The boys always wanted, he complained, "to do everything in a different way from mine," and they seemed entirely unwilling to exercise the care on which Hammond had always prided himself.[39]

The young Hammonds, in turn, chafed under this paternal domination. Spann yearned for his father to "place a little confidence in me." He and his brothers agreed that they were treated no better than overseers. When they urged Hammond to divide his lands and provide them with their own shares of his property, he refused. Until his death he retained ownership of all but the 133 acres of land he had given Spann to qualify for the legislature. His sons' "listlessness, indolence & selfishness," he explained, would lead them to squander their patrimony, leaving their mother and sisters with no support.[40]

Harry entreated his father to be more reasonable and defended their record of management as more than adequate, even if not as innovative as that of their father. But Paul and Spann were less conciliatory, complaining resentfully to their uncle Marcellus about their father's refusal to yield control. "The prospect which Father offers to us," Paul protested, "is to stay with him and attend to his business as long as he and Mother live and at their death inherit $50,000—and with this he thinks we ought to be satisfied. This I cannot be content to do."[41]

Hammond lamented that an "*abyss*" seemed to separate him from his sons, and he became so enraged by their demands that he threatened to disinherit them, sell the plantation and slaves, and invest the principle to support himself, his wife, and daughters. The Hammond boys and their father were on a collision course, and only the advent of war averted what might have become a permanent and irrevocable break. Eager to assume adult responsibilities, Harry, Spann, and Paul confronted during the late 1850s a father so accustomed to controlling others that he could not contemplate providing his sons with the financial bases for their independence. Yet he seemed not to recognize how threatened he felt by their desires for autonomy, and he insisted that he wished only to "abdicate" and to surrender his onerous plantation obligations. Bored and exasperated by the

---

39. Hammond, "Silver Bluff, Cathwood, Cowden, and Redcliffe," July 3, 1858; Hammond to Simms, December 19, 1859, in JHH Papers, LC.
40. Edward Spann Hammond Diary (MS vol. bd., 1856, Edward Spann Hammond Papers); Hammond to M. C. M. Hammond, October 11, 1858, in JHH Papers, SCL.
41. Paul Fitzsimons Hammond to M. C. M. Hammond, June 19, 1859, in JHH Papers, SCL.

minutiae of management with which he had occupied himself for nearly thirty years, Hammond at the same time clung jealously to his authority.[42]

Hammond and his sons never themselves arrived at any solution to their conflict; only external forces would mitigate the youths' bitterness. The war was to provide other sorts of responsibilities and othei meaningful roles for the young Hammonds; they would no longer have to await their father's acquiescence to become adults. The challenge of managing the plantation in wartime would in turn revive Hammond's interest, and he would resume close supervision of the agricultural enterprise until his final illness rendered him incapable of either continuing his mastery or complaining about the management of his sons. Hammonds, Paul once observed, "desire to govern whatever and whoever they come in contact with." James Henry Hammond and his sons indeed seemed almost destined by blood to struggle for mastery over one another and for dominion over Silver Bluff.[43]

With his two daughters, Hammond's relationships were far less problematic. More limited expectations reduced the scope for disappointment, and Hammond anticipated no challenge to his prerogative from his female offspring. In antebellum America, women were regarded as biologically inferior to men in intellectual and physical capacities, and Hammond could rest secure in the assumption that his authority over his daughters would never be questioned. But in spite of these differences in sex roles and expectations, Cattie grew up as spoiled as any of her brothers. Dissatisfied with the succession of boarding schools in which she was enrolled, Hammond's difficult and temperamental elder daughter resisted any imposition of authority. She "wont learn or submit to any other rule than her own will," Hammond reported to Harry in exasperation. "I shall bother no more with her education," he resolved after she was expelled from a fashionable Charleston finishing school in 1856. Indulged as a child, Cattie Hammond grew into a tragic adulthood. Married at the start of the war to James Gregg, scion of the Carolina cotton manufacturing family, Cattie was widowed in 1876 when one of the textile workers shot his employer. Her second husband, a manager from the factory, was generally viewed as an opportunist. Cattie died in her early forties while struggling to free herself from fifteen years of opium addiction.[44]

42. Hammond to M. C. M. Hammond, June 24, 1859, in JHH Papers, SCL; Hammond to Harry Hammond, July 16, 1859, in HBC Papers, SCL.
43. Paul Fitzsimons Hammond to M. C. M. Hammond, June 19, 1859, in JHH Papers, SCL.
44. Hammond to Harry Hammond, December 28, 1856, John McGehee to Hammond, Febru-

Courtesy of the South Caroliniana Library
Cattie Hammond, James's elder daughter.

Of all the Hammond offspring, Betty seems to have been the easiest and, in many senses, the most rewarding child. Born in 1849, nearly a decade younger than her nearest sibling, Bet was a naturally cheerful and winsome little girl whose laughter delighted her parents and her grown brothers alike. To her father she seemed the "light & life of the house." If any human being had been exempted from the evil Hammond believed to be struggling for dominance within

---

ary 23, 1857, both in JHH Papers, SCL; Loula Comer Hammond to Virginia Clay-Clopton, August 4, 1885, Clement C. Clay Papers. Opium addiction was not uncommon among middle- and upper-class women of this period who took opiate-based remedies for a variety of female complaints.

each individual, it was Betty. Reaching her teens during the war years, she in all likelihood never developed the expectations of wealth and position that so shaped the lives of her older siblings. In his unrepressed delight in this child, Hammond was perhaps less ambivalent, more open and demonstrative than in any other relationship of his life.[45]

But Bet was the exception to the troubled and stormy relationships that evolved between Hammond and all his kin. His instrumental view of family as the ultimate repository of status within the social order of the Old South shaped—indeed distorted—all his affective ties. Yet he produced sons who grew up without the ambition that their father never forgave them for escaping. "I don't ever care about being rich," Harry once apologetically confessed to his exasperated father. All but overwhelmed by the very force of paternal will, the young Hammonds grew up into an adult world of war, destruction and poverty very different from the privileged existence of their childhood. Yet perhaps their conflict- and sorrow-ridden prewar lives prepared them in some way for the painful future that awaited them. For, as Catherine Hammond sadly remarked in the flush times of the late 1850s, "With every thing to make us happy there are few families that are less so."[46]

45. Hammond to Harry Hammond, September 21, 1855, in JHH Papers, SCL.
46. Harry Hammond to Hammond, June 29, 30, 1859, in HBC Papers, SCL; Catherine Fitzsimons Hammond to M. C. M. Hammond, September 2, 1858, in JHH Papers, SCL.

CHAPTER 16

The Violation of Order

A S SOUTH CAROLINA flirted with secession during the 1850s, James Henry
Hammond confronted a paradox. Long the advocate of an independent
southern nation, Hammond found himself in the years after Nashville actively
opposed to his state's movement toward disunion. Although he had in no way
abandoned his commitment to southern independence, Hammond deplored the
"reckless & excited ignorance" of the Carolina secessionists in 1851–1852.
Throughout the years that remained before the outbreak of war, he would
continue to oppose what he regarded as dangerously irrational and demagogic
extremism.[1]

Hammond's professed allegiance to a politics of principle was hardly consistent with the mid-century foundations of American and even Carolinian public
life. The role of the elite within politics had been irrevocably altered since 1800.
Mass support, invoked by what Hammond regarded as corrupt self-interest, now
had routinely to be mobilized to advance any individual or position that sought
ascendancy. But Hammond never reconciled himself to the new character of
public life. Democracy seemed to him the "despotism of the monster multitude
. . . ruled . . . by the basest appetites, prejudices and vanities." For him the
means of political action mattered as much as any substantive end. His commitment to a southern nation arose from his long-cherished belief that by sealing
itself off from the increasingly modern, industrialized, and egalitarian North the
South could most effectively protect her special social order. To pursue secession

1. James Henry Hammond Diary (MS in JHH Papers, SCL), January 6, 1852.

without regard for these principles seemed to him self-defeating. Southern nationalism was in Hammond's view a means of retaining the traditional structure of regional society; his commitment to sectional independence was fundamentally conservative. "Order," he explained, "is a prime necessity in every community, especially an Agricultural one & most especially a slave-holding one. To the great body of the Southern People, the Union is the only tangible & appreciable Representative of Order, & it is solely on this account that they love & sustain it. . . . steps must be taken to carry on resistance & insure the rupture of the Union, *which do not in the first instance involve any violation of Order.*" Strict constitutionalism was the framework within which demagogic tendencies could be contained; constitutional principles had to serve as the guideposts as well as the legitimating force for southern actions.[2]

Such views isolated Hammond in Carolina political life of the 1850s, where public affairs seemed too often based in the "rules of Knight errantry." Hammond was at heart a secessionist alienated from the style that dominated Carolina's disunion party and from the faith in the federal government that characterized their more conservative opponents. Throughout the decade, he struggled to convert the secession movement to his conception of the purposes of separatism. But for the most part, whether hailed or condemned, he was misunderstood. The careful distinctions he wanted to draw between the means and ends of political action were too finely tempered for this new and fevered political age. The times had in a real sense passed him by.[3]

As Barnwell Rhett fanned the flames of resistance in Carolina during the winter of 1851, Hammond watched with alarm from Silver Bluff. A "reign of terror" seemed underway, for Carolina now required that "men must cease to speak unless they speak to stimulate the frenzy of the mob." The state legislature had called for the election in February of delegates to a convention to be held on some unspecified future date to consider secession, and Hammond was hardly surprised when extremists favoring separate state action by South Carolina won a substantial majority. But he saw this electoral victory as no triumph for his own ultimately disunionist views. Rhett, he believed, was acting imprudently, moving too fast, isolating Carolina from the rest of the region, and ensuring the ultimate failure of this movement for southern independence. If Carolina tried to secede and was defeated, she would "ruin the cause, perhaps forever, cer-

---

2. *Ibid.*, December 6, 1851.
3. Hammond, "Thoughts and Recollections" (MS vol. bd., 1852–53, JHH Papers, SCL), May 13, 1852.

tainly for our time." He worried that Rhett's revolution would "turn out an insurrection."[4]

But in spite of dramatic developments in Carolina politics, Hammond could not maintain his usual intensity of interest in the events at hand. Preoccupied with his rejection by the legislature for the senatorial vacancy in December, 1850, and beset by personal difficulties, he complained to Simms of a "nervous collapse" and of a "partial derangement" of his senses. He described as well the beginning of a process of "fattening" that resulted in a weight gain of fifty pounds over the next three years, an increase that might have been part of his response to the tensions that plagued him. Bitter about the course of events in Carolina, Hammond resolved to abandon any identification with his native state.[5]

Yet, as always, Hammond was unable to restrain his interest in politics. In "spite of myself," he wrote ruefully in his diary, "I feel constantly that public affairs are part of my vocation." Before long, he was interjecting his views into the crisis at hand. Certain that Rhett's call for separate state secession would only make Carolina look ridiculous, Hammond designed an alternative "Plan of State Action" to be submitted to a spring gathering in Charleston of a group called the Southern Rights Association. Printed anonymously in the Charleston *Mercury* on May 2, 1851, Hammond's proposal called for South Carolina to be "*in* but not *of* the union." The Palmetto State, the document asserted, desired an independent South and remained in the Union only to await the evolution of other states toward her secessionist views. In the meantime, however, she would appoint no presidential electors or congressmen, accept no federal appropriations, and work to encourage domestic manufacturing and economic independence. Adoption of such a plan, Hammond argued, would enable Carolina to appear strong and determined, but not foolhardy.[6]

The convention that took place in Charleston in May proved too solid in its support for immediate disunion to adopt Hammond's plan. But the body's very

4. James Henry Hammond to Nathaniel Beverley Tucker, February 25, 1851, in Tucker-Coleman Papers, Earl Gregg Swem Memorial Library, College of William and Mary, Williamsburg, Va.; Hammond to Edmund Ruffin, July 20, February 7, 1851, both in Edmund Ruffin Papers, Virginia Historical Society, Richmond; Hammond to William Gilmore Simms, February 14, 1851, in JHH Papers, LC. See also John Gibbes Barnwell, "'Love of Order': The Origins and Resolution of South Carolina's First Secession Crisis" (Ph.D. dissertation, University of South Carolina, 1979); Harold S. Schultz, *Nationalism and Sectionalism in South Carolina, 1852–1860: A Study of the Movement for Southern Independence* (Durham: Duke University Press, 1950).

5. Hammond to Simms, January 20, 1851, in JHH Papers, LC; Hammond to Ruffin, December 19, 1853, May 1, 1854, both in Ruffin Papers. VHS.

6. Hammond Diary (SCL), January 30, 1851; Charleston *Mercury*, May 2, 1851; Hammond to Tucker, April 8, 1851, in Tucker-Coleman Papers.

extremism provoked a conservative reaction that grew stronger as the summer wore on. Twelve hundred Charlestonians met on July 29 to endorse cooperation with other southern states in any secessionist move and to declare separate state action treasonous. Late in August, a group of moderates, finding "public senti- ment" in a "transition State," called upon Hammond to appeal to the "reason & common sense" of the people and to guide them back to the "right track. We know no one," they wrote, "who can address their understanding more power- fully than yourself." Hammond was delighted at the opportunity to decline this request with a blasting recitation of his grievances against Carolina. Instead of returning to active political involvement, he retreated once again and passed the summer and early fall disgruntledly reading novels "*ad nauseum.*"[7]

When the legislature, in its burst of radical enthusiasm the previous Decem- ber, had called for February elections to a state convention, it had also provided for an October vote for delegates to an anticipated southern congress. But as the fall canvass approached, Carolina knew that whatever decisions she made about secession, she would act alone. Complacency had once again settled over the rest of the South. No pan-southern gathering was going to meet; no other state was going to act in opposition to the outrages of 1850. Under these changed circumstances, the cooperationists and the immediate secessionists tacitly agreed to regard the already scheduled elections as a referendum on the issues that had so divided the state. When cooperationists won an overwhelming victory, the radicals began to acknowledge that Hammond's earlier perception of the situa- tion had been proved correct. His "Plan of State Action," derided as submission- ist in the spring, now seemed the most decisive measure for which they could win support. After all her threats, Carolina would be humiliated if she took no action to protest the Compromise of 1850. A rapprochement with the coopera- tionists had to be devised to save face. The "Plan of State Action" appealed to several radical leaders as a plausible peace offering to the moderates.

After a few feeble protests that he had "no heart for politics," Hammond agreed to revise and update his proposal in accordance with the suggestions of radical spokesman Maxcy Gregg. The situation offered "the opportunity . . . for a complete triumph and ample satisfaction for the past." Hammond fantasized about the gratification he would feel when the state called upon him in her "deepest disgrace" to "save her & as it were rule her from my deep retirement in

7. Joseph Dulles, A. G. McGrath, Nelson Mitchell, William D. Martin, and Charles Mar- berth to Hammond, August 28, 1851, Hammond to Simms, September 19, 1851, both in JHH Papers, LC.

these woods." But these long-cherished visions were not to be realized. In an ill-considered pamphlet circulated just before an all-important cooperationist caucus in Columbia in late November, Maxcy Gregg so insulted the moderates that any alliance became impossible. His support for Hammond's plan dictated its certain failure.[8]

When the state convention at last gathered in April, 1852, it was to preside over the death of the radical party. Rebuffed in his request to address the meeting, Rhett resigned his Senate seat and sailed for Europe. The gathering produced no decisive action—only the adoption of a report and an ordinance affirming the abstract right of secession. Hammond dismissed the proceedings as "too pitiful for comment." More prudent than the extreme secessionists, Hammond now found himself disgusted at the submissionism of the moderates. Again disillusioned, he turned to agriculture for consolation. "Reclaiming swamps has become my passion," he wrote Simms. "It is creative. It is exercising the highest functions without having to ask *votes*. I love their creep [and] gloom & their solemn silence." When Rhett's Senate successor was elected in December, Hammond was not even a candidate.[9]

But Hammond could not long survive without challenge. He threw himself into the effort to erect a mansion that would embody the wealth, taste, and refinement he had acquired in his years as plantation master. Within his private sphere, he would seek to compensate for what the public world had denied him.

By early 1854 Hammond had abandoned the idea of becoming a Georgian. His tentative efforts to sell Silver Bluff had failed, and he still spent most of his time in Carolina managing his affairs. As a diversion for himself and as a gesture of reconciliation to his wife, Hammond in 1855 purchased a four-hundred-acre tract of land near a settlement called Beech Island. On a red-clay ridge about six miles north of Silver Bluff, the site provided a vista across the surrounding countryside; Hammond boasted that on a clear day he could see every house in Augusta, more than five miles away. The property included a modest dwelling of eight rooms, with a striking flying staircase in the rear of the main hall. But the house was not the resplendent family seat Hammond envisioned for his old age. He intended to begin construction on an appropriate mansion as soon as possible. Hammond's design for his dwelling reflected the still fashionable Greek Revival style, as well as his penchant for display. Redcliffe was perched atop

8. Hammond Diary (SCL), November 8, 1851; James Jones to Hammond, November 16, 1851, in JHH Papers, LC; Hammond Diary (SCL), November 21, 1851.
9. Hammond to Simms, May 14, 1852, in JHH Papers, LC.

nine-foot brick pillars at the end of an avenue of carefully planted magnolias. Two-tiered piazzas adorned each side of the building, which boasted a rooftop observatory as well. A large center hall, fifty-three feet long, twenty feet wide, and fourteen feet high, provided an admirable setting for public receptions, and Hammond chose stylish Belgian tile and Brussels carpets to embellish the floors. Two rooms opened off to each side of the main hall, their doors carved from native sycamore and hinged with silver. The paintings Hammond had brought from Europe decorated the walls, except in the study, which he lined with bookcases crowned with marble busts of both classical and Carolina statesmen. Hammond himself occupied a room on the main floor of the house rather than one of the four bedchambers on the second story. Heavy green and gilt draperies trimmed large French windows in every room, and gas pipes ran throughout the house to provide an additional—and highly fashionable—source of light. Close behind the mansion stood the kitchen and four slave cabins to service this grandiose establishment.

The house itself was framed by elaborate gardens, largely the work of a Belgian landscape designer whom Hammond hired to terrace the hillside that sloped down to the Savannah River. Hammond never used the acreage of the Redcliffe tract for cotton or corn; this spot was to be "Arcadia." The property would serve as testimony to his ability to withdraw from the crass pursuit of material gain and to surround himself instead with orchards and vineyards. To a twentieth-century observer, the landscaping seems to have endured the past century somewhat better than the house itself. The trees set out in the 1850s are now magnificent, while the house appears almost ungainly, its opulent details too pretentious for its overall design. Soon after the family moved in, the ground-level pillars were connected to enclose a basement that would prevent cold winds from sweeping under the main floor. Wet rot in the 1880s forced the reconstruction of the piazzas and the removal of the second-story porches, and later a widow's walk replaced the airy cupola atop the dwelling. These changes imparted a heaviness the house originally lacked, and Redcliffe seems less elegant than Hammond would no doubt have liked it to appear. It is all too tempting to see the mansion as a fitting monument to its builder, to a man who never quite succeeded in convincing Carolina that he had transcended his "undistinguished" origins.[10]

10. Hammond to Simms, November, 1861, *ibid.*; Hammond to George deRenne, November 20, 1858, in George deRenne Papers, DU. See also National Parks Service, U.S. Department of the

Redcliffe in the late nineteenth century.

Hammond was, in fact, never able to involve himself as deeply in the design and construction of the house as he had originally intended. By the end of 1857, the climate of Carolina's public life had shifted once again, transforming Hammond's very isolation from a liability into his greatest political asset.

In the years that followed Rhett's 1852 humiliation, unionism gained steady support in the state under the able leadership of up-country congressman James L. Orr. Active participation in the national Democratic party, Orr argued, was

---

Interior, National Register of Historic Places Inventory Nomination Form: Redcliffe, 1973; John Shaw Billings, "Some Notes on the History of Redcliffe" (MS in HBC Papers, SCL).

the best means for Carolina to defend herself against federal encroachments. Orchestrating what came to be known as the convention movement because it called for Carolina's participation in the national Democratic nominating convention in 1856, Orr reaped the benefits of the Democrats' choice of James Buchanan, a candidate openly sympathetic to slavery and southern interests. But the mounting controversy over the status of slavery in the territories erupted into violence in Kansas and kept sectionalist feeling, expressed most actively in these years as anticonvention sentiment, very much alive throughout the state.[11]

When Senator A. P. Butler died suddenly in May, 1857, eyes turned to Hammond as a natural successor. His leading attribute seemed to be that no one was quite sure of his views. As a Charleston ally explained, "You have not been identified with any late party divisions, from Secession and Cooperation down to the Convention movement, and thus will be the most available *compromise* candidate." A less enthusiastic observer phrased the same point a bit more bluntly. "Hammond," he wrote, "is a big gun in this country from not having been fired off at any time since the Revolution."[12]

Despite Hammond's enforced exclusion from public life, faith in his extraordinary intellectual ability remained undiminished. And despite his hierarchical views and aristocratic pretensions, Hammond had won great popularity among the common people of the state, who identified with his humble origins. Hammond had cleverly—and given the nature of his own political views, cynically—cast many of his failures in almost populist terms. His past defeats, he maintained again and again, had been engineered by "cliques" thwarting popular will. Although the voters of South Carolina had no direct role in the choice of senator, their preference was evident to those who did. In selecting a replacement for Butler, Carolina's legislators may have viewed Hammond as a convenient means of satisfying popular demands without posing any real threat. Hammond, the Charleston *Evening News* reported, was "the people's candidate," and that fact "controlled the legislature and overrode all the efforts against him." By 1857, his petulant refusal to return to Nashville in 1850 was all but forgotten, and with Wade Hampton's removal to Mississippi, concern about Hammond's moral transgressions was fading as well. As Waddy Thompson, former

11. Roger P. Leemhuis, *James L. Orr and the Sectional Conflict* (Washington, D.C.: University Press of America, 1979).

12. John Cunningham to Hammond, June 20, 1857, in JHH Papers, LC; James Simons to John Manning, August 31, 1857, in Williams-Chesnut-Manning Papers, SCL.

up-country congressman, had remarked of the gossip that surrounded Hammond's name, "I have never been disposed to believe that anything really bad could be concealed under that beautiful face."[13]

Throughout the summer of 1857, Simms urged Hammond to go to Columbia and assert his claims to recognition. If he handled the situation wisely, Simms counseled, there might be presidential possibilities in the offing. "I believe I could make a better President than any we have had lately," the suggestible Hammond mused, but then determinedly dismissed Simms's entreaties. His years outside politics, he explained, "have *extinguished* every spark of ambition." On October 5 the Charleston *Mercury* printed the formal statement of his "determination not to be a candidate." But Hammond continued to brood about his ambitions. Late in October, as the legislative session approached, he complained of his worst attack of dyspepsia in years. "For all of my early life," he explained, "I thought I would as soon die as to make my final bow on the political stage. It seemed to me there was no life out of Affairs worth thinking of."[14]

In Columbia, Hammond's supporters were growing more confident of his election each day. On the eve of the November 27 senatorial vote, a group of followers held an anticipatory celebration. Hammond's letter declining to run, the *Mercury* asserted, should be "regarded as only the manly utterance of an independent proud man, and no positive refusal to serve the state, in case he was wanted." At home in Edgefield, Hammond reported himself "Dreadfully worried by apprehensions of being elected." Well ahead of his rivals Francis W. Pickens and James Chesnut on the first ballot, Hammond won a clear majority on the third. Spann, on the scene in Columbia, set out as soon as the final vote was counted and arrived at Redcliffe at midnight to wake his father with a jubilant announcement of his political rehabilitation.[15]

His election, Hammond's friends assured him, represented a new spirit in Carolina politics—a reinstatement of older values and a rejection of the techniques of demagoguery and electioneering that had in recent years made such remarkable inroads in the state. "This honor bestowed," Hammond's former gubernatorial secretary Beaufort Watts assured him, was "in the purity of that ancient Republic where Cincinnatus was called from his Farm to the head of the

13. Hammond Scrapbook (MS dated 1858–59, JHH Papers, LC); Waddy Thompson to Hammond, December 17, 1852, in JHH Papers, LC.
14. Hammond to Simms, August 13, 1857, in JHH Papers, LC; Charleston *Mercury*, October 5, 1857; Hammond to Simms, October 28, 1857, in JHH Papers, LC.
15. Edward McCrady to Mrs. McCrady, November 27, 1857, in McCrady Family Papers, SCL; Charleston *Mercury* clipping, Hammond Scrapbook (1858–59).

nation." The Charleston *Evening News* proclaimed that "The dynasty of mind had been again restored in South Carolina. The voice of the people has gone forth, that the reign of cliques and mediocrity shall cease." It was the fulfillment of all Hammond's fantasies of triumphant vindication.[16]

Yet his ambivalence about public life persisted. His election, he confided to his diary, "is to me a sentence of death. But it proves that no man ever had such friends & that SoCa is still capable of the utmost generosity." Others explained the victory differently; the defeated Pickens attributed his failure to Hammond's supporters' loud claims of *"persecution. . . .* Most all," Pickens consoled himself, "openly said that I ought to be elected, if public considerations were to guide, but it was necessary to put down aristocracy in the state and raise a persecuted man up." Benjamin Perry remarked upon the peculiar alliance of radicals and moderates, of proconvention and anticonvention men that had elected Hammond, and he speculated that the only explanation for the coalition was that many of the new senator's supporters had "mistaken his political views."[17]

Whatever the reason for his electoral success, Hammond was by mid-December packing for Washington. Despite the distractions of little Betty's measles and his own efforts "to beat into Harry & Spann's heads my instructions" about managing plantation affairs, Hammond had already begun to ponder the issues he faced in his new role. He wrote to a number of prominent Carolinians seeking their advice on the Kansas question already under heated debate in the Senate, confessing himself "sadly ignorant of the men & details that I must deal with." But his general remarks about programs and policies in a December 19 letter to Simms indicated decidedly moderate intentions. The violent sectionalism of his early career had been replaced by qualified unionist leanings. "I believe the slaveholding states *if united* are able to set up for themselves, but I am not in favour of their doing it so long as we can preserve the Union & the Constitution, without submitting to gross insult or permanent oppression."[18]

When Hammond arrived in Washington early in January, 1858, with his wife, son Paul, and daughters Cattie and Bet, he found a city strikingly changed from the rude capital he remembered from the 1830s. The growth in size and

16. Samuel Tupper to Hammond, December 2, 1857, William Lawton to Hammond, December 1, 1857, both in JHH Papers, LC; Charleston *Courier*, December 2, 1857; Beaufort T. Watts to Hammond, 1857, in Beaufort T. Watts Papers, SCL.

17. Hammond, "Silver Bluff, Cathwood, Cowden and Redcliffe" (MS vol. bd., 1856–87, JHH Papers, SCL), November 30, 1857; Francis W. Pickens to Lucy Holcombe, December 6, 1857, in Francis W. Pickens Papers, SCL; Benjamin F. Perry, *Reminiscences of Public Men, with Speeches and Addresses*, Second Series (Greenville, S.C.: Shannon, 1889), 107.

18. Hammond to Simms, December 19, 1857, in JHH Papers, LC; Hammond to Benjamin F.

James Henry Hammond from a photograph by Matthew Brady taken during
Hammond's term in the United States Senate.

opulence of the governmental seat could only have reminded him of the ominous expansion in federal power that it symbolized. The muddy Mall of the thirties had been transformed by the landscaping undertaken by Andrew Jackson Downing in the early 1850s, and new structures now surrounded a grassy open park. The Treasury Building, begun in 1838, the Patent Office, the Smithsonian, and the stub of the Washington monument had all been erected since his departure, imparting to the city a newly substantial and even imposing character. The Capitol itself was being expanded again, with a new extension to the House just completed and the Senate renovations still underway.[19]

Washington's society had changed almost as markedly as the city's physical setting. The emergence of political parties to replace state delegations as the units of cohesion in Congress had reduced the importance of the boardinghouse, and a number of new hotels had appeared by way of substitute. Hammond installed himself and his family in the newly remodeled Brown's, located on Pennsylvania Avenue between the Capitol and the White House.

Hammond's reputation had preceded him to Washington. The unsolicited nature of his election, remarkable even in Carolina, provoked great curiosity among legislators used to the turbulent democratic electioneering now standard throughout most of the nation. Almost at once Hammond was showered with invitations. At first these came chiefly from other southerners, men such as James Orr, Howell Cobb, and Robert Toombs of Georgia, and John Slidell of Louisiana. But soon Hammond won entree into the dinners and receptions even of such antislavery Republicans as William Seward.[20]

Washington society in the 1850s manifested a cosmopolitanism unimagined a generation earlier. A "reckless gaiety," as one Washington hostess described it, seemed to prevail everywhere. Jewels were conspicuous on men as well as women, and both sexes sported rich satins and velvets. Hosts vied in their efforts to provide the most sumptuous feasts, and Hammond promptly sent to Redcliffe for native delicacies and homemade Carolina wine to distinguish his own entertainments.[21]

Perry, December 31, 1858, Hammond to Simms, December 19, 1857, both in Benjamin F. Perry Papers, State of Alabama Department of Archives and History, Montgomery.

19. On Washington in this period, see Casimir Bohn, *Bohn's Handbook of Washington* (Washington, D.C.: C. Bohn, 1856); Mary J. Windle, *Life in Washington and Life Here and There* (Philadelphia: Lippincott, 1859); Daniel D. Reiff, *Washington Architecture, 1791–1861: Problems in Development* (Washington, D.C.: U.S. Commission of Fine Arts, 1971); Virginia Clay-Clopton, *A Belle of the Fifties* (New York: Doubleday, Page, 1905).

20. Hammond Account and Memorandum Book (MS vol. bd., 1858, JHH Papers, SCL).

21. Clay-Clopton, *A Belle*, 86.

Catherine was overwhelmed by the sophistication and display. It "has been my endeavor," she confided in a letter to Marcellus, "to conform as much as possible to the customs of the place. . . . I began to despair of making anything but blunders & mistakes, & heartily wished myself at home before I should be disgraced." At one reception with Cattie and Paul, Catherine became so "confused & anxious" she was unable in conversation to name the members of the Carolina delegation. Surrounded by men, Cattie was annoyed when her mother insisted they had to leave at once. Hammond, home "snugly in bed," laughed at their "disaster," but Catherine so feared a repetition of her embarrassment at a dinner scheduled at the White House the following week that she consulted two other Carolina wives for instruction in etiquette. The evening with the president went off splendidly, and Catherine's only complaint was that she was not given the seat next to Buchanan. Her husband, however, received more attention from the president than any other guest, and Catherine was delighted with his triumph. "In a word," she summed up the situation in Washington, "he is in his place."[22]

Hammond himself was not so confident of his standing. His public demeanor was reserved, prompting one observer to describe him soon after his arrival as a "noble-browed, middle aged man, who maintains a species of dignity, of all dignities the most imposing—a self-seclusion." Hammond's apparent aloofness actually bespoke his feelings of ill ease. At home on the plantation his authority was long since established; here he had, as he recognized, to get "hold of the ropes" and win it anew.[23]

Hammond's anxieties focused most sharply on his role within the stormy world of the Senate chamber, for it was there he knew his reputation must be won. His first entry into the hall the day after his arrival reassured him somewhat, for the "great guns," he found, "do not look so awfully great as one might expect." The South, he soon discovered, was in political disarray, "unorganized & . . . demoralized." He sensed that most southern congressmen regarded him with suspicion, fearing him as a rival rather than welcoming him as an ally, even though the times demanded united and decisive action.[24]

The new South Carolina senator arrived in the midst of a session already

22. Catherine Fitzsimons Hammond to M. C. M. Hammond, February 6, 1858, in JHH Papers, LC.

23. Windle, *Life In Washington*, 281; Hammond to Harry Hammond, January 14, 1858, in JHH Papers, SCL.

24. Hammond to M. C. M. Hammond, January 10, 1858, Hammond to Simms, January 20, 1858, both in JHH Papers, LC.

disrupted by the bitter struggle over the status of slavery in Kansas. In May, 1854, Stephen Douglas, senator from Illinois, had secured passage of the Kansas-Nebraska Act, which proposed the organization of these two territories with the slavery issue to be determined by the principle of popular sovereignty. Even though it seemed unlikely, given the realities of climate and geography, that either of the territories in question would ever be a slave state, the act invited proslavery and antislavery forces to vie for control of Kansas. New Englanders formed immigrant aid societies to fill the area with settlers hostile to the peculiar institution; southerners moved across the Missouri border to lay their claims on the disputed land. Between 1854 and 1857, violence held sway as bands of ruffians from each side sought to consolidate their position. Attempts to establish governmental order produced only fraudulent elections, and separate proslavery and antislavery governments emerged, each claiming legitimacy and demanding federal recognition.

When James Buchanan entered the White House in 1857, he moved at once to settle the issue, for he feared that the violence could not long be contained in the West. Dispatching a trusted associate to serve as territorial governor, Buchanan called for a new popularly supported constitution to serve as the basis for Kansas statehood. In June, elections were held for a constitutional convention, but the antislavery forces, fearing intimidation at the polls, abstained from voting. The proslavery forces gathered at Lecompton, Kansas, to produce a document that provided essentially no option on the slavery issue, permitting the electorate a choice only in limiting the future immigration of unfree labor, but not challenging the status of those slaves who had already arrived. To the antislavery forces this seemed a violation of Buchanan's earlier promise to permit an open vote on the government instrument and the future of slavery. When the Lecompton Constitution was submitted to Congress as part of the territory's formal application for statehood, the battle over Kansas moved to the halls of the Capitol.[25]

Hammond came to Washington without firm views on the Kansas question. He was not, he emphasized in a letter to Simms, "in favour of any further extension of Slave Territory." The South's existing borders included "ample ground to make ourselves the Ruling Power of the World . . . our vocation should be to develop our resources & consolidate the South." Hammond indicated he would

25. For general background on the political crises of this period and on the Kansas issue in particular, see David Potter, *The Impending Crisis, 1848–1861* (New York: Harper and Row, 1976).

"vote with *indifference* for the L[ecompton] Cons[titution] & *repudiate* the question as a test on slavery." Simms quickly responded with a sharply worded warning. "You *cannot* vote with indifference upon a subject which, you admit, involves the honour, if not the safety of the South," he insisted. "It does not matter what value you put upon Kansas. It does not matter how erring were your predecessors in making a test of its *proslavery* conditions. . . . The fact is patent, that it is made so. . . . You cannot repudiate the test."[26]

More than a decade earlier Hammond had similarly regarded the Wilmot Proviso as a false issue. Territorial expansion, Hammond was convinced, was not the South's most pressing concern and indeed promised more dangers than benefits. The important issue in Hammond's mind was the distribution of power within the nation's existing boundaries. But when the controversy over the Wilmot Proviso had been transformed into a symbolic contest for political control in Congress, Hammond had at last agreed that the South could not yield. Similarly, he accepted Simms's judgment about the significance of Kansas. Sobered by his friend's warning against a lukewarm stand, Hammond conceded the issue's importance as a challenge to the South's power and her "honour."[27]

Beset by uncertainties, Hammond postponed making any statement of his position on the Senate floor. Instead he delivered dozens of "senatorial speeches—to myself" until he began to feel he could no longer keep silent. "I fear when I start I shall say too much." At last on March 4, nearly two full months after his arrival, he was ready. "Tall, long-limbed, bald-headed, spectacled, clothed in black," he arose to address his colleagues on the Kansas question. But his defense of the Lecompton Constitution departed rapidly from the details of territorial conflict to issues with which Hammond felt more comfortable. Responding to Stephen Douglas' recent denunciation of the proposed Kansas charter as a violation of his doctrine of popular sovereignty, Hammond attacked Douglas' position as demagoguery. No territorial legislature could prohibit slavery. This was a right reserved exclusively to the states. The actions of a constitutional convention, he argued, drawing further upon the states' rights theories in which he and every other educated Carolinian had been schooled, were the proper vehicle for popular expression and must be heeded.[28]

26. Hammond to Simms, January 20, 1858, Simms to Hammond, January 28, 1858, both in JHH Papers, LC.
27. Simms to Hammond, January 28, 1858, *ibid.*
28. Hammond to Simms, February 7, 1858, *ibid.*; Boston *Traveller* clipping in Hammond Scrapbook (1858–59).

But he warned the Senate that the purpose of this prolonged agitation over the legitimacy of the Lecompton Constitution had wider significance. The congressional opponents of Lecompton, he asserted, were more interested in destroying the Democratic party in the North than in defeating an allegedly fraudulent constitution. "The true object of the discussion . . . is to agitate the question of slavery" and to isolate the South from any northern sympathy. Destroying the Democratic party, with its moderate policies toward the South, would widen the sectional breach and array all the forces of the North against the peculiar institution. The real intentions of the free states, Hammond argued, had been made clear the previous day in Seward's pronouncement to the Senate that the South was now a "conquered province." How could his region long remain in such a Union, where she had to depend on the good will of the North rather than on a set of assured rights? "We cannot rely on your faith when you have the power." The South had to have constitutional guarantees of her safety.[29]

If the South chose direct confrontation, Hammond continued boldly, her fundamental power would become clear. The region's political weakness in the nation disguised the superior strength of her social and economic systems. "If we never acquire another foot of territory," Hammond insisted, the South was already powerful enough to win and sustain her independence. She had a militia of a million men, an export trade substantially larger than that of the North, and through the production of cotton, a hold on the economic well-being of the world. "No," he declared defiantly, "you dare not make war on cotton. No power on earth dares make war on it. Cotton *is* King."[30]

But the South's greatest strength lay in her social system, in the "harmony of her political and social institutions," in the ready availability of that class of low intelligence necessary to do the menial labor in any society. And by establishing this "mud-sill" class as slaves, the South had ensured their welfare in a manner far more humane than the North's treatment of its workers. The South, Hammond asserted, had sustained the nation economically, socially, and politically. This southern influence, he concluded, "has been the cause of your peace and prosperity." If, as Seward had threatened, the North was about to "take the Government from us," if the balance of power in the nation was irrevocably to shift, Hammond cautioned, "Time will show what you will make of her; but no time can diminish our glory or your responsibility."[31]

29. *Congressional Globe*, 35th Cong. 1st Sess., Appendix, 69–70.
30. *Ibid.*, 70.   31. *Ibid.*, 71.

Hammond intended his speech both as a warning to the North and as a rally-ing cry to the South; it was meant to generate the pride and confidence the sena-tor had long found lacking among his compatriots. "I have to-day made my de-but," he wrote Marcellus with satisfaction. "I did as well as I expected." Paul, seated in the Senate gallery, thought the address had been delivered so slowly as to ruin its effect. "I did it," Hammond explained, "partly because I was embar-rassed, partly that I wished to appear calm and unexcited & may have carried it too far." The New York *Tribune* agreed with Hammond's assessment of his or-atorical skills: he had neither the "graces" of Preston, nor the "fire" of McDuffie. His "pen," the paper concluded, "is a more persuasive instrument than his tongue."[32]

Whatever his oratorical deficiencies, Hammond achieved national promi-nence with his provocative speech. The South responded with enthusiasm, and a subscription for twenty-five thousand copies of the address was raised almost at once. The Memphis *Avalanche* awarded Hammond "the mantle of the illustrious Calhoun," and the Charleston *Courier* expressed exasperation at his "meta-physico-political" abstractions, but declared its support for the substantive por-tions of the address. With "one bold stroke of Senatorial eloquence," the *Mer-cury* noted, Hammond "leaps into the almost inaccessible niche occupied by Calhoun."[33]

Predictably, the North displayed no such enthusiasm. While critics objected to various points of Hammond's address, finding his constitutional doctrines faulty and his economic and trade statistics inaccurate, most attacks were di-rected against his "mud-sill" doctrine of social stratification. Newspapers as far away as San Francisco deplored his antidemocratic sentiments, while as close as the Senate chamber itself, colleagues of obscure origins took offense. Even one southerner, the humble former tailor, Andrew Johnson of Tennessee, protested vigorously against what he perceived as a personal affront. The North, Ham-mond wrote proudly to Simms, "is in arms against me. While the papers come down on me column after column, not a speech here since has not been over half in answer to me."[34]

32. Hammond to M. C. M. Hammond, March 4, 1858, in JHH Papers, LC; New York *Tribune* clipping in Hammond Scrapbook (1858–59).
33. Hammond to M. C. M. Hammond, March 9, 1858, in JHH Papers, LC; Memphis *Ava-lanche*, Charleston *Mercury* and Charleston *Courier* clippings in Hammond Scrapbook (1858–59).
34. Hammond to Simms, March 22, 1858, in JHH Papers, LC. A survey of southern news-papers reveals that Hammond's aristocratic statements elicited essentially no negative response from the South or Southwest.

Late in March, the Lecompton Constitution passed the Senate with Hammond voting in favor despite some reservations about the constitutionality of the wording of the bill. The new senator was exhausted by the long days of wrangling, by the hours spent in Finance and Naval Appropriations Committee meetings and by the extensive reading and preparation the senatorial debates :equired. "I feel worn down every day & don't get rested by morning," he complained. He had made his long-awaited speech, but he feared, "it will soon be said I can't make another, & the amount of it is that I have got to *work*, when I had made all my calculations never to work any more." Besides, he grumbled to Simms, who was urging him to speak again soon, "I don't feel at home here yet."[35]

Yet Hammond was welcomed into a round of almost constant parties; he had become a coveted guest in Washington's most prominent circles. Lord Napier, impressed by the March 4 oration, requested an introduction and invited the entire Hammond family to an elegant soiree at his residence. Spann, recently arrived from Carolina, accompanied his father and his mother, who laughingly complained herself "ruined" by the presence of a grown son whose age testified unmistakably to her own.

When he left Washington at the end of the session in June, 1858, Hammond still felt himself a stranger within the city's political and social world. He was disappointed in his failure to establish a more commanding reputation; he had not conquered Washington, yet he could not settle for less. "I have not put myself forward to lead," he explained to Simms. "If I come back I *must* do it."[36]

Despite his determination to triumph, he found himself at critical moments almost incapacitated, and he blamed his failures on the "mephitic air" of the dank Senate chamber. "Out of that hall I feel I have the power to do it. In it, I am stupefied by the infernal air." By the next session of Congress the Senate would be installed in new and well-ventilated quarters, and Hammond would have to find a different rationalization for his paralyzing conflicts. The "intense, compelling will of high ambition," he lamented, "is no more with me."[37]

Hammond's return to Carolina provided no release from these tensions. His

35. Hammond to M. C. M. Hammond, March 26, 1858, Hammond to Simms, May 3, 1858, both in JHH Papers, LC.
36. Catherine Fitzsimons Hammond to M. C. M. Hammond, June 8, 1858, Edward Spann Hammond to M. C. M. Hammond, June 11, 1858, both in JHH Papers, SCL; Windle, *Life in Washington*, 322; Hammond to Simms, June 20, July 3, 1858, both in JHH Papers, LC.
37. Hammond to Simms, July 3, 1858, in JHH Papers, LC.

constituents were eager for their senator's account of the sectional battles that had raged in Washington throughout the winter and spring and for an explanation of what many perceived as Hammond's hesitation on the Kansas issue. Hammond dreaded the obligatory stump speeches. Simms and other enthusiastic supporters had organized a barbecue for fifteen hundred guests at the clubhouse of the Beech Island Agricultural Society on July 22 as a homecoming celebration for him. After the oratory of visiting dignitaries from Charleston, Columbia, and Augusta, Hammond's own address on the status and prospects of the South within the Union climaxed the day.[38]

Hammond began by assuring his listeners of the pleasure he felt at being among friends and neighbors where he was free to speak with more frankness than in the Senate. But his candid remarks, reported at length by the press, produced an uproar in the state. The senator's positions were in fact little different from those he had shared privately with his closest friends over the several preceding years. But at Beech Island, he first made his new conservatism public and explicit. Concentrating on possibilities for the South within the Union, Hammond eschewed secessionist rhetoric and placed greater emphasis on the responsibilities of the South than upon the transgressions of the North. Sectional reform and uplift, he insisted as he had for more than a decade, were a necessary prerequisite to the true salvation of the South. As the Charleston *Evening News* summarized, Hammond insisted that "the real battle to be fought was a moral, not a physical one. The Senator desired to see that battle fought and won, and the South to *rule* the Union. He did not mean the mere party or sectional rule which spring from success in elections and holding of office, but the ascendancy of the civilization and doctrine upon which the South had placed its stamp—which it had peculiarly developed. It is the patriarchal system in organism and character." The South's ultimate triumph must be in the realm of spirit and mind—not in the arena of political power.[39]

To his old states' rights allies, Hammond's position seemed a betrayal. Even many moderates, as R. B. Rhett, Jr., explained, regarded Hammond's views as "calculated to give aid and strength to unmitigated unionists and submissionists

---

38. Hammond to M. C. M. Hammond, June 30, 1858, *ibid.* See Charleston *Mercury*, July 26, 1858. See also Hammond's explanation of why he voted for the compromise Conference Bill instead of insisting upon preservation of the Senate version of the bill for Kansas statehood in Hammond to William P. Miles, November 17, 1858, in William Porcher Miles Papers, SHC.

39. Charleston *Evening News*, July 29, 1858; Charleston *Mercury*, January 12, 1859.

. . . while depressing and weakening the earnest advocates of resistance." One such resister, Maxcy Gregg, reported "Something like despair . . . caused by so heavy a blow coming from such a quarter." Although Hammond himself expressed little overt sympathy for the national Democrats and continued to insist that all parties were instruments of political spoils and corruption, Gregg and his followers regarded the Beech Island address as an announcement of Hammond's defection to Orr's camp. As summarized in the press, the speech appeared to one alarmed Charleston friend to yield all claim to a southern share in the territories and to abandon as well the notion of a southern confederacy as ultimate recourse against further northern aggression.[40]

Hammond was at first bewildered by the denunciations that appeared in the press. But he soon dismissed the "fuss" as the work of a coterie of Carolina politicians agitating to reopen the African slave trade. Any voice of conciliation would weaken their cause—which Hammond viewed as "treasonable to the South"—because of the divisions it would inevitably promote. Nothing, he believed, especially not a goal as unnecessary as reviving slave importations, should interfere with slowly emerging southern unity. Carolinians who viewed his speech as a betrayal of the South, Hammond complained to Simms, had badly misunderstood his true position. "You deserve it," Simms retorted, explaining, "You have been too careless of public opinion." He urged Hammond to publicly clarify his stance. A number of Hammond's supporters agreed that the senator must appease the injured states' rights faction by offering a second, carefully worded address that would be simultaneously submitted to the press. Hammond began to prepare an oration to deliver at Barnwell on October 29. Whatever the import of the address, a friend warned the senator, this time he must ensure "that it be *clothed in the garb of States Rights.*"[41]

Despite his effort to dismiss the critics of his Beech Island address as a few extremists, Hammond had been deeply wounded by the hostility he had aroused.

40. Robert Barnwell Rhett to Hammond, August 2, 1858, in JHH Papers, LC; Maxcy Gregg quoted in Schultz, *Nationalism and Sectionalism*, 174; Oscar Lieber to Francis Lieber, August 3, 1858, in Francis Lieber Papers, SCL; Maxcy Gregg to Robert Barnwell Rhett, September 14, 1858, in Robert Barnwell Rhett Papers, South Carolina Historical Society, Charleston; Cunningham to Hammond, October 9, 1858, in JHH Papers, LC; Charleston *Mercury*, August 2, 1858.
41. Hammond to M. C. M. Hammond, August 10, 1858, in JHH Papers, LC; Simms to Hammond, in Mary C. Simms Oliphant, Alfred Taylor Odell, and T. C. Duncan Eaves (eds.), *The Letters of William Gilmore Simms* (5 vols.; Columbia: University of South Carolina Press, 1952–56), IV, 90; Cunningham to Hammond, October 9, 1858, in JHH Papers, LC. See Ronald T. Takaki, *A Pro-Slavery Crusade: The Agitation to Reopen the African Slave Trade* (New York: Free Press, 1971).

All summer, he reported to Simms, he found himself "bleeding or constipated by turns owing I believe to my condition of intense suspense in all matters public and private." He even described the return of "those nervous times" that had driven him from Congress more than two decades before. Yet throughout the stultifying days of July and August and even into early fall, Hammond knew "nothing can bring me right until after the crucifixion at Barnwell." Even then, resurrection was not assured. Hammond's views on the mounting sectional conflict were inconsistent with those of many of the most powerful men of his state. "For 15 or 20 of the best years of my life I was a disunionist—a disunionist *per se* if I may use that expression. But latterly I have changed my opinion." Having seen the South's successes in the Union—with banks, with the tariff, and even in the courts with the recent Dred Scott decision—Hammond felt far less commitment to sectional independence than he once had. Perhaps this shift in views was simply a logical reassessment of the South's changed position in the nation. But it represented an altered sense of his personal political strategy as well. In his attempt to assume the mantle of the dead Calhoun, Hammond had taken on the fallen statesman's role as mediator between state and nation. And although he almost always vehemently denied any ambition for higher office, Hammond, like Calhoun, may have been encouraged in his antisecessionist posture by unspoken presidential hopes.[42]

On a warm and rainy Friday, Hammond delivered his "long looked for speech" to an audience made up almost entirely of local Barnwell citizens. Maxcy Gregg and other prominent Carolina figures had declined to attend because of what Gregg described as Hammond's support for the "enemies of our old State Rights faith." Ravaged by the tensions of the preceding months, Hammond was unable to complete more than half his oration, and the remainder was read to the assembled crowd. Although it was a more precise statement of his views than had been included in the garbled reports of the Beech Island address, Hammond knew it still remained "too full of truth for present digestion."[43]

As at Beech Island, the senator advocated confident moderation. Defending

---

42. Hammond to Simms, September 21, October 26, 1858, both in JHH Papers, LC; Hammond to M. C. M. Hammond, October 22, 1858, in JHH Papers, SCL; Hammond, untitled manuscript, n.d., JHH Papers, LC.

43. Hammond, "Silver Bluff, Cathwood, Cowden, and Redcliffe," October 31, 1858; Maxcy Gregg to A. P. Aldrich and the Barnwell Committee, October 23, 1858, in JHH Papers, LC; Hammond to Miles, November 5, 1858, in Miles Papers; Hammond to Simms, November 3, 1858, in JHH Papers, LC.

his position on the Kansas question, explaining the impracticability of reopening the slave trade, Hammond challenged the hope that the South might extend her system of agriculture and of unfree labor into presently or potentially available territory. Slavery could not flourish in the deserts of the West. Nor, he insisted, would the conquest of Mexico, with its population of "mongrels," benefit the South. Instead of concentrating their attention on "visionary" schemes of recovering equality in Congress, southerners should "look every consequence of our position full in the face." As she now stood, Hammond emphasized, the South already possessed one of the "most powerful people who now flourish on the globe." To those who insisted that the South could protect her safety and achieve her destiny only through secession, Hammond responded, "Perhaps so. But permit me to suggest, not yet." The achievements of southern power in the nation since 1820 demonstrated unequivocally that "no measure has yet been strong enough to stand against the South when united." In an evocation of Jefferson's legendary 1800 call for a unity to transcend party divisions, Hammond declared himself at once a national Democrat and a "State-Rights man." The South, he concluded, could expect a "magnificent future" within the Union.[44]

Hammond's gestures toward northern allies did not pass unnoticed in the free states. The northern press responded with enthusiasm to the Barnwell address, hailing it as a basis for interregional cooperation and conciliation. Hammond seemed to be making a direct overture to northern moderates. "There has not lately been heard a more contemptuous, though quiet reproof," the New York *Times* reported, "of the whole body of extreme Southern men and measures," and the New York *Herald* suggested Hammond as a "Southern Union candidate" for the presidency in 1860. But radical Carolinians were even more alienated than they had been by the Beech Island address. The fire-eaters now regarded him as a "traitor."[45]

Hammond did not remain in Carolina long enough to make a full assessment of state reaction to his speech. At the end of November he departed once again for Washington, where he moved with his family into five rooms at the National

44. Hammond, *Selections from the Letters and Speeches of the Hon. James H. Hammond, of South Carolina* (New York: John F. Trow, 1866), 336, 339, 340, 343, 355.
45. New York *Times*, reprinted in Columbia *South Carolinian*, November 9, 1858; New York *Herald* clipping in Hammond Scrapbook (1858–59); Lewis Cass to Hammond, November 6, 1858, Hammond to M. C. M. Hammond, November 28, 1858, April 10, 1859, all in JHH Papers, LC. See Plain Truth's attacks on Hammond in the Charleston *Mercury*, January 12, 14, 21, 24, 28, February 1, 10, 21, 25, 1859.

Hotel. Although Catherine much preferred the ease of these public accommodations, Hammond persuaded her to set up housekeeping in a rented dwelling across from the Navy Office Building. Here Hammond sought to maintain at least a modicum of privacy despite the steady stream of callers who testified to his new national stature.

The Barnwell address, he wrote to Simms, had "secured to me the ear of the whole country & imposed upon it the belief that I am honest, disinterested, & fearless . . . not without a fair share of talent. The thinking & patriotic men want just such a man for the next Presidency. . . . But as it is," he quickly added, "I would as soon think of scaling the walls of heaven." If Hammond discounted talk of his candidacy, his opponents in Carolina were nevertheless sufficiently alarmed to launch a series of newspaper attacks intended to undermine their native son's chances for the presidency. A Carolinian in a position of national political prominence, they recognized, would inevitably weaken the state's commitment to disunion.[46]

Although Hammond continued to insist that he lacked the physical constitution necessary for higher office, he was clearly gratified by the national response to his Barnwell address. Carolina's radicals, it seemed to Hammond, were serving as *"recruiting sergeants* for Seward" and the black Republicans; their extremism served only to aid the abolitionist enemy. Once faltering for "want of fuel," abolition was by mid-1859, Hammond believed, entirely reenergized by southern radicalism. The illegal landing of a shipload of Africans in the Georgia up-country just across the river from Silver Bluff enraged Hammond as yet another example of regional folly, close enough to home to be viewed as a direct rebuke to his own anti-slave-trade views. With his intimates he began to discuss the possibility of resigning his Senate seat before the December, 1859, session. Unless he were to admit to presidential ambitions, Hammond could see no further heights to scale. And he was exasperated by the fire-eaters' continual sniping. "I am ready to throw up my hands & retire," he wrote Simms in July, 1859.[47]

The viability of moderation and the possibility of peaceful sectional compromise within the framework of the Constitution were fatally undermined by the

46. Hammond to Simms, January 1, 1859, Peyton Bowman to Hammond, January 24, 1859, both in JHH Papers, LC. The Savannah *Republican* nominated Hammond for president on February 26.
47. Hammond to M. C. M. Hammond, April 10, 1859, Hammond to Simms, April 22, July 30, 1859, all in JHH Papers, LC.

events of mid-October. John Brown, a fanatical abolitionist trained in the battles of Bleeding Kansas, and a band of twenty-two followers seized the federal arsenal at Harpers Ferry, Virginia, intending to trigger a slave insurrection in the South. Brown and his men were quickly captured, but expressions of sympathy from the northern press combined with revelations of abolitionists' financial support to confirm the South's worst fears. Brown's raid seemed to offer nearly irrefutable evidence of the northern conspiracy against the South that Hammond had denied. In the view of the radical Robert Barnwell Rhett, the Harpers Ferry incident was simply "fact coming to the aid of logic." Northern hostility seemed implacable and unbounded, hardly subject to the kinds of compromise Hammond had been advocating.[48]

In the atmosphere of crisis that prevailed in the late fall of 1859, Hammond could not refuse to return to the Senate. "I fear it would appear like shrinking from duty not to go," he confided to a friend. Yet Hammond knew well that unity did not exist, even within South Carolina. In Columbia the legislature was debating secession, and Governor William Gist had declared that with Brown's incursion the North had "crossed the Rubicon." Yet Hammond himself still dissented from the intensifying disunionist sentiment in his state. He postponed leaving for the capital again and again, and finally departed for Washington "more reluctantly than John Brown did to the gallows." He was, he feared, about to become a martyr to constitutionalism and moderation.[49]

The Thirty-sixth Congress convened in December, 1859, under a cloud of sectional hostility. When Hammond had first come to Washington nearly a quarter century before, he had thrown himself into the effort to gag congressional debate about slavery altogether. Now the legislative body seemed able to discuss nothing else. The choice of a Speaker of the House, usually a routine matter, evolved into a bitter and protracted sectional battle centered on the candidates' attitudes to Hinton Rowan Helper's *The Impending Crisis*, an antislavery publication that deeply offended the sensibilities of its author's native South. Discussion of naval appropriations was quickly diverted into a consideration of suppression of the illegal African slave trade; debate on the Homestead Bill prompted a resumption of the struggle over the status of slavery in the territo-

---

48. Charleston *Mercury*, October 31, 1859.
49. Hammond to Watts, December 6, 1859, in Watts Papers, SCL; Hammond to Simms, December 19, 1859, in JHH Papers, LC. Gist quoted in Steven A. Channing, *Crisis of Fear: Secession in South Carolina* (New York: W. W. Norton, 1970), 95.

ries. Members of Congress had begun to arm. "The only persons who do not have a revolver and a knife," Hammond reported, "are those who have two revolvers." The Carolinian kept a pistol in his desk, but could not bring himself to carry it with him about the Capitol.[50]

This constant agitation of the slavery issue, Hammond complained, directly undermined the constitutional principles that formed the South's strongest defense. Congressional discussion of human bondage implied the possibility of legislative action, which Hammond believed the Constitution prohibited. Moreover, deliberation about slavery in Congress suggested that there was an issue to debate. Hammond insisted that any questions that had ever existed about the peculiar institution had long been settled by southerners themselves, the only Americans who had either jurisdiction or responsibility over slavery. "We have made up our minds." What the North might think, he declared, mattered little, for it was the South that bore the duty and burden of her domestic institutions.[51]

Opposed to every approach to the slavery issue that did not insist upon absolute congresssional nonintervention, Hammond despaired both of the North's meddling and of the South's failure to uphold those states' rights constitutional principles that served as the region's strongest defense. The resolutions of Senator Jefferson Davis of Mississippi calling for a congressional slave code for the territories subverted the South's power and legitimacy as surely as did any direct attack from the North. As the lengthy congressional session stretched into the oppressive Washington summer, Hammond found a new role, employing the motion for adjournment again and again as a weapon to silence Senate discussion of slavery. He intended his procedural gambit as a latter-day gag rule, but in the changed political atmosphere it more often interrupted than terminated what was fast becoming a marathon debate.

Over all of Washington hovered an anxious expectancy about the approaching presidential contest. The Republicans seemed certain to nominate abolitionist William Seward, who had proclaimed the existence of an "irrepressible conflict" between slave and free states. Could the Democrats settle on a candidate who could prevent the breakup of the Union? Stephen Douglas, the most prominent member of the party, had alienated the South with his opposition to the Lecompton Constitution, and many southerners, like Hammond, found unacceptable his advocacy of "squatter sovereignty" as the principle for determin-

50. Potter, *The Impending Crisis*, 389.
51. *Congressional Globe*, 36th Cong. 1st Sess., p. 1633.

ing the status of slavery in the territories. Not only did this doctrine smack of "mobocracy"; it gave territorial governments, agents of Congress, powers that rightfully belonged only to states.[52]

By spring Hammond had abandoned his own presidential hopes. The initial suggestion of his name by the press had generated no powerful movement for his nomination, and he now pled ill health as an explanation for not pursuing the nation's highest office. Robert M. T. Hunter, he believed, would make the best Democratic choice, for the Virginian might possibly unite North and South. As the Democratic Convention gathered in Charleston late in April, Hammond expressed confidence that the party would recognize Hunter as the solution to the sectional crisis. Although Hammond insisted upon his continuing opposition to the demagoguery represented by party nominating conventions, he wired the leader of South Carolina's delegation, urging him to support Hunter and to withdraw entirely if two other cotton states walked out in objection to either the nominee or the platform.

The Charleston convention never reached the point of considering nominees. When William Yancey of Alabama demanded that a federal slave code for the territories be included as a plank in the party platform, northern Democrats refused to comply. Unable to break the deadlock, Yancey and his delegation stalked out of the hall, followed by all the lower South, including South Carolina. Even as the cords of union were snapping about him, Hammond sought to remain optimistic about his own position. Carolina had been the third state to withdraw—just as he had counseled, Hammond noted with satisfaction, regarding this as a clear vindication of the power and influence he still held over the state. He seemed not even to notice that the issue on which the South had chosen to take her stand—the demand for a federal slave code—was one he had bitterly opposed. The senator had begun struggling to retain his identification with the South as she moved toward the impending crisis.

When Carolinians gathered in Charleston late in May to discuss policy for the southern Democratic Convention now scheduled for Richmond, Hammond forwarded an official declaration of his continuing confidence in the strength of the South, within or—he prudently added—without the Union. With "our surplus productions of cotton, rice, sugar &c. and our substructure of black slaves, *we are safe.*" Mounting southern fear, he argued, had no foundation in reality; this was a time for calm deliberation, not for the hysteria of "wild resolves" and

---

52. *Ibid.*, 2213, 2211–212; Hammond to Simms, April 8, 1860, in JHH Papers, LC.

"absurd bravados." Above all, he warned, nothing should be done to threaten the region's emerging unity.[53]

Late in June the strife-ridden congressional session at last drew to a close and Hammond headed wearily toward home, grateful for a release from the capital's incessant demands. But within a fortnight of his return, he had begun to complain of the boredom of life at Redcliffe, where he had neither politics nor plantation management to occupy his mind. He began to anticipate his return to Washington and to contemplate standing for reelection in December when the seat he had filled upon A. P. Butler's death came again before the legislature. But South Carolina's radicals had begun to move against Hammond, branding him a defector and attempting to expose the extent of his conservatism by demanding in the press that he specify the steps he would advocate in the case of a Republican presidential victory. Hammond sought to evade this question, for he knew his views would only fuel the hostility of the states' rights faction. Instead he continued to emphasize his confidence that Breckinridge and Lane, the candidates chosen by the rump Democratic convention in Richmond, would be elected and would preserve the Union by destroying black republicanism. In private, he confided to friends that Lincoln's election seemed a poor excuse for secession, for in itself it embodied no constitutional violation. He worried that South Carolina might once again act in foolish radical isolation.[54]

By October confusion over his position had reached such heights and seemed so threatening to his election that Hammond began to draft a letter on his views of the current crisis to present to the legislature when it convened in November. If Carolina seceded, he pledged in an appeal to his detractors, he would support her. But he urged his compatriots to moderate their radicalism. If they were to secede, they must choose a constitutional issue that would provide the strongest ideological basis for separation. Otherwise, "we throw from us and trample upon the aegis of the Constitution." And above all they should yield the leadership in disunion to another state untarnished by Carolina's reputation for impotent extremism.[55]

His support for the Union, Hammond explained, arose from his conviction of the South's strength within it, and he cited as evidence the victories the

53. Hammond to H. D. Lesesne, May 15, 1860, printed in Charleston *Mercury*, May 21, 1860.
54. G. D. Tillman to Hammond, October 9, 1860, in JHH Papers, LC; Hammond to Milledge Luke Bonham, October 3, 1860, in Milledge Luke Bonham Papers, SCL; Lawrence M. Keitt to Hammond, October 23, 1860, in JHH Papers, LC.
55. Hammond to Aldrich, November 8, 1860, in JHH Papers, LC.

South had achieved in recent years. If united, he insisted as he had for nearly a decade, the South could dictate national policy. His dread of secession arose not from anxieties about war with the North, which he thought very unlikely, but from his concern that disorder would give demagogues within the South an opportunity to restructure the region's political institutions. "The little great men who would seek notoriety by proposing to elect Judges, Senators and Representatives annually and perhaps by universal suffrage, must be kept from putting their hands upon our Constitution or we shall soon have the guillotine at work upon good men."[56]

Early in November a group of legislators in Columbia officially requested the statement on the current crisis that Hammond had nearly completed. Two days after Lincoln's election, he forwarded it to the state capital. But before the legislators had time even to consider Hammond's views, the senator had resigned. On the morning of November 11, twenty minutes after receiving a notification from James Chesnut that he had withdrawn from Carolina's other Senate seat, Hammond penned his own resignation. The gesture implied more decisiveness than Hammond truly felt. He confided to Simms that he was uncertain why Chesnut had acted, and he confessed that he had followed his lead simply in the interests of solidarity. "You know the Japanese have an *ancient* custom, which therefore must have its uses, of ripping up their own bowels to revenge an insult." The Carolina delegation, he mused, had "done pretty much that" in resigning. Hammond's moderate statement, sent off to Columbia less than a week before, no longer had any relevance in the rising tide of secession. Its conservative tone seemed so out of place that Hammond's friends in Columbia suppressed the document.[57]

As citizens gathered in Beech Island and other communities throughout the state to form cavalry patrols and vigilance committees to meet the crisis, Hammond began to adjust to the reality of radical triumph. Addressing a political meeting at nearby Hamburg, he delivered a stirring call for southern unity behind Carolina, which seemed certain to secede before Christmas. The southern nation he had so long envisioned was coming into existence almost in spite of him, under circumstances he had proclaimed unwise and inauspicious. "I have not incurred one iota of the responsibility of the move," he observed with rueful

56. *Ibid.*
57. Hammond to Simms, November 13, 1860, in JHH Papers, SCL. See also Hammond to M. C. M. Hammond, November 12, 1860, in JHH Papers, LC.

irony. Yet this would not prevent him from regarding the infant confederacy as his own offspring. "I will support it with all the strength I have." But sadly for Hammond, the new nation would not look to him as a progenitor. His moderation of the preceding decade had undermined his influence and legitimacy with the secessionists who now claimed victory.[58]

58. Hammond to Simms, November 13, 1860, in JHH Papers, SCL.

CHAPTER 17

The Time to Die

HAMMOND SOON ABANDONED all reservations about secession. The prompt response of other states to Carolina's lead surprised and delighted him, and he hastened to embrace the separatism he had so recently deplored. "The moment I saw that it was a movement of the *People* of the South" and not just a "bullying movement of the politicians," he explained, "I went into it with all my Soul." Once the first step had been taken, he insisted that no compromise should halt progress toward the southern confederacy that he still regarded as "the cherished dream and hope of my life."[1]

Hammond's enthusiasm seemed at first almost boundless. Belittling the likelihood of war with the North, he confidently expected diplomatic recognition from England and France within forty days. He rejoiced at the successful resistance of the Confederate Constitutional Convention to pressures for democratization, and even defended the new Confederate tariff as a necessary revenue measure free from any taint of despised protectionism. But this optimism was not long to last. The appointment of Jefferson Davis to the Confederate presidency brought the first appearance of Hammond's disenchantment, for the former Mississippi senator had snubbed him in Washington, and Hammond judged him the "most irascible man I ever knew. . . . [He was] as vain as a peacock as ambitious as the Devil." Perhaps even more important to Hammond's growing disaffection, however, was the gradual recognition that his belated enthusiasm would not compensate in the public eye for his years of opposition to the movement for

1. James Henry Hammond to Dear Sir, January 18, 1861, Hammond to J. D. Ashmore, April 2, 1861, both in JHH Papers, LC.

southern independence. Hammond could not ignore the failure of any constituency within the state to advance his name for office under the new regime, and he noted as well that the secession convention had not so much as sought his views. He insisted publicly that ill health had compelled his complete withdrawal from political life, but in private he could not help but regard his treatment in this hour of crisis as a "censure upon me and my Senatorial career."[2]

But Hammond's growing isolation was not entirely the result of his nationalist past. Throughout the war he would carp at Confederate policies, certain that his own notions of finance, military strategy, and constitutional government would far more effectively serve the southern cause. The crisis he had identified in the antebellum years seemed only intensified under the pressures of the conflict. He complained that there was not "a Statesman, a General or a Financier & in the South no qualities whatever to carry out consistently & persistently any policy or plan of action, whether in the field or in the Senate." The Confederacy's neglect of his own talents, he believed, bespoke a more general failure of leadership, which legitimated his reluctance to yield customary prerogative and submit to government direction. Like many other southern planters trained in the "habit of command," Hammond was temperamentally a general, not a common soldier. Denied the position of authority he felt he deserved, Hammond resisted the discipline rendered necessary even among civilians by this first modern war. Instead, Hammond maintained that his protests against Confederate taxes on his produce, against impressment of his slaves and crops, against conscription of his sons represented his dedication to a southern nation based in the principles of individual rights for which he had fought so long.[3]

To many Carolinians, Hammond's behavior during the war years seemed less like principled independence than disloyalty. Tolerated in the prewar era, his idiosyncratic views of men and measures appeared in the hour of southern crisis as evidence of an already suspected indifference to the southern cause; the invo-

2. Hammond to M. C. M. Hammond, March 1, 1861, Hammond to A. B. Allen, February 2, 1861, Hammond to William Gilmore Simms, March 24, 23, 1861, Hammond to I. W. Hayne, April 21, 1861, Hammond to Ashmore, April 2, 1861, Hammond to M. C. M. Hammond, February 6, 1861, all *ibid.* Hammond's nephew reported some interest in Charleston in sending his uncle to the secession convention, but this came to nought, as did the discussion among some of Hammond's friends of pressing his name for governor in 1862. Christopher Fitzsimons to Hammond, November 29, 1860, James Henry Hammond Diary, September 20, 1862, both in JHH Papers, SCL.
3. Hammond to Simms, July 10, 1862, in JHH Papers, LC. See Paul D. Escott, *After Secession: Jefferson Davis and the Failure of Confederate Nationalism* (Baton Rouge: Louisiana State University Press, 1978); Emory M. Thomas, *The Confederate Nation, 1861–1865* (New York: Harper and Row, 1979); Clement Eaton, *A History of the Southern Confederacy* (New York: Free Press, 1965).

cation of transcendent justifications for his behavior did not hide what many observers viewed as a reluctance to make personal sacrifices for the South. Apart from heavy investment in bonds that would ultimately prove worthless, Hammond made comparatively few contributions to the war effort, which he constantly attacked as badly conceived and poorly executed. From the Confederacy, as from his children and even himself, Hammond perhaps expected too much. When his anticipations were not fully realized, he was all too ready to denounce the sources of his disappointment. Inevitably, his censoriousness estranged him from the causes and the individuals he most cherished. His personality ironically seemed always to guarantee the continued isolation he tried so desperately to escape. Neither the personal ties he established nor the measure of public acclaim he achieved ever proved sufficient to satisfy his need for validation and love. Only death and Confederate defeat could rescue Hammond from his tragic alienation within the southern nation that had been the "hope" of his life.

As early as the spring of 1861, Hammond's behavior toward his brother John aroused doubts among his friends and neighbors about the depth of the former senator's commitment to the southern cause. Long a worrisome burden to his older brother, John had in the 1850s at last found a place for himself as a physician in the army. Secession and the possibility of war between Union forces and the South confronted the young officer with a difficult choice. Soon after Lincoln's election, John told James of his preference to be "with the state and with the South." Yet he confessed his reluctance to abandon a career in which he was, after a long struggle, just beginning to reap the rewards of success. Nevertheless, he wrote tentatively offering his services to both the governor of South Carolina and the Confederacy, but he received no reply. Given the alternatives of unemployment or Union service, James urged John to remain in the northern army. Otherwise, Hammond feared, "He will come back here to squat on Mother & the rest of us, requiring $2500 a year & doing nothing. Let him hold on. Damn patriotism if it dont pay."[4]

John's situation seemed to his older brother in many ways like his own, and his bitterness reflected his personal feelings of rejection. Hammond was certain that Jefferson Davis and South Carolina Governor Francis Pickens had ignored John's application "out of hostility to me," and James urged his brother to express a resentment his own investment in southern success did not permit him to dis-

4. John Fox Hammond to Hammond, November 19, 1860, Hammond to M. C. M. Hammond, March 1, 1861, both in JHH Papers, LC.

play. As the incident with John demonstrated, Hammond's ambivalence about his region was deep-seated. The South had made him what he was, but at the same time it had prevented him from becoming all he hoped to be. Even before 1861 he had complained that his services had been too frequently rebuffed, his sacrifices too often ignored by his region. The wartime situation greatly intensified these feelings of rejection. Hammond never doubted that his involvement in the nullification and Bluffton movements, his vigorous defenses of slavery and the southern way of life had earned him certain rights of seniority in the movement for southern independence. In a sense he felt he was entitled to partial ownership of the new Confederacy. When his claims were ignored, he lashed out with anger against those who had spurned him, defending himself by seizing the offensive, making himself the aggressor rather than the victim. His determination to move to Georgia after his defeat by the Carolina legislature in 1850 had been a similar gesture. But this time Hammond could not so directly express his indignation. Any owner of three hundred slaves had to remain committed to southern victory; unlike the short trip across the Savannah, a move across the Potomac would have been an act of willful self-destruction. Out of his ambivalence, Hammond therefore fixed upon John as a weapon of partial retribution. John's service as a field medical officer in the Army of the Potomac symbolized a part of James Henry Hammond that wished the defeat of the region that had failed to recognize his talents.[5]

John's failure to resign did not pass unnoticed. The *Mercury* declared the refusal of a number of southern citizens to withdraw from federal service to be "hideous moral delinquency, ingratitude, dishonor and treachery," and a resolution introduced in the state legislature late in 1861 specifically named young Dr. Hammond as one of a group of "infamous . . . false hearted traitors." Few doubted the elder Hammond's influence over his brother's decisions, and the former senator was widely criticized for his willing acceptance of disloyalty within the very bosom of his family.[6]

With the outbreak of hostilities in Charleston harbor in April, however, Hammond temporarily forgot his feelings of rejection in a burst of patriotic fer-

---

5. Kenneth Stampp also argues for the notion that many southerners wished for defeat, but he attributes this desire to rather different causes. See "The Southern Road to Appomattox," in Kenneth M. Stampp, *The Imperiled Union: Essays on the Background of the Civil War* (New York: Oxford University Press, 1980).

6. Charles Edward Cauthen, *South Carolina Goes to War, 1860–1865* (Chapel Hill: University of North Carolina Press, 1950), 76.

vor. His original confidence that the North would not take arms against the Confederacy was replaced by a new assurance that the South would easily triumph on the field of battle. He hastened to offer his advice to aid in her victory. Since the days of "Anti-Debt," Hammond had styled himself a financial expert, and it was in this area that he felt his insights would be most valuable to the inexperienced Confederate leadership.

Hammond's views of the South's economic prospects had long been clear and remained essentially unchanged by the outbreak of hostilities. Throughout the fifties, he had argued that cotton gave the region international economic power that could be wielded for political advantage. In March of 1861, Hammond had published a series of four pseudonymous articles in the Charleston *Mercury* advocating an export duty on cotton as the soundest financial basis for the new Confederate nation. The intense world demand for the South's staple, he contended, would lead foreign consumers to pay this tariff willingly, thereby relieving the southern nation of the burden of either direct taxes or import duties. With the outbreak of overt conflict, Hammond's faith in the efficacy of King Cotton only increased, and he began to argue for a total cotton embargo as a certain means of pressuring European nations into supporting the South. If the government purchased the entire cotton crop, he asserted, as well as large amounts of other produce, it would then control the cotton market and establish a basis as sound as specie for its currency.[7]

When the battle of Manassas in the summer of 1861 provided the first real indication of the North's intention to wage full-scale war against the South, Hammond was no longer content simply to pen his advice from the isolated tranquillity of Redcliffe. Late in July he departed for Richmond to lay his plans before the administration. For five days Hammond remained in the Confederate capital, regaling his old Senate associate R. M. T. Hunter, now secretary of state, with his financial schemes. But President Davis took no notice of the visiting Carolinian, and Hammond, ruefully acknowledging "there was no special need of me," soon turned toward home.[8]

7. Cent-a-Pound [James Henry Hammond], "An Export Duty on Raw Cotton, and Free Trade in Cotton Fabrics, the True Policy for the Southern Confederacy," Charleston *Mercury*, March 12, 13, 14, 15, 1861. See also Hammond to Lewis M. Ayer, Jr., February 10, 1863, in Lewis M. Ayer Papers, SCL, and three articles by Hammond in the press, "A Countryman," in the Charleston *Courier*, September 8, 1862, "A Back Countryman," and "Views of a Statesman," in the Charleston *Mercury*, clippings in Hammond Scrapbook (MS dated 1858–59, JHH Papers, LC).
8. Hammond Account Book (MS vol. bd., 1852–64, in JHH Papers, SCL), July 23–August 8, 1861; Hammond to M. C. M. Hammond, August 11, 1861, in JHH Papers, LC.

Filled with anger at Davis and his henchmen, who had "scornfully trampled" on his ideas, Hammond abandoned his mood of generous enthusiasm and returned to his attacks upon the Confederate leadership. The feebleness of their military preparations was matched, he contended, by the weakness of their financial plans, which depended upon inadequately supported loans as the only basis for Confederate currency. The imposition of a Union blockade late in the spring destroyed the feasibility of Hammond's notion that an export tax might serve as the chief source of revenue. But he only partially revised his views and continued to urge that Confederate notes be issued on the basis of government purchase of the entire cotton crop. The direct war tax that Secretary of the Treasury Memminger supported seemed to Hammond an unwarranted intrusion into individual rights. "It is too prying. . . . I am unwilling to let any stranger know how many forks, spoons &c I have." Such a measure could be enforced, he warned, only by "police and standing Army."[9]

The illogic of Hammond's position reveals the emotional basis of his discontent. Complaining of the inadequate support that would be provided Confederate currency by a system of loans, Hammond at the same time opposed the tax that would have provided the firmest basis for national finances. Legitimating his stance with the cherished notion that "cotton is King," Hammond demanded a government support for the staple—and its producers—that Memminger considered unconstitutional. What Hammond advocated as best for the Confederacy happened at the same time to be what was best for Hammond. He returned to Redcliffe even more alienated from the Confederate cause.[10]

Always before Hammond had responded to political rebuff by retreating into the preoccupations of plantation administration. This time, the exigencies of war combined with his own need for diversion to turn his attentions to Cowden and Silver Bluff. Since the mid-fifties Hammond had allocated ever-increasing responsibility for management to his sons. During his absence in the Senate, they had assumed nearly total control, and Hammond confessed he had been to Cowden only twice since 1858. But in June, Spann departed for Virginia to as-

9. Hammond to James L. Orr, December 11, 1863, in JHH Papers, LC; Hammond to Ayer, Jr., February 10, 1863, in Ayer Papers; Hammond to M. C. M. Hammond, August 11, 1861, Hammond to Herschel Johnson, September 2, 1861, both in JHH Papers, LC.

10. On Confederate financial policy, see Richard C. Todd, *Confederate Finance* (Athens: University of Georgia Press, 1954); Ralph L. Andreano, "A Theory of Confederate Finance," *Civil War History*, II (1956), 21–28; Eugene M. Lerner, "Money, Prices and Wages in the Confederacy," *Journal of Political Economy*, LXIII (February, 1955), 20–40; Eugene M. Lerner, "Monetary and Fiscal Programs of the Confederate Government," *ibid.*, LXII (December, 1954), 506–522.

Harry Hammond, James's eldest son, in his Confederate uniform

sume a position on the staff of South Carolina general Milledge Bonham. By September to Hammond's consternation, Harry had joined the army as well, offering his services as commissary to a Carolina regiment encamped at nearby Aiken. He "goes off," Hammond complained to Simms, "leaving 40000 bushels of corn & more than as many of Hay to be gathered by a drinking overseer." On October 20 Hammond resumed daily entries in the plantation journal he had a year earlier relinquished to Paul; he had officially reassumed control.[11]

The unexpected and "extraordinary proportions" of the war soon required sweeping adjustments in agricultural production. Military conflict, Hammond quickly recognized, would force upon the South that economic independence he had so tirelessly advocated, and he moved at once to prepare for anticipated shortages. Throughout the summer of 1861, Hammond purchased sheep, cattle, and pigs, until he was confident that within a year he would be free from any need to buy bacon. In fact, he for once underestimated his success, for by the following spring he reported more than twelve hundred head of livestock, including eight hundred hogs and growing sheep and cattle herds. Soon he began to make regular sales to neighbors and to the army. His experiments in cultivation paid their own wartime dividends, providing him with wine both to satisfy his own needs and to encourage the continuing loyalty of his slaves. His efforts with vegetables contributed as well; the harvest included a twenty-one-pound cabbage and a fine cauliflower that Hammond proudly displayed to the members of the Beech Island Agricultural Society, who had never seen or heard of such a plant before.[12]

Hammond's acute business sense served him in war as it had in peace. By late 1861 he was chiding the ever-improvident Simms for not having stocked up on plantation and household necessities like sugar, coffee, and salt that already cost three times as much as they had a year before. "I laid in my supplies," he explained smugly. Throughout the war Hammond would turn a good profit selling salt to less foresighted neighbors at a price as much as thirty times its cost to

11. Hammond to Simms, September 28, 1861, in JHH Papers, LC; Hammond Redcliffe Journal (MS vol. bd., 1861–64, JHH Papers, SCL), October 20, 1861.
12. Hammond to Simms, March 15, 1862, Hammond to M. C. M. Hammond, May 5, 1862, Hammond to F. W. Byrdsall, July 8, 1861, Hammond to Simms, September 28, 1861, all in JHH Papers, LC; Hammond Account Book (1852–64), October 17, 1863 (on purchase of livestock, see July 15, August 25, October 1, 14, 15, December 26, 1861); Hammond Redcliffe Journal, May 12, 1862, December 25, 1861, March 1, 1862; Hammond to Simms, December 22, 1861, in JHH Papers, LC.

him. And he would make generous donations of expensive necessities to the deserving and destitute as well.[13]

In spite of these rewards for his prudence, Hammond could not help but be distressed at what the war was doing to the cotton market. He could not sell any of his 1861 crop, and finally the following April offered his 442 bales to the Confederate Produce Loan in return for bonds in the amount of $32,778.25. Because he had already pledged ten thousand bushels of corn to the government, he held almost $45,000 in Confederate debt by late 1862. Even though the government was not buying the cotton crop outright as he continued to maintain "*it should*," he at least had received bonds in exchange for his produce. But Hammond found himself short of cash by spring, compelled to liquidate bank stock in order to meet his obligations in the inflationary wartime economy. The lesson was not lost upon him. In 1862 he planted only one-tenth as much cotton as he had the previous year. Corn, required to feed soldiers and civilians alike, would replace cotton at Cowden and Silver Bluff.[14]

If cotton had been one foundation of Hammond's prewar wealth, slaves had certainly been the other, and the military conflict threatened their value as well. Even during the mounting sectional strife of the forties and fifties, Hammond had seen a threat to his domination in the propaganda assaults of the North. Somehow it seemed impossible to keep knowledge of abolitionism from his bondsmen. Secession, he had hoped, would serve to seal off the South from the insidious influences of northern antislavery sentiment. Yet when disunion came it proved less a remedy than a further exacerbation of the problem. At first, Hammond was uncertain about his slaves' sympathies. As news drifted up from the low country of the fall of Port Royal to Union forces in November, 1861, Hammond noted that his bondsmen appeared "*anxious*," but he remarked, "Cant tell which side." Federal armies continued to exert pressure along the Georgia and Carolina coastline, and as the fighting grew closer in 1862 Hammond began to fear that the sound of cannon from Savannah, clearly audible on the plantation, would promote increasing disloyalty among his slaves.[15]

By spring the challenge to his control no longer remained limited to the

13. Hammond to Simms, November 26, 1861, in JHH Papers, LC; Hammond Account Book (1852–64), January 27, 1863, April 1, 11, 1862; Hammond Redcliffe Journal, November 1, 1861; Hammond to M. C. M. Hammond, May 5, 1862, in JHH Papers, LC.
14. Hammond Account Book (MS vol. bd., 1834–64, JHH Papers, SCL), April 7, 1862; Hammond Redcliffe Journal, April 6, 1862; Hammond to C. G. Memminger, April, 1862, in JHH Papers, LC. See Hammond Account Book (1852–64), March 13, 1863.
15. Hammond Redcliffe Journal, November 10, 1861, January 30, 1862.

threat of Union emancipation. Growing fear of the fall of Charleston prompted the state to introduce a system of slave impressment to provide labor for the city's defenses. Late in April, Hammond was formally requested to send sixteen male hands for four weeks work in the low country. Hammond considered the requisition to be nearly as dangerous as the Federal armies themselves. Impressment, he argued, challenged the very foundation on which the South's peculiar institution rested, for it threatened the all-important relationship between master and bondsman. Slavery, he had long believed, was not an anonymous labor system based in raw power. Any individual bondsman was induced to work largely out of ties—of both fear and affection—to a particular master. An owner, in turn, maintained control over a slave through a highly personalized combination of intimidation and manipulation. Any master's authority depended for its effectiveness on an appearance of omnipotence. To seize slaves from their owners destroyed those ties and permanently weakened the master's control by baring the limitations of his power. Impressment, Hammond declared, was "wrong every way & odious."[16]

In order to minimize the impact of the law upon his slave force, Hammond endeavored to hire free negroes to stand in for his slaves. But he could not find enough laborers willing to fill his quota, and he was compelled to supply six workers from his own force. In order to provide a constant reminder of his own power, Hammond hired a local white farmer to go with the slaves to Charleston in the role of deputy overseer. A year later Hammond was required to send another five of his workers and in the spring of 1864, six more. His elaborate theories about the peculiar institution provided him no protection from the intrusions of the law into what he had liked to regard as his private domain. War and the South's slavery system were beginning to seem increasingly incompatible.[17]

Even on the plantation, Hammond felt constant challenges to his control. Through networks of communication he could not discern, his bondsmen seemed always well apprised of war news. With the string of Confederate victories in Virginia in the spring of 1863 and the effective repulse of the Union attack on Charleston, the slaves grew "utterly subdued as if by blasted hopes." A "heavy gloom" settled "on all the negro faces." After two years of war, Hammond retained few illusions about the willing devotion of his slaves. No longer did he believe himself surrounded by docile fawning Sambos, whose prewar attentions

16. Hammond Redcliffe Journal, July 7, 1862.
17. Hammond Account Book (1852–64), June 18, July 19, 1862.

and manipulations had long deceived him into accepting, almost without question, the benevolent paternalistic version of southern slavery that had served his emotional and intellectual needs so well. He no longer assumed the blacks to be content with their lot; their "cheerful greetings" had ceased; they had "shut up their faces" and were retreating into a world of their own that Hammond had never before fully acknowledged. Now their demeanor was marked by a "peculiar furtive glance with which they regard me & a hanging off from me that I do not like."[18]

When Gettysburg and Vicksburg reversed the tide of Confederate fortunes in the summer of 1863, it became clear to Hammond that the slaves were eagerly awaiting "some great change." In spite of his orders for "much more discipline," control became nearly impossible, and the "demoralized" slaves began "Stealing right & left." Christmas brought no communal festival, "no smiling faces & merry hearts." Instead of offering the usual barbecue, Hammond simply distributed an extra week's allowance and left the slaves to organize their own celebration. Independent black festivities replaced the customary ritual of black and white interaction. The symbolic reinforcement of master-slave ties represented by the owner's traditional gift offerings no longer held any meaning within the fragmenting structure of white control. Hammond was convinced that despite his slaves' apparent passivity "the roar of a single canon of the Federal's would make them frantic savage cutthroats and incendiaries." Long before Union victory Hammond knew that the war had already destroyed the relationship of master and slave that had served as the chief support for the peculiar institution.[19]

Hammond's indignation at Confederate failures to defend slavery was compounded by his disgust with southern military policy and by his more general sense of alarm at the kind of warfare sectional confrontation had unleashed. The magnitude of the conflict, the mass mobilization of men and industry, the unprecedented numbers of deaths seemed to herald a new and terrible era, distinguished by a heightened ability to destroy. Here, Hammond believed, lay the war's most dangerous challenge to traditional values and assumptions. Chivalry, honor, even virtue seemed absurd in face of this new mechanized warfare; the materialism of the age had reached its logical and terrifying conclusion. The bat-

18. Hammond Redcliffe Journal, June 28, 1863.
19. *Ibid.*, August 8, April 9, August 30, 1863, August 6, 1864, December 25, June 28, 1863. See James L. Roark, *Masters Without Slaves: Southern Planters in the Civil War and Reconstruction* (New York: Norton, 1977).

tle of the ironclad ships *Monitor* and *Merrimac* in 1862 dramatically symbolized these changes for Hammond, who greeted the naval skirmish as "the forerunner of Armageddon & the Millenium [*sic*]." He felt, he reported, "very very sad more so than I have felt in many years," in large part because of "our lamentable victory of the Virginia or Merrimac. If that thing answers expectation it will be the greatest curse that has befallen man since the fall of Adam. Nations unable to resist assaults, must make reprisals & ravage each others coasts. Sea Coasts & Ports, must be abandoned to mere piracy. . . . The Yankees can build 3 of these Machines to our 1, & take our Coast & Ports. . . . & our only & poor recompense will be to shell their cities & Coast. Horrible Warfare!!²⁰

As frightening as he found these general reflections upon modern war, Hammond felt more immediately threatened by what he viewed as the inexcusable stupidity of day-to-day Confederate military policy. As Union naval forces battled for control of the Carolina and Georgia seacoast in 1862 and 1863, Hammond believed his situation on the navigable Savannah to be extremely vulnerable. Yet he could not persuade Confederate officials of the dangers threatening up-country communities. Instead, authorities continued to deplete Barnwell and Edgefield of their resources for defense, taking almost every able-bodied man for service elsewhere and even impressing up-country slaves to work in Charleston instead of on fortifications closer to home.²¹ Hammond's own sons quickly deserted him as well. Perhaps they regarded army service as a means of at last escaping their father's resented domination, for their commitment to the Confederate military endeavor seems to have been somewhat less than total. Spann's initial enthusiasm diminished after Manassas, and when his six-month enlistment expired in the fall he turned his attentions back to planting. But he did not give Hammond the satisfaction of returning to Redcliffe. Instead, he purchased a tract of land in Mississippi and departed with the twenty-six slaves his father had advanced him as a wedding present the previous June. When the Confederacy instituted conscription in the spring of 1862, Spann was home with his wife in Richmond, and his Virginia in-laws willingly purchased a substitute to keep him out of the army. Federal successes in the West rendered continua-

20. Hammond to M. C. M. Hammond, March 24, 1862, in JHH Papers, LC; Hammond Redcliffe Journal, April 6, 1862.
21. See Hammond to Miller B. Grant, March 3, 1862, Hammond to John C. Pemberton, April 28, 1862, Hammond to Roswell S. Ripley, April 30, 1862, all in JHH Papers, LC; Hammond to George W. Rains, May 21, 1862, in George Washington Rains Papers, SHC.

tion of his Mississippi enterprise impossible, and Spann began to write for the Richmond *Whig.*[22]

Harry was more intensely involved in the war, first confronting the chaos that Union seizure of Port Royal brought to the low country in 1861. Later, as an aide-de-camp to his father's old political enemy Maxcy Gregg at Fredericksburg, Harry had his horse shot from under him. Officially exempt from conscription because of a childhood accident that had left one leg shorter than the other, Harry nevertheless remained in the army as a noncombatant, serving as quartermaster in the Virginia theater until the end of the war.

Despite his complaints about Paul's ineffectiveness as a manager, Hammond "held him back" to aid in plantation affairs until early 1862. Under the pressure of the new conscription law, Paul at last left home to serve, to his father's dismay, as a common soldier in Tennessee. Hammond's entreaties to his friend John Breckinridge finally won the youth a reprieve from the front lines by securing him a position on the Kentucky general's staff. Paul began almost at once to discuss the possibility of a hired substitute but lingering scruples kept him in the army until fall. On a visit home in November, Paul at last agreed not to return to the battle, and his father sent an alternate, at a cost of eleven hundred dollars, to his regiment in Virginia. "We are all rejoiced," Hammond recorded.[23]

The hiring of substitutes was an issue that generated much controversy within the new southern nation. In response to poorer citizens' resentment of the practice, the Confederacy gradually eliminated many draft exemptions and finally declared the substitution system illegal late in 1863. In South Carolina the question had provoked especially vigorous public debate. The ideology of this most hierarchical of southern states was in certain ways consistent with this example of privilege, even though the number of Carolinians who actually escaped service by hiring alternates was comparatively small. At the time the system ended late in 1863, official reports showed only 791 such Carolinians, as contrasted with 15,000 Virginians.[24]

Hammond's support for substitution was both personal and ideological. When Paul was compelled to return to the front early in 1864, even the comparatively safe quartermaster's post his father had secured for him did not dimin-

22. Edward Spann Hammond, Elmwood Plantation, Bolivar Co., Mississippi, Stock and Crop Book (MS vol. bd., 1862, Edward Spann Hammond Papers, SCL).
23. Hammond to Harry Hammond, November 17, 1861, in HBC Papers, SCL; Hammond Redcliffe Journal, March 6, 1862; Paul Fitzsimons Hammond to Hammond, May 2, 1862, in JHH Papers, LC; Hammond Redcliffe Journal, January 12, 1863.
24. Cauthen, *South Carolina Goes to War*, 172.

ish Hammond's anger about Confederate policy. The new measure left Paul's father "helpless & heartless." Prohibition of substitution, like slave impressment or even conscription itself, seemed to Hammond another betrayal of the precepts upon which the southern nation had been founded. "This war," he protested to Confederate Senator James Orr, "is based on the principle & *fact* of the inequality of mankind—for policy we say *races*, in reality, as all history shows it, the truth is *classes* & to that *we* must come. *Here* under our Institutions it is so easy to rise from the lowest to the highest class by merit that this thing of forever grinding at wealth & place should be stopped." War was destroying the class as well as the racial basis of order that had structured the society of the Old South.[25]

Hammond's fears of a direct challenge to the rights of property were soon fulfilled. In March of 1863 the Confederate Congress passed a measure legalizing army impressment of civilian property necessary to the conduct of the war. A schedule of prices allotted for animals and foodstuffs was established, but the stated fees inevitably lagged behind the ever-escalating wartime market. From the first, Hammond protested the low assessments given his meat and grain and appealed to higher authorities for greater remuneration.

To avoid their seizure, Hammond hid his mules in the interior of the plantation and worked to foil the impressing officers in every way possible. But an eventual confrontation seemed inevitable as Confederate needs mounted and Hammond's patience declined. By 1864 even Hammond was feeling the effects of the failing southern economy, for, he explained, he had "believed in a short war & been lavish." His stores were all gone, and he feared the new Confederate direct tax passed in February, 1864, would draw "all the blood out of us" before the Yankees got a chance. But Hammond could still rely on sales of his corn to provide the income to support him and his establishment. The nearby manufacturing town of Graniteville, owned by William Gregg, Hammond's old friend and since fall, 1861, Cattie's father-in-law, provided a guaranteed market, for the mill workers had to purchase nearly all of their food supplies. The certainty of these sales combined with Hammond's personal ties to Gregg to make the planter determined to furnish the grain he had pledged. But in the summer of 1864, the Confederate impressors decided otherwise. When Hammond informed the officers that his corn had been already promised, the impressors took

25. Hammond Redcliffe Journal, January 13, 1864; Hammond to Orr, December 11, 1863, in JHH Papers, LC. See Albert Burton Moore, *Conscription and Conflict in the Confederacy* (New York: Macmillan, 1924).

little notice, insisting upon their prerogatives. Through July and August, Hammond engaged in near warfare with the authorities, challenging their right to his corn as well as the particular price they offered. When a Confederate captain left an official notice of impressment on Hammond's desk, he "tore [it] up & threw it out the window in his presence saying I paid no respect to the order of—his principal & simply defied him—not meant to offend & not offending I hope." After discouraging the impressors twice with his rage, Hammond feared that the next confrontation would go "to bloodshed." Catherine tried to keep him in the house and calm him down when the officers next arrived; Simms wrote urging him to regain his reason on the matter.[26]

The battle over impressment in the summer of 1864 released all Hammond's pent-up frustrations about Confederate policy and about the betrayal of those principles of individualism that he had regarded as central to the southern cause. Seizing his corn, he contended, was equivalent to "branding upon my forehead 'Slave'"; it seemed a direct challenge to the position he had dedicated his life to achieve. He could never have conceived, he bemoaned to Simms, "that I should be subjected to such humiliation & degradation at the hands of the Southern people." His own rejection by Confederate leadership, followed by the apostasies of conscription and impressment, and now compounded by the growing likelihood of military subjugation was simply too much for Hammond to bear. It was "terrible," he protested, "to see SoCa admired as the most Conservative & law-abiding people now regardless of constitutions & laws, plundering her own people." The Confederate armies had not yet been annihilated. But Hammond's dreams certainly had.[27]

Hammond's neighbor Thomas Davies despaired of his old friend. Hammond's attitude towards his brother John's unionism had alienated many people, but the "fact of the business is . . . [Hammond] has held aloof to such extent and his sons likewise" that "people are thinking all sorts of things. . . . for every man who does not go into this rebellion . . . [on] whom the country has any claims

26. Hammond Redcliffe Journal, March 28, 1864; Hammond to Simms, February 19, 1863, February 21, 1864, both in JHH Papers, LC. See Hammond Account Book (1834–64), February 6, 1864; Hammond to William Gregg, June 8, 1864, in JHH Papers, LC; Hammond Redcliffe Journal, July 20, August 8, 1864; Hammond to Simms, August 24, 1864, Simms to Hammond, July 28, 1864, both in JHH Papers, LC. See Harrison A. Trexler, "The Opposition of Planters to the Employment of Slaves as Laborers by the Confederacy," *Mississippi Valley Historical Review*, XXVII (September, 1940), 221–24; Bernard H. Nelson, "Confederate Slave Impressment Legislation, 1861–1865," *Journal of Negro History*, XXXI (October, 1946), 392–410.

27. Hammond Redcliffe Journal, August 1, 1864; Hammond to Simms, August 24, 1864, Hammond to Captain Elford, August 30, 1864, both in JHH Papers, LC.

whatever, is held up in [pub]lic opinion & will not soon be forgotten." Davies was certain Hammond was aware of the resentment his behavior had provoked. "He knows it well and . . . tries to douse himself of the reflections by whiskey potations."[28]

By the end of his losing battle with the impressors in mid-August, Hammond was "quite unwell." He had not, he explained, been sleeping for some time. "The War, the Impressment," the futility of his efforts in every arena of his life had "altogether used me up." His mother's death in June had further weakened and exasperated him. His wishes for a private funeral were disregarded, and pleading ill health, he refused to attend the crowded public ceremony in Augusta. In the course of the summer, as the contents of her will were revealed, Hammond became even more agitated. Unbeknownst to her eldest son and lifetime financial advisor, she had added a "secret codicil" leaving her house, seventy-one acres of land, and all her personal possessions to Kate Hyde, her nineteen-year-old granddaughter, the child of Hammond's deceased sister Caroline. His mother's decision to bequeath this property directly to the young girl seemed to evidence a lack of trust in her son's willingness to provide for his niece; her secrecy made James certain that she had intended it as a rebuke. For decades, Hammond believed, he had conscientiously tried to meet the truculent old woman's demands upon him, providing her a residence near his own, regularly supplementing her small income, and hiring a suitable companion. Yet she too had evidently chafed under the yoke of his oppression. In his already agitated state, Hammond regarded his mother's will as yet another attack upon his prerogative, another challenge to the patriarchal image already under siege, a betrayal from within the family to accompany those assaults already launched from without by the exigencies of war.[29]

In his isolation and bitterness, Hammond was by late summer, 1864, losing all ability to view events with reasoned judgment. Yet with his health and his world near collapse, his feeling of being under constant direct threat was perhaps not unwarranted. Certainly he was not a well man. But more than his physical constitution was in jeopardy. The achievements of his life were evaporating: his sons were under enemy fire; his plantation prey to hostile forces; his political views ignored; his principles abandoned by the southern nation that he had re-

---

28. [Thomas Davies] to Dear Brother, n.d., in JHH Papers, SCL.
29. Hammond Redcliffe Journal, August 9, June 2, 1864; Hammond to M. C. M. Hammond, July 6, 1864, in JHH Papers, SCL; Will of Catherine Fox Hammond, Will Book E, Edgefield County Will Book, 1852–66, pp. 524–25, Edgefield County Courthouse, Edgefield, S.C.

garded as the "hope" of his life. As he confided to Spann, it was the "time for me to die."[30]

As early as May, 1861, Hammond had begun to fear that his ever-precarious health had at last "failed me completely." By early 1863, he complained he could hardly walk across a room, and by the end of the year he was spending, he reported, twenty out of every twenty-four hours lying on his back. Never doubting that his persistent physical ailments reflected the tensions of his life, Hammond claimed a hereditarily "defective nervous system" that rendered his body unusually sensitive to emotional distress. He had experienced debilitating nightmares as a child; "anxiety" had caused his breakdown in 1836; and the horrors of war would hasten his demise. In the 1860s, as often before in Hammond's life, illness served as a refuge from a reality too difficult to bear.[31]

But Hammond's acknowledged "hypochondria" arose not only from the intense pressures created by his hopes and ambitions. Another fundamental aspect of his character made its own contribution to the destruction of his health, providing what may well have been the underlying physiological cause of his death. Hammond's need for absolute control over the world around him encompassed not only his slaves, his children, and his agricultural operations. He strived as well for a kind of "despotic sway" over his own physical being and most particularly over those excretions that were the focus of the mid-nineteenth century's attention to bodily processes. Prevailing therapeutics concerned itself with maintaining the proper balance of bodily intake and outflow, the correct equilibrium of fluids in the sum of all physiological activities. Like many others of his era, Hammond was obsessed with his bowels. Their daily operation was the surest sign of good health and had to be encouraged when necessary through pharmacological intervention. "Keep your Bowels open," Elisha had early warned his eldest son. Hammond transmitted this paternal admonition to his brother John. "Make it a point to have a copious evacuation *every day* after breakfast," he advised, and "When you fail," turn to medicine—as Hammond himself did with increasing frequency. By the time of his trip to Europe in 1836, he admitted that he was making "free use of enemas and shall the balance of my life." On his sea voyage home he found it necessary to take medicine every other day in order

30. Edward Spann Hammond, "Last Moments of J. H. Hammond, November, 1864" (MS vol. bd., 1861–1909, Edward Spann Hammond Papers, SCL).

31. Hammond Diary (SCL), September 20, 1862; Hammond to M. C. M. Hammond, January 21, 1863, in JHH Papers, SCL; Hammond Redcliffe Journal, December 27, 1863; Hammond Medical Diary (MS vol. bd., 1836–37, JHH Papers, SCL), May 3, 1863.

to have any movement of his bowels at all. Even when his overall health improved upon his return to America, Hammond continued to complain about constipation and, by the 1850s, severe hemorrhoids as well.[32]

His views on therapeutics and actual plantation practice shifted frequently during the years as he turned first to Thomsonianism and then to homeopathy, but he never abandoned his attentions to his bowels. His complaint that all his sufferings arose from "horse dosing in my childhood" indicates that in accordance with his abandonment of heroic treatment on the plantation after the mid-thirties, he reduced his own intake of medicine as well. Under the homeopathic regime he adopted in 1854, he probably reduced his own ingestion of drugs to meet the requirement for infinitesimal dosages prescribed by this fashionable therapeutic movement. But he still recorded routine doses of mercury-based laxatives, and he "habitually" used enemas, which were in all likelihood composed of drug solutions containing mercury.[33]

Although he reported some bleeding from hemorrhoids in the late fifties, in 1861 Hammond began at intervals to hemorrhage from the bowels, losing as much as a pound of blood in a single day. Yet he continued to intervene to maintain regular excretions. Three years of intermittent bleeding at last culminated in November, 1864, in a final "attack" that his family believed had been brought on by a drug overdose. It is not unlikely that the hemorrhaging that eventually killed him was the result of a level of mercury poisoning induced by the laxatives he had taken regularly for the past four decades. Many of the symptoms of which he regularly complained—a metallic taste in his mouth, digestive difficulties, dizziness, tingling and numbness, visual problems, mental depression, and irritability—are characteristics of chronic mercury poisoning. Hammond's need for control may ironically have contributed to his physical destruction at the same time that it proved the ruination of his hopes for public acclaim and his longing for familial love.[34]

32. Hammond to Simms, November 5, 1852, in JHH Papers, LC. See J. Hume Simons, *The Planter's Guide, and Family Book of Medicine* (Charleston: M'Carter and Allen, 1848), 12; Elisha Hammond to Hammond, March 4, 1827, in HBC Papers, SCL; Hammond to John Fox Hammond, September 21, 1839, Hammond European Diary, II (MS vol. bd., 1837), November 1, 1837, both in JHH Papers, SCL; Hammond to Milledge Galphin, January 8, 1837, in HBC Papers, SCL.
33. Hammond to Simms, July 17, 1861, June 16, 1857, both in JHH Papers, LC; Hammond, Medical Records (MS vol. bd., 1854, JHH Papers, SCL).
34. Hammond, "Silver Bluff, Cathwood, Cowden, and Redcliffe" (MS vol. bd., 1856–87, JHH Papers, SCL), July 9, 1858; Hammond Redcliffe Journal, November 1, 1861, February 19, 1862, October 3, 1864, November 26, 1862; Hammond to M. C. M. Hammond, January 21, 1863, in JHH Papers, LC; Edward Spann Hammond, "Last Moments." At the time of his death, Ham-

In Hammond's view the experience of war itself had brought a revolution to the South, overturning the values and assumptions of the cause he had championed so long. Before secession, Hammond had feared that a decisive movement for southern independence might well threaten the broader bases of social order in the region. But he little imagined the dimensions the North-South conflict would assume, nor did he anticipate the enormous changes that this first "modern" war would wreak. Like the many other southern planters who resisted conscription and impressment, Hammond never truly grasped how the necessity of mobilizing mass armies had changed the relationship of civilians to war. Nor did he understand that the personalism through which planters had controlled social interaction in the Old South had in these changed circumstances to give way to bureaucratic structures that made no allowance for the intricate webs of obligation and dependence that had served as the bases of planter power. Impressment officers ignored Hammond's ties with Gregg, undermined his ability to provide food for his needy neighbors, challenged his image of omnipotence before his slaves. The foundations of a social world built on concepts of duty and deference had been destroyed; the bureaucratic wartime state made patriarchy all but irrelevant; a father could not exercise his responsibility for a family that was being conscripted and impressed.

Hammond greeted death as a "relief." As his condition worsened during the first week of November he stopped dressing and moved only from a bed in his own chamber to one in the library and back again. On the twelfth he declined markedly and began to talk of death. Late in the day he summoned the black children from the yard to sing to him. Catherine and Spann sat up with him through the night, and he died just before ten the next morning.

When Simms heard of Hammond's death, he composed an elegy that showed how truly he had understood and sympathized with his departed friend in his feelings of barrenness and exile. The futility Hammond had felt so long had at last overwhelmed him.

> O Brave One! Thou has tilled a barren soil,
> Thou reap'st no fruit, though thou did'st sow the seed,

---

mond was consulting both homeopathic and regular physicians. The lack of precise information about which compounds he used, how frequently, and in what dosages makes it impossible to be certain about the diagnosis of Hammond's illness or the cause of his death. However, I am grateful to Albert Rizzo, M.D., for making some informed and helpful judgments on the basis of the information available.

Thou hast but exile for thy years of toil,
    No voice in council, though thy children bleed.
. . . .
Faction and party stilled thy mighty voice
    Which yet would teach us wisdom could we hear.
. . . .
So all earth's teachers have been overborne
    By the coarse crowd, and fainting droop or die;
They bear the cross, their bleeding brows the thorn,
    And ever hear the clamor, "Crucify!"[35]

35. Hammond to Pemberton, May 29, 1862, in JHH Papers, LC; Edward Spann Hammond, "Last Moments"; William Gilmore Simms, "O Tempore, O Mores," in Hammond Scrapbook (1858–59).

Epilogue

HAMMOND LIVED A LIFE of irony and contradiction. Caught in the rapidly changing world of the early nineteenth century, he was lured by the future, yet clung to the past. As a result, his design for self-aggrandizement, for fame, fortune, and dynastic achievement crumbled under the weight of the illusions on which it was based. As slaveowner, politician, plantation manager—even as father and husband—Hammond sought to impose an order that reality could not sustain.

In the realm of public affairs, Hammond vowed an allegiance to republican values not only at odds with the altered substance of Carolina political life but directly opposed to his own boundless aspirations. His image of a permanent, stable, and fixed social order hardly fit with his own career of rapid upward mobility. This paradox created enormous and unrelenting stress; Hammond's aggressive ambition tormented him, and left part of him always longing to retreat into the more transcendent satisfactions of intellectual life. Yet he knew that in the South only politics could bring him the recognition he craved. Within the public realm, Hammond was so torn between promoting his irrepressible desires for office and appearing the disinterested statesman that he succeeded in both displeasing those genuine unionists with whom he disagreed and alienating the advocates of the states' rights cause he regarded as the "hope" of his life. Not only was Hammond too rigid to accept the concessions and compromises required by the nation's democratizing party politics, he often seemed to regard contentious isolation as the only sure hallmark of the principled purity that he had come to identify as the essence of republican virtue. His inability either to abandon or to implement these traditional notions of public life rendered Hammond unable to fully comprehend or manipulate the political environment in which he functioned; his style of political behavior left him alone and misunderstood.

In his family life, Hammond seemed torn as well between older notions of patriarchal dominance and an undeniable need to be not just feared but loved. He desired a wife who would be both vassal and companion; he could not admit that these goals were hardly compatible. With his children too, Hammond's dynastic designs made him incapable of satisfying emotional longings that his romantic era had encouraged him to recognize and articulate. Imprisoned within these unyielding and contradictory expectations, Hammond was doomed to frustration, futility, and perhaps worst of all in his view, ineffectiveness.

Yet the dimension of Hammond's life in which his illusions were most fully and dramatically destroyed was undoubtedly his commitment to a social order based in black slavery. His ideas about human bondage were not simply an intellectual position he had developed for his proslavery essays, nor a political stance to advance his career. Hammond's feelings about the peculiar institution and about the duties and burdens of masterhood made up an important part of his own self-image and sense of personal worth. No one believed his arguments about the benevolence of human bondage more completely than he. The ideology of southern slavery offered him legitimation in his never-ending quest for despotic sway at the same time it promised that as paternalist he would be both revered and loved. Hammond's conceptions about the peculiar institution implied a resolution of these conflicting imperatives so central to his emotional and psychological constitution.

But this too was an illusion, as the disintegration of slavery under wartime pressures showed Hammond all too well. He did not have to live until the actual hour of southern surrender and black emancipation to know that the system as he had understood it was destroyed—had indeed probably never existed. Hammond came to what was perhaps the most painful realization possible: his slaves regarded him with, at best, indifference. They preferred their Christmas celebrations without him; their decades of cheerful greetings had been simply calculated manipulations now rendered unnecessary by impending Union victory. The people at Silver Bluff did not rise in revolution against those who had oppressed them for so long. Unlike many bondsmen who fled during the war itself, the Hammond slaves did not depart even when freedom was proclaimed. "We have not lost many negroes," the widowed Catherine complained in September, 1865, as she worried about having too many mouths to feed. "I wish we could get clear of many of the useless ones." These blacks were seemingly more concerned about remaining together in a group than fleeing white domination; the positive meaning of the web of slave interrelationships and the dedication to the black community at Silver Bluff were more central influences than the intrusions of a master's power. The plantation had been home to many of these slaves before Hammond arrived; the community had preceded him and now it outlived him.[1]

Although Hammond indicated throughout the war that he had begun to understand the illusions at the heart of his beliefs about the master-slave relationship, ultimately he felt compelled to deny these difficult truths. In the end, he preferred to die comforted by the assumptions that had guided him for so long. When he called the slave children from the yard to sing spirituals at his death bed, Hammond identified himself and his life with the myths of the Old South, even as it crumbled around him.

1. Catherine Fitzsimons Hammond to M. C. M. Hammond, September 3, 1865, in JHH Papers, SCL. The official inventory of Hammond's estate listed 297 slaves by name, although the probate officer counted these as totaling 303. The list, if accurate, represented declines of 18 slaves from the 1860 census figures and 52 from the total Hammond reported in 1861. (See Appendix, Charts 6 and 7.) Hammond's transfer of 23 slaves to Spann partially accounts for the sharp decline between 1861 and 1863, but other changes are not so clear, and his wartime records do not explain the shifts. Plantation books show no preponderance of either births or deaths during the period, and Hammond, who so carefully recorded his slaves' reactions to the war, never mentioned runaways. Of course, the declining percentage of male and female slaves aged twenty to thirty during the war years could be seen as evidence that slaves did indeed flee, for this was the age group most likely to run away. But it was also the age group most likely to be impressed, and the impact of this Confederate policy on Hammond's slave force should not be discounted. The dislocations of wartime may also have contributed. Acquaintances from the coast asked Hammond to shelter the slaves they had rescued from invading armies, and some of these bondsmen may have been included in the high 1861–1862 count. The nature of the surviving evidence makes it impossible to do more than speculate about the changing size of Hammond's slave force during the war. Given the obvious errors made in the death inventory, it is not even clear how reliable the wartime slave censuses are. Inventory, Estate of James Henry Hammond, Box 89, Package 3569, 1864, Edgefield County Courthouse, Edgefield, S.C.

Appendix

Charts and Tables

Chart 1   Sex and Age Pyramid of Hammond's Slaves, 1831

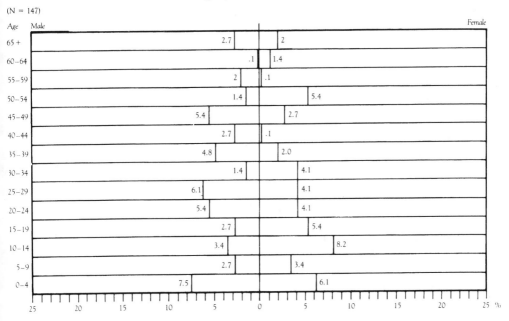

(N = 147)

Age   Male   Female

Age	Male	Female
65 +	2.7	2
60–64	.1	1.4
55–59	2	.1
50–54	1.4	5.4
45–49	5.4	2.7
40–44	2.7	.1
35–39	4.8	2.0
30–34	1.4	4.1
25–29	6.1	4.1
20–24	5.4	4.1
15–19	2.7	5.4
10–14	3.4	8.2
5–9	2.7	3.4
0–4	7.5	6.1

25   20   15   10   5   0   5   10   15   20   25 %

Chart 2   Crude Death Rate of Hammond's Slaves
(Five-Year Averages)

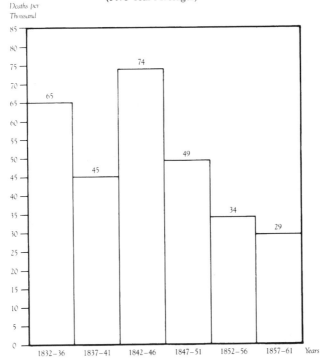

Deaths per
Thousand

Years	Deaths per Thousand
1832–36	65
1837–41	45
1842–46	74
1847–51	49
1852–56	34
1857–61	29

Years

Chart 3   Crude Birth Rate of Hammond's Slaves
(Five-Year Averages)

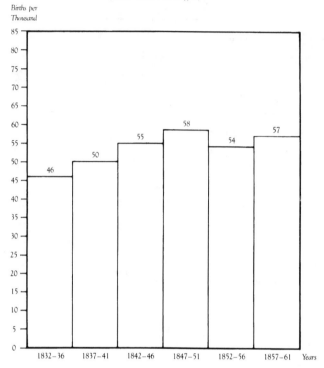

Births per Thousand

Chart 4   Birth-to-Death Ratio of Hammond's Slaves
(Five-Year Averages)

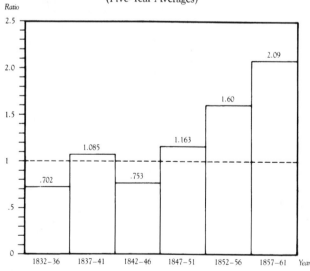

Ratio

Chart 5   Child Mortality Among Hammond's Slaves

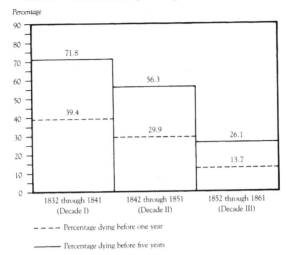

Percentage

90
80
      71.8
70
60   56.3
50
      39.4
40
30   29.9   26.1
20   13.7
10
0
   1832 through 1841   1842 through 1851   1852 through 1861
      (Decade I)   (Decade II)   (Decade III)

- - - - Percentage dying before one year

——— Percentage dying before five years

Chart 6   Sex and Age Pyramid of Hammond's Slaves, 1850

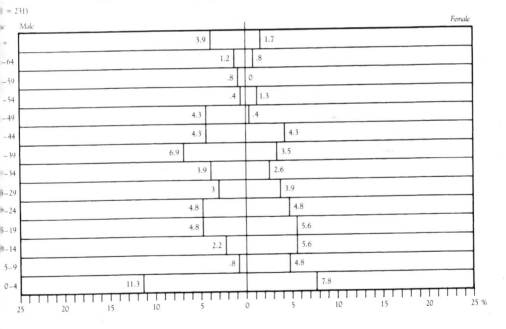

= 231)

Male   Female

+	3.9	1.7
–64	1.2	.8
–59	.8	0
–54	.4	1.3
–49	4.3	.4
–44	4.3	4.3
–39	6.9	3.5
–34	3.9	2.6
–29	3	3.9
–24	4.8	4.8
–19	4.8	5.6
–14	2.2	5.6
5–9	.8	4.8
0–4	11.3	7.8

25   20   15   10   5   0   5   10   15   20   25 %

Chart 7 Sex and Age Pyramid of Hammond's Slaves, 1860 and 1864—Wartime Changes

(1860 N = 315; 1864 N = 297)

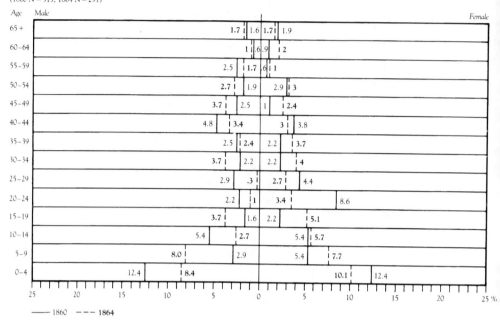

| Age | Male | | Female |

Age				
65 +		1.7 1.6 1.7 1.9		
60–64		1 1.6 .9 2		
55–59	2.5 1.7 .6 1			
50–54	2.7 1.9 2.9 3			
45–49	3.7 2.5 1 2.4			
40–44	4.8 3.4 3 3.8			
35–39	2.5 2.4 2.2 3.7			
30–34	3.7 2.2 2.2 4			
25–29	2.9 .3 2.7 4.4			
20–24	2.2 1 3.4 8.6			
15–19	3.7 1.6 2.2 5.1			
10–14	5.4 2.7 5.4 5.7			
5–9	8.0 2.9 5.4 7.7			
0–4	12.4 8.4 10.1 12.4			

25   20   15   10   5   0   5   10   15   20   25 %

——— 1860   – – – 1864

Chart 8 The Changing Size of Hammond's Slave Force

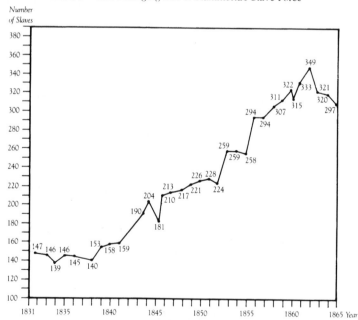

Number of Slaves

380
360
340
320
300
280
260
240
220
200
180
160
140
120
100

1831   1835   1840   1845   1850   1855   1860   1865 *Year*

147 146 146 139 145 140 153 158 159 190 204 181 210 213 217 221 224 226 228 259 259 258 294 294 307 311 315 322 333 349 320 321 297

Note: The dots placed off actual date lines represent counts made by Hammond at times other than the beginning of the year.

Chart 9   Number of Children Under Ten per Thousand Women
Ages Fifteen to Forty-nine

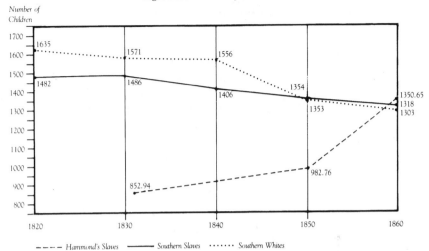

Source: Aggregate data from Richard H. Steckel, "Slave Mortality, Analysis of Evidence from Plantation Records," *Social Science History*, III (October, 1979), 86–114, and Richard H. Steckel, "The Economics of U.S. Slave and Southern White Fertility" (Ph.D. dissertation, University of Chicago,
1977).

Chart 10   Cotton-Corn Ratio at Silver Bluff in Acres Planted

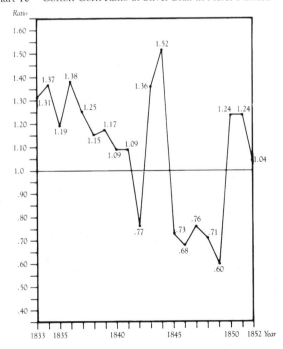

Chart 11   Per-Acre Cotton Productivity at Silver Bluff

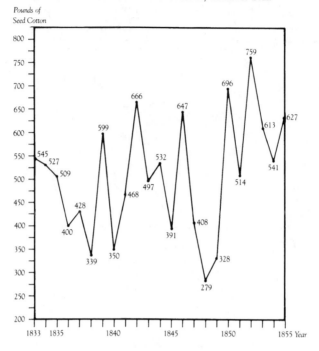

Chart 12   Per-Acre Corn Productivity at Silver Bluff

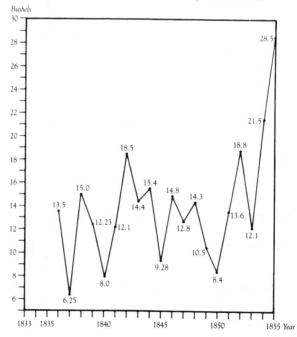

Chart 13 Cotton and Corn Acreage at Silver Bluff

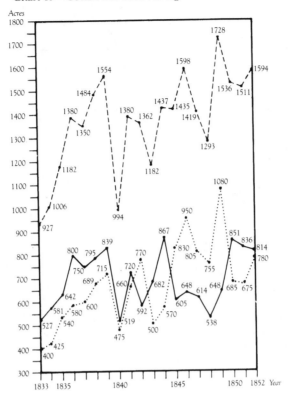

.... Corn Acreage

———— Cotton Acreage

— — — — Combined Acreage

Table 1 Kinship Naming Patterns Among Hammond's Slaves

N = 51

Namesake		Percentage
Father 17		33.3
Mother 3		5.9
Grandfather 11		21.6
Paternal 5	9.9	
Maternal 6	11.8	
Grandmother 10		19.7
Paternal 3	5.9	
Maternal 6	11.8	
Unspecified 1	2.0	
Maternal uncle 2		3.9
Maternal aunt 2		3.9
Paternal aunt 1		2.0
Deceased sibling 2		3.9
Mother's maiden name 1		2.0
Maternal grandmother's maiden name 1		2.0
Maternal cousin 1		2.0
Summary		
Named for paternal relatives 26		50.98
Named for maternal relatives 22		43.13
Other 3		5.88

Table 2 Hammond's Agricultural Wealth

	1850	1860	Percentage Change
Improved acreage	3,000	9,100	+203.0
Unimproved acreage	7,000	2,360	−66.0
Total acreage	10,000	11,460	+14.6
Cash value	$100,000	$255,000	+155.0
Value of farm implements and machines	$5,000	$3,000	−40.0
Value of livestock	$8,000	$16,400	+105.0
Number of cattle	130	154	+18.5
Number of pigs	360	595	+65.0
Number of mules	32	22	−31.2
Number of horses	22	51	+132.0
Bales of ginned cotton	160	315	+96.9
Bushels of corn	11,500	63,000	+447.8

Bibliographical Essay

Manuscript Materials

James Henry Hammond's almost obsessive record-keeping left extraordinarily rich materials for the historian. The great bulk of his papers are divided between two repositories: the Library of Congress has a James Henry Hammond Collection of 33 volumes and 17 manuscript boxes, which is also available on twenty reels of microfilm; the South Caroliniana Library of the University of South Carolina at Columbia has a James Henry Hammond Collection of 36 boxes and 170 volumes. The Hammond Papers in the Library of Congress tend to represent his public and political life, the South Caroliniana collection to be more personal in nature, but the distinction is by no means clearly drawn. Both collections, for example, include agricultural records and plantation books, and some of Hammond's most intimate reflections, such as his letters to William Gilmore Simms, are located in the Library of Congress. The South Caroliniana Library also has the Hammond-Bryan-Cumming Collection of 7,085 manuscripts, which includes some material relevant to Hammond but is devoted chiefly to the papers of his descendants. Twelve letters from his wife are available as the James Henry Hammond Letters in the Southern Historical Collection at the University of North Carolina, Chapel Hill, and the William R. Perkins Library at Duke also has a small James H. Hammond Collection, made up chiefly of his correspondence with William Hodgson.

There are important Hammond manuscripts in a number of other collections. The Edmund Ruffin Papers at the Virginia Historical Society in Richmond contain a group of Hammond's letters, especially rich on agricultural subjects. Hammond's wide-ranging speculations to Nathaniel Beverley Tucker are in the Tucker-Coleman Papers at the Earl Gregg Swem Memorial Library of the College of William and Mary. Significant letters from Hammond on political questions can be found in the William Porcher Miles Papers in the Southern Historical Collection, in the Benjamin F. Perry Papers, State of Alabama Department of Archives and History, Montgomery, in the John C. Calhoun Papers, Clemson University, and in the Lewis M. Ayer and Beaufort T. Watts Papers, both at the South Caroliniana Library. Hammond's extraordinary exchange concerning his slave son Henderson is documented in the Alexander H. Stephens Papers, Library of Congress.

In my research on Hammond's political career, I turned to a number of manuscript collections for background material. Among the most helpful were the Robert Barnwell Rhett Papers at the South Carolina Historical Society in Charleston, the Francis W. Pickens Papers in the South Caroliniana Library, the Francis W. Pickens and Milledge Luke Bonham Collection in the Library of Congress, the Milledge Luke Bonham Papers at South Caroliniana, the Robert F. W. Allston Papers at South Caroliniana, and the James Hamilton Papers at both the South Caroliniana and the Southern Historical Collection. The Franklin Harper Elmore Papers at the Library of Congress contain a particularly useful annotated scrapbook documenting Elmore's struggle with Hammond over the state bank.

Hammond's student days at South Carolina College are illuminated in manuscript materials at the University of South Carolina Archives, especially in the records of the Euphradian Society in its Minute Book (1823–33), Debate Book (1820–38), and Treasurer's books (1818–24). Although few governors' records have been preserved for the antebellum period, the South Carolina Department of Archives and History in Columbia has invaluable but largely uncatalogued information on Hammond's gubernatorial term in Legislative Papers (1831–1859). The manuscript returns for the Agricultural Schedules of the United States Census in 1850 and 1860 are also available at the Department of Archives. Because the microfilm copies at the National Archives in Washington were in part illegible, I found these originals indispensable. Manuscript returns for the Slave and Free Population Schedules for Barnwell and Edgefield Districts can be read on film at the National Archives. These documents provide detailed information about Hammond's slave property and plantation productivity.

Published Primary Materials

Newspapers were an important source for this study. The Charleston *Mercury* and Charleston *Courier* were both published throughout Hammond's adult life. They offer perhaps the best portrait available of South Carolina politics and provide useful background on the state's cultural and commercial life as well. The Edgefield *Advertiser* gave me a more local perspective on the political developments relevant to Hammond. The Columbia *South Carolinian* has not survived as well as the preceding papers, but the issues I was able to obtain offered insights on state developments as viewed from the capital city. The Columbia *Southern Times and State Gazette* during Hammond's editorship (1830–31) is, of course, essential not only for his positions on nullification and related political turmoil but for the variety of essays he wrote on nonpolitical subjects as well. These are not signed, but Hammond elsewhere identifies himself as having sole responsibility for the editorial department during his tenure at the paper.

Hammond was an avid reader of contemporary periodicals, and I found these provided valuable background for understanding his intellectual and scientific outlook. The *Southern Quarterly Review*, published in South Carolina and edited between 1849 and 1854 by William Gilmore Simms, offers a portrait of the cultural life of the state during the period when Hammond was most deeply involved in speculation and writing. The *Farmer's Register* (1833–1843), edited by another of Hammond's intimates, Edmund Ruffin, influenced the planter's agricultural thought and practice, as did the *Southern Agriculturist* (1841–1846), *Carolina Planter* (1840–1841) and *Farmer and Planter* (1850–1861).

Official Records

The behavior of the legislature towards Governor Hammond between 1842 and 1844 is best recorded in the *South Carolina House Journal*, the *South Carolina Senate Journal*, and the *Reports and Resolutions of the General Assembly of South Carolina*. Hammond's actions in Congress are documented in the *Congressional Globe* (24th Cong., 1st Sess., 35th Cong., and 36th Cong.).

Published Reminiscences

A number of Hammond's contemporaries made revealing observations about him in published memoirs. Virginia Clay-Clopton's *A Belle of the Fifties* (New York: Doubleday, Page, 1905) describes Washington social life during the 1850s as well as a number of visits to Redcliffe during the war. Benjamin F. Perry comments on Hammond in *Reminiscences of Public Men, with Speeches and Addresses,* Second Series (Greenville, S.C.: Shannon, 1889). Mary J. Windle, a Washington hostess of the 1850s, describes the South Carolina senator in *Life in Washington and Life Here and There* (Philadelphia: Lippincott, 1859). Solon Robinson recounts a visit to Silver Bluff in "Mr. Robinson's Tour," *American Agriculturist* IX (February, 1850), 49–51.

Hammond's Published Works

During his lifetime Hammond thought about which of his writings he might wish to have published in a collected edition. Even though no such volume was completed until after his death, the selections included are chiefly those Hammond himself had designated as his most important works. In all probability, William Gilmore Simms served as the volume's editor, for he corresponded with Hammond's widow about undertaking such a project soon after his friend's death. *Selections from the Letters and Speeches of the Hon. James H. Hammond of South Carolina* (New York: John F. Trow, 1866) has been recently reprinted by the Southern Studies Program of the University of South Carolina with an Introduction and Notes by Clyde N. Wilson. This collection contains Hammond's most important public statements, including his gag-rule speech, his governor's messages, his proslavery tracts, his South Carolina College and South Carolina Institute addresses, his eulogy for Calhoun and his Barnwell Courthouse oration. The major omissions, as Clyde Wilson points out, are his significant agricultural writings. Among these I would include "Anniversary Oration of the State Agricultural Society of South Carolina . . . 25th November, 1841," in *Proceedings of the Agricultural Convention and of the State Agricultural Society of South Carolina from 1839 to 1845 Inclusive* (Columbia: Sumner and Carroll, 1846); *Marl: A Letter Addressed to the Agricultural Society of Jefferson County, Georgia* (Augusta: J. McCafferty, 1846); "Overseers," *Carolina Planter,* I (August, 1844), 25–30. Significant other writings omitted from *Letters and Speeches* are *The Railroad Mania: And Review of the Bank of the State of South Carolina* (Charleston: Burges, James, and Paxton, 1848), which Hammond came to think was too partisan, and *The North and the South: A Review of the Lecture on the Same Subject, Delivered by Mr. Elwood Fisher before the Young Men's Mercantile Association of Cincinnati, Ohio* (Charleston: James S. Burges, 1849), reprinted from the *Southern Quarterly Review* of 1849.

Secondary Works on James Henry Hammond

Hammond's letters and diaries have often been used by historians pursuing top-ics touched upon in his voluminous papers, but few scholars have written about Hammond as a subject in his own right. Elizabeth Merritt's biography, *James Henry Hammond, 1807–1864* (Baltimore: Johns Hopkins University Press, 1923) was the first full treatment of his life. It is brief and largely political in orientation. Robert Cinnamond Tucker's "James Henry Hammond: South Carolinian" (Ph.D. dissertation, University of North Carolina, 1958) is more satis-factory and provides a complete, although somewhat unanalytical account of his public and private life, including considerable detail on plantation activities. Tucker gives short shrift, however, to Hammond's last decade. The most com-prehensive treatment of Hammond's political role appears in Charles Wiltse's *John C. Calhoun, Nullifier, 1829–1839* (Indianapolis: Bobbs-Merrill, 1949) and *John C. Calhoun, Sectionalist, 1840–1850* (Indianapolis: Bobbs-Merrill, 1951), although these of course give no coverage of the important events in Ham-mond's career after Calhoun's death in 1850.

Clement Eaton provides an intriguing sketch of Hammond, which draws particular attention to his intellectual capabilities in "The Hamlet of the Old South," *The Mind of the Old South* (Baton Rouge: Louisiana State University Press, 1964). Carol K. Bleser's *The Hammonds of Redcliffe* (New York: Oxford University Press, 1981), a collection of excerpts from the letters and personal papers of the Hammond family between 1855 and 1938, begins with a brief por-trait of "The Founder." My own *A Sacred Circle: The Dilemma of the Intellectual in the Old South, 1840–1860* (Baltimore: Johns Hopkins University Press, 1977) treats Hammond as one of a group of southern thinkers seeking a place for their talents within the Old South.

Because Hammond's interests and involvements ranged so widely, brief dis-cussion of the secondary literature on American agriculture, intellectual trends, slavery, politics, economics, and social life that informed this study would be of little value. The most pertinent information on such sources is to be found in the footnotes.

Index

management, 72–73, 74–75, 82–88, 89–90

—travels of: to Europe, 186–203; to Florida, 109; on honeymoon, 62–63; to New York, 220, 291; to Philadelphia, 183; to Richmond, 364

—views of: on agriculture, 213, 231–32, 236, 258, 272–73, 276, 335; on history, 263, 273, 280; on religion, 193, 246, 247, 249, 258, 261, 262–63, 265, 274, 279–80; on riches, 27, 147–48, 261, 265, 320; romanticism and, 11–12, 187, 225, 227; on science, 260–61, 263, 264, 269; on war, 371; on women, 29, 33, 230, 313, 325–26, 328. *See also* Hammond, James Henry: political positions of

—writings of: on agriculture, 115, 117, 124, 258, 273–74, 276; as editor, 44–58; on Confederate finances, 364; as governor, 250; *Letter . . . to the Free Church of Glasgow*, 246, 248, 259; letter to the South Carolina legislature (1860), 357–58; *The North and the South: A Review*, 294–95; on Oregon, 259, 286; "Plan of State Action," 333; on popular election of governor and president, 272; *Railroad Mania*, 276–78; *Two Letters on Slavery*, 259, 267, 278–82, 283, 284; "Untitled Thoughts," 258; in youth, 11–12, 24, 29. *See also* Hammond, James Henry, orations of

Hammond, James Henry (Harry): birth of, 139; character of, 322, 325; and Confederate army, 367, 372; education of, 230, 315, 323, 325; and European trip, 185, 187, 190, 192; and father, 87, 230, 313, 319, 320–21, 325, 326–27, 340

Hammond, John Fox, 10, 147, 157, 184, 201, 208, 230, 308, 310–11, 317, 320, 362–63, 374, 376

Hammond, Juliana, 9

Hammond, Marcella Morris, 324

Hammond, Marcus Claudius Marcellus: birth of, 9; career of, 184, 230; character of, 146–47, 308–309; education of, 146–47, 157, 158n; and relationship with James Henry Hammond, 277, 302, 309–10, 321, 324; mentioned, 40, 107, 167, 181, 197, 208, 221, 234, 294, 296, 316, 325, 343, 347

Hammond, Paul Fitzsimons, 208, 302, 315, 322, 323, 324, 326–27, 328, 340, 343, 347, 367, 372

Hammond, William Cashel, 163, 315–16, 321, 324

Hammond Guards, 286

Hampton, Ann, 241, 290

Hampton, Ann Fitzsimons, 204, 221

Hampton, Caroline, 241, 290

Hampton, Catherine, 221, 241, 242, 243, 290

Hampton, Harriet, 241, 290

Hampton, Wade, II, 30, 58, 204, 221, 241, 242–43, 283, 284, 287, 288–89, 295, 302, 307, 314, 315, 338

Hampton, Wade, III, 241

Hampton family, 206, 243–44, 257

Hannah (slave), 84

Harper, William, 24, 64, 142, 176

Harpers Ferry, 354

Harrison, William Henry, 219

Harvard University, 325

Hayne, I. W., 30, 35, 52, 61, 145, 160, 226, 229

Hayne, Robert Y., 47, 49, 54, 142, 153

Helper, Hinton Rowan, 354

Henderson (slave), 87, 317–19

Henry, Robert, 14–15

Hercules (slave), 84

History, 263, 264, 270, 273, 280

Hoar, Samuel, 181, 251–52

Holmes, George Frederick, 264, 267, 282

Homeopathy, 77–78, 82n, 100n, 325, 377, 378n

Homer, 14

Homestead Bill, 354

Homosexuality, 18–19n

Hook, Henry, 34–35

Horses, Thoroughbred, 158–59

Hotspur, Hammond as, 53, 297, 299

Hudson (slave), 97

Huger, Daniel, 236, 285

Hunter, Robert M. T., 356, 364

Hyde, Caroline Augusta Hammond, 9, 39, 146, 311, 375

Hyde, Kate, 375

Imphee, 122–23

Impressment, 369, 373

Intellectuals, role of, 227–28, 238–39, 250, 259–60, 264, 266–67, 278–82, 301, 340

Internal improvements, 161, 285, 291

Ireland, 201–202

Italy, 191–97

Jackson, Andrew, 37, 49, 142, 144, 167, 171, 205, 247

Jackson, Dr. Samuel, 80

Jackson, William, 169